SUBLETHAL AND CHRONIC EFFECTS OF POLLUTANTS ON FRESHWATER FISH

SUBLETHAL AND CHRONIC EFFECTS OF POLLUTANTS ON FRESHWATER FISH

EDITED BY

R. MÜLLER AND R. LLOYD

Published by arrangement with
the Food and Agriculture Organization of the United Nations
by
Fishing News Books

Copyright © 1994 by FAO
Fishing News Books
A division of Blackwell Science Ltd
Editorial Offices:
Osney Mead, Oxford OX2 0EL
25 John Street, London WC1N 2BL
23 Ainslie Place, Edinburgh EH3 6AJ
238 Main Street, Cambridge,
    MA 02142, USA
54 University Street, Carlton,
    Victoria 3053, Australia

Other Editorial Offices:
Arnette Blackwell SA
1 rue de Lille
75007 Paris
France

Blackwell Wissenschafts-Verlag GmbH
Kurfürstendamm 57
10707 Berlin
Germany

Blackwell MZV
Feldgasse 13
A–1238 Wien
Austria

First published 1994

Set by Florencetype Ltd, Stoodleigh, Devon
Printed and bound in Great Britain by
The University Press, Cambridge

DISTRIBUTORS

Marston Book Services Ltd
PO Box 87
Oxford OX2 0DT
(*Orders:* Tel: 0865 240201
        Fax: 0865 721205
        Telex: 83355 MEDBOK G)

USA
  Blackwell Science, Inc
  238 Main Street
  Cambridge, MA 02142
  (*Orders:* Tel: 800 759–6102)

Canada
  Oxford University Press
  70 Wynford Drive
  Don Mills
  Ontario M3C IJ9
  (*Orders:* Tel: (416) 441–2941)

Australia
  Blackwell Science Pty Ltd
  54 University Street
  Carlton, Victoria 3053
  (*Orders:* Tel: (03) 347–5552)

British Library
Cataloguing in Publication Data

A Catalogue record for this book is
available from the British Library

ISBN 0-85238-207-3

The designations employed and the presentation of material in this publication do not imply the
expression of any opinion whatsoever on the part of the Food and Agriculture Organization of the
United Nations concerning the legal status of any country, territory, city or area or of its authorities,
or concerning the delimitation of its frontiers or boundaries.

Contents

v

viii   *Contents*

Introduction

The European Inland Fisheries Advisory Commission (EIFAC) was founded as a Regional Commission by a decision of the Council of the Food and Agriculture Organization of the United Nations (FAO) in 1957. At the first EIFAC session held in Dublin in 1960, 11 main areas of fisheries interests were identified by the participating countries; among these the effect of pollution on freshwater fisheries was ranked fourth. In those days, fish kills caused by the constituents of sewage and industrial wastes and by the misuse of agricultural chemicals were common. The research in this area was confined mainly to identifying the acute toxicity of a large number of chemicals, and also environmental parameters, to fish.

In order to collate this information into a useful form, a Working Party on Water Quality Criteria for European Freshwater Fish was established in 1962 (subsequently attached to Sub-Commission III, Fish and Polluted Water, formed in 1964) with the objective of critically reviewing the available data for specific chemicals and parameters that were known to be causing damage to European fisheries, and to propose advisory water quality standards. During the following years, reports were published on suspended solids, pH, temperature, dissolved oxygen, ammonia, nitrite, phenols, zinc, copper, cadmium, chlorine, nickel, aluminium, and mixtures of toxicants. In 1990, it was recognised that competent reviews of the appropriate literature were being carried out for a wide range of other substances by other national and international organisations, and so because the original objective had been satisfied, the working party was disbanded.

The water quality standards proposed by this working party have played a major role in restoring and improving the fisheries of Europe and to some extent worldwide. However, in some waters and with some fish species, no significant recovery of the fishery has been seen, even though there is no evidence of pollution. In other cases, fish have been found to accumulate high concentrations of heavy metals and organochlorine compounds such as polychlorinated biphenyls, which may have deleterious effects on fish populations either directly or as a terminal link in the food chain, as well as being of hygienic importance for man. This has led to a considerable research effort being directed to studies of sublethal effects of pollutants on fish, both to provide information relevant to the setting of water quality criteria, and as a field monitoring tool to identify the cause of a depleted fishery in natural waters.

It was for this reason that Sub-Commission III proposed the theme of 'Sublethal and chronic effects of pollutants on freshwater fish' for the Symposium to be held in conjunction with the Seventeenth Session of EIFAC in 1992. The objectives of the Symposium were to collate the present information in this field, to assess the ways by which fish fauna can be impacted, to identify gaps in existing knowledge, and to propose avenues of research which may be fruitful. A secondary aim, and of equal importance in the context of the objectives of EIFAC, was to provide a forum for the exchange of scientific information from all European countries and in particular between scientists from the East and those from the West.

It was stressed at the outset that papers submitted to the Symposium should describe concepts and hypotheses by which concentration–effects data can be used to predict effects on fish communities. Effects of pollution on fish can be measured at different levels of biological organisation, i.e. cellular (change in cell structure, enzyme induction, immunology), organ (physiology, respiration, osmoregulation), individual (mortality, scope for growth, activity and reproduction), population (growth rate, reproduction) and community (species interactions). Effects measured at the community level are the most relevant for the purposes of fisheries protection; effects at the cellular level are the most relevant for a basic understanding of the processes involved and perhaps also as a tool for monitoring water quality.

To be of practical use, the information obtained at all these levels of organisation has to be capable of integration into a form which can assist management decisions taken within a legislative framework. In particular, it should lead to the setting of valid, accurate water quality standards or provide evidence on the extent to which a fish population or community has been damaged. In this latter respect, it is necessary to separate effects which are adaptive or which fall within a normal range for the organism, from those that are harmful and which can cause damage at higher levels of biological organisation.

Clearly, this is an ambitious goal and most of the 39 papers accepted for the Symposium fell short of this ideal. However, the 32 papers published in these proceedings show individually the regional differences in the approach to this problem and collectively how effects at different levels of biological organisation may be integrated in a useful manner. But it must be recognised, too, that it is difficult to categorise individual research projects within this holistic approach. The original intention was to separate them according to the level of biological organisation investigated, but some of the papers received fell more naturally into a more specific classification of life cycle and population effects (related to standard toxicity tests) and aluminium toxicity together with acid waters.

Therefore, although the papers have been separated into four groups for convenience of presentation, the subject matter of some of them may cross (or indeed should cross) one or more of the boundaries. Thus, the four sections of these proceedings represent a somewhat artificial division, and some of the papers could easily have been allocated differently. For this reason, all the papers should be considered together in order to gain a broad (even if to some extent partial) overview of the present status of European research in this field.

Each section is preceded by a short summary prepared by the Chairmen and Vice-Chairmen of each of the four sessions, and a brief overview of the Symposium by the Chairman and the Convenor is given as a conclusion. These formed part of a report which was agreed and approved by the Seventeenth session of EIFAC.

R. Müller, Symposium Chairman
R. Lloyd, Symposium Convenor

SECTION A
MORPHOLOGICAL AND PHYSIOLOGICAL EFFECTS AT CELL AND TISSUE LEVELS

A wide variety of subjects was dealt with, using morphological, biochemical and physiological parameters, *in vivo* and *in vitro* techniques; the major topics were pesticide and heavy metal toxicity and immunotoxic effects. The most commonly used fish species were rainbow trout and carp. In evaluating the papers presented in this section, a few conclusions and recommendations can be made; some of these comments will be equally applicable to papers in other sections because of overlapping subject matter.

A considerable amount of research is being carried out in Europe in the field of freshwater toxicology. Knowledge and technical infrastructure can also be derived from classical toxicology, and this may promote the speed of scientific development in this field. For the study of morphological and physiological effects at cell and tissue level, disciplines such as pathology, physiology, immuno(toxico)logy, biochemistry, haematology, etc., are used. In some papers a single methodology was applied while in others authors have used combinations of methodologies. The latter approach is to be encouraged, since it may facilitate mutual comparisons of results and may place the relative relevance of methods and data into a proper perspective.

A major difference and difficulty, compared with classical mammalian toxicology, is the fact that the protection of the population/ecosystem is the ultimate target and not the organism. This requires a further, difficult, extrapolation stage in the progression of molecules – cell – tissue – organisms – population. In this section we were presented with field studies, as well as laboratory studies, both *in vivo* and *in vitro*. In quite a few chapters, the laboratory studies were clearly linked to real-world field situations, which increases their relevance.

Another difficulty is that major differences between species may occur also at the cell/tissue level. This should be taken into account when selecting a test species and in making extrapolations from the data to fish in general.

There seems to be a need for a definition of the term 'sublethal effects'; some investigators apparently consider this to be an effect which occurs in individuals that manage to survive potentially lethal toxic concentrations (sublethal at the individual level) while others use this for long-term effects at concentrations that do not cause significant mortality in the population (sublethal at the population level). There seems to be also a difference in interpretation of the term 'chronic'. These definitions should be established and adhered to in order to allow for comparisons and exchange of data and interpretations among various investigators.

Immunotoxicology is currently an important field within the scientific community of toxicologists. It is relevant that in aquatic toxicology the toxic impairment of immunological defence should be taken into consideration, in particular as resistance to external infectious disease is a major element in ecology. There seems, however, to be in some instances a disagreement as to the definition of immunotoxicity. In immunotoxicology the compound is called immunotoxic when there is a functional impairment of immune parameters, particularly of the specific immunity (cellular/humoral), with a certain degree of specificity, i.e. when the immune system is the major target without any overt, non-specific toxic effects on other vital organs.

The study of morphological and physiological effects at the tissue and cell level are very relevant in identifying the mechanism of action of (groups of) unknown chemicals, which then helps in the identification of causes of damage in field populations.

In conclusion, the main recommendation could be that progress in various wider fields of science should be utilised in research on the toxicology of fish, and the important need is for the integration and communication between the different fields of expertise.

P. W. Wester, Session Chairman
J. Szakolczai, Session Vice-Chairman

Chapter 1
Monitoring of sublethal chronic effects in fish: the pathomorphological approach

P.W. WESTER and C.J. ROGHAIR

*National Institute of Public Health and Environmental Protection,
PO Box 1, 3720 BA Bilthoven, The Netherlands*

1.1   Introduction

In ecotoxicology, the effect of toxic compounds on the fate and dynamics of populations and biomass is studied. This is a difficult and complicated process, and therefore parameters by which it is measured are quantitative and relatively basic, such as survival and mortality. With acutely toxic effects, these parameters are quite appropriate, whereas for long-term effects caused by sublethal concentrations the relevant parameters are difficult to ascertain. As sublethal effects are in general more subtle and qualitative, it is difficult to monitor these at the population or community level, due to the complexity of an ecosystem and the specificity of the induced effect. Therefore, for the lower toxic concentrations, laboratory studies at the level of organisms are indispensable for the identification of relevant effects. This avoids the complexity of population dynamics and focuses on the study of more specific and mechanistic actions.

After determining the general toxicological parameters, the next step is to identify and to localise an effect, if any. As in mammalian toxicology, this is achieved by an overall screening of the various compartments of the organisms by light microscopy, which may then reveal organ and tissue abnormalities. Furthermore, indications can be obtained of the mechanism of action, which is important for our understanding of toxic events and for the assessment of possible implications at the population level, for example, when the reproductive system appears to be affected. Moreover, if a specific effect of a certain compound or group of compounds is found, this may be used as a monitoring tool in field studies (Hinton and Lauren, 1990). In contrast to the situation in freshwaters, field studies in which histopathology is incorporated are nowadays quite common in coastal water monitoring programmes (Overstreet, 1988; Vethaak *et al.*, 1993).

In this chapter, the histopathological studies which we have carried out with small freshwater fish in our laboratory are evaluated (Wester and Canton, 1986; 1987; 1992; Wester *et al.*, 1985; 1988; 1990; Wester and Roghair, 1992). These studies were made to investigate the utility of this approach in aquatic toxicity studies, with special emphasis on sublethal effects occurring after chronic exposure.

1.2   Materials and methods

The methodology used has been described in detail in the various papers dealing with individual compounds (Wester *et al.*, 1985; 1988; 1990; Wester and Canton, 1986; 1987; 1992; Wester and Roghair, 1992). The main techniques are briefly described below.

1.2.1   *Animals*

The test fish were guppy (*Poecilia reticulata*), medaka (*Oryzias latipes*) and three-spined stickleback (*Gasterosteus aculeatus*) obtained from the Institute's breeding colonies. They were used in the experiments at the egg or juvenile stage; this permitted the study of the development of, for example, reproductive organs and was aimed to prevent inhomogeneity due to sexual dimorphism.

1.2.2   *Chemicals*

Chemicals were selected according to their relevance for the environment and, as far as possible, the knowledge and experience in our Institute with their toxicology in rodents, in view of the extrapolation and the interpretation of the relevance of the findings. The compounds used in the study with guppy and medaka were β-hexachlorocyclohexane (β-HCH), bis(tri-n-butyltin)oxide (TBTO), di-n-butyltindichloride (DBTC), methylbromide, sodium bromide, and methylmercury chloride. Stickleback and medaka were exposed to the fabric softener ditallow dimethyl ammonium chloride (DTDMAC). Chemicals which were poorly soluble in water were applied in dimethylsulphoxide (DMSO) as a vehicle at a maximum concentration of 0.1 ml.l^{-1}.

1.2.3   *Experimental procedure*

Guppies (a live-bearing species) were exposed from the age of 4 weeks after birth, and medaka and stickleback from the egg stage. Exposure periods were in general one and three months. Besides a control and a solvent (DMSO) control, a concentration range was chosen after a pilot study to provide a significant expected mortality in the highest concentration in order to ensure that histopathological changes occurred. Ten surviving fish per concentration group and exposure period were processed routinely for paraffin embedding, with five fish per tissue block, and examined histopathologically in total-body sections at 10–15 section intervals. For further characterisation of the findings additional investigations were carried out (enzyme histochemistry, electron microscopy, and biochemistry).

1.3   Results

With the histological procedures used, all relevant organs could be studied *in situ* in the series of sections containing groups of animals (Fig. 1.1). The effects and target

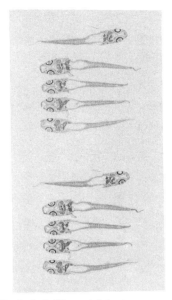

Fig. 1.1   Histological slide containing two consecutive H&E-stained sections of five guppies as used in these studies.

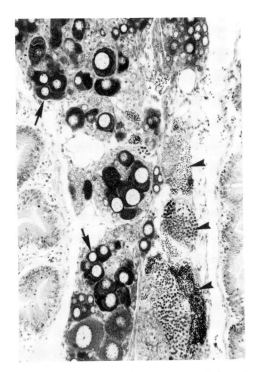

Fig. 1.2   Gonad of a male medaka in which both spermatogenesis (arrowheads) and oocytes (arrows) are present, indicative of hyperestrogenism. (From: Wester and Canton, 1986).

organs are described in the papers previously mentioned, in which for each species and/or compound the qualitative and quantitative data are given in greater detail. The major results are summarised in this chapter. Only those effects for which a clear dose-and-effect relationship could be established were considered to be important. These included an estrogenic activity of β-HCH (excessive vitellogenesis, testis atrophy, hermaphroditism, pituitary changes) (Fig. 1.2). TBTO induced thymus atrophy in guppies (Fig. 1.3) and affected the glycogen metabolism in both guppies and medaka. The same findings were observed after DBTC exposure, which appeared to be due to TBTO-contamination whereas DBTC itself was apparently far less toxic. Bromide interfered with thyroid and muscle function, possibly by competition with iodine, whereas methylbromide appeared to be a superficial irritant. Methylmercury was specifically toxic for cells in mitosis, which was attributed to an effect on the mitotic spindle proteins, and was also toxic for the gas gland and gall bladder epithelium. Moreover, the occurrence of granulomas was a typical finding following exposure to this compound. In the study with DTDMAC a teratogenic effect in the gas gland was demonstrated resulting in an ineffective swim bladder (Fig. 1.4), which was reflected by an abnormal swimming behaviour. In Table 1.1 the quantitative data expressed as no-observed-effect concentrations ('NOECs') are summarised and compared with data from conventional aquatic toxicology parameters (not for DTDMAC-studies). This table shows that for some compounds significant differences exist in the comparative sensitivity of routine aquatic toxicology and histopathology. Moreover, it shows that apparently no advantage exists in terms of sensitivity in extending a 1-month exposure period to 3 months.

1.4   Discussion

These studies have shown that histopathology can reveal specific structural toxic effects in a variety of organs of small laboratory fish. This is a useful tool in the risk assessment of toxic chemicals that may be discharged to the aquatic environment. The main applications of histopathology are discussed below.

From the qualitative point of view, some effects at the level of organisms clearly might affect at the population level, in particular those that affect energy metabolism, growth and reproduction (McDowell Capuzzo *et al.*, 1988). Thus, effects observed in our studies that may be important in population dynamics are the estrogenic effect of β-HCH or the sperm necrosis caused by methylmercury chloride (Wester, 1991). These effects will not be revealed by classical toxicity studies where only mortality, growth and general condition are monitored as in the case of β-HCH, but an impairment of sexual function is indeed incompatible with procreation of a species. Other effects that obviously impair normal physiology are, for example, muscle degeneration and paralysis after bromide exposure (Wester *et al.*, 1988), teratological abnormalities in the swim bladder by DTDMAC (Wester and

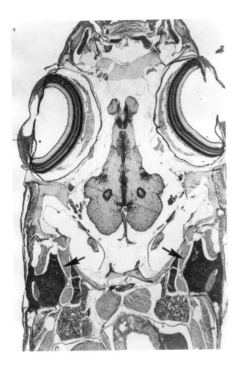
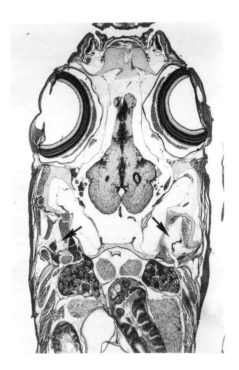

Fig. 1.3 Low power histological picture of a control (left) and TBTO-exposed guppy (right). The paired thymus (arrows) has almost completely disappeared in the exposed fish.

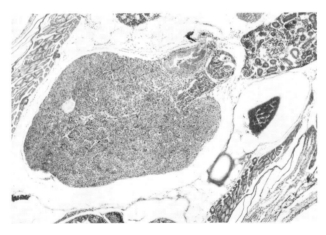

Fig. 1.4 Medaka exposed to DTDMAC, with an abnormally developed massive gas gland resulting in an ineffective swim bladder. (From: Wester and Roghair, 1992).

Table 1.1 No-observed-effect concentrations (NOEC) for general toxicological parameters and histo-pathology in *P. reticulata* and *O. latipes*.

		P. reticulata		O. latipes	
		Gen. toxicity	Histopathology	Gen. toxicity	Histopathology
β-HCH (mg.l^{-1})	1 month	⩾1.0	0.032	0.056	0.056
	3 months	0.1	0.032	0.032	0.10
TBTO (μg.l^{-1})	1 month	1.0	0.01	1.0	0.32
	3 months	0.32	0.01	3.2	0.32
DBTC (μg.l^{-1})	1 month	1800	<320	1800	<320
NaBr (mg.l^{-1})	1 month	32	10	320	<180
	3 months	32	32	320	<180
MeBr (mg.l^{-1})	1 month	0.1	a	0.56	a
	3 months	–	–	0.18	a
MeHg (μg.l^{-1})	1 month	3.2	1.0	1.0	a
	3 months	1.0	1.0	–	–

Notes: a   no significant effects observed
       –   not performed

Roghair, 1992) and ocular lesions by organotins (Wester and Canton, 1987; Wester *et al.*, 1990).

Of particular interest is the atrophy of the thymus which was observed in guppies exposed to organotins (Wester and Canton, 1987) and is likely to result in immune suppression. This immune suppression (e.g. decreased resistance to infectious agents) has been demonstrated in the rat exposed to TBTO (Vos *et al.*, 1984), and similar studies with fish are foreseen in the near future. It is generally accepted that immune impairment is an important factor in fitness at the ecological level (Anderson *et al.*, 1984; Vos *et al.*, 1989).

For effects such as damage to mitotic spindles, changes in thyroid activity or in glycogen metabolism, the impact at a higher level of biological organisation may be less obvious, although conceivable. Surprisingly, no significant lesions were seen in the gills in contrast to results obtained from acute studies (Wester *et al.*, 1988). This supports the conclusion of Mallatt (1985) that (non-specific) hyperplastic gill lesions which are commonly observed in acute studies are less important in chronic sublethal toxic exposures.

Apart from the assessment of functional relevance for the population of toxicological effects found in the individual, histopathology can be used as a tool to obtain insight into the specific mode of action of chemicals. This can then be used to guide the direction of further research.

From the quantitative point of view the NOECs obtained from histopathological examination were compared for the 1 and 3-months exposed fish, and with those from routine toxicology parameters; these are summarised in Table 1.1. In general, one month appeared to be an adequate exposure period, and in quite a number of cases, a significant increase in sensitivity could be achieved as compared with routine parameters. If this is the case, the histopathological NOECs could then be used in extrapolation methods such as that used by the EPA (OECD, 1991). However, these laboratory data still need to be translated to the field situation. In the laboratory experiments, the concentrations tested and the NOECs determined were frequently in the upper range of, or higher than, concentrations which could be measured in the aquatic environment.

To compare these crude data, however, is a rather simplistic approach. First, the animals were exposed to waterborne toxicants in order to standardise the experimental procedure. This implies that the uptake would probably have taken place mainly through the gills, which is not always the case under field conditions; uptake as (bio)concentrated toxicants in the food or on sediment particles may be more important in some cases. Where such uptake occurs, extrapolation can be carried out, for example, by measuring and comparing the body burden of the compound in question. Another point is that accumulation in the adipose tissue might occur, which then becomes hazardous under catabolic conditions. Also there may be other natural stress conditions present which might influence the impact of toxic compounds and which were not measured, including the toxic interaction of multiple combined exposures (synergism, antagonism).

A limitation of the use of pathomorphological data is that structural effects might be functionally of lesser relevance, for example, in the case of endocrine disturbances; on the other hand, the absence of pathological lesions at sub-NOEC level does not exclude functional disturbances at those levels. This is illustrated by the immune suppression found in rats which occurred at lower concentration than that at which thymus atrophy could be observed (Vos *et al.*, 1984).

Finally, as is the case with models in general, it is not yet established whether the model species chosen are the most representative (or sensitive?) test animals for any field situation. Therefore, data from laboratory studies as described above should be extrapolated with care, especially when used for quantitative extrapolation. Their usefulness lies predominantly in the insight which they provide on the toxic action of the contaminant, which can be helpful in establishing the relevance of the effect for fitness and survival. Knowledge of fundamental toxicological and pathological processes is not only important for the regulators of chemicals that are potentially aquatic pollutants, but also for researchers involved in field studies.

Acknowledgements

The authors wish to thank Drs J.G. Vos and A.D. Vethaak for critical reading and comments on the manuscript.

References

Anderson, D.P., W.B. Van Muiswinkel and B.S. Robertson, 1984. Effects of chemically induced immune modulation on infectious diseases of fish. In: Liss, A. R. (Ed.) *Chemical Regulation of Immunity in Veterinary Medicine*, pp. 187–211. New York.

Hinton, D.E. and D.L. Lauren, 1990. Integrative histopathological approaches to detecting effects of environmental stressors on fishes. *Am.Fish.Soc.Symp.*, **8**: 51–66.

Mallatt J., 1985. Fish gill structural changes induced by toxicants and other irritants: a statistical review. *Can.J.Fish.Aquat.Sci.*, **42**: 630–648.

McDowell Capuzzo, J., M.N. Moore and J. Widdows, 1988. Effects of toxic chemicals in the marine environment; predictions of impact from laboratory studies. *Aquat.Toxicol.*, **11**: 303–311.

OECD, 1991. Draft report of the OECD workshop on the extrapolation of laboratory aquatic toxicity data to the real environment. Organization for Economic Cooperation and Development, Paris, 83 p.

Overstreet, R.M., 1988. Aquatic pollution problems, Southeastern U.S. coasts: histopathological indicators. *Aquat.Toxicol.*, **11**: 213–239.

Vethaak, A.D., D. Bucke, T. Lang, P.W. Wester, J. Jol and M. Carr, 1993. Spatial trends of gross disorders and hepatic lesions in dab (*Limanda limanda* L.) sampled along a pollution gradient in the German Bight. *Marine Ecol.Prog.Series*, in press.

Vos, J.G., A. De Klerk, E.I. Krajnc, W. Kruizinga, B. Van Ommen and J. Rozing, 1984. Toxicity of bis(tri-n-butyltin)oxide in the rat. II. Suppression of thymus-dependent immune responses and of parameters of nonspecific resistance after short-term exposure. *Toxicol.Appl.Pharmacol.*, **75**: 387–408.

Vos, J.G., H. Van Loveren, P.W. Wester and A.D. Vethaak, 1989. The effects of environmental pollutants on the immune system: experimental evidence and field observations. In: Krieps, R. (Ed.) *Environment and Health: a Holistic Approach*, 50–60. Avebury, Aldershot.

Wester, P.W., 1991. Histopathological effects of environmental pollutants β-HCH and methylmercury on reproductive organs in freshwater fish. *Comp.Biochem.Physiol.*, **110C** (1/2): 237–238.

Wester, P.W. and J.H. Canton, 1986. Histopathological study of *Oryzias latipes* (medaka) after long-term β-hexachlorocyclohexane exposure. *Aquat.Toxicol.*, **9**:21–45.

Wester, P.W. and J.H. Canton, 1987. Histopathological study of *Poecilia reticulata* (guppy) after long-term exposure to bis(tri-n-butyltin)oxide (TBTO) and di-n-butyltindichloride (DBTC). *Aquat.Toxicol.*, **10**: 143–165.

Wester, P.W. and J.H. Canton, 1992. Histopathological effects in *Poecilia reticulata* (guppy) exposed to methylmercury chloride. *Toxicol.Pathol.*, **20**: 81–92.

Wester, P.W. and C. Roghair, 1992. Teratogenic effect in the gas gland of fish induced by the fabric softener ditallow dimethyl ammonium chloride. *Dis.Aquat Org.*, **12**: 207–213.

Wester, P.W., J.H. Canton and A. Bisschop, 1985. Histopathological study of *Poecilia reticulata* (guppy) after long-term β-hexachlorocyclohexane exposure. *Aquat.Toxicol.*, **6**: 271–296.

Wester, P.W., J.H. Canton and J.A.M.A. Dormans, 1988. Pathological effects in freshwater fish *Poecilia reticulata* (guppy) and *Oryzias latipes* (medaka) following methylbromide and sodium bromide exposure. *Aquat.Toxicol.*, **2**: 323–344.

Wester, P.W., J.H. Canton, A.A.J. Van Iersel, E.I. Krajnc and H.A.M.G. Vaessen, 1990. The toxicity of bis(tri-n-butyltin)oxide (TBTO) and di-n-butyltindichloride (DBTC) in the small fish species *Oryzias latipes* (medaka) and *Poecilia reticulata* (guppy). *Aquat.Toxicol.*, **16**: 53–72.

Chapter 2
Detection of environmentally relevant concentrations of toxic organic compounds using histological and cytological parameters: substance-specificity in the reaction of rainbow trout liver?

T. BRAUNBECK

Department of Zoology I, University of Heidelberg, Im Neuenheimer Feld 230,
D-W-6900 Heidelberg, Germany

2.1   Introduction

The global production of organic chemicals has risen from 7.5 megatonnes in 1950 to over 150 megatonnes in 1980 (Nagel, 1988). To a certain extent, either on purpose or accidentally, man-made toxic chemicals are released into the environment during production, transportation as well as utilisation, and thus pose a threat to living biota. Therefore, the assessment of environmental hazards due to toxic substances is an important challenge to toxicologists and ecotoxicologists. The acute toxicity of chemicals to fish may be easily evaluated in a short-term fish test, and death still represents an unequivocal endpoint in toxicology. However, the assessment of sublethal effects of concentrations of organic pollutants low enough to be of relevance for the environment requires more subtle techniques. From an ecological point of view, survival, growth, reproduction, spawning and hatching success provide endpoints of undoubted significance. Since reaction and adaptation to environmental parameters, regardless of whether they are natural or man-made, are hierarchical processes involving different levels of biological organisation (Lloyd, 1992; Stebbing, 1985; Vogt, 1987), macroscopically overt signs of toxicity are almost always preceded by changes at the organ, tissue, cellular, and molecular levels (Segner and Braunbeck, 1990). A capability for investigating toxicant-induced changes at lower levels of biological organisation occurring prior to organismic changes should, therefore, provide a rapid 'early warning system' (cf. Moore, 1985).

The methods of established value in the evaluation of environmental impact at the organ and cellular levels are histology and cytology, and, in the aquatic system, fish liver ultrastructure has proved to be particularly susceptible to low levels of environmental contaminants (see Braunbeck *et al.*, 1990a). In the course of more comprehensive investigations on the plasticity of fish hepatocytes, the sublethal effects of several organic reference chemicals and pesticides have recently been studied in collaboration with other laboratories (Braunbeck *et al.*, 1989, 1990a–c, 1992, 1993). Hepatocellular reactions to chemicals were shown to depend on sex (Braunbeck *et al.*, 1989, 1990b), species (Braunbeck *et al.*, 1990a, 1993), age (Braunbeck *et al.*, 1992), and physiological preconditioning (Braunbeck and Segner, 1992).

A further crucial point for the potential value of cytological monitoring of chemical-induced damage concerns the substance-specificity of hepatocellular reaction. From a thorough evaluation of published data, specific syndromes produced in fish liver as responses to particular pesticides appear to be few in number. In zebrafish, however, it is possible that hepatocellular reactions to 4-nitrophenol, 4-chloroaniline, lindane, and atrazine could be used to differentiate between these compounds (Braunbeck *et al.*, 1989, 1990a, b, 1993).

In an attempt to evaluate further the substance-specificity of morphological reactions of fish liver to environmental contaminants, this chapter provides a comparative account of ultrastructural alterations in the liver of rainbow trout (*Oncorhynchus mykiss*) subjected for prolonged periods to sublethal concentrations of the reference chemical 4-chloroaniline, the pesticides endosulfan, atrazine, diazinon, disulfoton and linuron, as well as the mycotoxin ochratoxin.

The primarily qualitative nature of morphological studies imposes serious restrictions on their potential integration with more quantitatively oriented disciplines in environmental sciences (Hinton *et al.*, 1987; Braunbeck and Segner, 1992). As a consequence, in mammalian histology and pathology, quantitative stereological methods have been used since the late 1960s (e.g. Blouin, 1977; Blouin *et al.*, 1977; Bolender, 1979; Bolender and Weibel, 1973; Hess *et al.*, 1973; Loud, 1968; Pfeifer, 1973; Rohr *et al.*, 1973; Stäubli *et al.*, 1969; Weibel, 1979; Weibel *et al.*, 1969). In contrast, quantitative approaches have been scant in teleost histology (Braunbeck and Storch, 1992; Hampton *et al.*, 1989; Hinton *et al.*, 1985; Peute *et al.*, 1985; Segner and Braunbeck, 1990). Thus, the second purpose of this chapter is to illustrate the potential of quantitative morphology in an experiment on sublethal 4-chloroaniline toxicity in rainbow trout.

2.2   Experimental design

In collaboration with Dr H. Bresch (Federal Research Centre for Nutrition, Karlsruhe, Germany: diazinon, 4-chloroaniline), Dr R.D. Negele (Bavarian Agency for Water Research, Wielenbach, Germany: atrazine, linuron) and Dr H.J. Pluta (Federal Health Institute, Berlin, Germany: endosulfan, disulfoton), fingerling rainbow trout (*Oncorhynchus mykiss*) were exposed to 4-chloroaniline (40, 200, 1000 $\mu g.l^{-1}$), endosulfan (1, 10, 50, 100 $ng.l^{-1}$), atrazine (10, 20, 40, 80, 160 $\mu g.l^{-1}$), diazinon (8, 40, 200 $\mu g.l^{-1}$), disulfoton (0.1, 1, 5, 20 $\mu g.l^{-1}$), linuron (30, 120, 240 $\mu g.l^{-1}$) and ochratoxin (0.1, 1 $\mu g.kg^{-1}$ food).

Although the experiments were carried out in different laboratories, the test conditions were comparable in all experiments. Fish from 5 to 20 g body-weight were kept in batches of 20–25 individuals in 40–60 l all-glass aquaria with water exchange rates of 30–100 ml.min^{-1} (10–11 mg.l^{-1} O$_2$; 400 mg.l^{-1} CaCO$_3$; 10–15°C; pH 7.2–7.6). Ammonia, nitrite, and nitrate were kept below detection limits. Photoperiod was 12 hr light and 12 hr dark. Fish were fed with commercially available trout food at a daily rate of 3–4% body-weight throughout the experiments. Exposure times were 4–5 weeks.

Since sexual differences are not yet apparent in hepatocytes of fingerling rainbow trout of this size, no differentiation could be made on the basis of sex. For each treatment, four fish were studied.

Fixation was carried out by cardiac perfusion (Braunbeck *et al.*, 1992). Peroxidatic activity of catalase was visualised by incubation in alkaline diamino-benzidine (pH 10; Braunbeck *et al.*, 1989). Liver stereological analysis followed the procedure of Weibel (1979) as described in detail by Segner and Braunbeck (1990).

2.3   Results

Nucleus

The major results from the rainbow trout experiments are listed in Table 2.1. In contrast to control animals which are almost free of binucleate cells, stimulation of mitosis and subsequent augmentation of binucleate cells were observed for all toxicants except endosulfan and disulfoton and thus appear to be a common feature of rainbow trout intoxication. Among unspecific symptoms, multiple nucleoli are frequent and, in parallel to corresponding alterations in the cytoplasm, the nuclear envelope is often distorted. In contrast, free macrovesicular lipid inclusions (not membrane-bound) could only be observed after exposure to 4-chloroaniline, linuron, and ochratoxin; intranuclear steatosis (membrane-bound lipid accumulation) is restricted to ochratoxin.

Rough endoplasmic reticulum (RER)

Control rainbow trout are characterised by a remarkably regular arrangement of extensive stacks of non-fenestrated RER cisternae forming an almost continuous sheath around the central nucleus. Occasionally, a single layer of spherical to ovoid mitochondria is interposed between the nucleus and the RER. This pericentral portion of organelle-containing cytoplasm is strictly separated from peripheral areas of glycogen and lipid storage by a layer of mitochondria and peroxisomes ('cytoplasmic compartmentation', Braunbeck *et al.*, 1989).

Increased RER heterogeneity characterised by dilation, fragmentation, vesiculation and, eventually, reduction is one of the most common and earliest reactions of rainbow trout hepatocytes to chemical toxicants. Exceptions are diazinon, which

Table 2.1 Cytological alterations in the liver of rainbow trout after prolonged sublethal exposure to 4-chloroaniline, endosulfan, atrazine, diazinon, disulfoton, linuron and ochratoxin. Data presented as lowest concentration (in μg.l^{-1}) inducing the respective alteration.

	4-Chloro-aniline	Endo-sulfan	Atrazine	Diazinon	Disul-foton	Linuron	Ochra-toxin
Concentrations in μg.l^{-1} (mmol.l^{-1})	200 (1562) 1000 (7812)	0.001 (0.003) 0.01 (0.025) 0.05 (0.122) 0.1 (0.245)	10 (46.4) 20 (92.7) 40 (185.4) 80 (370.9) 160 (741.8)	8 (26.3) 40 (131.4) 200 (657.2)	0.1 (0.36) 1 (3.64) 5 (18.22) 20 (72.88)	30 (120) 120 (481) 240 (963)	0.1 mg.kg^{-1} 1 mg.kg^{-1} (food doses)
Nuclei							
Stimulation of mitosis	200		160	40		30	1
Augmentation of binucleate cells	200		160	40			1
Free nuclear lipid inclusions	1000					120	0.1
Intranuclear steatosis							1
Intranuclear myelin formation	200						
Deformation of nuclear envelope	200	0.01	80			30	
Inflation of nuclear envelope	200						
Augmentation of nucleoli	200	0.01	160	40		120	
Rough endoplasmic reticulum							
Increased heterogeneity	200	0.01	40			120	0.1
Reduction	200		160		0.1*		0.1
Fragmentation, vesiculation	200	0.05	40			120	0.1
Dilation of cisternae	200	0.01	40			120	0.1
Fenestration of cisternae							1
Collapse of cisternae							0.1
Steatosis						120	0.1
Formation of RER whorls						30	1
Transformation into myelin body(ies)							1
Smooth endoplasmic reticulum							
Proliferation		0.05	160	40	5	30 ?	1
Golgi apparatus							
Increased heterogeneity	200	0.05		200		120	
Hypertrophy				200	5	120	
Fenestration of cisternae		0.05					
Dilation of cisternae				200			
Stimulation of VLDL synthesis						120	
Decrease of VLDL synthesis	200	0.05					1
Reduction of Golgi vesicles							1
Augmentation of Golgi vesicles				200			
Collapse of cisternae							1
Mitochondria							
Proliferation	200				0.1 *	120	
Increased heterogeneity	200	0.05	40	40		120	0.1
Increase in volume				40			
Dilation of intermembranous space		0.05				30	
Induction of longitudinal cristae			40				
Collapse of mitochondria							1
Intramitochondrial myelin formation		0.05	160				
Partial lysis		0.1					

Table 2.1 Continued.

	4-Chloro-aniline	Endo-sulfan	Atrazine	Diazinon	Disul-foton	Linuron	Ochra-toxin
Peroxisomes							
Proliferation		0.01		200		120	
Reduction	200						
Increased heterogeneity		0.05		200		120	
Increased catalase activity		0.05					
Reduction in catalase activity	200						
Heterogeneity in catalase distribution		0.05					
Cluster formation		0.01		40?		120	
Tail formation (division?)						120	
Myelin formation in matrix		0.05					
Accumulation around lipid						120	
Lysosomal elements							
Proliferation		0.05	80	200	0.1	30	
Reduction	200						
Induction of new lysosome types			160			120	
Crystal formation in matrix							
Phospholipidosis				200		120	
Myelinated bodies		0.05	40			30	1
Induction of autophagosomes		0.01	40	40		30	
Induction of multivesicular bodies		0.05	160			120	
Induction of glycogenosomes	200 ?			40			
Storage materials							
Increase of lipid deposits						30	
Perisinusoidal polarisation of lipids						30	
Steatosis						120	0.1
Increased electron density of lipid droplets							0.1
Formation of cholesterol crystals	200						
Formation of lipid clusters						120	
Nuclear lipid inclusions						120	
Decrease in glycogen stores	200	0.1	40		5	120	0.1
Glycogen condensation	200						
Intracellular compartmentation							
Disturbance of compartmentation	200	0.1	40				0.1
Perisinusoidal vacuolation				40			
Peribiliary vacuolation				40			
Non-parenchymal cells							
Immigration of macrophages	200	0.05	40	200		30	1
Formation of macrophage centres	200	0.1	80			120	1
Immigration of granulocytes			40				
Increased glycogen phagocytosis	200	0.05	80			120	
Phagocytosis of entire cells		0.1	80			30	1
Proliferation of Ito cells				40			
Variability of liver parenchyma							
Increased intraindividual parenchyma		0.1	40	40		30	0.1
Increased interindividual parenchyma		0.05	40			30	0.1

* 0.1 and 1 $\mu g.l^{-1}$ only

fails to induce any RER alterations, and ochratoxin, which stimulates additional modifications such as fenestration, fusion of opposite cisternal membranes and transformation of the entire RER into huge myelin bodies. Steatosis in RER is observed with linuron and ochratoxin. As a consequence of all these RER changes, disturbance of the cytoplasmic compartmentation is commonly seen in exposed rainbow trout.

Smooth endoplasmic reticulum (SER)

In control fish, typical SER as an irregular network of undulating, anastomosing tubular and vesicular profiles is restricted to tiny areas close to Golgi fields. Except for 4-chloroaniline, all the substances induce an SER augmentation; the degree of proliferation, however, varies from low in the linuron experiment to appreciable with diazinon. Also, it should be noted that in many cases (especially with ochratoxin) differentiation between degranulated RER and true (functionally active) SER is practically impossible.

Golgi fields

In non-exposed rainbow trout, the RER sheath is interrupted by strongly developed Golgi fields, which consist of up to five barely fenestrated cisternae displaying marked polarity and budding off many vesicles of varying dimensions and containing numerous very low density lipoprotein (VLDL) granules. A typical, but unspecific, attribute of contaminated rainbow trout liver is increased Golgi heterogeneity which, however, in contrast to the RER reaction, is of a diverse nature. Thus, 4-chloroaniline and endosulfan induce reduced VLDL secretion, whereas linuron stimulates VLDL production in hypertrophic Golgi fields; diazinon provokes an increased number of Golgi vesicles without stimulation of VLDL production; endosulfan prompts fenestration, linuron dilation of Golgi cisternae; finally, ochratoxin apparently causes complete morphological disintegration and cessation of normal Golgi functions.

Mitochondria

In healthy fish, mitochondria are predominantly located as spherical to elongated profiles in intimate association with RER lamellae and peroxisomes close to the nucleus or the edges of RER stacks. Again, increased heterogeneity is the sole feature common to all treatments. Both linuron and 4-chloroaniline produce a conspicuous proliferation of mitochondria; endosulfan exposure results in a dilation of the intermembranous space, the formation of extended myelin-like membrane whorls and eventually mitochondrial lysis; elongated longitudinal cristae and myelin formation in the matrix and the intermembranous space are typical of atrazine contamination; diazinon results in megamitochondria; and, with ochratoxin, mitochondria appear to collapse, i.e., the matrix volume is reduced to zero.

Peroxisomes

Normally, peroxisomes appear as small spherical particles without a matrix core. Peroxisomal proliferation is weak after diazinon and linuron treatment, but is most conspicuous after endosulfan exposure. In most cases, proliferation of peroxisomes is accompanied by the formation of slender tail-like projections, which might be interpreted as the morphological expression of peroxisome division. In hepatocytes of rainbow trout subjected to endosulfan, peroxisomes also form aggregates of up to 20 profiles and display intensely staining matrix portions very reminiscent of the core typical of mammalian peroxisomes. In contrast, the number of peroxisomes is reduced with 4-chloroaniline.

Lysosomal elements

Lysosomes are rare in control rainbow trout; they are restricted to the peribiliary complex. Except for 4-chloroaniline (reduction) and ochratoxin (no reaction), all chemicals tested induce a proliferation of lysosomes accompanied by an augmentation of other lysosomal elements (myelinated and multivesicular bodies, autophagosomes and glycogenosomes). Following exposure to 4-chloroaniline, lysosomes display long, slender crystalline inclusions in their matrix; with both diazinon and linuron, lysosomes contain stacks of obliterating membrane fragments, a phenomenon very reminiscent of what has been described as phospholipidosis in mammals (see Phillips *et al.*, 1987). Glycogenosomes, i.e. organelles degrading glycogen within membrane-bound vacuoles most likely derived from lysosomes (Gas and Serfaty, 1972), can be observed after rainbow trout exposure to diazinon and, much more conspicuously, to 4-chloroaniline (Braunbeck *et al.*, 1990a).

Hepatic storage products

In control hepatocytes, the cell periphery of rainbow trout hepatocytes is occupied by extensive glycogen fields; lipid droplets are sparse. Except for linuron and ochratoxin, which stimulate an augmentation of cytosolic lipid deposits (macrovesicular lipid accumulation, i.e., aggregation of lipoid materials to cytoplasmic vacuoles without a limiting membrane) and steatosis (microvesicular lipid accumulation, i.e., within cisternae of the rough and smooth endoplasmic reticulum; Baglio and Farber, 1965), very little change can be observed with respect to lipid reserves. With linuron, hepatocytes display a conspicuously inhomogeneous distribution of lipid droplets, which accumulate at the basal (sinusoidal) face of the hepatocytes. In contrast, glycogen stores are depleted after exposure to 4-chloroaniline, endosulfan, atrazine, linuron and ochratoxin. In particular, 4-chloroaniline is further marked by accumulation of cholesterol-like crystals and conspicuous condensation of glycogen into very dense masses, which eventually end up in glycogenosome-like particles.

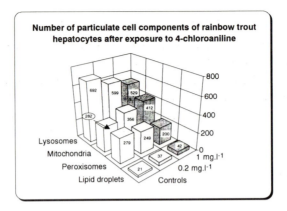

Fig. 2.1 Numerical changes of mitochondria, peroxisomes. lysosomes and lipid droplets in rainbow trout hepatocytes induced by exposure to 4-chloroaniline. Multistage sampling and morphometric evaluation were performed according to the principles of Weibel (1979). At all tiers, the hepatocyte was selected as the reference space. At each tier, a total of 12 micrographs taken from four animals per treatment were evaluated. For details of sampling for stereological analysis, see Segner and Braunbeck (1990).

Non-parenchymal cells

The liver of unimpaired rainbow trout is almost free from migrating phagocytic cells. In all experiments, however, toxicant exposure results in varying degrees of macrophage immigration and subsequent formation of macrophage centres. Elevated phagocytic activity, both of glycogen, cellular debris and entire hepatic cells, is evident. Exceptional, however, are the immigration of granulocytes following atrazine exposure, and the proliferation of Ito cells in rainbow trout exposed to diazinon.

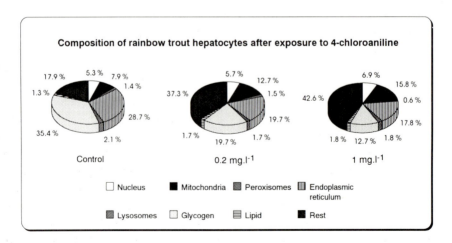

Fig. 2.2 Alterations in rainbow trout hepatocyte composition after exposure to 4-chloroaniline.

Quantification of chemical-induced cytological alterations

In order to also evaluate the species-specificity of toxicant-induced hepatocellular changes, the liver from carp fed with endosulfan-contaminated food was investigated by stereological techniques. Peroxisomal proliferation, SER induction and glycogen depletion found in rainbow trout is paralleled in carp. As an example of the technique, quantitative alterations in hepatocyte composition of rainbow trout exposed to 4-chloroaniline are illustrated in Figures 2.1 and 2.2.

2.4   Discussion

Relative sensitivity of cytological techniques

Table 2.2 compares LC_{50}, LOEC and NOEC data obtained with conventional methods with cytological LOECs reported here, and shows the clearly greater sensitivity of the latter. This sensitivity may be enhanced further by the introduction of quantitative morphological techniques. In particular, minute alterations such as those observed in the liver of carp exposed to dietary endosulfan can only be safely diagnosed by means of stereology.

Substance-specificity of cytological alterations

As a rule, structural acclimation to environmental conditions is only rarely based on the introduction of newly formed structures, but more often consists of qualitative and quantitative alterations of pre-existing characteristics (Forbus, 1952). When considering the rather limited set of hepatocellular structural variables, it is evident that specificity is likely to be based on relative changes. Mainly based on light microscopical investigations, this led several authors to the conclusion that *all* structural alterations are unspecific (Couch, 1975; Sindermann, 1984).

However, our data demonstrate that at least within a given set of experiments, specific structural responses do exist. In Figure 2.3, all cytopathological effects observed in at least three experiments have been classified as 'unspecific'. According to this list, the typical reaction of a rainbow trout hepatocyte exposed to organic toxicants is likely to include (1) disturbance of the highly regular cytoplasmic compartmentation; (2) augmentation of nucleoli and nuclear deformation in conjunction with a stimulation of karyokinesis, but not of cytokinesis; (3) reduction and graduated disintegration of RER; (4) proliferation of SER, peroxisomes and lysosomal elements; (5) increased heterogeneity of mitochondria and peroxisomes; (6) glycogen depletion; and (7) an immigration of macrophages. In contrast, numerous changes could only be seen for one or two substances (Fig. 2.4). In particular, the pathological syndrome induced by ochratoxin includes numerous apparently specific effects such as RER transformation into huge membrane whorls or the 'collapse' of mitochondria and Golgi cisternae. Other unique alterations include induction of peroxisomal cores after endosulfan exposure, granulocyte

Table 2.2 A comparison of the toxicological data for the organic toxicants tested.

	LC$_{50}$ value	'Conventional' NOEC	'Conventional' LOEC	Cytological LOEC
4-Chloroaniline	rainbow trout: 14 mg.l^{-1} zebrafish: 46 mg.l^{-1}	zebrafish: 1.8 mg.l^{-1}	zebrafish: 3.2 mg.l^{-1}	zebrafish: 40 μg.l^{-1} rainbow trout: 200 μg.l^{-1}
Endosulfan	striped bass: 0.1 μg.l^{-1} rainbow trout: 0.3 – 1.9 μg.l^{-1} carp: 0.9 – 7 μg.l^{-1}	carp: 0.14 μg.l^{-1} guppy: 0.6 μg.l^{-1} tilapia: 0.63 μg.l^{-1}	carp: 0.33 μg.l^{-1} tilapia: 0.44 μg.l^{-1}	rainbow trout: 10 ng.l^{-1} carp: 1 ng.l^{-1}
Atrazine	larval catfish: 0.2 – 0.3 μg.l^{-1} rainbow trout: 1 – 9 mg.l^{-1} zebrafish 37 mg.l^{-1}	zebrafish: 80 μg.l^{-1} brook trout: 60 – 120 μg.l^{-1}	zebrafish: 100 μg.l^{-1} carp: 100 μg.l^{-1}	rainbow trout: 40 μg.l^{-1} zebrafish: 1 mg.l^{-1}
Diazinon	brook trout: 1.6 mg.l^{-1} bluegill sunfish: 0.46 mg.l^{-1}	fathead minnow: < 3.2 μg.l^{-1} brook trout: < 0.55 μg.l^{-1}	brook trout: 0.55 μg.l^{-1} fathead minnow: 3.2 μg.l^{-1}	rainbow trout: 40 μg.l^{-1}
Disulfoton	bluegill sunfish: 0.3 mg.l^{-1} rainbow trout: 1.85 mg.l^{-1}			rainbow trout: 0.1 μg.l^{-1}
Linuron	harlequin fish: 0.6 – 4.6 mg.l^{-1} rainbow trout: 5 –16 mg.l^{-1} carp: 20 μg.l^{-1}		rainbow trout: 30 μg.l^{-1}	rainbow trout: 30 μg.l^{-1}
Ochratoxin	rainbow trout: 4.67 mg.kg^{-1} (LD$_{50}$!)			rainbow trout: 100 μg.kg^{-1}

	4-Chloroaniline	Endosulfan	Atrazine	Diazinon	Disulfoton	Linuron	Ochratoxin
Nuclei							
Stimulation of mitosis	▨		▨	▨		▨	▨
Augmentation of binucleate cells	▨		▨	▨		▨	▨
Free nuclear lipid inclusions	▨					▨	
Deformation of nuclear envelope	▨	▨	▨			▨	▨
Augmentation of nucleoli	▨	▨				▨	▨
Rough endoplasmic reticulum							
Increased heterogeneity	▨	▨	▨			▨	▨
Reduction	▨	▨	▨		▨	▨	▨
Fragmentation, vesiculation	▨	▨	▨			▨	▨
Dilation of cisternae	▨	▨	▨			▨	▨
Smooth endoplasmic reticulum							
Proliferation		▨	▨	▨	▨	▨	▨
Golgi apparatus							
Increased heterogeneity	▨	▨					
Decrease of VLDL synthesis	▨	▨					▨
Mitochondria							
Increased heterogeneity	▨	▨	▨	▨	▨	▨	▨
Peroxisomes							
Proliferation		▨		▨		▨	
Increased heterogeneity		▨		▨		▨	
Cluster formation		▨		▨		▨	
Lysosomal elements							
Proliferation		▨	▨	▨	▨	▨	
Myelinated bodies		▨	▨	▨	▨	▨	
Induction of autophagosomes		▨	▨	▨	▨	▨	
Induction of multivesicular bodies		▨	▨			▨	
Storage materials							
Decrease in glycogen stores	▨	▨	▨		▨	▨	▨
Intracellular compartmentation							
Disturbance of compartmentation	▨					▨	▨
Non-parenchymal cells							
Immigration of macrophages	▨	▨	▨	▨		▨	▨
Formation of macrophage centres	▨	▨	▨	▨		▨	▨
Increased glycogen phagocytosis	▨	▨				▨	▨
Phagocytosis of entire cells	▨	▨				▨	▨
		▨	▨	▨		▨	▨
		▨	▨	▨		▨	▨

Fig. 2.3 Compilation of unspecific cytological alterations in the liver of rainbow trout after prolonged sublethal exposure to 4-chloroaniline, endosulfan, atrazine, diazinon, disulfoton, linuron and ochratoxin. (A cytological alteration was termed 'unspecific', if it was found after exposure to at least three test chemicals.)

invasion with atrazine or condensation of tremendous amounts of glycogen in multinucleate hepatocytes of 4-chloroaniline-contaminated rainbow trout. However, it should be borne in mind that the electron microscopical analysis of the liver of fish from further toxicological experiments will elucidate histo- and cyto-pathological phenomena similar to those now termed 'specific', and that the term 'specific' is, therefore, only valid under the definition given above within the given set of compounds tested, and under the given experimental context and methodology.

In conclusion, the hepatocytic reaction to xenobiotics consists of an intricate complex of unspecific and specific alterations. However, in each of the experiments conducted so far, at least the *combination* of cytological variations proved substance-specific. As a consequence, from a cytopathological point of view, a

	4-Chloroaniline	Endosulfan	Atrazine	Diazinon	Disulfoton	Linuron	Ochratoxin
Nuclei							
Intranuclear steatosis							�
Intranuclear myelin formation	▪						
Inflation of nuclear envelope	▪						
Rough endoplasmic reticulum							
Fenestration of cisternae							▪
Collapse of cisternae							▪
Steatosis						▪	▪
Formation of RER whorls						▪	▪
Transformation into myelin body(ies)							▪
Golgi apparatus							
Hypertrophy				▪		▪	
Fenestration of cisternae		▪					
Dilation of cisternae				▪			
Stimulation of VLDL synthesis						▪	
Reduction of Golgi vesicles							▪
Augmentation of Golgi vesicles				▪			
Collapse of cisternae							▪
Mitochondria							
Proliferation	▪						
Increase in volume					▪	▪	
Dilation of intermembranous space		▪					
Induction of longitudinal cristae			▪				
Collapse of mitochondria							▪
Intramitochondrial myelin formation		▪					
Partial lysis		▪					
Peroxisomes							
Reduction	▪						
Increased catalase activity	▪	▪					
Reduction in catalase activity	▪						
Heterogeneity in catalase distribution		▪					
Tail formation (division?)						▪	
Myelin formation in matrix		▪					
Accumulation around lipid						▪	
Lysosomal elements							
Reduction	▪						
Induction of new lysosome types			▪			▪	
Crystal formation in matrix							
Phospholipidosis				▪		▪	
Induction of glycogenosomes							
Storage materials							
Increase of lipid deposits						▪	
Perisinusoidal polarisation of lipids						▪	
Steatosis						▪	▪
Increased electron density of lipid droplets							▪
Formation of cholesterol crystals	▪						
Formation of lipid clusters						▪	
Glycogen condensation	▪						
Non-parenchymal cells							
Immigration of granulocytes			▪				
Proliferation of Ito cells				▪			

Fig. 2.4 Compilation of 'specific' cytological alterations in the liver of rainbow trout after prolonged sublethal exposure to 4-chloroaniline, endosulfan, atrazine, diazinon, disulfoton, linuron and ochratoxin. (A cytological alteration was termed 'specific', if it was found after exposure to less than three test chemicals.)

generalisation of observations on pathological alterations made for one particular substance to apply to any other compound appears to be fragile, if not impossible.

Functional significance and diagnostic value of cytological alterations

According to the principle of the relationship and mutual interaction between structure and function, an alteration of liver structure may be expected to also imply an alteration of liver function (Hinton *et al.*, 1987). However, the functional interpretation of hepatic structural alterations in fish is hampered by the lack of appropriate data on xenobiotic metabolism in fish. At present, it is particularly the unspecific phenomena we are able to interpret. One example of structure–function relationship in toxicology is the correlation between SER proliferation and induction of xenobiotic biotransformation (Hacking *et al.*, 1978; Klaunig *et al.*, 1979; Braunbeck and Völkl, 1991, 1993). Among the substances investigated in rainbow trout liver in the present study, endosulfan and diazinon have to be regarded the strongest inducers.

On the other hand, specific morphological changes at least give an indication of the location of the toxic attack or even to the mode of toxic action. Moreover, specific structural modifications of hepatocytes are doubtless of increased diagnostic value with respect to the identification of the substance.

In an attempt to evaluate the significance of cytological and histological alterations at the next higher tier of biological organisation, i.e. at the level of the individual, a classification may be made into regenerative (adaptive) reactions, i.e. processes to be regarded as expression of defence mechanisms, or, alternatively, into symptoms of irreversible damage, i.e. plainly degenerative phenomena (cf. Sindermann, 1984). At present, SER proliferation, lysosomal and peroxisomal proliferation, and immigration of macrophages are assumed to be of adaptive nature. In contrast, reactions such as RER fractionation, dilation, vesiculation and transformation into membrane whorls are likely to express the onset of degenerative processes related to functional disturbance or dysfunction. The combination of sensitivity, accuracy and the fact that cytology is capable of simultaneously providing evidence of adaptive reactions, of truly pathological responses *and* of transitions from adaptation to degeneration, certainly represents the major advantage of the use of histo- and cytopathological alterations as biomarkers of environmental pollution by organic chemicals.

References

Baglio, C.M. and E. Farber, 1965. Reversal by adenine of the induced lipid accumulation in the endoplasmic reticulum of the liver. *J.Cell Biol.*, **27**: 591–601.

Blouin, A., 1977. Morphometry of liver sinusoidal cells. In: Wisse, E. and D.L. Knook (Eds.) *Kupffer Cells and Other Liver Sinusoidal Cells*, pp. 62–70. Elsevier, North-Holland Biomedical Press.

Blouin, A., R.P. Bolender and E.R. Weibel, 1977. Distribution of organelles and membranes between hepatocytes and non-hepatocytes in the rat liver parenchyma. *J.Cell Biol.*, **72**: 441–455.

Bolender, R.P., 1979. Morphometric analysis in the assessment of the response of the liver to drugs. *Pharmacol.Rev.*, **30**: 429–443.

Bolender, R.P. and E.R. Weibel, 1973. A morphometric study of the removal of phenobarbital-induced membranes from hepatocytes after cessation of treatment. *J.Cell Biol.*, **56**: 746–761.

Braunbeck, T. and H. Segner, 1992. Preexposure temperature acclimation and diet as modifying factors for the tolerance of golden ide (*Leuciscus idus melanotus*) to short-term exposure to 4-chloroaniline. *Ecotox.Environ.Safety*, **24**: 72–94.

Braunbeck, T. and V. Storch, 1992. Senescence of hepatocytes isolated from rainbow trout (*Oncorhynchus mykiss*) in primary culture. An ultrastructural study. *Protoplasma*, **170**: 138–159.

Braunbeck, T. and A. Völkl, 1991. Induction of biotransformation in the liver of eel (*Anguilla anguilla* L.) by sublethal exposure to dinitro-*o*-cresol: an ultrastructural and biochemical study. *Ecotox.Environ.Safety*, **21**: 109–127.

Braunbeck, T. and A. Völkl, 1993. Cytological alterations in the livers of golden ide (*Leuciscus idus melanotus*) and eel (*Anguilla anguilla*) induced by sublethal doses of dinitro-o-cresol. In: Braunbeck, T., W. Hanke and H. Segner (Eds.) *Fish in Ecotoxicology and Ecophysiology*, pp. 55–80. Weinheim, VCH.

Braunbeck, T., V. Storch and R. Nagel, 1989. Sex-specific reaction of liver ultrastructure in zebrafish (*Brachydanio rerio*) after prolonged sublethal exposure to 4-nitrophenol. *Aquat.Toxicol.*, **14**: 185–202.

Braunbeck, T., V. Storch and H. Bresch, 1990a. Species-specific reaction of liver ultrastructure in zebrafish (*Brachydanio rerio*) and trout (*Salmo gairdneri*) after prolonged exposure to 4-chloroaniline. *Arch.Environ.Contam.Toxicol.*, **19**: 405–418.

Braunbeck, T., G. Görge, V. Storch and R. Nagel, 1990b. Hepatic steatosis in zebrafish (*Brachydanio rerio*) induced by long-term exposure to γ-hexachlorocyclohexane. *Ecotox.Environ.Safety*, **19**: 355–374.

Braunbeck, T., P. Burkhardt-Holm and V. Storch, 1990c. Liver pathology in eels (*Anguilla anguilla* L.) from the Rhine river exposed to the chemical spill at Basle in November 1986. *Limnologie aktuell*, **1**: 371–392.

Braunbeck, T., S.J. Teh, S.M. Lester and D.E. Hinton, 1992. Ultrastructural alterations in hepatocytes of medaka (*Oryzias latipes*) exposed to diethylnitrosamine. *Toxicol.Pathol.*, **20**: 179–196.

Braunbeck, T., P. Burkhardt-Holm, G. Görge, R. Nagel, R.D. Negele and V. Storch, 1993. Regenbogenforelle und Zebrabärbling, zwei Modelle für verlängerte Toxizitätstests: relative Empfindlichkeit, Art- und Organspezifität in der cytopathologischen Reaktion von Leber und Darm auf Atrazin. *Schriftenr.Ver.Wasser-, Boden-, Lufthygiene*, in press.

Couch, J.A., 1975. Histopathological effects of pesticides and related chemicals on the liver of fishes. In: Ribelin, W.E. and G. Migaki (Eds.) *The Pathology of Fishes*, pp. 559–584. Madison, University of Wisconsin Press.

Forbus, W.D., 1952. *Reaction to Injury: Pathology for Students of Disease*. Baltimore, Williams & Wilkins.

Gas, N. and A. Serfaty, 1972. Cytophysiologie du foie de la carpe (*Cyprinus carpio* L.). Modifications ultrastructurales consécutives au maintien dans les conditions de jeûne hivernal. *J.Physiol.*, *Paris*, **64**: 57–67.

Hacking, M.A., J. Budd and K. Hodson, 1978. The ultrastructure of the liver of the rainbow trout: normal structure and modifications after chronic administration of a polychlorinated biphenyl Aroclor 1254. *Can.J.Zool.*, **56**: 477–491.

Hampton, J.A., R.C. Lantz and D.E. Hinton, 1989. Functional units in rainbow trout (*Salmo gairdneri*, Richardson) liver: III. Morphometric analysis of parenchyma, stroma, and component cell types. *Am.J.Anat.*, **185**: 58–73.

Hess, F.A., E.R. Weibel and R. Preisig, 1973. Morphometry of dog liver: normal base-line data. *Virchows Arch.Abt. B Zellpathol.*, **12**: 303–317.

Hinton, D.E., J.A. Hampton and R.C. Lantz, 1985. Morphometric analysis of liver in rainbow trout quantitatively defining an organ of xenobiotic metabolism. *Mar.Environ.Res.*, **17**: 238–239.

Hinton, D.E., R.C. Lantz, J.A. Hampton, P.R. McCuskey and R.S. McCuskey, 1987. Normal versus abnormal structure: considerations in morphologic responses of teleosts to pollutants. *Environ.Health Perspect.*, **71**: 139–146.

Klaunig, J.E., M.M. Lipsky, B.F. Trump and D.E. Hinton, 1979. Biochemical and ultrastructural changes in teleost liver following subacute exposure to PCB. *J.Environ.Pathol.Toxicol.*, **2**: 953–963.

Lloyd, R., 1992. *Pollution and Freshwater Fish.* Oxford, Fishing News Books.

Loud, A.V., 1968. A quantitative stereological description of the ultrastructure of normal rat liver parenchymal cells. *J.Cell Biol.*, **37**: 27–46.

Moore, M.N., 1985. Cellular responses to pollutants. *Mar.Pollut.Bull.*, **16**: 134–139.

Nagel, R., 1988. Fische und Umweltchemikalien. Beiträge zu einer Bewertung. University of Mainz.

Peute, J., R. Huiskamp and P.G.W.J. Van Oordt, 1985. Quantitative analysis of estradiol-17β-induced changes in the ultrastructure of the liver of male zebrafish, *Brachydanio rerio. Cell Tissue Res.*, **242**: 377–382.

Pfeifer, U., 1973. Cellular autophagy and cell atrophy in the rat liver during long-term starvation. A quantitative morphological study with regard to diurnal variations. *Virchows Arch.Abt.B Zellpathol.*, **12**: 195–211.

Phillips, M.J., S.J. Poucell, J. Patterson and P. Valencia, 1987. *The Liver: an Atlas and Text of Ultrastructural Pathology*, pp. 159–238. New York, Raven Press.

Rohr, H.P., H.R. Brunner, Y.M. Rasser, Ch.A. von Matt and U.N. Riede, 1973. Einfluss des Hungers auf die quantitative Cytoarchitektur der Rattenleberzelle. I. Absoluter Hunger und Wiederauffütterung. *Beitr.Pathol.*, **149**: 347–362.

Segner, H. and T. Braunbeck, 1990. Adaptive changes of liver composition and structure in golden ide during winter acclimatization. *J.Exp.Zool.*, **255**: 171–185.

Sindermann, C.J., 1984. Fish and environmental impact. *Arch.Fisch.Wiss.*, **35**: 125–160.

Stäubli, W., R. Hess and E.R. Weibel, 1969. Correlated morphometric and biochemical studies on the liver cell. II. Effects of phenobarbital on rat hepatocytes. *J.Cell Biol.*, **42**: 92–112.

Stebbing, A.R.D., 1985. A possible synthesis. In: Bayne, B.L. (Ed.) *The Effects of Stress and Pollution on Marine Animals*, pp. 301–314. New York, Praeger Publishers.

Vogt, G., 1987. Monitoring of environmental pollutants such as pesticides in prawn aquaculture by histological diagnosis. *Aquaculture*, **67**: 157–164.

Weibel, E.R., 1979. *Stereological Methods*. Vol. I. New York, London, Academic Press.

Weibel, E.R., W. Stäubli, H.R. Gnägi and F.A. Hess, 1969. Correlated morphometric and biochemical studies on the liver cell. I. Morphometric model, stereologic methods, and normal morphometric data for rat liver. *J.Cell Biol.*, **42**: 68–91.

Chapter 3
Herbicides in water: subacute toxic effects on fish

I. ELEZOVIĆ,[1] M. BUDIMIR,[2] V. KARAN[1] and N.K. NEŠKOVIĆ[2]

[1] *Faculty of Agriculture, Department of Pesticides, Nemanjina 6,*
11080 Zemun, Belgrade-Zemun, former Yugoslavia
[2] *Institute of Plant Protection, Department of Toxicology, T. Drajzera 9, PO Box 936,*
11001 Belgrade, former Yugoslavia

3.1   Introduction

There is a continued widespread use of pesticides, despite their potential to cause harmful effects on the environment and ecosystems. The methods used for pesticide application (spraying and dusting) enable them to enter, and to pose a risk to, the aquatic ecosystem (Johnson, 1973).

Due to their widespread distribution and toxic nature, pesticides may have a serious impact on the aquatic environment and have been shown to exert adverse effects on the associated organisms (e.g. Nešković *et al.*, 1992; Beusen and Neven, 1989; Singh and Reddy, 1990; Nemcsok *et al.*, 1987; Radhaiah *et al.*, 1987; Holcombe *et al.*, 1983). Also, the extensive use of herbicides has increased the incidence of environmental pollution; these chemicals are among the most significent causes of water contamination because they are used on or near the soil and in many instances in water for aquatic weed control.

Atrazine   (2-chloro-4-ethylamino-6-isopropylamino-s-triazine) is a selective triazine-based herbicide used at pre-emergence and early post-emergence, for weed control in corn, orchards, sorghum, non-cultivated areas, etc. It may also be used in stagnant and slow running water for submerged vegetation control.

Dichlobenil   (2,6-dichlorobenzonitrile) is an aromatic nitrile compound used as a pre-emergence selective herbicide for weed control in apples, citrus, grapes, pears, plums, alfalfa, non-cultivated areas, etc. It is used also for aquatic weed control and total vegetation control (Thompson, 1982).

2,4-D   (2,4-dichlorophenoxyacetic acid) is a selective translocated phenoxy herbicide used in apples, pears, grass, barley, wheat, sorghum, corn, oats, rice, sugar cane, etc. for weed control. Used also to control aquatic plants, for brush control, as a growth stimulator, and on turf (Thompson, 1982).

Glyphosate   (N-/phosphonomethyl/glycine) is a broad-spectrum, post-emergence, translocated herbicide used primarily for weed control in corn, sorghum, soybean, rice, cotton, orchards, groves, vineyards, etc. It may also be used in the vicinity of potable water supplies (Thompson, 1982).

These four compounds have been registered for use in Yugoslavia (Mitić), 1990).

Bearing in mind that herbicides may be toxic to mammals and freshwater organisms (Nešković *et al.*, 1992; Marchini *et al.*, 1988; Elezović *et al.*, 1988; Budimir *et al.*, 1987) their mode of toxic action is of major interest. To obtain a better understanding of the mode of action of herbicides, more information is required on the biochemical changes which they cause. Therefore, the study of their toxicity should be more concerned with sublethal than with lethal effects.

The objective of this study was to investigate the acute toxicity, as well as subacute toxic effects, of different concentrations of atrazine, dichlobenil, 2,4-D and glyphosate herbicides to carp (*Cyprinus carpio*), one of the commercially most important fish species in Yugoslavian freshwaters.

3.2   Materials and methods

3.2.1   *Chemicals*

The following compounds were used.

Atrazine	Technical grade, purity 93.7%, supplied by 'Zorka', Šabac, Yugoslavia.
Dichlobenil	Technical grade, purity 75%, supplied by 'Galenika', Belgrade, Yugoslavia.
2,4-D	Technical grade, purity 98%, supplied by 'Galenika', Belgrade, Yugoslavia.
Glyphosate	Technical grade, purity 62%, supplied by ICI, England.

Dilutions of these herbicides, including stock solutions, were made in water.

3.2.2.   *Test fish*

Carp of 3.8–5.5 g in body weight and 3.6–4.5 cm in body length (for acute toxicity) and 51.0–58.0 g in body weight and 13.0–18.2 cm in body length (for subacute tests) were used in the experiments and were purchased from 'Ribokombinat', Belgrade. They were acclimated to laboratory conditions for 10 days prior to the experiments in 10 l glass aquaria (55 × 25 × 20 cm). During the experiment the fish were fed once a day (the quantity of food supplied was 1.5% of body weight) with 'Rihran', a special aquaria fish mixture, purchased from 'Florine', Maribor, Slovenia.

3.2.3   *Water characteristics*

Chlorine-free tap-water having the following physical and chemical characteristics was used: pH 7.0–7.5, total hardness 141–223 mg.l^{-1} (as $CaCO_3$), and dissolved oxygen 7.5–11.5 mg.l^{-1}. The water temperature was kept at 20 ± 1.0°C. Test solutions were changed every 24 hours, followed by the addition of fresh herbicide solution.

3.2.4   *Toxicity testing*

Acute toxicity tests were performed according to the OECD Guideline No.203 for semi-static tests (OECD, 1981). Fish were exposed to a range of herbicide concentrations for 96 hours. Mortality was recorded after 24, 48 and 96 hours. The lethal concentration causing 50% mortality (LC_{50}) was calculated by the Litchfield and Wilcoxon method (1949).

For subacute toxicity tests (14 days), fish were randomly divided into groups of 10 fish each. One group served as control while the remaining groups were exposed to different herbicide concentrations. At the end of the 14-day period blood samples were taken before sacrificing the fish. Liver and kidneys were collected, their fresh weight recorded and then prepared for biochemical analysis.

3.2.5   *Biochemical analysis*

Liver, kidneys and serum of fish from each group were used for biochemical analysis. Total lipids in serum and organs were determined by the vaniline method, using 'Radonja', Sisak, kits.

Glucose and glycogen were determined spectrophotometrically (625 nm) using the ortho-toluidine method and test kits from 'Radonja', Sisak.

3.2.6   *Statistical analysis*

The mean and the standard deviation were calculated for each test group. The mean of the test and control groups were compared using Student's t-test with the significance level set at $P = 0.05$.

3.3   **Results**

3.3.1   *Acute toxicity*

The results of the acute toxicity tests with the herbicides atrazine, dichlobenil, 2,4-D and glyphosate, and carp are given in Table 3.1.

The acute toxicity varied depending on the type of the compound tested and the duration of exposure. Acute toxicity (LC_{50}) for 48-hour exposure was 11.2 mg.l^{-1} for dichlobenil, 41.0 mg.l^{-1} for atrazine, 295 mg.l^{-1} for 2,4-D and 645.2 mg.l^{-1}

Table 3.1 Acute toxicity (LC_{50} in mg.l^{-1}) of the herbicides atrazine, dichlobenil, 2,4-D and glyphosate to carp.

| Herbicide | LC_{50} | | |
	24h	48h	96h
Atrazine	41.0	41.0	18.8
	(36.2–45.0)*	(37.5–44.1)	(15.7–20.2)
Dichlobenil	14.3	11.2	10.9
	(11.9–16.1)	(9.7–13.2)	(9.1–12.3)
2,4-D	310.0	295.0	270.0
	(268.5–343.0)	(262.0–312.5)	(259.2–286.5)
Glyphosate	–	645.2	620.0
		(632.5–655.0)	(607.0–638.5)

* 95% confidence limits

for glyphosate. After 96 h the toxicity was somewhat greater, with LC_{50}s of 10.9 mg.l^{-1} for dichlobenil, 18.8 mg.l^{-1} for atrazine, 270.0 mg.l^{-1} for 2,4-D and 620.0 mg.l^{-1} for glyphosate.

3.3.2   *Subacute toxicity*

In the subacute toxicity tests, the effects of atrazine, dichlobenil, 2,4-D and glyphosate on some blood and tissue constituents were studied. The results are given in Tables 3.2 to 3.5.

Changes were found in the level of total lipids, glucose and glycogen in fish exposed to different atrazine concentrations (Table 3.2).

A statistically significant increase in the total lipids concentration of liver and kidney was obtained at atrazine concentrations of 3.0 and 6.0 mg.l^{-1} as well as a statistically significant ($P < 0.01$) increase in the glucose and glycogen level in the serum. At the same time, the total lipids in the serum (at all three concentrations tested) as well as glucose and glycogen level in liver, were at the same level as the control fish.

With dichlobenil (Table 3.3) a statistically significant ($P < 0.05$ and $P < 0.01$ respectively) increase in total lipid content of liver and kidneys (at all three concentrations tested) was obtained as well as an increase in the level of glucose and glycogen in the serum of fish exposed to 2.5 mg.l^{-1}. In all other measurements, statistically significant differences compared to the control were not observed.

The effects of different concentrations of 2,4-D on biochemical changes in serum and organs of carp are given in Table 3.4. The increase of glucose and glycogen level in liver and serum of carp exposed to 250.0 mg.l^{-1} was statistically different from the controls ($P < 0.05$). The differences found for total lipids in liver, kidneys and serum at all three concentrations tested, and for glucose and glycogen in liver

Table 3.2 Biochemical changes in liver, kidney and serum constituents of carp exposed to various atrazine concentrations during the experiment (14 days).

	Treatment	Conc.	Total lipids		Glucose		Glycogen	
		$(mg.l^{-1})$	$g.l^{-1}$	% of control	$mg.kg^{-1}$	% of control	$mg.g^{-1}$	% of control
Liver	Control	0.0	14.2	100.0	30.9	100.0	28.1	100.0
	Atrazine	1.5	15.7	110.6	29.5	95.5	26.8	95.4
		3.0	16.9	119.0*	28.7	92.5	26.1	92.9
		6.0	16.6	116.9*	27.9	90.3	25.4	90.4
Kidney	Control	0.0	15.3	100.0				
	Atrazine	1.5	16.9	110.4				
		3.0	20.1	131.4**				
		6.0	17.3	113.1*				
Serum	Control	0.0	13.0	100.0	23.0	100.0	20.9	100.0
	Atrazine	1.5	12.8	98.5	25.5	110.9	23.2	111.0
		3.0	12.1	93.1	29.0	126.1**	26.4	126.3**
		6.0	13.4	103.1	28.1	122.2**	25.6	122.5**

*   Significantly different from control, $P<0.05$
**   Significantly different from control, $P<0.01$

Table 3.3 Biochemical changes in liver, kidney and serum constituents of carp exposed to various dichlobenil concentrations during the experiment (14 days).

	Treatment	Conc.	Total lipids		Glucose		Glycogen	
		$(mg.l^{-1})$	$g.l^{-1}$	% of control	$mg.kg^{-1}$	% of control	$mg.g^{-1}$	% of control
Liver	Control	0.0	11.2	100.0	28.9	100.0	26.3	100.0
	Dichlobenil	2.5	13.0	116.1*	26.3	91.0	23.9	91.0
		5.0	13.9	124.1*	26.5	91.7	24.1	91.6
		10.0	13.6	121.4*	27.4	94.8	24.5	93.1
Kidney	Control	0.0	10.6	100.0				
	Dichlobenil	2.5	13.5	127.3**				
		5.0	12.8	120.7*				
		10.0	14.3	134.9**				
Serum	Control	0.0	13.0	100.0	23.0	100.0	20.9	100.0
	Dichlobenil	2.5	12.7	97.7	27.8	120.9*	25.3	121.0*
		5.0	11.1	89.2	22.1	96.1	20.1	96.2
		10.0	11.8	90.8	23.6	102.6	21.5	102.9

*   Significantly different from control, $P<0.05$
**   Significantly different from control, $P<0.01$

Table 3.4 Biochemical changes in liver, kidney and serum constituents of carp exposed to various 2,4-D concentrations during the experiment (14 days).

	Treatment	Conc.	Total lipids		Glucose		Glycogen	
		$(mg.l^{-1})$	$g.l^{-1}$	% of control	$mg.kg^{-1}$	% of control	$mg.g^{-1}$	% of control
Liver	Control	0.0	17.8	100.0	35.0	100.0	31.8	100.0
	2,4-D	150.0	17.9	100.6	35.2	100.6	32.0	100.6
		200.0	18.3	102.8	35.4	101.1	32.2	101.3
		250.0	19.1	107.3	40.7	116.3*	37.0	116.5*
Kidney	Control	0.0	16.5	100.0				
	2,4-D	150.0	15.2	92.1				
		200.0	16.7	101.2				
		250.0	16.2	98.2				
Serum	Control	0.0	15.9	100.0	36.7	100.0	33.4	100.0
	2,4-D	150.5	17.8	111.9	36.2	98.6	32.9	98.5
		200.0	17.2	108.2	36.5	99.4	33.2	99.4
		250.0	17.7	111.3	41.9	114.2*	38.1	114.1*

* Significantly different from control, $P<0.05$

Table 3.5 Biochemical alterations in liver, kidney and serum of carp exposed to various glyphosate concentrations during the experiment (14 days).

	Treatment	Conc.	Total lipids		Glucose		Glycogen	
		$(mg.l^{-1})$	$g.l^{-1}$	% of control	$mg.kg^{-1}$	% of control	$mg.g^{-1}$	% of control
Liver	Control	0.0	17.8	100.0	34.3	100.0	31.2	100.0
	Glyphosate	2.5	17.2	96.6	34.2	99.7	31.1	99.7
		5.0	19.2	107.9	33.8	98.5	30.1	98.4
		10.0	20.4	114.6*	33.9	98.8	30.8	98.7
Kidney	Control	0.0	16.5	100.0				
	Glyphosate	2.5	15.7	95.1				
		5.0	17.8	107.8				
		10.0	17.9	108.5				
Serum	Control	0.0	15.9	100.0	39.1	100.0	35.6	100.0
	Glyphosate	2.5	15.6	98.1	40.1	102.5	36.5	102.5
		5.0	16.6	104.4	42.7	109.2	38.8	109.0
		10.0	17.2	108.2	46.9	119.9*	42.7	119.9*

* Significantly different from control, $P<0.05$

and serum at 150.0 and 200.0 mg.l^{-1} between test and control fish were not statistically significant.

Similar results were obtained with glyphosate (Table 3.5). Only an increase in the glucose and glycogen content in serum, and in the total lipids in liver, was obtained at 10.0 mg.l^{-1}. In all other cases the differences recorded were not statistically significant.

3.4   Discussion

The effects of pesticides on fish differ widely and depend on the type of the compound, the concentration and the exposure time. However, other factors may influence these effects, in particular environmental conditions.

Blood glucose concentration appears to be a sensitive, reliable indicator of environmental stress in fish. Glucose levels in blood and tissues may be used to indicate the toxicological significance of a substance in the aquatic environment.

The acute toxicity of the herbicides studied to carp (Table 3.1) shows a considerable variation between the compounds tested, ranging from 10.9 (dichlobenil) to 620.0 mg.l^{-1} (glyphosate). Based on their acute toxicity, all four compounds (even the most toxic, dichlobenil) are listed in the group of weakly toxic substances for fish (Clarke *et al.*, 1970).

On the basis of the results which were obtained for subacute (14 days) toxicity effects, it may be concluded that atrazine (Table 3.2) and dichlobenil (Table 3.3) effects may be reflected in an increase in the total lipids in fish liver and kidney, as well as in glucose and glycogen levels in the serum. Effects of 2,4-D (Table 3.4) and glyphosate (Table 3.5) are less pronounced and may be reflected in an increase of serum glucose and glycogen content.

Other authors have also examined the harmful effects of sublethal pesticide concentrations on some fish blood and tissue constituents. A relationship between glucose content and the exposure of fish and mammals to organochlorine insecticides (Kraybill, 1969; Olivereau, 1964) has been noted. Subsequently, Silberberg (1974) studied the effects of sublethal concentrations (2.33 ppb) of the organochlorine insecticide dieldrin on fish and noted significant increases (after 5 days of treatment) in blood glucose to more than 133% of control levels. However, 15 days following the treatment, the blood glucose levels in treated fish returned to the initial levels. Another organochlorine insecticide (heptachlor) induced a decrease of blood and kidney glucose level in *Tilapia mossambica* (Radhaiah *et al.*, 1987). An increase in blood glucose concentration in carp exposed 24 and 48 hours to different concentrations of the organophosphorus pesticide methadation has also been recorded (Nemcsok *et al.*, 1987). Further, in tests on eel (*Anguilla anguilla*) an increase in the liver and muscle glucose, e.g. a decrease in the muscle glycogen content (Ferrando and Andreu-Moliner, 1991) has been detected following the exposure of fish to sublethal lindane concentrations (0.335 mg.l^{-1}) in water.

Heavy metals may, in addition to pesticides, induce biochemical and enzymatic changes in fish as well, leading to an increase in glucose and a decrease in glycogen level in catfish (*Clarias batrachus*) liver and kidneys, as is the case with lithium (Goel *et al.*, 1985). Eventually, even environmental factors may affect the toxic response of fish. Water temperature has been found to increase phenol toxicity to fish as measured by blood and tissue glucose and glycogen changes (Gluth and Hanke, 1983). Differences in the reported experimental results obtained for biochemical effects of toxicants to fish, obtained by various authors, may be explained by variations in the environmental conditions, and this should be borne in mind when conducting experiments and evaluating the results obtained.

Results from the experiments reported here, together with the results obtained by other authors, demonstrate the significance of these studies in gaining a better understanding of the harmful effects of pesticides, including herbicides, on aquatic organisms.

Acknowledgement

This study was supported by the Scientific Research Fund of Serbia on the Project 'Pesticides and the Environment' (Contract No.1809).

3.5   References

Beusen, J.M. and B. Neven, 1989. Toxicity of dimethoate to *Daphnia magna* and freshwater fish. *Bull.Environ.Contam.Toxicol.*, **42**: 126–133.

Budimir, M., I. Elezović, V. Karan and N. Nešković, 1987. Akutni i subakutni toksični efekti pesticida na ribe. Jugoslovensko savetovanje o primeni pesticida, Opatija (Abstract: *Glasnik zaštite bilja*, **10–11**: 406–407).

Clarke, F.E., D.G. Harvey and D.J. Humphreys, 1970. *Veterinary Toxicology*. London, Bailliere Tindall.

Elezović, I., V. Poleksić, V. Mitrović-Tutundžić and M. Budimir, 1988. Die Auswirkung von Dichlobenil und Atrazin auf den morphologischen Kiemenbau beim Karpfen (*Cyprinus carpio* L.). Internal report, XXVII. Arbeitstagung Internationale Arbeitsgemeinschaft Donauforschung der Societas Internationalis Limnologiae, Constanta-Mamaia.

Ferrando, M.D. and E. Andreu-Moliner, 1991. Effects of lindane on fish carbohydrate metabolism. *Ecotoxicol.Environ.Safety*, **22**: 17–23.

Gluth, G. and W. Hanke, 1983. The effect of temperature on physiological changes in carp, *Cyprinus carpio* L. induced by phenol. *Ecotoxicol.Environ.Safety*, **7**: 373–389.

Goel, K.A., S.D. Sharma and Maya, 1985. Biochemical and enzymological changes in liver and kidney of *Clarias batrachus* following lithium intoxication. *Arh.hig rada toksikol.*, **36**: 249–253.

Holcombe, G.W., G.L. Phipps and J.T. Fiandt, 1983. Toxicity of selected priority pollutants to various aquatic organisms. *Ecotoxicol.Environ.Safety*, **7**: 400–409.

Johnson, D.W., 1973. Pesticides residues in fish. In: Edward, C.A. (Ed.) *Environmental Pollution by Pesticides*, pp. 181–212, London, Plenum.

Kraybill, H. (Ed.), 1969. Biological effects of pesticides in mammalian systems. *Annals N.Y.Acad.Sci.*, **160**: 1.

Litchfield, J.T. and F. Wilcoxon, 1949. A simplified method of evaluating dose–effect experiments. *J.Pharmacol.*, **96**: 99–113.

Marchini, S., L. Passereni, D. Cesareo and M.L. Tosato, 1988. Herbicidal triazines: acute toxicity on *Daphnia*, fish and plants and analysis of its relationships with structural factors. *Ecotoxicol.Environ.Safety*, **16**: 148–157.

Mitić, N. (Ed.), 1990. Pesticidi u poljoprivredi i šumarstvu u Jugoslaviji. Belgrade, Privredni pregled.

Nemcsok, J., B. Asztalos, E. Vig and L. Orban, 1987. The effect of an organophosphorus pesticide on the enzymes of carp (*Cyprinus carpio* L.). *Acta Biol.Hung.*, **38**: 77–85.

Nešković, N., I. Elezović, V. Karan, V. Poleksić and M. Budimir, 1992. Acute and subacute toxicity of atrazine to carp (*Cyprinus carpio* L.). *Ecotoxicol.Environ.Safety*, 25.

Olivereau, M., 1964. *Texas Rept.Biol.Med.*, **22**: 1.

OECD, 1981. OECD Guidelines for testing of chemicals. Guidelines 203 and 204 (adopted in 1984). Paris, OECD.

Radhaiah, V., M. Girija and J.K. Rao, 1987. Changes in selected biochemical parameters in the kidney and blood of the fish *Tilapia mossambica* exposed to heptachlor. *Bull.Environ.Contam.Toxicol.*, **39**: 1006–1011.

Silberberg, E.K., 1974. Blood glucose: a sensitive indicator of environmental stress in fish. *Bull.Environ.Contam.Toxicol.*, **11**: 20–25.

Singh, H.S. and T.V. Reddy, 1990. Effect of copper sulfate on hematology, blood chemistry and hepato-somatic index of an Indian catfish, *Heteropneustes fossilis* (Bloch), and its recovery. *Ecotoxicol.Environ.Safety*, **20**: 20–35.

Thompson, W.T., 1982. Agricultural chemicals. Book II: Herbicides. Fresno, California, Thompson Publications. 214 pp.

Chapter 4
The effects of pollutants on selected haematological and biochemical parameters in fish

Z. SVOBODOVÁ, B. VYKUSOVÁ and J. MÁCHOVÁ
Research Institute of Fish Culture and Hydrobiology, 389 25 Vodňany, Czech Republic

4.1   Introduction

The effects of pollutants on fish are evaluated by acute and chronic toxicity tests. The methods for acute toxicity tests are standardised in many cases and the final evaluation, i.e. the calculation of the LC_{50}, and subsequent categorisation of pollutants into their individual class of toxicity, is based solely on the mortality of fish (ISO 7346/1, ON 46 6807 and others).

From the results of such acute toxicity tests, predictions can be made of the concentration range which would include sublethal effects and the maximum admissible level. Chronic toxicity tests are then performed within this concentration range. The measurement of the maximum admissible concentration of substances is, from the point of view of fish culture, the basic requirement of this test. The methods used for chronic toxicity tests are not yet standardised, and a variety of different methods have been recommended (Lesnikov, 1979; Svobodová and Vykusová, 1989). Mortality of fish is generally not recorded in chronic toxicity tests. During the course of the test, the effects of sublethal concentrations are evaluated on the basis of the condition and behaviour of fish, food consumption and weight increase. At the end of the test, the following parameters are evaluated:

(a) Physical condition factors (weight of fish, Fulton's coefficient, relative weight of hepatopancreas, etc.);
(b) Health condition (pathoanatomical and histopathological changes, parasitic and/or bacteriological state, etc.);
(c) Residues of substances and their metabolites in organs and tissues of fish, or changes in the sensory properties of muscle;
(d) Haematological state;
(e) Biochemical condition of blood plasma;
(f) Non-specific immunological parameters.

This chapter summarises the results of fish toxicity tests carried out in recent years at the Department of Aquatic Toxicology and Fish Diseases of the Research Institute of Fish Culture and Hydrobiology in Vodňany, Czech Republic. The focus is on the extent to which changes in the various individual parameters (particularly haematological and biochemical) are useful measurements in chronic toxicity tests.

4.2   Material and methods

The acute toxicity tests using carp and rainbow trout fingerlings were performed in accordance with the standard ON 46 6807; the chronic toxicity tests with the same species were carried out using the methods of Svobodová and Vykusová (1989). A well-water with the following physical and chemical characteristics was used for acute and/or chronic toxicity tests: pH 6.5–7.0; acidity (up to pH 4.5) 0.3–0.5 mmol.l^{-1}; alkalinity (up to pH 8.3) 0.16–0.20 mmol.l^{-1}; Σ Ca + Mg 2.6–3.0 mmol.l^{-1}; COD$_{Mn}$ 3.0–3.5 mg.l^{-1}; ammonia in traces. Haematological and biochemical parameters were measured according to the 'Unified methods for haematological examination of fish' (Svobodová *et al.*, 1986); analysis of blood plasma to evaluate the lysozyme content was made by the method of Studnicka *et al.* (1986); acetylcholine esterase activity in fish brain was measured by a modification of the colorimetric method proposed by Hestrin (1949); histopathological examination of fish organs and tissues (after staining the paraffin sections with haematoxylin and eosin); and metal residues in organs and tissues were measured by AAS after prior mineralisation of samples by a dry method using nitric acid and hydrochloric acid at a maximum temperature of 500°C. Triazine residues in fish organs and tissues were determined by gas chromatography.

4.3   Results and discussion

4.3.1   *Effects of acute toxic action*

Pronounced changes occur in fish tissues during the course of acute toxic action. Significant changes in the values for haematological, biochemical and other parameters appear after acute exposure (usually in 48 hours) to different pollutants at concentrations near to the LC$_{50}$ level.

Red blood cells

Significant increases in the erythrocyte count was found in carp after toxic exposure to organophosphorus pesticides and with CuSO$_4$.5H$_2$O (control group of fish 1.64 ±0.0059 and 1.17 ±0.11 T.l^{-1}, test fish after exposure 1.84 ±0.050 and 1.58 ±0.033 T.l^{-1}, respectively). On the other hand, a decrease in erythrocyte count in fish is generally found after toxic exposure to pesticides based on triazines.

Changes in the haematocrit value are closely connected with changes in both erythrocyte count and erythrocyte volume. A significant increase in the haematocrit value of carp was found after acute toxic exposure to organophosphorus pesticides, $CuSO_4.5H_2O$, and $ZnSO_4.7H_2O$ (control group of fish 30.0 ±0.7, 29.0 ±0.4, and 27.0 ±2.0%; test fish after exposure 36.0 ±1.0, 39.0 ±0.5, and 38.0 ±2.0%, respectively). On the other hand, a significant decrease in the haematocrit value was found in carp after acute toxic exposure to pesticides based on triazines (control group of fish 43.0 ±2.1%, test fish after exposure 25.0 ±1.2%).

A significant increase or a decrease in haemoglobin concentration also occurred in fish during the course of acute toxic action. For example, an increased level was found in carp exposed to toxic concentrations of $CuSO_4.5H_2O$ (control group 62.4 ±1.12 g.l^{-1}, test fish after exposure 83.2 ±1.44 g.l^{-1}). A pronounced decrease in haemoglobin level is regularly found in fish exposed to toxic concentrations of pesticides based on triazines. An increased volume of erythrocytes, mean corpuscular volume (MCV) and a decreased level of mean corpuscular haemoglobin concentration (MCHC) are among the other changes in the pattern of red blood parameters found in fish after acute toxic exposure. These changes are very typical for fish exposed to organophosphorus pesticides (MCV: control group 176 ±4 fl, test fish after exposure 210 ±5.7 fl; MCHC: control group 0.24 ±0.003 l.l^{-1}, test fish after exposure 0.21 ±0.008 l.l^{-1}).

These results suggest that toxic substances can significantly damage the haemopoetic system of fish and in some cases they can even cause an increased disintegration of erythrocytes. Furthermore, some changes may be the result of a disorder in erythrocyte cell membrane permeability and/or the result of the activation of protective mechanisms. These mechanisms may include the release of erythrocytes from blood deposits and/or from haemopoetic tissues into the blood stream. In support of our data, Komarovskiy (1969) showed that a pronounced decrease in haemoglobin volume and erythrocyte count in fish occurred after toxic exposure to pesticides based on triazines. On the other hand, McKim *et al.* (1970) and Christensen *et al.* (1972) reported that an increase in erythrocyte count, haemoglobin volume and haematocrit level occurred in brook trout and catfish (*Ictalurus nebulosus*) exposed to acute toxic concentrations of copper. Adámek and Pravda (1986) found increased haematocrit levels in fish after acute toxic exposure to organophosphorus pesticides; Waiwood (1980) and Williams and Wootten (1981) demonstrated an increased level in these parameters in rainbow trout exposed to formaldehyde and copper sulphate.

Leucocytes and lymphocytes

A decrease in leucocyte count and changes in differential leucocyte count are very characteristic findings in fish after toxic exposure to different pollutants. The data in Table 4.1 show the regularity of this occurrence in carp.

The leucocrit value (based on the leucocyte count) is markedly decreased in carp after acute toxic exposure to pesticides based on diazines (control group 1.6 ±0.2% and 1.5 ±0.2%; test fish after exposure 0.7 ±0.2% and 1.0 ±0.1%).

Using the differential leucocyte count expressed both as a percentage and as

Table 4.1 Leucocyte count (mean ±standard error) in carp after acute toxic exposure to different pollutants (n = number of fish. C = concentration in mg.l^{-1}).

Substance	C	n	Control group	n	Fish after exposure
			Leucocyte count G.1^{-1}		
$CuSO_4.5H_2O$	1.5	30	50.5 ± 3.97	30	17.7 ±1.30
$ZnSO_4.7H_2O$	164	10	58.5 ± 8.66	8	30.7 ±3.35
	140	10	56.0 ± 7.65	9	31.7 ±4.71
	108	9	78.7 ± 4.91	5	32.0 ±6.50
	88	9	75.6 ±11.2	4	33.0 ±5.13
$K_2Cr_2O_7$	244	10	53.8 ± 8.44	10	48.7 ±1.60
p-nitrophenol	28.0	6	95.5 ± 1.23	8	50.9 ±5.13
	28.6	10	53.2 ± 5.16	8	42.5 ±4.19

Table 4.2 Changes in differential leucocyte count (mean ±standard error) in carp after acute toxic exposure to $ZnSO_4.7H_2O$ at 140 mg.l^{-1} (n = number of fish).

		Control group $n = 10$	Fish after exposure $n = 9$
Leucocytes	G.1^{-1}	56.0 ± 7.65	31.7 ± 4.71
Small lymphocytes	%	96.4 ± 0.56	62.2 ±10.05
	G.1^{-1}	48.4 ±12.76	23.4 ± 5.16
Neutrophilic granulocytes with elongated nucleus	%	1.4 ± 0.52	32.7 ± 9.87
	G.1^{-1}	0.5 ± 0.17	9.2 ± 3.54

absolute numbers, a decrease in the level of small lymphocytes and an increase in granulocytes (particularly in neutrophilic granulocytes) is very characteristic in all cases of acute toxicity. Typical changes in the differential leucocyte count of carp after acute toxic exposure to $ZnSO_4.7H_2O$ are shown in Table 4.2.

These changes in the leucocyte count and in the differential leucocyte count lead to a decrease in the non-specific immunity of affected fish. Small lymphocytes are active in the increase, build-up and transport of globulins (some of which act as antigens). A significant decrease in leucocyte numbers and particularly of small lymphocytes in fish may cause a decrease in antigen production and thus a reduced resistance to disease. A significant decrease in the leucocyte count of fish exposed to ammonia was also found by Waluga and Flis (1971) and by Wlasow and Dabrowska (1990). Similarly, a significant decrease in the leucocrit value of salmonids under stress from exposure to pulp mill effluent has been reported by McLeay and Gordon (1977). When characterising the effects of stress in fish, Peters (1986) gave as a cause the decreased percentage of lymphocytes and increased percentage of granulocytes. Neutrophilia was reported by Grizzle (1977) to be the most important haematological response in fish exposed to malachite green. A similar pattern of changes in the differential leucocyte count in fish after toxic exposure to phenols and ammonia has been described by Wlasow (1985) and Wlasow and Dabrowska (1990), respectively.

Blood biochemistry

An increase in the blood plasma glucose level in fish after acute toxic exposure is the most frequent and most pronounced change found among the biochemical parameters. For example, a plasma glucose value of 22.8 ± 1.23 mmol.l^{-1} was found in carp after acute toxic exposure to CuSO$_4$.5H$_2$O, compared to a value of only 9.4 ± 0.26 mmol.l^{-1} found in the control group. Apart from such general biochemical changes, specific changes can be found in fish exposed to different pollutants. For example, an average level of 1533 μg N-ammonia was found in 100 ml blood plasma of farmed carp showing clinical signs of acute ammonia poisoning; this level decreased to 203 μg N-ammonia in 100 ml blood plasma after a 24-hour recovery period in fresh water.

Inhibition of acetylcholine hydrolase activity in fish brain after toxic exposure to organophosphorus pesticides is a very specific effect which can be utilised for diagnostic purposes. Various organophosphorus pesticides at concentrations close to their LC$_{50}$ values can induce a decrease in the enzyme level to 60–20% of their normal physiological activity in fish. Similar changes were found and used by various authors to evaluate the effects of these pesticides on fish (e.g. Kozlovskaya *et al.*, 1984; Kozlovskaya and Tsuiko 1985; Salte *et al.*, 1987, and others).

Pathoanatomical and histopathological changes, and bioaccumulation

Apart from haematological and biochemical effects pathoanatomical and histo-pathological changes in fish tissues and pollutant accumulation in fish are also investigated as part of the toxicity test procedure. Pathoanatomical and histopatho-logical changes in fish after acute toxic exposure can be very pronounced in many cases but they are not specific for individual pollutants. Based on the results of post-mortem examinations of poisoned fish, a common feature is a much increased production of skin and gill mucus. Because of this mucous covering, the colour of the gills is changed to a grey-red. Even when slightly damaged, gills can show heavy bleeding. The inner part of the operculum is usually heavily coated with mucus. Liver blood vessels are prominent in the body cavity. These features form the pathoanatomical picture for carp and rainbow trout after toxic exposure to CuSO$_4$.5H$_2$O. Considerable circulatory disorders are the dominant histopathologi-cal changes in all the organs (particularly the gills) of the above-mentioned fish species. These disorders contribute to the respiratory epithelium and liver tubule epithelium vacuolisation and disintegration, in hepatocyte vacuolisation, and in damage to the brain nerve cells (wrinkling and hyperchromasia). These dystrophic

Table 4.3 Levels of copper (mean ±standard error) in tissues of carp after acute toxic exposure to $CuSO_4.5H_2O$ at 1.5 mg.l^{-1} (number of fish in each group = 30).

Tissue	Cu in dry matter of tissue (mg.kg^{-1})	
	Control group	Fish after exposure
Skin	4.80 ±0.144	5.07 ±0.748
Muscle	4.68 ±0.179	4.59 ±0.088
Gills	6.90 ±0.911	24.35 ±1.386
Hepatopancreas	40.03 ±1.893	53.69 ±4.357
Kidney	11.20 ±0.402	12.22 ±0.549

changes are caused by disorders in the blood supply. A heavy secretion of mucus on the skin is another feature of carp and rainbow trout poisoned by $CuSO_4.5H_2O$; very similar pathological changes can be found after acute toxic exposure to many other pollutants.

Concentrations of of copper found in the organs and tissues of carp after acute toxic exposure to $CuSO_4.5H_2O$ are presented in Table 4.3. The highest copper accumulation was found in fish gills. Therefore, in cases of acute poisoning by copper, a diagnosis can be based on chemical analysis of gills where the copper content will be several times higher than that in non-affected fish.

A total mortality of pond fish occurred after acute poisoning by the herbicide Zeazin DP 50 (active substance: 50% atrazine). Atrazine concentrations of 0.21 and 0.505 mg.kg^{-1} were found in the muscle and hepatopancreas respectively of dead carp.

4.3.2   *Effects of chronic toxic exposure*

In tests for chronic toxicity, the long-term effects of pollutants on fish are studied. These tests usually continue for 90 to 100 days. The effects of pollutants within the sublethal and maximum admissible concentration range are examined. These concentrations are usually estimated to be 3, 10, 30, 100 and 300 times and/or 5,10, 50, 100 and 500 times lower than the 48hLC$_5$ value. After evaluating all the results obtained within a chronic toxicity test, the concentration which, when compared with the control fish, did not cause any significant changes in the test fish is regarded as the maximum admissible concentration.

From an analysis of the results from a series of chronic toxicity tests, the conclusion can be reached that changes in haematological and biochemical parameters are not as significant as they are in cases of acute poisoning. On the other hand, histopathological changes and increases in pollutant residue concentration become more important effects, particularly at concentrations which are near to the maximum admissible values especially from the point of view of fish culture requirements.

Red blood cells

As can be seen in Table 4.4, changes in the haemoglobin level and haematocrit values are not very pronounced in carp and rainbow trout during the course of the chronic toxicity tests. Significant decreases in these values were found very infrequently, and then usually only on exposure to the highest pollutant concentration tested ($48hLC_5 \div 3$). More pronounced changes were found in carp and rainbow trout after long-term exposure to sublethal concentrations of Zeazin DP 50.

Contrary to the acute effect of pollutants, the very pronounced decrease in leucocyte count is found much less frequently in chronic toxicity tests (Table 4.5). A significant decrease in the leucocyte count was found only in carp and rainbow trout exposed to the highest concentration tested of p-nitrophenol ($48hLC_5 \div 5$). In other cases, the leucocyte count fluctuated within the range found for the control group of fish. An interesting exception was a significant decrease in the small lymphocyte count found in carp after chronic exposure to p-nitrophenol at most of the sublethal concentrations tested, even at a concentration of 0.195 mg.l^{-1} which is $48hLC_5 \div 100$.

Blood chemistry

The level of total proteins in the blood plasma has a tendency to decrease in fish after a long-term exposure to pollutants. This is particularly characteristic for carp in chronic toxicity tests with both $ZnSO_4.7H_2O$ and p-nitrophenol (Table 4.6). It was presumed that blood plasma enzymes would be an indicator of damage in fish after long-term exposure to toxic substances, similar to that found for warm-blooded animals. Therefore, the activity of ALT, AST, LDH, GGT and ALP enzymes in carp and rainbow trout was measured at the end of the chronic toxicity tests. The results did not reveal any increase in their activity as a result of the toxic exposure, in spite of dystrophic changes occurring in the parenchymal organs of fish within the general histopathological pattern. From these results, it may be concluded that the blood plasma enzymes in fish do not have the same degree of diagnostic potential as that found in warm-blooded animals. This is probably due to the more limited response by lower animals to pathological stimulation.

Non-specific resistance

Apart from these traditional clinical haematological and biochemical methods, there are other methods that can be used to indicate the effect of sublethal concentrations of pollutants on fish. Of these, the parameters associated with non-specific resistance in fish after long-term exposure to toxic substances seem to be very important. Results of a 90-day chronic toxicity test with carp exposed to $ZnSO_4.7H_2O$ shown in Table 4.7, indicate the long-term effect of low concentrations on non-specific resistance (these results were obtained in cooperation with

Table 4.4 Haemoglobin level (Hb g.l⁻¹) and haematocrit value (Hk %) in carp and rainbow trout at the end of chronic toxicity tests (mean ±standard error of 20 fish in each group; C = concentration of toxicant).

$K_2Cr_2O_7$			$ZnSO_4.7H_2O$			p-nitrophenol			Zeazin DP 50		
C(48hLC5÷) mg.l⁻¹	Hb	Hk	C(48hLC5÷) mg.l⁻¹	Hb	Hk	C(48hLC5÷) mg.l⁻¹	Hb	Hk	C(48hLC5÷) mg.l⁻¹	Hb	Hk
					CARP						
71.8 (÷3)	63.5 ±1.77	29.9 ±1.23	30.9 (÷3)	71.2 ±3.01[+]	34.6 ±1.08	3.9 (÷5)	83.8 ±1.41	40 ±0.7	11.0 (÷3)	69.3 ±1.56[++]	
21.5 (÷10)	56.1 ±3.37	29.6 ±1.61	9.27 (÷10)	85.1 ±3.08	36.9 ±0.96	1.95 (÷10)	85.9 ±1.08	41 ±0.8	3.3 (÷10)	70.8 ±7.01[+]	28 ±1.0
7.18 (÷30)	65.0 ±2.33	37.0 ±0.70	3.09 (÷30)	85.3 ±2.37	36.9 ±0.15	0.39 (÷50)	83.5 ±1.41	37 ±0.8	1.1 (÷30)	84.8 ±2.04	39 ±0.9
2.15 (÷100)	61.5 ±2.06	33.5 ±0.91	0.927 (÷100)	75.5 ±2.34	34.7 ±1.03	0.195 (÷100)	82.6 ±1.60	37 ±0.9	0.33 (÷100)	73.9 ±2.93	37 ±0.9
0.72 (÷300)	68.0 ±2.00	34.9 ±0.91	0.31 (÷300)	87.8 ±2.02[+]	39.2 ±0.72	0.04 (÷500)	85.1 ±1.51	40 ±0.6	Control	82.0 ±2.16	38 ±0.7
Control	59.7 ±2.52	31.8 ±1.17	Control	79.5 ±2.66	37.1 ±1.12	Control	82.5 ±1.18	39 ±0.6			
					RAINBOW TROUT						
12.5 (÷10)	59.1 ±1.69[+]	37.1 ±1.49	3.65 (÷3)	61.1 ±2.94[++]	38.2 ±1.93	2.4 (÷5)	49.3 ±4.36[+]	31.2 ±2.20	5.4 (÷2)	44.3 ±2.34[++]	27.6 ±1.29[++]
4.2 (÷30)	72.5 ±2.51[+]	44.9 ±1.17	0.365 (÷30)	68.6 ±1.89	43.1 ±1.10	1.2 (÷10)	68.3 ±2.04[+]	40.2 ±0.95	1.08 (÷10)	58.9 ±2.12[+]	37.8 ±1.11
1.25 (÷100)	76.8 ±2.62	45.6 ±1.26	0.11 (÷100)	69.3 ±2.01	41.7 ±0.81	0.24 (÷50)	67.0 ±4.01	38.2 ±2.10	0.215 (÷50)	61.3 ±3.56[+]	37.1 ±2.63
0.42 (÷300)	69.0 ±3.41	41.0 ±1.88	0.036 (÷300)	66.5 ±1.38[+]	40.2 ±1.05[+]	0.12 (÷100)	72.9 ±2.02[+]	44.9 ±0.95[+]	0.11 (÷100)	68.6 ±2.94	39.7 ±1.25
Control	71.8 ±3.50	41.4 ±1.59	Control	73.5 ±3.17	44.6 ±1.35	0.025 (÷500)	69.4 ±1.93[+]	45.5 ±0.92[+]	0.045 (÷250)	65.8 ±2.18	38.6 ±1.09
						Control	62.3 ±1.82	40.1 ±1.19	Control	69.7 ±1.20	42.0 ±0.58

[+] $P < 0.05$
[++] $P < 0.01$

Table 4.5 Leucocyte count (Leuco-G.l^{-1}, mean ±standard error) in carp and rainbow trout at the end of chronic toxicity tests (C = concentration of toxicant; number of fish in each group = 20).

$K_2Cr_2O_7$		$ZnSO_4.7H_2O$		p-nitrophenol	
		Carp			
C(48hLC$_5\div$) mg.l^{-1}	Leucocyte count	C(48hLC$_5\div$) mg.l^{-1}	Leucocrit value	C(48hLC$_5\div$) mg.l^{-1}	Leucocyte count
71.8 ($\div$3)	35.1 ±5.33	30.9 ($\div$3)	0.65 ±0.100	3.9 ($\div$5)	28.4 ±3.12[+]
21.5 ($\div$10)	56.0 ±5.95	9.27 ($\div$10)	0.76 ±0.056	1.95 ($\div$10)	32.9 ±2.82[+]
7.18 ($\div$30)	48.9 ±7.31	3.09 ($\div$30)	0.78 ±0.092	0.39 ($\div$50)	35.5 ±4.73
2.15 ($\div$100)	42.5 ±4.06	0.927 ($\div$100)	0.90 ±0.109	0.195 ($\div$100)	36.8 ±3.09
0.72 ($\div$300)	50.0 ±6.42	0.31 ($\div$300)	0.72 ±0.093	0.04 ($\div$500)	38.1 ±2.52
Control	36.0 ±4.65	Control	0.73 ±0.079	Control	52.3 ±4.44
		Rainbow trout			
C(48hLC$_5\div$) mg.l^{-1}	Leucocyte count	C(48hLC$_5\div$) mg.l^{-1}	Leucocyte count	C(48hLC$_5\div$) mg.l^{-1}	Leucocyte count
		3.65 ($\div$3)	18.6 ±6.87	2.4 ($\div$5)	7.6 ±2.75[+]
12.5 ($\div$10)	14.8 ±2.18			1.2 ($\div$10)	17.8 ±2.76
4.2 ($\div$30)	14.0 ±1.78	0.365 ($\div$30)	20.8 ±2.41	0.24 ($\div$50)	13.2 ±2.44
1.25 ($\div$100)	15.8 ±3.47	0.11 ($\div$100)	12.7 ±2.16	0.12 ($\div$100)	19.5 ±3.58
0.42 ($\div$300)	11.3 ±0.78	0.036 ($\div$300)	16.5 ±2.23	0.025 ($\div$500)	28.2 ±4.10
Control	19.6 ±3.12	Control	19.1 ±2.66	Control	21.7 ±4.49

+ $P<0.05$

two Polish authors, M. Studnicka and A. Siwicki, 1987). A pronounced sensitivity of myeloperoxidase in carp was found in chronic toxicity tests with $K_2Cr_2O_7$; markedly lower values of this enzyme were found even at a concentration of 2.15 mg.l^{-1} (i.e. 48hLC$_5\div$:100). Based on these results, a significant decrease in non-specific immunity values in fish seems to occur after sublethal exposure to toxic substances. This confirms a generally valid assumption that there is an increased risk of a greater immunological insufficiency as a result of a change in environmental quality. The results add further weight to the importance of immunotoxicological methods in this field.

A very promising result was obtained in cooperation with two Hungarian authors (G. Jeney and Z. Jeney, 1988) when examining rainbow trout for collagen volume in the spine after chronic exposure to Zeazin DP 50. The analytical data are presented in Table 4.8. A significant decrease in spinal collagen volume was found even at the lowest test concentration (i.e. 48hLC$_5\div$250).

Histopathology and bioaccumulation

As stated earlier in connection with chronic toxicity tests, histopathological changes in fish tissue and residue levels of test substances in fish are very important parameters for deriving the maximum admissible concentrations of chemicals in the

Table 4.6a The level of total proteins (TP g.l^{-1}, mean ±standard error) in blood plasma of carp at the end of chronic toxicity tests with $ZnSO_4.7H_2O$ and p-nitrophenol (C = concentration of toxicant in mg.l^{-1}; number of fish in each group = 20).

C	$ZnSO_4.7H_2O$	C	p-nitrophenol
30.9	15.3 ±1.80[+]	3.9	27.7 ±0.80[+]
9.27	16.9 ±1.70[+]	1.95	33.1 ±0.61[+]
3.09	18.5 ±1.50[+]	0.39	29.8 ±0.41[+]
0.927	22.1 ±1.40	0.195	35.9 ±0.67
0.31	23.2 ±1.60	0.04	35.2 ±0.71
Control	25.4 ±1.50	Control	37.7 ±0.55

+ $P<0.05$

Table 4.6b The level of total proteins (TP g.l^{-1}, mean ±standard error) in blood plasma of rainbow trout at the end of chronic toxicity tests with $K_2Cr_2O_7$ and p-nitrophenol (C = concentration of toxicant in mg.l^{-1}; number of fish in each group = 20).

C	$K_2Cr_2O_7$	C	p-nitrophenol
12.5	52.0 ±2.95	2.4	32.4 ±5.91[+]
4.2	59.3 ±2.95	1.2	47.3 ±1.61
1.25	53.7 ±3.66	0.24	53.6 ±2.38
0.42	56.4 ±6.31	0.12	51.1 ±1.28
Control	52.0 ±2.97	0.025	50.9 ±1.45
		Control	46.9 ±2.08

+ $P<0.05$

Table 4.7 Values of selected parameters (mean ±standard error) in blood plasma of carp at the end of a chronic toxicity test with $ZnSO_4.7H_2O$ (C = concentration of toxicant; TP = total proteins; number of fish in each group = 20).

C(48hLC5÷) mg.l^{-1}	TP g.l^{-1}	Globulin g.l^{-1}	Lysozyme g.l^{-1}
30.9 (÷30)	15.3 ±1.80[+]	3.5 ±0.50[++]	0.25 ±0.04[+]
9.27 (÷10)	16.9 ±1.70[+]	3.6 ±0.07[++]	0.27 ±0.05[+]
3.09 (÷30)	18.5 ±1.50[+]	4.7 ±0.60[++]	0.29 ±0.03[+]
0.927 (÷100)	22.1 ±1.40	6.2 ±0.50[+]	0.30 ±0.05[+]
0.31 (÷300)	23.2 ±1.60	6.5 ±0.70[+]	0.31 ±0.04
Control	25.4 ±1.50	8.5 ±0.50	0.36 ±0.04

+ $P<0.05$
++ $P<0.01$

Table 4.8 Collagen volume (mean $\pm$standard error) in spine of rainbow trout at the end of a chronic toxicity test with Zeazin DP 50 (C = concentration of toxicant; number of fish in each group = 20).

$C(48LC_5\div)$ $mg.l^{-1}$	Collagen $mg.l^{-1}$
5.4 ($\div$2)	314.7 $\pm$42.2[++]
1.08 ($\div$10)	313.4 $\pm$70.4[++]
0.11 ($\div$100)	262.8 $\pm$57.1[++]
0.045 ($\div$250)	258.0 $\pm$38.5[++]
Control	382.4 $\pm$41.3

[++] $P<0.01$

Table 4.9 Copper residues (Cu $\mu g.g^{-1}$ dry weight, mean value of 12–20 fish in each group) in tissues of carp and rainbow trout at the end of a chronic toxicity test with $CuSO_4.5H_2O$ (C = concentration of toxicant in $mg.l^{-1}$).

Carp				Rainbow trout			
$C(48hLC_5\div)$	Muscle	Gills	Liver	$C(48hLC_5\div)$	Muscle	Gills	Liver
0.28 ($\div$2.5)	4.66	28.0	262	0.2 ($\div$2.5)	2.68	69.3	1168
0.14 ($\div$5)	7.91	25.2	223	0.1 ($\div$5)	2.42	64.0	1369
0.07 ($\div$10)	5.88	26.8		0.05 ($\div$10)	3.21	44.3	1029
0.014 ($\div$50)	2.99	21.9	137	0.01 ($\div$50)	1.64	28.1	871
0.007 ($\div$100)	6.02	9.6	77	0.005 ($\div$100)	1.93	10.1	367
Control	6.37	10.4	79	Control	2.77	13.6	390

context of fish culture requirements. Significant changes in these parameters can be found even at concentrations of 100, 300 and sometimes even 500 times lower than the 48hLC$_5$. For example, histopathological changes were found in chronic toxicity tests with $CuSO_4.5H_2O$ even at the minimum test concentrations (0.007 $mg.l^{-1}$ in carp, 0.005 $mg.l^{-1}$ in rainbow trout). These changes were based on increased activity of connective tissue, particularly near the kidney tract and liver bile duct. Circulatory disorders and dystrophic changes in the epithelium of kidney tubules were found in fish from a chronic toxicity test with Zeazin DP 50 after exposure to the minimum concentration used (i.e. 48hLC$_5\div$300). Limited dystrophic changes of the respiratory epithelium, venostasis in liver and gills, and increased secretory activity of mucous cells in the skin were found after long-term exposure to $ZnSO_4.7H_2O$ at a very low (48hLC$_5\div$300) concentration. Limited dystrophic changes of the respiratory epithelium and slight dystrophic changes in kidney tubules, together with hypersecretion of the mucous cells in the skin, were also characteristic of a long-term effect of $K_2Cr_2O_7$ at a concentration of 48hLC$_5\div$300. Slight dystrophic changes in the epithelium of kidney tubules and a pronounced activity of large eosinophilous cells with granulated cytoplasm in the submucosa of the gut wall were found as a long-term effect of p-nitrophenol at a concentration of 48hLC$_5\div$500.

Table 4.10 Atrazine residues (mg.kg^{-1} wet weight, mean value of 14–20 fish in each group) in tissues of carp at the end of a chronic toxicity test with Zeazin DP 50 (C = concentration of toxicant in mg.l^{-1}).

C(48hLC$_5$÷)	Muscle	Liver	Gills
11.0 (÷3)	7.35	4.44	7.20
1.1 (÷30)	0.95	2.44	0.70
0.33 (÷100)	0.30	0.82	0.86
Control	0	0	0

Table 4.11 Chromium residues (Cr µg.kg^{-1} wet weight, mean values) in tissues of carp and rainbow trout at the end of a chronic toxicity test with K$_2$Cr$_2$O$_7$ (C = concentration of toxicant in mg.l^{-1}; number of fish in each group = 8–12).

	Carp				Rainbow trout			
C(48hLC$_5$÷)	Muscle	Gills	Liver	Kidney	C(48hLC$_5$÷)	Muscle	Gills	Liver
71.8 (÷3)	12.2	270.7	225.2	164.5				
21.5 (÷10)	1.5	90.7	109.8	114.8	12.5 (÷10)	6.15	19.47	24.79
7.18 (÷30)	12.9	41.4	20.5	42.3	4.2 (÷30)	0.52	9.18	9.38
2.15 (÷100)	0.27	21.7	6.2	18.2	1.25 (÷100)	0.31	8.48	5.06
0.72 (÷300)	0.04	7.1	2.5	7.0	0.42 (÷300)	0.32	5.79	1.97
Control	1.13	0.2	1.7	0.7	Control	0.31	0.39	0.37

The residues found in fish from chronic toxicity tests with CuSO$_4$.5H$_2$O, Zeazin DP 50 and K$_2$Cr$_2$O$_7$ are shown in Tables 4.9 to 4.11. The concentration of copper in the muscle of all the experimental fish were similar to those of the control group (Table 4.9), as they were for the gills and liver of carp and rainbow trout exposed to the minimum test concentration of 0.005 mg.l^{-1} CuSO$_4$.5H$_2$O. When these fish species were exposed to a concentration of 0.01 mg.l^{-1} CuSO$_4$.5H$_2$O, the concentration of copper in the gills and liver were roughly twice as high as in the controls. In other groups of fish, the higher the CuSO$_4$.5H$_2$O concentration in the water, the higher was the level of copper found in the gills and liver.

The atrazine content in carp tissues at the end of a chronic toxicity test with Zeazin DP 50 is shown in Table 4.10. The data show that high levels of atrazine residues occur in fish exposed to even the minimum test concentration used (48hLC$_5$÷100). Again, the higher the concentration of Zeazin DP 50 in the water, the higher are the residues found in fish tissues. Chromium residues in the gills, liver and kidney of carp and rainbow trout responded very sensitively to K$_2$Cr$_2$O$_7$ exposure, being higher by about one order of magnitude even at a 48hLC$_5$÷300 concentration compared to the control fish (Table 4.11).

4.4   Conclusions

As the data presented here have shown, histopathological changes and residue levels of test substances in fish tissues are the most sensitive parameters for the evaluation of chronic toxicity test effects and thus also for the derivation of maximum admissible concentrations. Routine clinical haematological and bio-chemical examinations are an important tool in the evaluation of chronic toxicity test results, but they are insufficiently sensitive to reflect the other changes found in fish that contribute to the derivation of a minimum effective concentration. On the other hand, the evaluation of some parameters (e.g. those of non-specific resistance and/or the collagen content in fish spine) after a long-term exposure to low concentrations of toxic substances may be very important. Apart from these examples, other parameters should be sought which can be used to quantify the harmful effects of low concentrations of pollutants on fish so that maximum admissible concentrations in the water can be set to meet fish culture requirements.

4.5   References

Adámek, Z. and D. Pravda, 1986. Hematologické aspekty intoxikací ryb pesticidními přípravky. (Haematological aspects of fish intoxication with pesticides.) First Ichthyohaematological Conference, Litomysl, 97–100.

Christensen, G.M., J.M. McKim and W.A. Brungs, 1972. Changes in the blood of the brown bullhead (*Ictalurus nebulosus*) following short- and long-term exposure to copper. *Toxic.Appl.Pharmac.*, **23**: 417–427.

Grizzle, J.M., 1977. Hematological changes in fingerling channel catfish exposed to malachite green. *Progr.Fish-Cult.*, **39**: 90–93.

Hestrin, S., 1949. The reaction of acetylcholine and other carboxylic acid derivates with hydroxylamine and analytical application. *J.Biol.Chem.*, **180**: 249.

Komarovskiy, F.J., 1969. Tez. dokl. sympoz. po vodnoi toksikologii. In: Osetrov, V.S. *et al.* (Eds.) Spravochnik po Boleznam Ryb. (Handbook of Fish Diseases.) Moscow, Kolos, 351 pp.

Kozlovskaya, V.I. and G.M. Tsuiko, 1985. Deistvie phosphoorganicheskih pesticidov na acetilcholines-terazu mozga ryb. (Effect of organophosphorus pesticides on acetylcholine esterasis activity in fish brain.) *Eksper.Vod.Toksikol., Riga*, **10**: 67–72.

Kozlovskaya, V.I., F.L. Mayer and D.D. Petti, 1984. Aktivnost acetilcholinesterazy mozga i soderjanie kolagenov v pozvonochnike karasia pri intoksikacii chlorofosom. (Activity of acetylcholine-esterasis in brain and collagen volume in spine of crucian carp after chlorophos intoxication.) *Gidrobiol.J.*, **20**: 56–58.

Lesnikov, L.A., 1979. Razrabotka normativov dopustimogo soderjania vrednyh veshchestv v vode rybohoziaistvennyh vodoiemov. (Elaboration of standards of acceptable concentration of pollu-tants in the water of fish culture units.) *Sborniknauch.trudov, GosNIORCH, Leningrad*, 144: 3–41.

McKim, J.M., G.M. Christensen and E.P. Hunt, 1970. Changes in the blood of brook trout (*Salvelinus fontinalis*) after short-term and long-term exposure to copper. *J.Fish.Res.Bd.Can.*, **27**: 1883–1889.

McLeay, D.J., and M.R. Gordon, 1977. Leucocrit: a simple hematological technique for measuring acute stress in salmonid fish, including stressful concentration of pulpmill effluent. *J.Fish.Res.Bd.Can.*, **34**: 2164–2175.

Peters, G., 1986. Stress as a defense disturbing factor in aquaculture. International Symposium on Ichthyopathology in Aquaculture, Dubrovnik, 38–39.

Salte, R. *et al.*, 1987. Fatal acetylcholinesterase inhibition in salmonids subjected to a routine organo-phosphate treatment. *Aquaculture*, **61**: 173–179.

Studnicka, M., A. Siwicki and B. Ryka, 1986. Lysozyme level in carp (*Cyprinus carpio* L.). *Bamidgeh*, **38**: 22–25.

Svobodová, Z. and B. Vykusová, 1989. Stanovení nejvyšších přípustných koncentrací (NPK) látek ve vodě z hlediska požadavků chovu ryb. (Determining the maximum admissible concentrations of substances in water from the point of view of fish culture requirements.) , VÚRH Vodňany, Czech Republic, Edice Metodik.

Svobodová, Z., D. Pravda and J. Paláčková, 1986. Jednotné metody hematologického vyšetřování ryb. (Unified methods of haemathological examination of fish.) VÚRH Vodňany, Czech Republic, Edice Metodik.

Waiwood, K.G., 1980. Changes in hematocrit of rainbow trout exposed to various combinations of water hardness, pH and copper. *Trans.Am.Fish.Soc.*, **109**: 461–463.

Waluga, D. and J. Flis, 1971. Zmiany we krwi obwodowej karpia (*Cyprinus carpio* L.) pod wplywem wody amoniakalnej. (Changes in the peripheral blood in carp (*Cyprinus carpio* L.) under the influence of ammonium liquor.) *Rocz.Nauk roln.*, **93**: 87–94.

Williams, H.A. and R. Wootten, 1981. Some effects of therapeutic levels of formalin and copper sulphate on blood parameters in rainbow trout. *Aquaculture*, **24**: 341–353.

Wlasow, T., 1985. The leucocyte system in rainbow trout, *Salmo gairdneri* Rich., affected by prolonged subacute phenol intoxication. *Acta Ichthyol.Piscator.*, **15**: 83–94.

Wlasow, T. and H. Dabrowska, 1990. Hematology of carp in acute intoxication with ammonia. *Pol.Arch.Hydrobiol.*, **37**: 419–428.

ISO 7346/1 Water quality – Determination of the acute lethal toxicity of substances to a freshwater fish (*Brachydanio rerio* Hamilton-Buchanan (Teleostei, Cyprinidae)) – Part 1: Static method of 1984, Geneva, International Organization for Standardization.

ON 46 6807 Test akutní toxicity na rybách a dalších vodních živočiších. (Acute toxicity test on fish and other aquatic organisms.) Prague, ÚNM, 1989. 31 p.

Chapter 5
Sublethal effects of cadmium on carp (*Cyprinus carpio*) fingerlings

J. PALÁČKOVÁ,[1] D. PRAVDA,[2] K. FAŠAIC[3] and O. ČELECHOVSKÁ[4]

[1] *Department of Fisheries and Hydrobiology, University of Agriculture, Zemědělská 1, 613 00 Brno, Czech Republic*
[2] *Department of Reproduction and Veterinary Preventive Medicine, University of Agriculture, Zemědělská 1, 613 00 Brno, Czech Republic*
[3] *Research Development Centre for Fisheries, University of Zagreb, B. Adžije 2/IV, 41000 Zagreb, Croatia*
[4] *Department of Chemistry, Physics and Biochemistry, University of Veterinary Sciences, Palackého 1/3, 612 42 Brno, Czech Republic*

5.1 Introduction

Because of its harmful effects at low concentrations on living organisms (Eisler, l985), cadmium is one of the most hazardous environmental pollutants.

Various types of toxic effect of cadmium on fish have been reported with different results. The effects on haematology, ion balance and carbohydrate metabolism have been investigated in rainbow trout (*Oncorhynchus mykiss*) (Haux and Larson, 1984), an anaemic response was demonstrated in flounder (*Pleuronectes flesus*) (Johansson-Sjöbeck and Larson, 1978), haematological and/or biochemical changes were also recorded in carp (*Cyprinus carpio*) (Pravda *et al.*, 1989), tilapia (*Oreochromis mossambicus*) (Ruparelia, 1990) and other species (Larson, 1975). On the other hand no significant haematological differences were found between controls and cadmium exposed dogfish (*Scyliorhinus canicula*) (Tort and Hernández-Pascual, 1990) and winter flounder (*Pseudopleuronectes americanus*) (Calabrese *et al.*, 1975).

The present investigation was carried out to determine values for haematological and biochemical parameters in the blood, and levels of cadmium in the muscle and hepatopancreas tissues, of carp fingerlings exposed to a sublethal concentration of cadmium and after a partial recovery. The aim of the study was to contribute to the knowledge of sublethal responses of fish to cadmium.

5.2 Material and methods

The experiment was carried out at the Department of Fisheries and Hydrobiology, University of Agriculture, Brno, Czech Republic.

The experimental organisms were 170 carp (*Cyprinus carpio*) fingerlings with an average initial weight of 25.6 ±8.8 g. The fish were kept under laboratory conditions in 400 l tanks for 2 weeks prior to the experiment. Since the values for weight–length coefficients (condition factor), and an ichthyopathological examination, did not show any distinct pathological symptoms, it was assumed that the fish were in a good condition and in a good state of health. After an acclimation period, fish were exposed to a sublethal concentration of cadmium (as $CdCl_2.2\frac{1}{2}H_2O$) in tap water, using a static water system with a filter and aeration, under controlled laboratory conditions and at a water temperature of 20 ±1°C. The exposure medium was continuously replenished and partly exchanged to maintain the concentration of cadmium at 0.02 mg $Cd.l^{-1}$. Once a week, hydrochemical parameters such as temperature, salinity, dissolved oxygen levels and pH were measured according to the 'Unified methods of chemical analyses of water' (1965); the concentration of cadmium in the water was measured by atomic absorption spectrophotometry.

Except for the day before blood sampling, fish were fed with a standard pelleted diet both during the acclimation and the entire experimental period. The weight of fish per litre of water and the amount of food provided per gram of fish were equal for both the control and experimental groups. Samples of 10 fish were analysed at intervals of 4, 11, 19, 25, 39, 53 and 67 days and these formed Group 1. After an elapsed exposure period of 25 days, a proportion of the fish stock was transferred into cadmium-free tap-water for a subsequent recovery period in two aquaria; Group 2 continued on the diet and Group 3 was not fed. From these two tanks fish were further sampled for analysis at the intervals given above. Fish in the control Group 4 were kept in cadmium-free tap-water, fed and analysed at the beginning and at the end of the experiment.

Blood was sampled by cardiac puncture using heparinised glass Pasteur pipettes (Jirásek *et al.*, 1980) immediately after capture and without anaesthesia. Values for the haematological and biochemical parameters studied were measured using the 'Unified methods of haematological investigation in fish' (Svobodová *et al.*, 1986). The concentrations of calcium and chloride in the plasma were determined by colorimetric methods (with o-Cresolphthalein Complexone and Thiocyanate respectively). Electrophoretic separation of blood protein was performed on Cellogel strips under the conditions for 'micro-long' electrophoresis, with an instrument supplied by the Chemetron Company; transparent films were read using a Supercello 3 densitometer. Concentrations of glycogen in the hepatopancreas were determined by the method described by Edler (1968). During the course of the experiment, levels of cadmium in muscle and hepatopancreas tissues of fish were measured by a standard method using atomic absorption spectrophotometry (Perkin Elmer 5000 instrument) and concentrations are expressed as mg.kg^{-1} wet weight of the tissue.

Data were analysed for statistical significance using analysis of variance (ANOVA) and Student's t-test.

5.3   Results and discussion

The results of the experiment are presented in Tables 5.1 to 5.4. Values for the parameters studied showed some changes that were more or less related to the exposure time. Similar changes in selected parameters were observed in carp fingerlings exposed to a similar level of cadmium in the water, in a previous experiment (Pravda *et al.*, 1989). Because there are no other data for carp fingerlings in the available literature, the results presented here can be only compared with published data for other fish species exposed to different levels of cadmium.

A significant decrease in the glycogen content of the hepatopancreas at the beginning of the experimental period was followed by a continuous increase after 19 days of exposure (Table 5.1). Dose-dependent changes in liver glycogen content were found in rainbow trout exposed to 0.01 and 0.10 mg $Cd^{2+}.l^{-1}$ and after recovery by Haux and Larson (1984).

Concentrations of glucose in blood plasma varied and their values showed a hypoglycaemic trend. Values measured in experimental groups at the end of the experiment were significantly lower by comparison with the control (Table 5.1). Dose-dependent differences in blood glucose have been observed in flounders, where a significant increase was found after an exposure to 0.05 mg $Cd^{2+}.l^{-1}$ but no significant changes were recorded when they were exposed to 0.50 mg $Cd^{2+}.l^{-1}$ (Larson, 1975). Cadmium caused a hyperglycaemia that persisted throughout the recovery period in rainbow trout (Haux and Larson, 1984).

The concentrations of total lipids and cholesterol in blood plasma fluctuated. Mean values assessed in fish transferred into cadmium-free water for recovery (Group 2) did not differ significantly from the control at the end of the experiment (Table 5.1).

The decrease in plasma calcium content during the initial 19 days was followed by an increase to values similar to that of the control. Hypocalcaemia in blood plasma was also found in flounders (Larson, 1975) and in rainbow trout (Haux and Larson, 1984) exposed to various sublethal levels of cadmium.

Cadmium also reduces the plasma chloride content; no significant differences were found within the experimental Groups 1–3 at the end of the experiment, but the values were significantly lower than those of the control Group 4 (Table 5.1).

There was a fluctuation in the values for total protein and protein fractions in the blood plasma during the course of the experiment (Table 5.2). Comparing the values obtained at the final sampling time, significantly lower values in plasma protein were found in the fish from Groups 1 and 3; further changes included a decrease in albumin and A/G ratio and the increase in α-globulin fraction.

Only a few significant changes were observed for the erythrocytes count, haemoglobin level, haematocrit value and red blood cell indices such as MCH, MCV and MCHC (Table 5.3). At the final sampling time, the only significant difference, a decrease, was observed in the haemoglobin and haematocrit values for the unfed fish in the recovery period (Group 3). Cadmium has been shown to cause anaemia

Table 5.1 Glycogen content in hepatopancreas and biochemical parameters in blood plasma of carp fingerlings exposed to a sublethal concentration of cadmium, and after recovery. Values given are means ±standard deviation for groups of 8–10 fish.

Parameter	Group	Exposure period (days)							
		0	4	11	19	25	39	53	67
Glycogen in hepatopancreas mg.100 mg^{-1}	1	12.52 ± 0.84^{e}	$5.45 \pm 0.78^{a.b}$	4.24 ± 0.59^{a}	$6.34 \pm 0.61^{b.c}$	7.78 ± 0.64^{c}	9.76 ± 0.96^{d}	$10.44 \pm 0.36^{d.e}_{x}$	$11.82 \pm 0.71^{e}_{x}$
	2						$8.69 \pm 1.24_{x}$	$9.74 \pm 0.53_{x}$	$10.13 \pm 0.56_{x}$
	3	$.12.52 \pm 0.84$					$4.92 \pm 0.73^{a}_{y}$	$3.16 \pm 0.55^{b}_{y}$	$2.96 \pm 0.36^{b}_{y}$
	4	12.52 ± 0.84							$9.66 \pm 0.91^{*}_{x}$
Glucose mmol.l^{-1}	1	8.07 ± 0.80^{c}	5.79 ± 0.44^{b}	3.75 ± 0.17^{a}	$6.75 \pm 0.64^{b.c}$	3.50 ± 0.51^{a}	$3.64 \pm 0.49^{a}_{x}$	2.87 ± 0.25^{a}	$3.98 \pm 0.31^{a}_{x}$
	2						$3.36 \pm 0.35^{a}_{x.y}$	2.60 ± 0.29^{a}	$5.38 \pm 0.33^{b}_{y}$
	3	8.07 ± 0.80					$2.33 \pm 0.17^{a}_{y}$	2.51 ± 0.25^{a}	$4.11 \pm 0.43^{b}_{x}$
	4	8.07 ± 0.80							7.69 ± 0.52
Total lipids g.l^{-1}	1	4.84 ± 0.28^{d}	$3.72 \pm 0.65^{b.c}$	2.48 ± 0.28^{a}	2.29 ± 0.16^{a}	$2.74 \pm 0.29^{a.b}$	$5.21 \pm 0.47^{d}_{x}$	$4.23 \pm 0.39^{c.d}_{x}$	$3.75 \pm 0.22^{b.c}_{x}$
	2						$3.89 \pm 0.49^{a}_{x.y}$	$4.44 \pm 0.36^{a}_{x}$	$7.15 \pm 0.53^{b}_{x}$
	3	4.84 ± 0.28					$3.55 \pm 0.45^{a}_{y}$	$1.89 \pm 0.19^{b}_{y}$	$1.63 \pm 0.22^{b}_{y}$
	4	4.84 ± 0.28							$6.99 \pm 0.34^{**}_{x}$
Cholesterol mmol.l^{-1}	1	2.63 ± 0.15^{e}	$2.71 \pm 0.22^{b.c.e}$	1.85 ± 0.14^{a}	$2.95 \pm 0.33^{c.e}$	$3.25 \pm 0.08^{c.d}$	3.74 ± 0.25^{d}	$2.11 \pm 0.25^{a.b.e}_{x}$	$2.15 \pm 0.19^{a.b.e}_{x}$
	2						3.45 ± 0.27^{a}	2.37 ± 0.23^{b}	$5.38 \pm 0.25^{c}_{y}$
	3	2.63 ± 0.15					3.38 ± 0.12	2.82 ± 0.19	$3.30 \pm 0.30_{z}$
	4	2.63 ± 0.15							$5.13 \pm 0.51^{**}_{y}$
Calcium mmol.l^{-1}	1	1.88 ± 0.06^{f}	$1.81 \pm 0.12^{c.d.f}$	1.61 ± 0.05^{c}	1.02 ± 0.05^{b}	1.37 ± 0.11^{b}	2.25 ± 0.07^{e}	$2.13 \pm 0.10^{e.f}_{x}$	$1.86 \pm 0.08^{d.f}_{x}$
	2						2.32 ± 0.08^{a}	$2.33 \pm 0.07^{a}_{x}$	1.93 ± 0.08^{b}
	3	1.88 ± 0.06					2.16 ± 0.14^{a}	$1.73 \pm 0.09^{b}_{y}$	$1.70 \pm 0.09^{b}_{y}$
	4	1.88 ± 0.06							2.01 ± 0.08
Chloride mmol.l^{-1}	1	138.1 ± 4.8^{f}	$113.3 \pm 5.2^{d.e}$	116.0 ± 2.7^{e}	$85.4 \pm 3.5^{a.b}$	80.8 ± 6.3	$102.3 \pm 1.5^{c.d}$	$93.6 \pm 4.9^{b.c}_{x}$	$90.9 \pm 2.8^{a.b.c}_{x}$
	2						95.5 ± 3.5	$95.8 \pm 3.3_{x}$	$96.5 \pm 2.5_{x}$
	3	138.1 ± 4.8					102.0 ± 1.5^{a}	$61.9 \pm 6.8^{b}_{y}$	$85.5 \pm 2.7^{a.b}_{x}$
	4	138.1 ± 4.8							$120.2 \pm 7.0_{y}$

Groups: 1 = fish exposed to water with Cd^{2+} at 0.02 mg.l^{-1} for 67 days, fed
   2 = fish transferred from Group 1 into cadmium-free water after the exposure period of 25 days, fed
   3 = fish transferred from Group 1 into cadmium-free water after the exposure period of 25 days, without feeding
   4 = fish of the control group

Note: Dissimilar sub/superscripts denote means significantly different at $P<0.05$ (LSD analysis) within rows (a.b.c.d.e.f) and columns (x.y.z).
   * $P<0.05$, ** $P<0.01$, Student's t-test.

Table 5.2 Total protein and percent proportions of various protein fractions in blood plasma of carp fingerlings exposed to a sublethal concentration of cadmium, and after recovery. Values given are means ±standard deviation for groups of 8–10 fish. Group treatments and denominations as in Table 5.1.

Parameter	Group	Exposure period (days)							
		0	4	11	19	25	39	53	67
Total protein g.l^{-1}	1	22.8 ± 1.4^{a}	23.9 ± 1.3^{a}	18.9 ± 0.5^{b}	27.1 ± 1.3^{c}	31.6 ± 1.5^{d}	$29.4 \pm 0.9^{c,d}_{x}$	$23.7 \pm 1.3^{a}_{x}$	$32.8 \pm 1.3^{d}_{x}$
	2						$30.9 \pm 2.2^{d}_{x}$	$25.9 \pm 0.8^{b}_{x}$	$35.7 \pm 1.0^{c}_{x,y}$
	3						$24.1 \pm 0.9^{a}_{y}$	$19.6 \pm 0.5^{b}_{y}$	$14.7 \pm 1.4^{c}_{z}$
	4	22.4 ± 1.4							$38.8 \pm 2.2^{**}_{y}$
Albumin %	1	39.2 ± 1.8^{e}	30.6 ± 1.7^{a}	32.6 ± 1.3^{a}	32.7 ± 1.2^{a}	19.9 ± 1.4^{b}	15.3 ± 1.2^{d}	$13.9 \pm 1.1^{d}_{x}$	$25.0 \pm 1.0^{c}_{x}$
	2						$24.8 \pm 0.9^{a}_{y}$	$16.4 \pm 1.1^{b}_{x}$	$25.6 \pm 0.6^{a}_{x}$
	3						$25.1 \pm 1.4^{a,b}_{y}$	$26.0 \pm 0.7^{c}_{y}$	$22.3 \pm 0.9^{b}_{y}$
	4	39.2 ± 1.8							$40.1 \pm 0.7_{z}$
α-globulin %	1	19.3 ± 2.5^{a}	19.8 ± 0.7^{a}	19.0 ± 1.3^{a}	19.9 ± 1.3^{a}	32.2 ± 1.5^{c}	$23.9 \pm 2.3^{a,b}_{x}$	$27.6 \pm 1.6^{b,c}$	$32.8 \pm 3.8^{c}_{x}$
	2						$30.9 \pm 0.8^{a}_{y}$	27.4 ± 1.7^{a}	23.4 ± 1.2^{b}
	3						$29.4 \pm 1.0^{a}_{y}$	22.8 ± 2.4^{b}	$24.5 \pm 1.3^{a,b}_{y}$
	4	19.3 ± 2.5							$15.7 \pm 0.6_{z}$
β-globulin %	1	23.7 ± 3.5^{c}	29.5 ± 1.5^{a}	27.3 ± 0.8^{a}	$26.9 \pm 0.8^{a,c}$	12.5 ± 1.1^{d}	16.9 ± 1.9^{b}	$22.5 \pm 2.2^{c}_{x}$	$16.5 \pm 1.3^{b,d}_{x}$
	2						13.4 ± 0.6^{a}	$14.8 \pm 1.2^{a}_{x}$	$28.0 \pm 2.9^{b}_{y}$
	3						14.8 ± 0.7	$17.7 \pm 1.7_{x,y}$	$21.9 \pm 3.2_{x,y}$
	4	23.7 ± 3.5							$20.6 \pm 1.2_{x}$
τ-globulin %	1	17.8 ± 1.1^{d}	$20.1 \pm 1.4^{a,d}$	$21.1 \pm 1.4^{a,d}$	$20.5 \pm 1.1^{a,d}$	35.4 ± 2.4^{b}	$43.9 \pm 3.0^{c}_{x}$	$36.0 \pm 2.9^{b}_{x}$	$25.7 \pm 2.3^{a}_{x}$
	2						$30.9 \pm 1.4^{a}_{y}$	$41.4 \pm 1.5^{b}_{x}$	$23.0 \pm 2.2^{c}_{x}$
	3						$30.7 \pm 1.8_{y}$	33.5 ± 2.4	31.3 ± 2.9
	4	17.8 ± 1.1							$23.6 \pm 1.3^{**}$
Albumin/globulin	1	0.64 ± 0.02^{e}	0.45 ± 0.04^{a}	0.49 ± 0.03^{a}	0.49 ± 0.03^{a}	0.25 ± 0.02^{c}	$0.18 \pm 0.02^{c,d}_{x}$	$0.16 \pm 0.02^{d}_{x}$	$0.34 \pm 0.02^{b}_{x}$
	2						$0.33 \pm 0.02^{a}_{y}$	$0.19 \pm 0.02^{b}_{x}$	$0.34 \pm 0.01^{a}_{x}$
	3						$0.34 \pm 0.02^{a,b}_{y}$	$0.35 \pm 0.01^{a}_{y}$	$0.27 \pm 0.02^{b}_{y}$
	4	0.64 ± 0.02							$0.67 \pm 0.02_{z}$

Table 5.3 Haematological parameters in carp fingerlings exposed to a sublethal concentration of cadmium, and after recovery. Values given are means ±standard deviation for groups of 8–10 fish. Group treatments and denominations as in Table 5.1.

Parameter	Group	Exposure period (days)							
		0	4	11	19	25	39	53	67
Haemoglobin g.l^{-1}	1	48.2 ±2.9^d	43.9 ±3.1$^{a.d}$	54.5 ±3.6$^{b.d}$	61.2 ±3.6$^{b.c}$	63.1 ±1.8^c	63.4 ±2.3^c	59.2 ±1.1$^{b.c}_x$	64.8 ±4.5^c_x
	2						63.2 ±3.6	58.7 ±2.6$_x$	61.8 ±3.9$_x$
	3						56.4 ±3.3^a	37.8 ±4.4$_y$	25.1 ±4.6^c_y
	4	48.2 ±2.9							59.5 ±1.7$^{**}_x$
Hematocrit l.l^{-1}	1	0.23 ±0.17^c	0.20 ±0.01$^{a.c}$	0.22 ±0.01$^{a.c}$	0.27 ±0.02$^{b.c}$	0.29 ±0.01^b	0.31 ±0.03^b	0.29 ±0.01^b_x	0.27 ±0.01$^{b.c}_x$
	2						0.29 ±0.01	0.28 ±0.01$_x$	0.29 ±0.02$_x$
	3						0.28 ±0.02^a	0.18 ±0.01^b_y	0.11 ±0.01^c_y
	4	0.23 ±0.17							0.31 ±0.02**
Erythrocytes T.l^{-1}	1	1.03 ±0.13^e	1.21 ±0.02$^{a.b.e}$	1.37 ±0.12$^{b.c.e}$	1.86 ±0.12^d	1.36 ±0.18$^{b.c.e}$	+	1.62 ±0.12$^{c.d}$	0.94 ±0.09$^{a.e}$
	2						+	1.40 ±0.07	1.08 ±0.19
	3						+	1.67 ±0.08	0.61 ±0.13
	4								0.82 ±0.08
MCH pg	1	48.1 ±6.4^d	36.4 ±2.1$^{a.d}$	40.5 ±3.9$^{a.b.d}$	33.2 ±1.8$^{a.d}$	49.9 ±5.7$^{b.d}$	+	37.5 ±2.7$^{a.d}_x$	70.3 ±4.7^c
	2						+	42.4 ±3.4$_x$	60.8 ±3.6
	3						+	22.6 ±2.6$_y$	43.7 ±2.2
	4	48.1 ±6.4							75.3 ±6.6*
MCV fl	1	223.2 ±28.2^d	169.9 ±13.5$^{a.d}$	165.1 ±14.2$^{a.d}$	148.5 ±8.9^a	226.1 ±25.7$^{b.d}$	+	148.0 ±10.9$^{a.b.d}_x$	298.4 ±18.7$^{c.d}$
	2						+	200.6 ±10.3$_x$	318.8 ±48.3
	3						+	107.8 ±6.9$_y$	202.7 ±46.2
	4	223.2 ±28.2							373.5 ±53.3*
MCHC l.l^{-1}	1	0.22 ±0.02	0.22 ±0.01	0.25 ±0.01	0.22 ±0.01	0.22 ±0.01	0.21 ±0.01	0.20 ±0.01	0.24 ±0.01
	2						0.22 ±0.02	0.21 ±0.01	0.21 ±0.01
	3						0.21 ±0.01	0.21 ±0.02	0.21 ±0.02
	4	0.22 ±0.02							0.19 ±0.01

+ no analysis made

Table 5.4 White blood cell counts, percent proportions of various leucocytes in blood, and cadmium levels in muscle and hepatopancreas tissues in carp fingerlings exposed to a sublethal concentration of cadmium, and after recovery. Values given are means ±standard deviation for groups of 8–10 fish. Group treatments and denominations as in Table 5.1.

Parameter	Group	Exposure period (days)							
		0	4	11	19	25	39	53	67
Leucocytes G.l-1	1	72.3 ± 6.3^{b}	$78.9 \pm 10.1^{b,c}$	96.6 ± 11.3^{c}	66.7 ± 9.1^{b}	66.2 ± 11.2^{b}	+	36.3 ± 5.6^{a}	28.3 ± 3.8^{a}
	2						+	38.0 ± 5.5	21.5 ± 7.3
	3						+	36.7 ± 4.7	$20.0 \pm 2.9^{*}$
	4	72.3 ± 6.3					+		$19.8 \pm 1.8^{**}$
Lymphocytes %	1	93.4 ± 1.3	96.3 ± 1.1	94.6 ± 1.2	89.5 ± 4.2	95.6 ± 1.1	93.8 ± 2.7	$89.0 \pm 1.9_{x}$	92.7 ± 2.0
	2						91.3 ± 1.9	$94.3 \pm 1.5_{x,y}$	96.3 ± 1.2
	3						94.7 ± 1.4	$95.8 \pm 1.9_{y}$	95.2 ± 0.6
	4	93.4 ± 1.3							94.0 ± 2.4
Monocytes %	1	2.87 ± 0.83	1.70 ± 0.52	3.88 ± 1.09	1.33 ± 0.80	2.00 ± 0.53	1.35 ± 0.42	1.50 ± 0.56	2.16 ± 0.65
	2						4.86 ± 1.89	2.35 ± 0.49	1.16 ± 0.48
	3						3.16 ± 0.60^{a}	0.67 ± 0.33^{b}	$2.15 \pm 0.65^{a,b}$
	4	2.87 ± 0.83							2.50 ± 0.67
Granulocytes %	1	3.73 ± 0.99^{a}	2.00 ± 0.76^{a}	1.52 ± 0.33^{a}	9.17 ± 2.56^{b}	2.40 ± 0.97^{a}	$4.85 \pm 2.61^{a,b}$	9.50 ± 2.29^{b}	$5.14 \pm 1.40^{a,b}$
	2						3.84 ± 0.91	$3.35 \pm 1.23_{y}$	2.54 ± 0.89
	3						2.14 ± 1.22	$3.53 \pm 1.80_{y}$	2.65 ± 0.76
	4	3.73 ± 0.99							5.50 ± 1.80
Cadmium in muscle mg.kg-1	1	0.017 ± 0.003^{a}	0.018 ± 0.004^{a}	0.018 ± 0.003^{a}	$0.027 \pm 0.004^{a,b}$	0.030 ± 0.004^{b}	$0.036 \pm 0.004_{x}^{b,c}$	0.044 ± 0.003^{c}	$0.059 \pm 0.005_{x}^{d}$
	2						$0.045 \pm 0.006_{x,y}$	0.047 ± 0.003	$0.046 \pm 0.007_{x}$
	3						$0.049 \pm 0.003_{y}$	0.048 ± 0.003	$0.055 \pm 0.005_{x}$
	4	0.017 ± 0.003							$0.028 \pm 0.002_{y}^{*}$
Cadmium in hepatopancreas mg.kg-1	1	0.023 ± 0.005^{a}	0.035 ± 0.008^{a}	0.039 ± 0.008^{a}	0.157 ± 0.015^{b}	0.167 ± 0.009^{b}	$0.329 \pm 0.019_{x}^{c}$	$0.287 \pm 0.018_{x}^{c}$	$1.212 \pm 0.039_{x}^{d}$
	2						$0.223 \pm 0.031_{y}^{a}$	$0.198 \pm 0.024_{y}^{a}$	$0.130 \pm 0.013_{y}^{b}$
	3						$0.318 \pm 0.016_{x}^{a}$	$0.526 \pm 0.022_{z}^{b}$	$0.620 \pm 0.019_{z}^{c}$
	4	0.023 ± 0.005							$0.018 \pm 0.004_{y}$

+ no analysis made

in several fish species; a reduction in haemoglobin and haematocrit values was found in eel, flounder and perch (Larson, 1975). Significant reductions in haemoglobin level, haematocrit value and red blood cells count, but no differences in the MCHC, MCH or MCV indices, were observed between the controls and cadmium exposed (0.05–0.50 mg $Cd^{2+}.l^{-1}$) flounders (Johansson-Sjöbeck and Larson, 1978). Changes, but with no specific trend, in haematological parameters were observed in tilapia during a prolonged exposure to 0.1–10 mg $Cd^{2+}.l^{-1}$ (Ruparelia, 1990). Cadmium exposure caused an anaemia in rainbow trout (Haux and Larson, 1984). No significant changes, with the exception of the increase in erythrocytes count, were observed in the majority of haematological parameters examined in dogfish after a short-term exposure to 50 mg $Cd^{2+}.l^{-1}$ (Tort and Hernández-Pascual, 1990). No significant haematological differences were found between winter flounder exposed to 0.005 and 0.01 mg $Cd^{2+}.l^{-1}$ for 60 days and control fish (Calabrese *et al.*, 1975).

The significant increase in leucocyte count found after 11 days of exposure was followed by a significant decrease that occurred in all experimental groups, including the control (Table 5.4). No significant changes were observed in the percentage proportion of lymphocytes and monocytes, and few changes were recorded in granulocytes. No differences between the control and experimental groups were found for these parameters at the end of the experiment (Table 5.4). An increase in leucocyte count was found in flounders (Johansson-Sjöbeck and Larson, 1978). As with the results presented here, a prolonged exposure resulted in lower values (including those in the control) than those measured at the earlier sampling time. The reduction in the total leucocyte count was attributed to a lower number of lymphocytes (Johansson-Sjöbeck and Larson, 1978).

The cadmium exposure resulted in a continuous accumulation that was more rapid in the hepatopancreas than in the muscle tissues. At the end of the experiment, the content of cadmium in fish in Group 1 was 3.5 times higher in muscle and as much as 53 times higher in the hepatopancreas by comparison with the initial values. During the period of recovery (Table 5.4), there was a decrease in cadmium levels in the hepatopancreas, but no such elimination was detected in muscle tissue. A dose-dependent accumulation of cadmium in muscle and liver tissues was found in rainbow trout exposed to 0.01 and 0.10 mg $Cd^{2+}.l^{-1}$ for 30 weeks; the levels recorded in the liver were about 100 times higher than those in the muscle (Haux and Larson, 1984).

5.4   Conclusions

The exposure of carp fingerlings to a sublethal level of cadmium causes physiological disturbances such as the decrease and the subsequent increase in glycogen content in hepatopancreas, hypoglycaemia, hypocalcaemia, a reduction in plasma chloride, and changes in the plasma protein spectrum, associated with an accumulation of cadmium which is more rapid in the hepatopancreas than in the muscle tissue.

The results obtained both during the exposure and the subsequent recovery periods demonstrate that carp fingerlings have an ability to compensate for some of the disturbances and return these physiological processes to normal, despite the presence of accumulated cadmium in the body.

The discrepancies between the results obtained by various authors might be explained by the use of different conditions including the fish species, cadmium concentrations, and the exposure period. Because of this variability between the various studies, it is difficult to establish any specific effect of cadmium that would be useful especially for the monitoring of field conditions. It should be emphasised that the results obtained are valid only for the conditions of the experiment carried out.

References

Calabrese, A. *et al.*, 1975. Sublethal physiological stress induced by cadmium and mercury in the winter flounder, *Pseudopleuronectes americanus*. In: Koeman, J.H. and J.J.T.W.A. Strik (Eds.) *Sublethal Effects of Toxic Chemicals in Aquatic Animals*, 15–21. Amsterdam, Elsevier.

Edler, D., 1968. Das Verhalten der Konzentration des Leberglykogens und des Blutzuckers bei Kälbern von der Geburt an bis zu einer Alter von drei Monaten und Erprobung der Aspirationsbiopsie der Leber bei Kälbern. Brno-Leipzig. Dissertation. 85 p.

Eisler, R., 1985. Cadmium hazard to fish, wildlife and invertebrates: a synoptic review. *Biol.Rept.*, **85** (2): 1–46.

Haux, C. and A. Larson, 1984. Long-term sublethal physiological effects on rainbow trout, *Oncorhynchus mykiss*, during exposure to cadmium and after subsequent recovery. *Aquat.Toxicol.*, 5: 129–142.

Jirásek, J., D. Pravda and A. Hampl, 1980. An effective method of blood sampling for mass hematological examination of young fish. *Acta Univ.Agr.(Brno)*, **1**: 175–182.

Johansson-Sjöbeck, M.L. and A. Larson, 1978. The effects of cadmium on the hematology and on the activity of delta-aminolevulic acid dehydratase (ALA-D) in blood and hematopoetic tissues of the flounder, *Pleuronectes flesus*. *Environ.Res.*, **17**: 191–204.

Larson, A., 1975. Some biochemical effects of cadmium on fish. In : Koeman, J.H. and J.J.T.W.A. Strik (Eds.) *Sublethal Effects of Toxic Chemicals in Aquatic Animals*, 3–13. Amsterdam, Elsevier.

Pravda, D. *et al.*, 1989. Dynamics of changes of the haemogram and biochemistry of carp fingerling blood in experiments with diet containing PCBs and Hg and Cd admixtures in the water environment of fish. Second Ichthyohaematological Conference, Litcmysl, 24–35.

Ruparelia, S.G., 1990. Effect of cadmium on blood of tilapia, *Oreochromis mossambicus*, during prolonged exposure. *Bull.Envir.Contam.Toxicol.*, **45**: 305–312.

Svobodová, Z., D. Pravda and J. Paláčková, 1986. Jednotné metody hematologického vysetrování ryb. (Unified methods of haemathological examination of fish.) VÚRH Vodnany, Edice Metodik.

Tort, L. and M.D. Hernández-Pascual, 1990. Haematological effects in dogfish, *Scyliorhinus canicula*, after short-term sublethal cadmium exposure. *Acta Hydrochim.Hydrobiol.*, **18**: 379–383.

Unified methods of chemical analyses of water. 1965. Prague, SNTL, 449 pp.

Chapter 6
Interactions between copper and cadmium during single or combined metal exposures in the teleost fish *Oreochromis mossambicus*: heavy metal accumulation and endocrine events

S.M.G.J. PELGROM, L.P.M. LAMERS, A. HAAIJMAN, P.H.M. BALM, R.A.C. LOCK and S.E. WENDELAAR BONGA

Department of Animal Physiology, Faculty of Science, University of Nijmegen, Toernooiveld, 6525 ED Nijmegen, The Netherlands

6.1   Introduction

As a result of increased industrialisation, heavy metals are widespread in the freshwater environment. An increased body content of heavy metals in fish will contribute to the adverse effects of heavy metal exposure. Studies have shown that cadmium (Cd) exposure affects liver and kidney functions in fish (Friberg *et al.*, 1986) and calcium uptake in rainbow trout gills (Verbost *et al.*, 1987). Among other effects, copper (Cu) exposure affects growth and swimming performance in rainbow trout (Lett *et al.*, 1976; Waiwood and Beamish, 1978). During exposure to waterborne metals, the gills play an important role in metal uptake. Sublethal metal exposure results in both a disturbed ion balance, due to the ionregulatory function of gills, and an increased metal burden in the fish. During the process of adaptation, the endocrine system controls the mechanisms involved in the acclimation process (Fu *et al.*, 1989).

In many studies, the total amount of heavy metal in fish has been used as an indicator of metal exposure. However, natural freshwaters are generally contaminated by metal mixtures. The effects of such mixtures on aquatic organisms seem to be complex (Hamilton *et al.*, 1987). This is especially true for the interactions between copper and cadmium. In the literature, both addition and synergism as well as no effect after exposure to metal mixtures are described.

In this study we investigated the interaction between sublethal concentrations of Cu and Cd during single and combined exposure on the total amounts of body Cu and Cd in immature fish after a 96-hour period of exposure. To investigate whether these whole body results could be extrapolated to specific organs, we determined total amounts of Cu and Cd in selected organs of mature fish after 6 and 11 days of exposure. It has been demonstrated that the effects of heavy metals are organ-specific. However, the relation between the amount of metal accumulated and the function of target organs has received relatively little attention. Finally, this matter was addressed by studying the effect of metal exposure on interrenal cortisol production. Cortisol is a crucial factor in the adaptation to heavy metals by teleosts: at the branchial level, it restores the ionic imbalances caused by the metals, but it also induces the production of metal-binding proteins, thereby contributing to metal detoxification. In the present study, interrenal function was studied in relation to heavy metal accumulation.

6.2   Materials and methods

Tilapia (*Oreochromis mossambicus*) were obtained from our laboratory stock. Fish were kept in artificial fresh water without detectable Cu and Cd. The artificial fresh water consisted of demineralised water supplemented with 1.3 mM $NaHCO_3$, 0.5 mM $CaCl_2$, 0.06 mM KCl and 0.2 mM $MgCl_2$; the pH was 7.8. The water was continuously aerated and filtered. The light:dark regime was 12:12 hours and temperature 26°C. Fish were fed a commercial food for tropical fish (Tetramine[TM]) at 2% ($^w/_w$) of their body weight per day.

6.2.1   *Experiments with sexually immature fish*

Three days before starting the experiment, 15 groups of 15 fishes (one month old) were placed randomly in polyethylene 4.5 l aquaria filled with artificial fresh water, at 26°C. During acclimation, the water was continuously replenished by means of a flow-through system (flowrate: 0.24 $l.h^{-1}$). During acclimation and during the experiment, the fish were not fed. The experiment started with the connection of each aquarium to its own stock metal solution by means of a 16-channel peristaltic pump. During the first 6 hours of exposure, the flowrate was 0.66 $l.h^{-1}$ and for the following 90 hours 0.24 $l.h^{-1}$. Copper and cadmium concentrations in both the stock solutions and the aquaria were monitored daily by means of AAS (Atomair Absorption Spectrometer, Philips PU 9200). In the aquaria the Cu concentration ranged from 0 to 400 $\mu g.l^{-1}$; the Cd concentration ranged from 0 to 155 $\mu g.l^{-1}$.

After 96 h of exposure, fish were rinsed in artificial freshwater and immediately killed in ice-cold CO_2/acetone. Fish were weighed and lyophilised. After measuring the dry weight, complete destruction followed using nitric acid. Whole body Cu and Cd was determined by AAS.

6.2.2   *Experiments with sexually mature fish*

Mature female tilapia (mean weight 20 g, 5 months old) were kept in four groups of 12 fishes, in 80 l aquaria. In these fish, organs of choice can be excised successfully.

The artificial freshwater was continuously renewed (flowrate 0.36 $l.h^{-1}$) and filtered. The temperature was 26°C, and the light:dark regime was 12:12 h. During the experiment fish were fed (2% $^w/_w$) daily. The experiment was started by connecting (by means of a peristaltic pump) each of the four aquaria to its own reservoir filled with metal solutions in artificial fresh water. The metal concentrations in the aquaria were 50 μg.l^{-1} Cu and 20 μg.l^{-1} Cd singly, 50 μg.l^{-1} Cu + 20 μg.l^{-1} Cd, and no metals (control). The exposure regime was comparable with that used for the immature fish (first 6 h a flowrate of 4.5 l.h^{-1}, followed by a flowrate of 1.5 l.h^{-1}), and the exposure lasted 6 or 11 days. Feeding was ended the day before the fish were sacrificed. After exposure, the fish were killed by spinal section, and interrenal tissues (Nandi and Bern, 1960) were immediately prepared for micro-superfusion (described by Balm, 1986). Tissues (gills, liver and kidney) were prepared, weighed and lyophilised. After determination of the dry weights, tissues were completely dissolved with nitric acid.

With fish exposed to Cu or Cd for 6 days, the cortisol released by interrenal tissue (under basal and secretagogue, ACTH (adrenocorticotropic hormone) and 8-Br-cAMP stimulation) was determined by means of a RIA (Radio Immuno Assay, described by Balm, 1986). At the end of the superfusion of interrenal tissues, the adrenals were also weighed, lyophilised and dissolved in nitric acid. Total amounts of Cu and Cd in tissues were determined by means of AAS.

6.2.3   *Statistics*

Data are presented as means ±SEM (standard error of the mean). For statistical evaluation Student's t-test was applied. The degree of significance is indicated with asterisks, with * $P \leq 0.05$, ** $P \leq 0.02$, *** $P \leq 0.01$ and **** $P \leq 0.001$.

6.3   **Results and discussion**

No mortality occurred during the gradual exposure to the ranges of Cu and Cd used in this study. The metal concentrations used are not only sublethal, but also comparable with the Cu and Cd concentrations found in fresh waters. Although generally low, the environmental Cd concentration can reach 100 μg.l^{-1} during sporadic contamination (van Vuuren, 1989). The Cu concentrations used are also in the range that can be found in fresh waters; the limit for Cu concentration in drinking water is 50 μg.l^{-1}.

6.3.1   *Cu and Cd accumulation in immature fish*

Metal concentrations in the water increased gradually during the first 18 hours of exposure until they reached the final concentrations and then remained constant during the remainder of the exposure period (inserts of Fig. 6.1 and Fig. 6.2). Exposure of immature tilapia to Cu concentrations ranging from 100 to 400 μg.l^{-1} and Cd concentrations ranging from 35 to 155 μg.l^{-1} resulted in a dose-dependent increase in whole body Cu and Cd content respectively (Fig. 6.1 and Fig. 6.2).

Whole body Cd content in Cu exposed fish and whole body Cu content in Cd

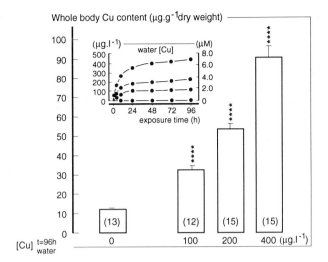

Fig. 6.1 Whole body copper content (in µg Cu per gram dry weight) in fish after exposure to 0, 100, 200 or 400 µg.l^{-1} Cu for 96 hours. Asterisks indicate significant differences between control and Cu-exposed fish. Numbers of fish per group are indicated in the bars.

Insert: copper concentrations in the aquaria (in µg.l^{-1} and µM) during exposure.

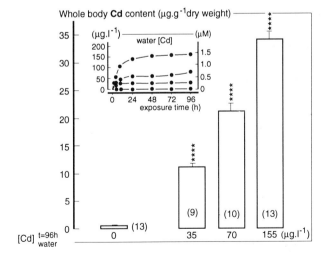

Fig. 6.2 Whole body cadmium content (in µg Cd per gram dry weight) in fish after exposure to 0, 35, 70 or 155 µg.l^{-1} Cd for 96 hours. Asterisks indicate significant differences between control and Cd-exposed fish. Numbers of fish per group are indicated in the bars.

Insert: cadmium concentrations in the aquaria (in µg.l^{-1} and µM) during exposure.

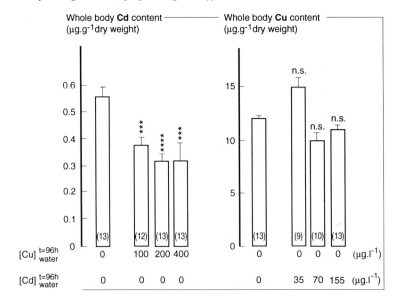

Fig. 6.3 Whole body cadmium content (in μg Cd per gram dry weight) in Cu exposed fish (left) and whole body copper content (in μg Cu per gram dry weight) in Cd exposed fish after 96 hours. Numbers of fish per group are indicated in the bars. Asterisks indicate significant differences between control and metal exposed fish.

exposed fish are shown in Figure 6.3. Copper exposure resulted in an accumulation of Cu as well as in a significantly decreased Cd content of fish, probably as a result of Cd excretion. Because the fish were reared in Cd-free water and not fed during the exposure period, the Cd present in fish at the start must originate from Cd ingestion from food during the period before the experiment. The elimination of Cd as a result of Cu exposure may be mediated by metallothioneins (MTs), metal binding proteins (Klaverkamp *et al.*, 1984). Concentrations of MTs increase in fish during metal exposure and are important for the recovery of physiological homeostasis (Giles, 1984). It is known that Cu is able to displace Cd from MTs. As a result of an increasing Cu load in MTs during Cu exposure, the Cd-binding capacity of MTs decreases (Laurén and McDonald, 1985, 1987; Scheuhammer and Cherian, 1986). Release of Cd as a result of Cu exposure has also been reported by Meshitsuka *et al.* (1983) who investigated effects of *in vitro* metal exposure on human KB-cells, a human carcinoma cell line. It might be expected that during Cu exposure, not only the Cu accumulation but also the release of Cd from MTs will affect physiological processes in fish.

No effect was observed on whole body Cu content after Cd exposure. This accords with the above mentioned suggestion concerning the involvement of MTs during metal exposure, since Cd is not able to displace Cu from MTs.

Besides the measurement of Cu and Cd in fish exposed to single metals, we also measured whole body metal content after exposure to Cu + Cd mixtures

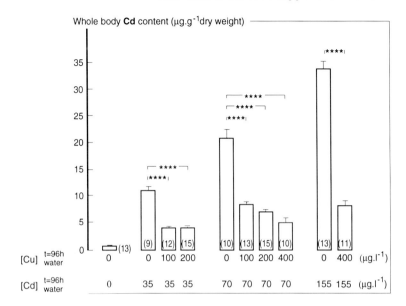

Fig. 6.4   Whole body cadmium content (in µg Cd per gram dry weight) in fish exposed to combinations of Cu + Cd concentrations for 96 hours. Numbers of fish per group are indicated in the bars. Asterisks indicate significant differences between Cd content of Cd + Cu exposed fish and fish exposed to Cd alone.

(Fig. 6.4). Co-exposure to Cu + Cd had no significant effect on the whole body Cu content when compared to the Cu content in fish exposed to Cu alone (data not shown). In contrast, co-exposure to Cu + Cd resulted in a significantly decreased Cd content compared to fish exposed to Cd alone. This decrease is most probably due to a combination of increased elimination and decreased uptake of Cd. Holwerda (1991) reported that Cu exposure had no effect on the *in vitro* uptake of Cd in gills of clams but only increased the elimination of accumulated Cd. However, in our fish it is more likely that Cu/Cd interactions also occur during uptake of Cd, in view of the fact that Cd elimination from teleosts is usually very slow, and therefore cannot possibly account for the effect observed. The increased excretion of Cd and interaction between Cu and Cd during exposure will probably result in an increased toxicity of the metal exposure, because during this period more Cd will be present in a toxic, not MT-bound, form. For trout hepatocytes (Denizeau and Marion, 1990) and human KB cells (Meshitsuka *et al.*, 1983, 1987) it has also been shown that *in vitro* exposure to Cu + Cd resulted in an increased toxicity, which was measured as a change in the protein content of the cells after exposure.

6.3.2   *Cu and Cd accumulation and interaction in organs of mature fish*

To investigate whether the results obtained for the metal content of the whole body are representative of those for specific organs, we investigated the Cu and Cd

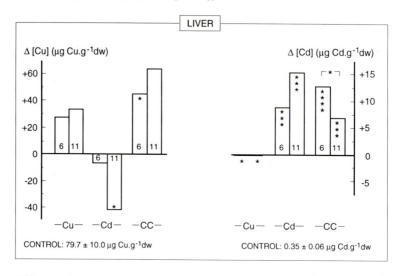

Fig. 6.5 Difference in metal content in livers of fish exposed to 50 μg.l⁻¹ Cu, 20 μg.l⁻¹ Cd and to 50 μg.l⁻¹ Cu + 20 μg.l⁻¹ Cd (CC) and metal content in control fish (Δ [Cu] or Δ [Cd]). Concentrations of Cu and Cd in livers of control fish are indicated at the bottom of the figure. Exposure time, 6 or 11 days, is indicated in the bars. Asterisks in the bars indicate significant differences between metal exposed and control fish; asterisks between bars indicate significant differences between 6 and 11 days of exposure.

accumulation in several organs of mature fish after 6 and 11 days of exposure to 50 μg.l⁻¹ Cu and/or 20 μg.l⁻¹ Cd. These concentrations were based on the results obtained with immature fish; in those experiments, the lowest concentrations of heavy metals caused an effect. In addition, these concentrations of Cu and Cd are environmentally relevant.

No mortality of the mature fish occurred during the exposure period and no changes in feeding behaviour were observed between the control and experimental groups of fish. Figures 6.5, 6.6 and 6.7 show the Cu and Cd content, expressed as the difference in metal concentration between metal exposed and control fish, in liver, kidney and gills, respectively. The metal content in organs of metal exposed fish is compared first with the metal content of control fish, and significant differences are indicated by asterisks in the bars. Second, differences in the metal content in organs between 6 and 11 days exposed fish are indicated by asterisks between the bars. To summarise, Figure 6.8 shows the difference in metal concentration in the organs of fish exposed to mixtures of Cu + Cd compared to metal content in organs of fish exposed to the metals singly.

In liver (Fig. 6.5), Cu exposure did not result in significantly increased Cu concentration. Cadmium exposure resulted in significantly increased Cd concentrations, as well as a decreased Cu concentration after 11 days of exposure, while co-exposure to Cu + Cd resulted in a significantly increased Cu content. Copper exposure resulted in a significantly decreased Cd concentration in liver, a phenomenon similar to the results obtained from experiments with immature fish.

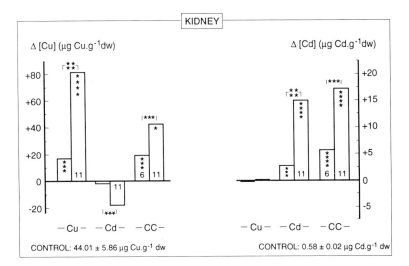

Fig. 6.6 Differences in metal content in kidneys of fish exposed to 50 μg.l⁻¹ Cu, 20 μg.l⁻¹ Cd and to 50 μg.l⁻¹ Cu+ 20 μg.l⁻¹ Cd (CC) and metal content in control fish (Δ [Cu] or Δ [Cd]). Concentrations of Cu and Cd in kidneys of control fish are indicated at the bottom of the figure. Exposure time, 6 or 11 days, is indicated in the bars. Asterisks are as indicated in Figure 6.5.

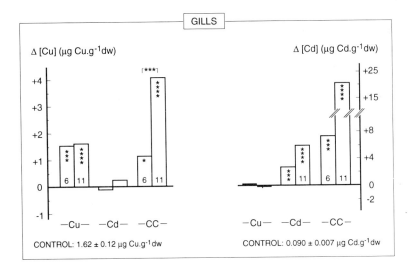

Fig. 6.7 Differences in metal content in gills of fish exposed to 50 μg.l⁻¹ Cu, 20 μg.l⁻¹ Cd and to 50 μg.l⁻¹ Cu+ 20 μg.l⁻¹ Cd (CC) and metal content in control fish (Δ [Cu] or Δ [Cd]). Concentrations of Cu and Cd in gills of control fish are indicated at the bottom of the figure. Exposure time, 6 or 11 days, is indicated in the bars. Asterisks are as indicated in Figure 6.5.

		COPPER CC ➡ Cu	CADMIUM CC ➡ Cd
LIVER	6 days	ns	ns
	11 days	ns	ns
KIDNEY	6 days	ns	⬆ ★★
	11 days	ns	ns
GILLS	6 days	ns	⬆ ★★
	11 days	⬆ ★★★	⬆ ★★

Fig. 6.8 Metal contents in liver, kidney and gills of tilapia co-exposed to Cu and Cd (CC) compared to the metal content of fish exposed to Cu and Cd separately. Comparisons are for both 6 and 11 days of exposure. Significantly increased metal content in tissues of fish exposed to the mixture compared to single-metal exposed fish is indicated by vertical arrows. Values are obtained from the experiment depicted in Figures 6.5, 6.6 and 6.7.

However, the liver of fish co-exposed to Cu + Cd during 6 days accumulated Cd to the same extent as fish exposed to Cd alone, although exposure during 11 days resulted in a decreased Cd concentration when compared to 6 days of exposure. No significant differences were observed between metal concentrations in liver of Cu + Cd co-exposed fish when compared to the concentrations in fish exposed to the metals separately (Fig. 6.8).

In kidney (Fig. 6.6), exposure to Cu or to Cu + Cd resulted in a time-dependent increase in Cu concentration. Cadmium exposure for 11 days resulted in a significantly decreased Cu concentration compared to exposure during 6 days. In contrast to the results obtained from experiments with immature fish, Cu exposure had no effect on Cd content in kidney. Cadmium exposure, alone or in combination with Cu, resulted in a time-dependent increased Cd concentration. A comparison of the metal concentrations in kidneys of Cu + Cd co-exposed fish with the metal concentration in kidneys of Cu or Cd exposed fish indicates that only the Cd concentration after 6 days of exposure was significantly increased (Fig. 6.8).

Exposure to Cu or Cd resulted, both after 6 and 11 days, in an increased concentration in gills of Cu and Cd respectively (Fig. 6.7). In gills, Cu exposure had no effect on Cd content, nor did Cd exposure affect the Cu content. Co-exposure to both metals resulted in increased concentrations of both Cu and Cd, after 6 and 11 days exposure. Figure 6.8 shows that Cu + Cd co-exposure during 6 days resulted in a significantly increased Cd concentration compared to the Cd concentration in gills of fish exposed to Cd alone. Co-exposure to Cu + Cd during 11 days resulted in significant increases of both Cu and Cd compared to the metal concentrations in gills of fish exposed to the metals separately. Figure 6.8 shows that of the organs studied, exposures to mixtures seem to be most detrimental to the gills.

Our results demonstrate that tissue-dependent interactions are involved in metal accumulation during exposure. Increasing the exposure time does not result in an increased metal content in all the organs. A positive relationship between metal concentration in the environment and metal concentration in organs of fish, as suggested by Buckley *et al.* (1984) seems to be too simplistic.

6.3.3   *In vitro cortisol release from interrenal tissue after exposure to Cu or Cd for 6 days*

To study the role of cortisol during the process of adaptation to increasing metal concentrations in fish, we measured the *in vitro* cortisol release by interrenal tissue after exposure to Cu or Cd during 6 days. Because of their extensive epithelial surface and their role in water and ion regulation, gills are sensitive targets for metals during exposure. Exposure to both Cu and Cd had resulted in a significantly increased metal concentration in the gills (Fig. 6.7). It is known that Cd exposure results in a disturbed ion balance in fish, and the cortisol is required for the activation of ion transporting ATPases which serves to restore the ionic balance. Generally, stressors increase the release of cortisol by adrenal tissue. Nevertheless, in this study Cd exposure resulted in a decreased *in vitro* secretagogue-stimulated cortisol release (Fig. 6.9). This seems to contradict the findings of increased plasma cortisol levels described by Fu *et al.* (1989). However, these authors determined the plasma cortisol levels after acute Cd administration, while this study deals with gradually exposed fish. The difference between the exposure methods is illustrated by the lethal concentration of Cd found during acute exposure (Fu, 1989), while during gradual exposure to the same Cd concentration no mortality was observed in the present study. However, it is still possible that an initially increased cortisol release, mediated by elevated ACTH levels upon exposure to Cd, had preceded the effect observed here. As a result, the interrenal tissue will have become less sensitive to ACTH, a general phenomenon observed in the study of adrenal function during stress. The negative effect on the interrenal function associated with exposure to Cd could contribute to the toxicity of the metal.

There is a striking difference in Cu concentration between the kidney (Fig. 6.6) and interrenal tissue (Fig. 6.10) of control fish, while the Cd concentrations are comparable in those tissues. More important, the amount of metal accumulation is small compared to metal accumulation in kidney. This indicates that the renal and interrenal tissue are two separate compartments with different functions; this is supported by the fact that interrenal tissue contains no renal tissue. Despite these differences, however, the two tissues have a common origin (Nandi and Bern, 1960). It also seems that metal accumulation in the interrenal is not directly related to the endocrine effect observed. Both Cu and Cd accumulated in interrenal tissue during exposure, whereas only Cd exposure had a significant effect on cortisol release (Fig. 6.10).

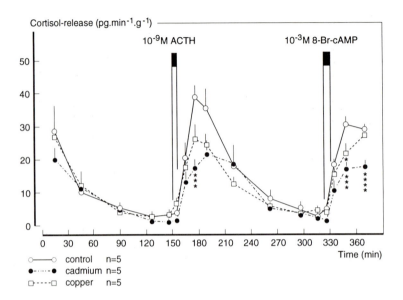

Fig. 6.9 Cortisol release (in picogram cortisol per minute per gram fish) during *in vitro* superfusion of interrenal tissue of *in vivo* exposed fish to 50 µg.l^{-1} Cu or 20 µg.l^{-1} Cd for 6 days. Secretagogue-stimulated cortisol release was investigated by means of stimulation with ACTH (5 min. 10^{-9} M) and 8-Br-cAMP (10 min. 10^{-3} M). Significant differences between control and metal exposed fish are indicated by asterisks.

6.4   Conclusions

To summarise, Cu and Cd interactions are complex, and results of metal concentrations in immature fish are not simply comparable with metal contents of organs of mature fish after exposure. Moreover, the complexity of Cu/Cd interaction is shown by the results of metal accumulation for fish co-exposed to Cu and Cd. The metal concentrations in fish exposed to mixtures of Cu and Cd are not simply a combination of the metal contents of fish exposed to the metals separately. Since in natural fresh waters a mixture of metals is usually present, these interactions will have confounding consequences if the metal content in fish is used as a monitor for metal exposure.

In this study, we have demonstrated that exposure to Cd resulted in a significantly decreased secretagogue stimulated cortisol release. It is known that endocrine mechanisms are involved in both metal uptake/elimination and regulation of MT synthesis. Further research on the involvement of (neuro-) endocrine regulation during acclimation to sublethal metal exposure is needed to obtain an insight into the mechanisms involved.

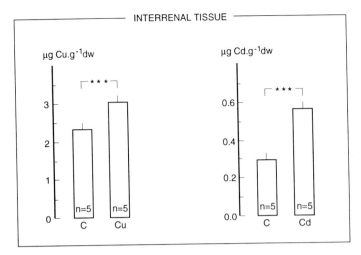

Fig. 6.10 Cu and Cd content (in μg per gram dry weight) of interrenal tissue of fish exposed to 50 μg.l^{-1} Cu or 20 μg.l^{-1} Cd for 6 days. Numbers of fish per group are indicated in the bars. Asterisks indicate significant differences between control (C) and metal exposed fish.

References

Balm, P.H.M., 1986. Osmoregulation in teleosts by cortisol and prolactin; adaptation to low pH environments. Ph.D. thesis, University of Nijmegen, Nijmegen, The Netherlands.

Buckley, J.A., G.A. Yoshida and N.R. Wells, 1984. A cupric ion–copper bioaccumulation relationship in coho salmon exposed to copper containing sewage. *Comp.Biochem.Physiol.*, **78C**: 105–110.

Denizeau, F. and M. Marion, 1990. Toxicity of cadmium, copper, and mercury to isolated trout hepatocytes. *Can.J.Fish.Aquat.Sci.*, **47**: 1038–1042.

Friberg, L., T. Fjellström and G.F. Nordberg, 1986. Cadmium. In: Friberg, L. *et al.* (Eds.) *Handbook on the Toxicology of Metals*, 2nd edn, Vol II, pp. 130–184. Amsterdam, Elsevier.

Fu, H., 1989. Hormonal responses of fish to cadmium. Ph.D. thesis, University of Nijmegen, Nijmegen, The Netherlands.

Fu, H., O.M. Steinebach, C.J.A. Van den Hamer, P.H.M. Balm and R.A.C. Lock, 1989. Involvement of cortisol and metallothionein-like proteins in the physiological responses of tilapia (*Oreochromis mossambicus*) to sublethal cadmium stress. *Aquat.Toxicol.*, **16**: 257–270.

Giles, M.A., 1984. Electrolyte and water balance in plasma and urine in rainbow trout (*Salmo gairdneri*) during chronic exposure to cadmium. *Can.J.Fish.Aquat.Sci.*, **41**: 1678–1685.

Hamilton, R.D., J.F. Klaverkamp, W.L. Lockhart and R. Wagemann, 1987. Major aquatic contaminants, their sources, distribution and effects. In: Healey, M.C. and R.R. Wallace (Eds.) *Canadian Aquatic Resources*, pp. 357–386. Ottawa, Department of Fisheries and Oceans Canada.

Holwerda, D.A., 1991. Cadmium kinetics in freshwater clams. V. Cadmium–copper interaction in metal accumulation by *Anodonta cygnea* and characterization of the metal-binding protein. *Arch.Environ.Contam.Toxicol.*, **21**: 432–437.

Klaverkamp, J.F., W.A. Macdonald, D.A. Duncan and R. Wagemann, 1984. Metallothionein and acclimation to heavy metals in fish: a review. In: Cairns, V.W. *et al.* (Eds.) *Contaminant Effects on Fisheries*, pp. 99–113. New York, Wiley.

Laurén, D.J. and D.G. McDonald, 1985. Effects of copper on branchial ionregulation in the rainbow trout, *Salmo gairdneri* Richardson. *J.Comp.Physiol.B.*, **155**: 636–644.

Laurén, D.J. and D.G. McDonald, 1987. Acclimation to copper by rainbow trout, *Salmo gairdneri*: biochemistry. *Can.J.Fish.Aquat.Sci.*, **44**: 104–111.

Lett, P.F., G.J. Farmer and F.W.H. Beamish, 1976. Effect of copper on some aspects of the bioenergetics of rainbow trout *Salmo gairdneri*. *J.Fish.Res.Bd.Can.*, **33**: 1335–1342.

Meshitsuka, S., T. Nose and M. Ishizawa, 1983. Specific effects of copper on the uptake and release of cadmium by KB cells. *Yonaga Acta Medica*, **26**: 87–98.

Meshitsuka, S., M. Ishizawa and T. Nose, 1987. Uptake and toxic effects of heavy metal ions: Interactions among cadmium, copper and zinc in cultured cells. *Experientia*, **43**: 151–156.

Nandi, J. and H.A. Bern, 1960. Corticosteroid production by the interrenal tissue of teleost fish. *Endocrinol.*, **66**: 295–303.

Scheuhammer, A.M. and M.G. Cherian, 1986. Quantification of metallothioneins by a silver-saturation method. *Toxicol.Appl.Pharmacol.*, **82**: 417–425.

Verbost, P.M., G. Flik, R.A.C. Lock and S.E. Wendelaar Bonga, 1987. Cadmium inhibition of Ca^{2+}-uptake of rainbow trout gills. *Am.J.Physiol.*, **253**: R216–R221.

Vuuren, W.E. van, 1989. Cadmium calamiteiten op de maas: een triest record in november 1988. *H_2O*, **22**: 23–25.

Waiwood, K.G. and F.W.H. Beamish, 1978. Effect of copper, pH and hardness on the critical swimming performance of rainbow trout (*Salmo gairdneri* Richardson). *Wat.Res.*, **12**: 611–619.

Chapter 7
Disulfoton as a major toxicant in the Rhine chemical spill at Basle in 1986: acute and chronic studies with eel and rainbow trout

H. ARNOLD and T. BRAUNBECK

Department of Zoology I, University of Heidelberg, Im Neuenheimer Feld 230, D-W-6900 Heidelberg, Germany

7.1   Introduction

The phosphate ester pesticide disulfoton (Solvirex®, Frumin® AL) was the toxicant spilt in the greatest quantity during the chemical accident at Basle on 1 November 1986. From a store of 287 tonnes of active ingredient, approximately 3–9 tonnes were released into the River Rhine while controlling the fire. In combination with several other chemicals discharged during this incident, it had a tremendous effect on aquatic organisms and on the Rhine ecosystem in general. In particular, the population of the European eel (*Anguilla anguilla*) was severely reduced, although this species had been previously regarded as fairly resistant towards xenobiotics (Amiard-Triquet *et al.*, 1987; Ferrando *et al.*, 1987).

Cytological changes in the hepatocytes of eels exposed to the chemical spill indicated an induction of both immunological and detoxification processes (Braunbeck *et al.*, 1990). Subsequent studies on the effects of dinitro-*o*-cresol, a phenolic pesticide released at the time of the accident, showed that it caused symptoms in eel liver similar to those found in the Rhine eel, but failed to provide a conclusive explanation for the lethal effects on the latter population of the River Rhine following the accident. In fact, even the highest tested concentration of this pesticide (250 µg.l^{-1}) did not affect the behaviour or macroscopical appearance of eels (Braunbeck and Völkl, 1991). However, a comparison with data from a similar experiment with golden ide *(Leuciscus idus melanotus)* indicated that eels were much more sensitive to sublethal impacts of dinitro-*o*-cresol than had been expected (Braunbeck and Völkl, 1993).

Fish are known to be susceptible to disulfoton; the LC$_{50}$ values given for rainbow trout *(Oncorhynchus mykiss)* vary from 1.85 mg.l^{-1} to 3 mg.l^{-1} (Holcombe *et al.*, 1982; Mayer and Ellersieck, 1986), and corresponding data for fathead minnow (*Pimephales promelas*), channel catfish (*Ictalurus punctatus*), bluegill sunfish (*Lepomis macrochirus*) and largemouth bass (*Micropterus salmoides*) are 4.3, 4.7, 0.3, and 0.06 mg.l^{-1}, respectively (Mayer and Ellersieck, 1986). Studies on the acute and sublethal toxicity of disulfoton to eels and rainbow trout were therefore carried out to obtain further information on the apparent exceptional reaction of eels to chemicals, especially organophosphate compounds, compared to that of other fish species. In order to investigate cytological and biochemical changes occurring in hepatocytes, the fish were exposed to sublethal concentrations of disulfoton for a prolonged period of time. In addition, in a preceding range-finding experiment, eels were exposed to acute toxic levels for up to 96 hours.

7.2   Experimental procedure

7.2.1   *Test fish*

Juvenile European eel with an average body weight of 95 g and a mean body length of 42 cm were obtained from a commercial fish dealer in Hamburg, Germany, and kept in batches of 20 in glass aquaria containing 60 l of continuously aerated water adjusted to 20 $\pm 1°C$ ($CaCO_3$ 400 ± 20 mg.l^{-1}; pH 7.40 ± 0.15; $NH_3 \leq 0.01$ mg.l^{-1}; O_2 10.5 ± 0.5 mg.l^{-1} equivalent to 90–95% saturation). Water was constantly replaced at a rate of 15 l.h^{-1} in a flow-through system giving a sixfold exchange of the total water volume per day. Fish were allowed to acclimate to the laboratory conditions for 8 weeks; no mortalities were recorded during this period. During adaptation, fish were fed with a mixture of minced spleen and commercially available trout food (Trouvit®) twice daily at 3–4% of the body weight. The light:dark period was 12:12 hours.

The sublethal experiment with immature rainbow trout (mean length 15 cm), obtained from the hatchery of the Institute for Water, Air and Soil Hygiene (Berlin, Germany) was carried out under similar laboratory conditions in collaboration with Dr H.J. Pluta (Federal Health Agency, Berlin, Germany).

7.2.2   *Test chemical and methods*

Disulfoton (Solvirex®, 98% purity, kindly provided by Sandoz, Basle, Switzerland), was dissolved in distilled water at 20°C with vigorous agitation for at least 72 hours to provide a stock solution of 10 mg.l^{-1} (the maximum solubility of disulfoton at 20°C is 25 mg.l^{-1}.

To measure acute toxicity, disulfoton concentrations of 0, 10, 25, 50, 80 and 100 μg.l^{-1} were prepared by differential dilution of the stock solution with water.

For sublethal exposure, the amount of toxicant in the aquaria was adjusted to 5 and 20 μg.l^{-1} by continuously adding disulfoton stock solution to the water inflow. Both contaminant and water inputs were controlled by peristaltic pumps. Feeding was suspended during the exposure period. At the end of this period, fish were anaesthetised by immersion in a saturated aqueous solution of ethyl-4-aminobenzoate (benzocaine; Merck, Darmstadt, Germany) and then processed for electron microscopy or biochemical analysis (four fish for each, respectively). After 4 weeks, the remaining animals were transferred to clean water and examined for electron microscopical changes two weeks after the termination of the disulfoton

treatment. To avoid possible effects of diurnal variations, all sampling was performed at midmorning. The actual concentrations of disulfoton in the aquaria were
measured by means of capillary gas chromatography (columns: 50 m CPSil 8 CB,
ID 0.32 mm, or 50 m DB-5, ID 0.22 mm, plus 50 m CPSil 19 CB, ID 0.32 mm) with
detection by flame photometry or NP detector.

7.2.3   *Electron microscopy*

From the control and from each concentration, four fish were fixed for electron
microscopy by means of *in situ* cardiac perfusion through the ventricular wall, using
hydrostatic pressure from a perfusion apparatus equipped with a 5 mm (ID)
polyvinyl tube and a blunt metal needle with a terminal opening of 1.5 mm (flow
rate 50 ml.min^{-1}), according to the procedure given by Braunbeck and Völkl
(1993).

7.2.4   *Cytochemistry*

For the discrimination of lysosomes, peroxisomes were visually identified by the
peroxidatic activity of catalase, using the alkaline 3,3'-diaminobenzidine (DAB)
method (Le Hir *et al.*, 1979).

7.2.5   *Biochemical procedures*

For biochemical measurement of enzymatic activity, the fish were perfused via the
ventricle with physiological saline free of PVP and procaine hydrochloride. After
dissection, total livers were weighed, minced with scissors in chilled homogenisation buffer (250 mM sucrose, 5 mM Mops, 1 mM EDTA, 0.1% ethanol, pH 7.4,
supplemented with 0.2 M phenylmethylsulfonyl fluoride (PMSF), 1 mM ε-amino
caproic acid and 0.02 mM dithiotreitol) and homogenised for 2 min by a single
stroke at 300 rpm in 8 ml ice-cold homogenisation buffer, using a Potter-Elvehjem
homogeniser held in an ice-water bath. The differential centrifugation procedure as
outlined by Braunbeck and Völkl (1991) was used to determine the different
enzyme activities in the respective fractions.

7.2.6   *Enzyme analyses*

Assays were run with a Pharmacia-LKB ultrospec III spectrophotometer. The
following standard procedures were employed for the measurement of enzyme
activities: uricase (E.C. 1.7.3.3) Priest and Pitts (1972); esterase (E.C. 3.1.1.1)
Beaufay *et al.* (1974) using *o*-nitrophenyl acetate as substrate; NADPH cytochrome
P450 reductase (E.C. 1.6.99.3) Sottocasa *et al.* (1967); UDP glucuronyltransferase
(E.C. 2.4.1.17) Castren and Oikari (1983); choline esterase (E.C. 3.1.1.18) Ellman
et al. (1961) using butyrylthiocholine as substrate; the protein content of the

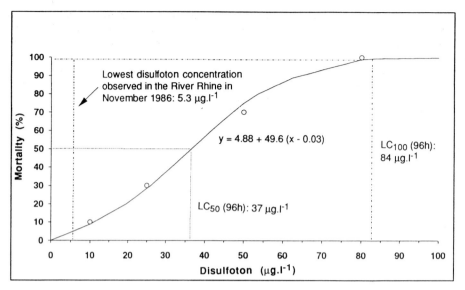

Fig. 7.1 Acute toxicity of disulfoton to eel.

fractions was estimated by the method of Bradford (1976), using ovalbumin as a standard.

7.3   Results

7.3.1   *Acute toxicity of disulfoton to eels*

Disulfoton proved to be extremely toxic to eels. Using probit transformation, the LC_{50} for 96 hours was estimated to be 37 $\mu g.l^{-1}$, i.e. three orders of magnitude below the LC_{50} of rainbow trout (Fig. 7.1). At 100 $\mu g.l^{-1}$, all the eels died within 25 hours (LC_{100}). During such an acute exposure, eels showed pronounced behavioural changes; they were incapable of normal swimming and made spasmic movements. A loss of integumental pigmentation was also observed. Most of the fish quickly recovered after transfer to clean water.

7.3.2   *Cytological features in control eels*

The hepatocytes of untreated eels were dominated by large lipid droplets as the major energy deposit. As a consequence of excessive lipid storage, the rough endoplasmic reticulum (RER), mitochondria, Golgi fields, peroxisomes and glycogen were randomly distributed throughout the entire cytoplasm. The spherical nucleus contained little heterochromatin with a patchy distribution and a scarcely visible nucleolus. The RER was arranged in parallel arrays, closely confined

Table 7.1 Semiquantitative evaluation of changes in various components of control eel hepatocytes and liver cells, and after exposure to disulfoton as well as after a two-week regeneration period following a four-week exposure to 5 μg.l^{-1} disulfoton. Data are given as mean estimates from four fish per treatment.

	Controls	100 μg.l^{-1} 48 hours	20 μg.l^{-1} 2 weeks	5 μg.l^{-1} 2 weeks	5 μg.l^{-1} 4 weeks	Regener. 2 weeks
SER	+	++	++	+++	+	++
RER	+++	++	+	+	++	+
Mitochondria	++++	++	+++	++	++	++
Peroxisomes	+	++	++	++	++	±
Myelinated bodies	+	+	+	++	−	−
Glycogen	++	±	−	++	+	++
Lipid	+++	++	++	++++	++	++

Abbreviations: − absent; ± rare; + occasionally; ++ regularly present; +++ frequent; ++++ very frequent

between the nucleus and lipid droplets. RER lamellae were slightly fenestrated; smooth endoplasmic reticulum (SER) was only poorly developed in control eels.

Together with lipid droplets and RER cisternae, mitochondria represented the most conspicuous cell components. They were of spherical to elongated shape and contained prominent cristae and intramitochondrial granules. There was a very intimate association with a collar of electron dense material around lipid droplets most likely consisting of phospholipids. Peroxisomes were of spherical appearance and displayed a homogenous matrix.

Golgi fields, glycogen, peroxisomes, lysosomes and myelinated structures were scarce in the control fish; they lacked a preferential localisation. The dictyosomes were arranged in stacks of 4–5 lamellae budding off large vesicles containing numerous VLDL particles. In close vicinity to the Golgi fields, bundles of microtubuli were prominent. Secondary lysosomes containing fibrillar and granular matrix components of variable electron density in a patchy distribution were concentrated in the peribiliary complex.

7.3.3 *Ultrastructural effects of disulfoton in eel liver*

Cytopathological effects occurring after exposure to different disulfoton concentrations are summarised in Table 7.1. At lower magnifications, the ultrastructure of eel hepatocytes appeared to be unaffected by disulfoton exposure. However, on closer inspection, all concentrations tested induced a vesiculation and a decrease in the amount of RER as well as a SER proliferation. In addition, there was a slight increase of peroxisomes and lysosomes in contrast to a decrease of mitochondria. At 5 and 100 μg.l^{-1} only, disulfoton was found to induce annulate lamellae, i.e. an extensive accumulation of nuclear pore-like structures within cisternae of the ER.

At concentrations ≥20 μg.l^{-1}, the hepatocellular glycogen contents were drastically depleted. At the highest concentration, Golgi fields were no longer discernible. Most conspicuously, during regeneration, hepatocytes extruded large membrane whorls resembling myelinated bodies into the intercellular space.

Particularly affected were fish exposed for two weeks to 5 μg.l^{-1} disulfoton where severe fenestration and a decrease in the amount of RER was observed. The parallel arrangement of RER lamellae, however, was mostly maintained. Conversely, there was an intensive transitory proliferation of small vesicular profiles of SER, which became the dominant element of the hepatocyte. When compared to the controls, the association of mitochondria and lipid droplets appeared to be less pronounced, and the number of mitochondria was also reduced. Most of these effects were reversed after 4 weeks.

After a recovery period of 2 weeks, most hepatocellular parameters had not returned to control values (Table 7.1). Only the glycogen stores appeared to be increased, indicating the onset of hepatocellular recovery.

7.3.4   *Biochemical alterations in eel liver after disulfoton exposure*

Deviations in enzyme activities in eel liver after exposure to disulfoton were greatest in fish exposed to the acute toxic concentration of 100 μg.l^{-1}, and during a transient period after 2 weeks' exposure to 5 μg.l^{-1} disulfoton (Tables 7.2–7.4). For example, uricase activities per gram liver, and per milligram protein in the homogenate, were significantly reduced at 5 μg.l^{-1} after 2 weeks. Likewise, NADPH cytochrome P450 reductase only showed a reduction at 5 μg.l^{-1} after 2 weeks; this finding coincided with the considerable increase in the endoplasmic reticulum under the same exposure conditions.

In contrast, whereas lower concentrations of disulfoton ($\leqslant$20 μg.l^{-1}) slightly stimulated allantoinase activities, both in respect to specific activities in the homogenate and in the peroxisomal fraction, there was an almost complete suppression of allantoinase activity at 100 μg.l^{-1}. Esterase activities were consistently reduced by a factor of 4–10 by disulfoton exposure at all the concentrations tested. Both with 5 and 20 μg.l^{-1} disulfoton, there was a stimulation of the conjugating enzyme UDP glucuronyl transferase, whereas no difference from the controls was seen at 100 μg.l^{-1}. Of the other enzymes, UDP glucuronyl transferase induction was more pronounced after a four-week exposure to 5 μg.l^{-1} than after two weeks.

There was a tendency for a reduction of choline esterase activities in the homogenate (per mg protein) at 20 μg.l^{-1}; the difference was significant at 100 μg.l^{-1}. In the cytosolic fraction, however, no significant change in choline esterase was found.

7.3.5   *Ultrastructure of control rainbow trout hepatocytes*

It was already evident from light microscopy that the liver parenchyma of control trout had a highly regular appearance, with hepatocytes showing large, intensely stained peripheral glycogen fields which were clearly separated from a central

Table 7.2 Activities of some key enzymes in the liver of eel exposed to disulfoton.

	Controls (day 0)	Controls (2 weeks)	Controls (4 weeks)	5 μg.l^{-1} (2 weeks)	5 μg.l^{-1} (4 weeks)	20 μg.l^{-1} (2 weeks)	100 μg.l^{-1} (2 days)
Uricase (mU per g liver)	515.05 ±72.41	415.62 ±140.91	343.45 ±25.46	114.09 ±23.083**	385.91 ±159.79	253.39 ±87.22	680.28 ±350.30
Allantoinase (mU per g liver)	114.46 ±18.00	96.35 ±10.71	64.40 ±15.41	67.04 ±11.05**	55.27 ±29.65	122.07 ±56.38	1.16 ±1.36***
Esterase (mU per g liver)	371.58 ±96.92	232.89 ±87.78	156.15 ±42.00	53.94 ±18.74**	32.69 ±13.54**	38.61 ±11.93**	37.70 ±14.01***
NADPH Cytochrome P450 reductase (mU per g liver)	6.18 ±1.14	4.07 ±0.95	4.22 ±1.23	1.83 ±0.54**	4.52 ±1.55	3.48 ±3.37	4.57 ±1.85
UDP glucuronyltransferase (μU per g liver)	196.75 ±91.13	72.5 ±10.6	75.00 ±35.55	108.25 ±70.27	130.00 ±55.98	160.00 ±72.57	167.81 ±127.71
Choline esterase (μU per g liver)	27.25 ±7.45	18.60 ±10.15	17.72 ±6.01	16.39 ±2.24	18.68 ±9.76	18.32 ±12.72	9.99 ±3.05**

Means ±SE ($n = 4$). Differences from control data were calculated by Student's t-test: * $P<0.05$; ** $P<0.01$; *** $P<0.001$

Table 7.3 Specific activities of selected enzymes in eel liver homogenate per mg protein, with exposure to disulfoton.

	Controls (day 0)	Controls (2 weeks)	Controls (4 weeks)	5 µg.l^{-1} (2 weeks)	5 µg.l^{-1} (4 weeks)	20 µg.l^{-1} (2 weeks)	100 µg.l^{-1} (2 days)
Uricase (mU.mg^{-1})	379.35 ±27.79	447.33 ±54.38	350.07 ±12.84	179.10 ±32.49***	475.80 ±47.58**	212.40 ±24.78***	522.18 ±60.92**
Allantoinase (mU.mg^{-1})	77.15 ±20.15	79.54 ±23.86	81.93 ±18.39	73.14 ±18.29	71.60 ±25.06	109.40 ±21.79	1.01 ±0.91***
Esterase (mU.mg^{-1})	85.45 ±22.51	77.35 ±30.94	74.35 ±18.59	18.84 ±4.71**	15.83 ±6.33***	10.33 ±7.23**	9.85 ±2.46***
NADPH Cytochrome P450 reductase (mU.mg^{-1})	4.11 ±0.55	2.75 ±0.04	6.03 ±0.50	2.33 ±0.23*	2.13 ±0.64***	5.80 ±0.80***	3.81 ±0.10
UDP glucuronyl transferase (µU.mg^{-1})	150.38 ±60.15	75.66 ±22.70	102.12 ±10.21	82.43 ±57.71	170.36 ±39.18*	107.59 ±39.81	60.29 ±18.09*
Choline esterase (µU.mg^{-1})	20.30 ±6.09	18.31 ±6.41	25.36 ±7.61	17.37 ±1.39	25.12 ±6.53	13.82 ±6.91	7.92 ±0.65**

Means ±SE ($n = 4$). Differences from control data were calculated by Student's t-test: * $P < 0.05$; ** $P < 0.01$; *** $P < 0.001$

Table 7.4 Specific activities of individual enzymes in specific fractions from the liver of eel exposed to disulfoton.

	Controls (day 0)	Controls (2 weeks)	Controls (4 weeks)	5 µg.l⁻¹ (2 weeks)	5 µg.l⁻¹ (4 weeks)	20 µg.l⁻¹ (2 weeks)
Uricase (mU per mg protein)	549.38 ±219.75	439.75 ±87.95	495.50 ±188.29	465.50 ±209.48	816.60 ±122.49*	517.91 ±139.84
Allantoinase (mU per mg protein)	86.25 ±35.36	112.90 ±57.58	92.27 ±30.45	52.71 ±16.87	123.58 ±42.45	41.81 ±29.26
Esterase (mU per mg protein)	405.00 ±170.10	235.76 ±10.61	255.30 ±125.09	48.15 ±21.32***	59.83 ±20.94*	24.24 ±10.91***
NADPH Cytochrome P450 reductase (mU per mg protein)	6.76 ±1.24	4.25 ±1.23	8.12 ±2.44	7.98 ±4.58	8.57 ±4.28	6.07 ±2.43
UDP glucuronyltransferase (µU per mg protein)	500.00 ±155.00	292.91 ±90.80	497.67 ±99.53	611.83 ±183.55*	1350.23 ±337.55**	371.68 ±144.95
Choline esterase (µU per mg protein)	23.78 ±1.90	30.84 ±9.25	25.63 ±7.69	24.98 ±9.99	26.07 ±12.64	36.19 ±10.13

Means ±SE ($n = 4$). Differences from control data were calculated by Student's t-test: * $P<0.05$; ** $P<0.01$; *** $P<0.001$

Table 7.5 Semiquantitative evaluation of disulfoton-induced alterations in trout hepatocytes. Data are given as mean estimates from four fish per treatment.

	Control	20 µg.l^{-1}	5 µg.l^{-1}	1 µg.l^{-1}	0.1 µg.l^{-1}
SER	+	+	++	++	++
RER	+++	+++	+++	++	++
Mitochondria	++	++	+++	+++	+++
Peroxisomes	++	++	+++	+++	+++
Lysosomes	+	+++	++	++	++
Myelinated bodies	+	±	+	±	++

Abbreviations: – absent; ± rare; + occasionally; ++ regularly present; +++ frequent; ++++ very frequent

perinuclear zone of organelle-containing cytoplasm. Lipid inclusions were rare in these control fish. At the ultrastructural level, the exceptionally standardised arrangement of the cellular components in these hepatocytes became even more evident. Extensive stacks of up to 30 highly ordered, non-fenestrated RER lamellae formed an almost continuous sheath around the centrally located, slightly irregular nucleus. Occasionally, a single layer of spherical to ovoid mitochondria appeared between the nucleus and the ER. In contrast, the typical development of SER as an irregular network of undulating and anastomosing tubular or vesicular profiles was restricted to minute areas adjacent to glycogen and Golgi fields.

The RER piles were regularly bordered by large amounts of spherical peroxisomes. We consistently failed to find a peroxisomal core. The uniform array of peroxisomes could be interspersed with small spherical to elongated mitochondrial profiles. Between the nucleus and the bile canaliculus, the RER sheath was interrupted by extensively developed Golgi fields consisting of several piles of 3–5 cisternae displaying a conspicuous polarity and budding off numerous vesicles and vacuoles of variable size containing numerous VLDL granules. The peribiliary area contained abundant lysosomes. The periphery of rainbow trout hepatocytes was occupied by extensive storage fields, mainly glycogen; lipid inclusions were rare. Glycogen fields were normally free of organelles.

7.3.6   *Hepatic ultrastructure of disulfoton treated rainbow trout*

The major cytopathological changes found in rainbow trout liver following exposure to disulfoton are listed in Table 7.5.

As with changes found in eels, most evident cytological effects were observed with exposure to 5 µg.l^{-1} disulfoton. There was an increase in the amount of SER at lower and intermediate disulfoton concentrations in contrast to a concentration-dependent RER decline. In both species, peroxisomes showed a slight increase over control values, whereas myelinated bodies in rainbow trout mainly appeared in the lowest concentration tested. Mitochondria in hepatocytes of exposed eels seemed to be slightly decreased, whereas rainbow trout hepatocytes showed a small augmentation.

7.4   Discussion

Organophosphates are widely used as pesticides; they are absorbed by skin and mucous membranes. In mammals, they are known to act primarily as choline esterase inhibitors. Disulfoton also causes significant reductions in choline esterase activity and a decrease in the number of muscarine receptors in various organs (Costa *et al.*, 1984, 1990). Moreover, several liver enzyme activities are modified (Costa and Murphy, 1983).

The results presented here clearly demonstrate the extreme sensitivity of eels to disulfoton. Although the eel is generally considered to be a relatively insensitive fish species (Amiard-Triquet *et al.*, 1987; Ferrando *et al.*, 1987), LC_{50} data for eel are three orders of magnitude lower for disulfoton than those for rainbow trout (Holcombe *et al.*, 1982; Mayer and Ellersieck, 1986). Also, at sublethal toxicant levels the effects on eels were more pronounced than those with rainbow trout, although both species showed conspicuous cytological effects with exposure to $5 \ \mu g.l^{-1}$ disulfoton.

In both eel and rainbow trout the hepatocellular reactions to sublethal disulfoton exposure appear to follow a biphasic pattern; responses to concentrations $\leqslant 5$ $\mu g.l^{-1}$ are mostly qualitatively and/or quantitatively different from changes observed at higher concentrations. This transition from adaptive/regenerative phenomena to degenerative reactions was also found in eels exposed to dinitro-*o*-cresol, which generally stimulated hepatic metabolism at exposure concentrations of up to $50 \ \mu g.l^{-1}$, whereas $250 \ \mu g.l^{-1}$ induced a suppression of most enzyme activities and a transition from adaptive changes in liver structure and function to degenerative symptoms (Braunbeck and Völkl, 1991). In contrast, dinitro-*o*-cresol failed to generate such a biphasic reaction in golden ide (Braunbeck and Völkl, 1993).

Apart from a report by Takase and Oyama (1985), who examined the uptake and metabolism of disulfoton in carp *(Cyprinus carpio)*, no data are available on the fate of this pesticide in fish. Takase and Oyama (1985) reported a degradation of disulfoton to sulfoxides, basically similar to that found in mammals (Yashiki *et al.*, 1990). From a biochemical point of view, the primary target of disulfoton toxicity is choline esterase (Costa *et al.*, 1984, 1990). However, other modes of toxic action associated with receptor effects have been postulated for mammals (Schwab *et al.*, 1983). This view is supported by our findings in eel liver; inhibition of choline esterase could only be found at acute toxic concentrations and no significant change was evident at $\leqslant 20 \ \mu g.l^{-1}$. Thus, all effects found at $\leqslant 20 \ \mu g.l^{-1}$ must be attributable to other toxic mechanisms of disulfoton.

While most hepatic microsomal enzymes in mice were found to be unaffected by disulfoton, Costa and Murphy (1983) reported a suppression of carboxyl esterase activities in the brain and liver. The significant reduction in esterase activities measured in eel liver probably parallels this observation. It is likely that the spasmic muscle contractions of eels following acute disulfoton exposure can be accounted for by a modulation of muscarinic receptor binding.

As a further parallel to biochemical findings in mammals, the mixed function oxygenase-associated enzyme NADPH cytochrome P450 reductase failed to be induced by disulfoton exposure, whereas there was an increase in the phase II enzyme UDP glucuronyl transferase. This is in accord with the findings of Hodgson (1982), as well as of Hajjar and Hodgson (1982) in pig liver microsomes, who reported disulfoton oxidation to the corresponding sulfoxide by FAD-dependent monooxygenases, but not by NADPH-dependent oxygenases.

As for the contribution of disulfoton to the fatal effects of the chemical spill at Basle in November 1986, the data presented here indicate that *disulfoton alone* can be held responsible for the reduction of at least the eel population. According to the Deutsche Kommission zur Reinhaltung des Rheins (1986), disulfoton was measured at concentrations of 5.3–600 $\mu g.l^{-1}$ in River Rhine water after the chemical spill. The 96hLC$_{50}$ of disulfoton to eel is only 37 $\mu g.l^{-1}$, and in our experiment, 100% mortality occurred in acute exposure to 83 $\mu g.l^{-1}$. In another experiment with rainbow trout simultaneously exposed to endosulfan and disulfoton (not reported here), the acutely toxic concentrations were also considerably reduced with a combination of the two pesticides, when compared to LC$_{50}$s for the single compounds. Thus, although synergistic effects may have played an important role in the fatal consequences of the chemical spill, disulfoton is likely to have been a major causative agent for the fish kill.

References

Amiard-Triquet, C., J.C. Amiard, A.C. Andersen, P. Elie and C. Metayer, 1987. The eel (*Anguilla anguilla* L.) as a bioindicator of metal pollution: factors limiting its use. *Water Sci.Techn.*, **19**: 1229–1232.

Beaufay, H., A. Amar-Costesec, E. Feytmans, D. Thinès-Sempoux, M. Wibo, M. Robbi and J. Berthet, 1974. Analytical study of microsomes and isolated subcellular membranes from rat liver. I. Biochemical methods. *J.Cell Biol.*, **61**: 188–200.

Bradford, M.M., 1976. A rapid and sensitive method for the quantitation of microgram quantities of protein utilizing the principle of protein-dye binding. *Anal.Biochem.*, **72**: 248–254.

Braunbeck, T. and A. Völkl, 1991. Induction of biotransformation in the liver of eel (*Anguilla anguilla* L.) by sublethal exposure to dinitro-*o*-cresol: an ultrastructural and biochemical study. *Ecotox.Environ.Safety*, **21**: 109–127.

Braunbeck, T. and A. Völkl, 1993. Cytological alterations in the livers of golden ide (*Leuciscus idus melanotus*) and eel (*Anguilla anguilla*) induced by sublethal doses of dinitro-*o*-cresol. In: Braunbeck, T., W. Hanke and H. Segner (Eds.) *Fish in Ecotoxicology and Ecophysiology*, pp. 55–80. Weinheim, VCH.

Braunbeck, T., P. Burkhardt-Holm and V. Storch, 1990. Liver pathology in eels (*Anguilla anguilla* L.) from the Rhine river exposed to the chemical spill at Basle in November 1986. *Limnologie aktuell*, **1**: 371–392.

Castren, M. and A. Oikari, 1983. Optimal assay conditions for liver UDP glucuronyltransferase from the rainbow trout, *Salmo gairdneri. Comp.Biochem.Physiol.*, **76**: 365–369.

Costa, L.G. and S.D. Murphy, 1983. Unidirectional cross-tolerance between the carbamate insecticide propoxur and the organophosphate disulfoton in mice. *Fund.Appl.Toxicol.*, **3**: 483–488.

Costa, L.G., M. Shao, K. Basker and S.D. Murphy, 1984. Chronic administration of an organophosphorus insecticide to rats alters cholinergic muscarinic receptors in the pancreas. *Chem.Biol.Interact.*, **48**: 261–269.

Costa, L.G., G. Kaylor and S.D. Murphy, 1990. *In vitro* and *in vivo* modulation of cholinergic muscarinic receptors in rat lymphocytes and brain by cholinergic agents. *Int.J.Immunopharmacol.*, **12**: 67–75.

Deutsche Kommission zur Reinhaltung des Rheins, 1986. Deutscher Bericht zum Sandoz-Unfall mit Meßprogramm. 69 p.

Ellman, G.L., K.D. Courtney, V. Andres and R.M. Featherstone, 1961. A new and rapid colorimetric determination of acetylcholinesterase activity. *Biochem.Pharmacol.*, **7**: 88–95.

Ferrando, M.D., E. Andreu-Moliner, M.M. Almar, C. Cebrian and A. Nunez, 1987. Acute toxicity of organochlorinated pesticides to the European eel *(Anguilla anguilla)*. The dependency on exposure time and temperature. *Bull.Environ.Contam.Toxicol.*, **39**: 365–369.

Hajjar, N.P. and E. Hodgson, 1982. Sulfoxidation of thioether-containing pesticides by the flavin-adenine dinucleotide-dependent monooxygenase of pig liver microsomes. *Biochem.Pharmacol.*, **31**: 745–752.

Hodgson, E., 1982. Production of pesticide metabolites by oxidative reactions. *J.Toxicol.Clin.Toxicol.*, **19**: 609–621.

Holcombe, G.W., G.L. Phipps and D.K. Tanner, 1982. The acute toxicity of kelthane, dursban, disulfoton, pydrin and permethrin to fathead minnows *Pimephales promelas* and rainbow trout *Salmo gairdneri. Environ.Poll.*, **29**: 167–178.

Le Hir, M., V. Herzog and H.D. Fahimi, 1979. Cytochemical detection of catalase with 3,3'-diaminobenzidine. A quantitative reinvestigation of the optimal assay conditions. *Histochem.*, **64**: 51–66.

Mayer, F.L. and M.R. Ellersieck, 1986. Manual of acute toxicity: interpretation and database for 410 chemicals and 66 species of freshwater animals. *US Dept.Int.Fish and Wildl.Serv.Res.Publ.*, 160.

Priest, D.G. and O.M. Pitts, 1972. Reaction intermediate effects on the spectrophotometric uricase assay. *Anal.Biochem.*, **50**: 195–205.

Schwab, B.W., L.G. Costa and S.D. Murphy, 1983. Muscarinic receptor alterations as a mechanism of anticholinesterase tolerance. *Toxicol.Appl.Pharmacol.*, **71**: 14–23.

Sottocasa, G.L., B. Kuylenstierna, L. Ernster and A. Bergstrand, 1967. An electron transport system associated with the outer membrane of liver mitochondria. A biochemical and morphological study. *J.Cell Biol.*, **32**: 415–438.

Takase, I. and H. Oyama, 1985. Uptake and bioconcentration of disulfoton and its oxidation compounds in carp, *Cyprinus carpio* L. *J.Pestic.Sci.*, **10**: 47–54.

Yashiki, M., T. Kojima, M. Ohtani, F. Chikasue and T. Miyazaki, 1990. Determination of disulfoton and its metabolites in the body fluids of a Di-Syston intoxication case. *Forensic Sci.Int.*, **48**: 145–154.

Chapter 8
The long-term effect of PCBs on fish

Z. SVOBODOVÁ,[1] B. VYKUSOVÁ,[1] J. MÁCHOVÁ,[1] M. HRBKOVÁ[2] and L. GROCH[3]

[1] Research Institute of Fish Culture and Hydrobiology, 389 25 Vodňany, Czech Republic
[2] Hygienic Station, Schneidera 32, 370 71 České Budějovice, Czech Republic
[3] Veterinary University, Palackého 1–3, 612 42 Brno, Czech Republic

8.1   Introduction

In recent years, polychlorinated biphenyls (PCBs) have become one of the most important pollutants in the living environment. PCBs are among the most stable of organic compounds; they are also highly to extremely toxic to fish, particularly to their early developmental stages (Mattheis *et al.*, 1984). The problems of PCBs in fisheries are important both in the rearing of fish and particularly in the hygienic requirements for edible fish flesh. Values for PCB residues in fish from flowing waters and reservoirs have been reported by many authors (e.g. Hattula, 1972; Krasnicki *et al.*, 1977; Peneva, 1980; Falkner and Simonis, 1982; Stechert and Jantz, 1983; Schüler *et al.*, 1985; Braun *et al.*, 1987; Kredl *et al.*, 1989; and Braun *et al.*, 1990). The results are usually compared to the hygienic standard set in the USA which corresponds to 2 mg PCB per l kg of fish muscle (Schüler *et al.*, 1985; Brunn, 1982). In the Czech Republic, the maximum admissible concentration in commercial fish has been set at 0.5 mg of PCB per 1 kg of edible fish tissue.

As part of the monitoring programme of Czech and Slovakian surface waters (including reservoirs and ponds), PCB residues in fish and other components of the aquatic ecosystem were determined. A search was made for components or organisms within the aquatic environment which could be used as indicators of water body contamination. Fish, particularly those with a high fat content, were found to be the most important indicators of aquatic environment contamination by PCBs (Svobodová *et al.*, 1989a, b).

This investigation can be separated into two parts: the investigation of PCB residues and their effects on fish in a polluted river, and laboratory experiments on the effects of PCBs on carp.

8.2   Histopathological changes and PCB residues in fish from a contaminated river

Fish were used to evaluate the level of contamination in the River Skalice which was polluted by PCBs in 1986. This river received a discharge of PCBs with a low

Fig. 8.1 Localities of fish sampling in the Skalice River.

chlorine content (Delor 103) from a chemical industry (for the processing and chemical treatment of gravel for road construction) in the town Rožmitál.

8.2.1 *Material and methods*

In 1989, fish were caught in the Skalice River (Fig. 8.1) by electric fishing at the following nine sites: upstream of the chemical industry at Rožmitál; downstream sites at Skuhrov; Zadní Poříčí; Březnice; Myslín; Mirovice; Nerestce; Čimelice; and Ostrovce (about 3 km before the river enters the Orlík Dam Lake); a map of the river and the sampling sites is given in Figure 8.1. The length of the Skalice River from Rožmitál to the Orlík Dam Lake is 53 km. Six to seven species of fish, mostly roach, tench, carp, bream, chub, eel, and pike, were caught at the individual sites. Five to ten specimens of the individual species were sampled and analysed. Using Delor 103 and 106 as the standards, PCB residues were determined in fish muscle, liver and gonads. Separation of PCB residues from the samples and the purification of extracts were carried out by the method of Hruška and Kociánová (1978) with additional techniques for PCB residues described by Kredl and Breyl (1984). A gas-chromatograph (Hewlett-Packard 5730A) with integrator HP 3390A with an electron-capture detector was used for the determination of PCB residues.

The values given for PCB residues in this paper represent the sum of compounds with both low and high chlorine content (Delor 103 and Delor 106). The livers of the fish caught were examined histologically. After fixation in a neutral 10%

formaldehyde, samples were processed by the standard method using paraffin sections stained with haematoxylin and eosin.

8.2.2   *Results and discussion*

Residues with a high chlorine content (i.e. similar to Delor 106) were dominant in the muscle of fish caught in the Skalice River at Rožmitál (above the chemical industry; Table 8.1). PCBs with a low chlorine content (i.e. similar to Delor 103) were present only in trace amounts. Except for eel, the levels found in fish were within the hygienic standard of 0.5 mg.kg^{-1} of edible tissue. On the other hand, at all the sites on the Skalice River below the chemical industry down to the site at Ostrovce, the hygienic standard was exceeded. At these sites, PCB residues with a low chlorine content dominated those with a high chlorine content. The highest levels of PCB residues were found in fish from the site at Skuhrov, just below the site of discharge; an extremely high value was found in eel (258.9 mg.kg^{-1} of muscle). At the sites further downstream, progressively lower residue levels were found. Despite this gradual decrease, the level of PCB in edible fish tissues exceeded the standard of 0.5 mg.kg^{-1} fresh weight. At the last sample site a concentration of 19.1 mg.kg^{-1} of PCB was found in the muscle of eel.

Within the individual fish species from the Skalice River sites, the highest level of PCB residues was found in the muscle of eel (where the fat content was 20–30%) and the lowest level in those fishes with a low muscle fat content (under 1%), for example in pike and perch. The values for PCB residues found in the liver and gonads of fishes (except eel and brown trout) greatly exceeded those in the muscle. In eel, the PCB residues in the liver (3–4% of fat) were found to be 4–7 times lower than those in the muscle (10–30% of fat). The most pronounced difference between PCB residue levels in muscle and liver were found in the pike. In this species, the PCB content in the liver (11–16% of fat) was found to be 50–100 times higher than that in muscle (0.5–0.8% of fat).

These results show that the ban on the consumption of fish from the River Skalice below the chemical industry in Rožmitál was fully justified.

Histopathological examination of liver samples from various fish species showed that damage to the liver parenchyma occurred to different degrees depending on the sampling site. It was found that the most significant harmful changes occurred in the liver of fishes from those sites immediately below the chemical industry, particularly from those at Skuhrov and Poříčí. Less significant histopathological changes were found in fish from the lowest downstream sites at Čimelice and Ostrovce. The most sensitive species to the chemical pollution appeared to be carp, followed by roach, tench and bream.

As an example of the extent of tissue damage, the histopathological picture of liver in carp from the Skuhrov and Ostrovce sites can be used. In the liver of carp from the Skuhrov site (PCB residues: 5.97 mg.kg^{-1}), distinct changes in the walls of the vessels and the bile duct were found, including hyperplasia, fibrinoid dystrophy and necrosis. The walls of the large vessels contained numerous invasive macrophages. Hyperplasia of the vessel endothelia, perivascular infiltration of lymphoid elements, hyperplasia of the walls of small blood capillaries in the liver parenchyma, and dystrophic changes of hepatocytes, were found. In the liver of carp caught in the Ostrovce-Avia locality (PCB residues: 2.17 mg.kg^{-1}), a mild perivascular cell infiltration and numerous macrophages around the vessels were found.

Liver haemorrhage was found in eels caught at the most contaminated sites of the Skalice River. Histopathological changes such as mild dystrophic changes in hepatocytes, individual perivascular cell infiltration and isolated bleeding in the liver parenchyma were found in pike associated with the high level of PCB residues in the liver.

Liver damage caused by contamination with PCBs, particularly those with low chlorine content (e.g. Delor 103), was generally shown as changes in the vessels and bile duct where hyperplasia of their walls and different levels of fibrinoid dystrophy were found to a varying extent. Melanomacrophages were clustered around the damaged vessels and acted as processors of the material thereby created. An inflammatory reaction in cells surrounding the vessels was another response of the organism to vessel wall damage. Different levels of dystrophic change were found in hepatocytes. The damage to the vessels leads to bleeding in the liver parenchyma. The macrophage activity in liver parenchyma is a defensive mechanism in fish. These histopathological changes found in the liver of fish from sites contaminated by Delor 103 are similar to those found in the liver of chickens receiving chronic low doses of Delor 103 (Halouzka *et al.*, 1990).

8.2.3   *Conclusions*

The measurement of xenobiotic residues in indicator organisms (in the case of PCB, mainly in fish) forms a basis for monitoring their occurrence as contaminants in surface waters. The information presented here has shown the important role which can be played by monitoring the state of health of fish, and in particular the histopathological changes occurring in their livers. Therefore, when designing a programme to monitor the contamination of surface waters by such substances, an examination of the state of fish health (particularly the histopathological changes occurring in parenchymal and other tissues) should be included as well as the monitoring for residue levels. However, these changes will probably not be specific to individual types of contamination. Nevertheless, they can provide strong evidence of the harmful degree of contamination, caused either by individual substances, or more usually by a complex of pollutants, the combined effects of which are impossible to predict precisely from a chemical analysis alone because of the possible additive and/or antagonistic interactions. In order to provide firm concentration–response relationships, definitive laboratory experiments have to be

Table 8.1 The content of PCB in muscle of fish caught in the Skalice River (sites Rožmitál-Březnice).

Locality and date	Species	n	Age (years) mean / range	Fish weight (g) mean ± SD / range	Fat cont. %	PCBs (mg.kg⁻¹) in fat of muscle 103	106	Σ103+106	in muscle (fresh wt.) 103	106	Σ103+106
Rožmitál (200 m upstream) 17 July 1989	Roach	10	7.7 / 6–10	198 ±10.8 / 145–215	2.00	+	15.5	15.5	+	0.31	0.31
	Tench	8	/ 5–8	457 ±48.7 / 300–700	1.06	+	8.51	8.51	+	0.09	0.09
	Eel	4	/ 5–10	360 ±26.8 / 300–430	30.40	+	4.21	4.21	+	1.28	1.28
	Pike	2	2	568 ±22.5 / 545–590	0.70	+	32.4	32.4	+	0.23	0.23
	Pike-Perch	1	4	1150	1.00	+	29.3	29.3	+	0.29	0.29
	Carp	5	3.7 / 2–4	1463 ±210.3 / 715–1950	1.04	+	9.62	9.62	+	0.10	0.10
Skuhrov (downstream) 17 July 1989	Carp	1	7	6050	1.07	+	6.57	6.57	+	0.07	0.07
	Roach	4	6.75 / 6–8	256 ±31.6 / 205–304	2.00	956	71.4	1027.4	19.12	1.43	20.55
	Tench	8	/ 6–13	735 ±80.9 / 490–1100	1.00	1560	65.9	1625.9	15.6	0.66	16.26
	Pike	1	2	600	0.70	1087	86.7	1173.7	7.6	0.61	8.21
	Eel	5	–	281 ±15.0 / 235–320	30.31	802	52.3	854.3	243	15.85	258.9
	Carp	6	2.7 / 2–4	1430 ±313.2 / 510–2500	1.00	182	17.0	199	1.82	0.17	1.99
	Bream	2	8	1075 ±25.0 / 1050–1100	2.00	3595	158.4	3753.4	71.9	3.17	75.1
	Rudd	3	4.3 / 4–5	187 ±22.4 / 155–230	0.50	150	13.9	163.9	0.75	0.07	0.82

Table 8.1 Continued.

Locality and date	Species	n	Age (years) mean range	Fish weight (g) mean ± SD range	Fat cont. %	PCBs (mg.kg⁻¹) in fat of muscle			in muscle (fresh wt.)		
						103	106	Σ103+106	103	106	Σ103+106
Zadní Poříčí 18 July 1989	Roach	10	4.3 2–8	120 ±18.3 55–235	2.00	291	38	329	5.28	0.76	6.58
	Eel	1	–	500	30.30	325	30.4	355.4	98.5	9.21	107.7
	Pike	4	2.5 2–4	788 ±311.2 300–1700	0.68	1424	123	1547	9.96	0.86	10.32
	Carp	2	4	2425 ±75.0 2350–2500	1.00	216	14.8	230.8	2.16	0.15	2.31
	Perch	6	2.2 2–3	28 ±8.9 65–130	1.00	218	16.0	234	2.18	0.16	2.34
Březnice (swimming pool) 18 July 1989	Roach	10	7.2 5–12	319 ±23.1 200–470	2.00	427	31.7	458.7	8.54	0.63	9.17
	Tench	3	5–8	500 ±115.5 300–700	1.00	298	18.0	316	2.98	0.18	3.16
	Pike	4	2.25 2–3	938 ±137.5 700–1300	0.70	579	80.4	659.4	4.05	0.56	4.61
	Carp	10	3.1 3–4	1610 ±93.9 1250–2300	1.00	266	15.8	281.8	2.66	0.16	2.82
	Bream	2	8	975 ±25.0 950–1000	2.00	466	65.9	531.9	9.32	1.32	10.64
	Chub	4	8 5–10	554 ±76.8 330–680	1.00	480	51.8	531.8	4.80	0.52	5.32

+ traces

carried out. The results of such an experiment with carp and PCBs are given in Section 8.3.

8.3   The effect of long-term PCB exposure on condition, haematological and histopathological parameters of carp

An experiment was performed to obtain similar levels of PCB residues in experimental fish as were found at polluted field sites, and thus enabling a more precise assessment of changes in the values occurring in some of these parameters.

8.3.1   *Material and methods*

Carp in their second year were used to study the effects of long-term PCB treatment. The experiment was carried out in the laboratory; water temperature was in the range 17–20°C in May and June 1991. Twenty-seven and 28 carp were stocked in the control and experimental aquaria, respectively. Fish were acclimated to the laboratory conditions for 14 days and fed *ad libitum* with live zooplankton. Both during the acclimation period and in the experiment, all fish were transferred daily after feeding into fresh solutions at the same temperature. Prior to starting the experiment, i.e. before the beginning of PCB treatment, the fish were weighed; the average weight of carp in the control and experimental group was 74.9 ±5.3 g and 67.9 ±4.3 g, respectively. PCB was given intraperitoneally, using Delor 103 (manufacturer: Chemko Strážske) with a chlorine content of 42%. Fish in the control group were injected with sunflower oil at the same dosage. The treatment was carried out once a week, with a dose of 0.1–0.2 ml of Delor 103 and/or sunflower oil depending on the weight of fish; six doses were given during the 42 days of the experiment. No mortalities of fish occurred as a result of the normal Delor 103 and/or sunflower oil treatment during the course of the experiment. However, five control and four experimental carp died immediately after treatment with Delor 103 and/or sunflower oil as a result of a poor intraperitoneal injection technique.

The examination of the fish condition, blood sampling for haematological examination, sampling and fixing of tissue samples for histological and pathological examination, and muscle sampling for determination of PCB residues, were carried out at the end of the test. The haematological examination followed the 'Unified methods of haematological examination of fish' (Svobodová *et al.*, 1986); the liver, spleen and kidney of the experimental fish were examined histologically, and PCB residues were determined by the gas-chromatography method, as is described in Section 8.2.

8.3.2   *Results and discussion*

The results of the examination of the condition and haematological parameters of fish after the long-term exposure to Delor 103 are presented in Table 8.2. As these data show, experimental fish had a lower weight gain, a significantly decreased value of Fulton's coefficient of condition [weight (g) × 100/body length^3 (cm)] and a lower weight of hepatopancreatic tissue compared with control group. The relative weight of the hepatopancreas in the experimental fish was also lower. The haematocrit value and particularly the number of leucocytes was significantly lower in the experimental group. A decrease in the non-specific immunity in fish due to a considerably lower number of leucocytes (expressed in absolute numbers) and a significant decrease in the values for small lymphocytes, was very characteristic. Small lymphocytes are active in globuline production and transport, some of them acting as antibodies. Thus, a considerable decrease in the value for small lymphocytes in fish is followed by a decrease in potential antibody production, i.e. a decrease in fish disease resistance. These effects may indicate that PCBs have an immunosuppressive effect. It might be expected that the same changes would occur in fish from a contaminated natural environment as the Skalice River. However, in field conditions, these changes cannot be so precisely assessed as in the laboratory experiment because of the great natural variability of haematological values and biochemical parameters (Hlavová, 1993).

Considerable histopathological changes were found in the parenchymal organs of these fish. The changes found in the hepatopancreas were confined to the vascular system where proliferative hyperplastic processes occur. Endothelial swelling, expansion of adventitious tissue and its cell infiltration is seen in the blood vessels. Progressive homogenisation of the walls of larger vessels occurs as a consequence of fibrinoid dystrophy or necrosis. Similar changes are found in the wall of the bile duct. Cell infiltration (mostly in a spherical nucleus form) can be found in the portobiliar space. Dystrophic changes of differing intensity and extent are found in the hepatocytes of most of the fish examined. Similar histopathological changes to those found in the liver vessels occurred also in the spleen vessels; i.e. endothelial swelling, fibrinoid dystrophy of the wall and proliferation of adventitious cells. Dystrophic changes were seen in the epithelium of the distal parts of the kidney tubules, such as vacuolisation and epithelium detachment from the basal membrane. Necrotic changes in the tubule epithelium occurred in individual cases.

The values of PCB residues in muscle and in fat of muscle (both in mg.kg^{-1}) are given in Table 8.3. Values similar to those found at sites on the Skalice River for 12 km below the source of pollution downstream towards the town of Březnice (Table 8.1) were found in the experimental fish. In fish from this locality, a considerable immunosuppressive effect of PCB can be expected irrespective of the histological and pathological changes shown to occur. Considerable immuno-suppressive effects have been found in mammals (Safe *et al.*, 1987) and birds (Piskač *et al.*, 1990) after PCB administration. However, similar changes in the white blood cell picture found in fish after PCB treatment have been found as a response to other pollutants, e.g. malachite green (Grizzle, 1977), phenols (Wlasow, 1985), triazines and diazines (Svobodová and Pečená, 1987), and/or different

Table 8.2 The effect of long-term treatment with PCB (Delor 103) on the condition and haematological parameters in carp (n = number of fish). For experimental procedure see text.

Parameters	Units	Control			Experiment		
		n	mean ±SD	range	n	mean ±SD	range
Start fish weight	g	27	74.9 ±5.31	40–130	28	67.9 ±4.28	45–130
Final fish weight	g	23	77.4 ±5.74	44.6–134	23	63.4 ±4.33	43.5–129.8
Body length	cm	23	14.0 ±0.35	11.5–16.7	23	13.4 ±0.26	11.5–16.5
Fulton's coefficient		23	2.72 ±0.035	2.4–3.1	23	2.59 ±0.054	1.98–3.3*
Weight of liver	g	22	3.38 ±0.268	1.9–6.2	23	2.65 ±0.230	1.5–6.4*
Rel. weight of liver	%	22	4.34 ±0.158	3.1–6.2	23	4.13 ±0.130	2.8–5.5
Haematocrit (PCV)	l.l^{-1}	23	33.72 ±0.769	24.5–39.5	22	29.89 ±0.824	23–38*
Haemoglobin (Hb)	g.l^{-1}	23	76.80 ±1.624	65–92	23	75.22 ±2.700	44–102.5
MCHC	l.l^{-1}	23	0.30 ±0.072	0.2–1.9	22	0.26 ±0.011	0.13–0.38
Total protein (TP)	g.l^{-1}	10	3.12 ±0.033	3.0–3.2	10	3.04 ±0.04	3–3.4
Leucocrit (BC)	l.l^{-1}	23	0.78 ±0.063	0.3–1.5	18	0.63 ±0.026	0.4–0.9
Leucocytes	G.l^{-1}	20	34.03 ±3.632	14–69	22	12.88 ±1.188	0.4–21.5*
Small lymphocytes	%	20	92.52 ±0.691	86.2–96.7	22	92.79 ±1.110	83.8–100
	G.l^{-1}	20	31.5 ±3.379	12.7–65.9	22	12.09 ±0.34	0.3–89.9*
Large lymphocytes	%	20	0.41 ±0.112	0–2	22	1.29 ±0.276	0–5.3
	G.l^{-1}	20	0.13 ±0.035	0–0.5	22	0.10 ±0.042	0–0.9
Neutrophilic granulocytes with rod-like nucleus	%	20	4.60 ±0.556	1–11.2	22	3.71 ±0.781	0–12.4
	G.l^{-1}	20	1.62 ±0.321	0.3–5.8	22	0.36 ±0.070	0–1.2*
Neutrophilic granulocytes with segmented nucleus	%	20	0.96 ±0.197	0–0.3	22	0.74 ±0.261	0–4.8
	G.$^{-1}$	20	0.26 ±0.051	0–0.7	22	0.09 ±0.031	0–5
Monocytes	%	20	1.52 ±0.272	0–5	22	2.00 ±0.524	0–8.5
	G.l^{-1}	20	0.52 ±0.123	0–2.5	22	0.24 ±0.062	0–1.2

* $P < 0.05$

Table 8.3 PCB residues (mean values) in carp muscle after long-term application of Delor 103
(n = number of fish). For experimental procedure see text.

Group	Expressed in	PCB residues (mg.kg^{-1})					
		n	D 103	n	D 106	n	Total
Control	Muscle (fresh wt)	27	<0.004	27	0.017	27	0.017
	Fat of muscle	27	<0.004	27	1.209	27	1.029
Experiment	Muscle (fresh wt)	28	9.325	28	0.918	28	10.243
	Fat of muscle	28	782.42	28	76.993	28	859.41

stress factors (Peters, 1986). Therefore, such changes are not specific to PCBs, but they can confirm the harmfulness of measured tissue concentrations.

8.3.3   Conclusions

Carp were treated with polychlorinated biphenyls (Delor 103) by intraperitoneal injection during a 42-day experiment. The values of PCB residues produced in experimental fish were similar to those found in fish from the polluted Skalice River. Lower weight gain, a significant deterioration of condition parameters and significant changes in the white blood cell picture were found in the experimental fish. Considerable histopathological changes were found in the parenchymal organs (e.g. liver, spleen and kidney) of these fish.

References

Braun, F. *et al.*, 1987. Organische Schadstoffe. Polychlorbiphenyle (PCB) und Pesticide im Kreislauf des Wassers: Bilanzierung und Bewertung. Munich, Bayer. Landesanst. Wasserforsch., Bericht. 79 pp.

Braun, F. *et al.*, 1990. Neue Untersuchungen zur Analytik und Verbreitung von Polychlorbiphenylen (PCB) und Pflanzenbehandlungsmitteln. Munich, Bayer. Landesanst. Wasserforsch., Bericht. 103 pp.

Brunn, H., 1982. Höchstmengenverordnung für PCB in tierischen Rohstoffen und daraus hergestellten Nahrungsmitteln. *Fischwirt.*, **62**: 1178–1181.

Falkner, R. and W. Simonis, 1982. Polychlorierte Biphenyle (PCB) im Lebensraum Wasser (Aufnahme und Anreicherung durch Organismen – Probleme der Weitergabe in der Nahrungspyramide). Ein Literaturbericht für den Zeitraum 1972–1979. *Ergebn.Limnol.*, **17**: 1–74.

Grizzle, J.M., 1977. Hematological changes in fingerling channel catfish exposed to malachite green. *Progr.Fish-Cult.*, **39**: 90–93.

Halouzka, R., J. Ruprich and A. Piskač, 1990. Účinek polychlorovaných bifenylůna organismus kuřat: patologické změny orgánů po krátkodobém a dlouhodobém příjmu Deloru 103. (The effects of polychlorinated biphenyls on chick organisms: pathological changes in the organs after a short-term or long-term intake of Delor 103.) *Vet.Med.(Praha)*, **35**: 303–312.

Hattula, M.L., 1972. The levels of PCB in some Finnish fish. In: *Gewässer und Pflanzenschutzmittel*, pp. 109–111. Stuttgart, G. Fischer Verlag.

Hlavová, V., 1993. Reference values of the haematological indices in brown trout, *Salmo trutta m. fario* L. *Folia zool.*, 42(1) (in press).

Hruška, J. and M. Kociánová, 1978. Stanovení reziduí chlorovaný pesticidů v potravinách, biologickém materiálu a vode metodou plynové chromatografie. (Determination of PCB concentrations in food products, biological materials and water by the gas chromatography method.) *Průmysl potravin*, **29**: 49–51.

Krasnicki, K. *et al.*, 1977. Residues of organochlorine pesticides and polychlorinated biphenyls (PCB) in flesh of fish from Mazurian lakes. *Zesz.Nauk.ART, Olsztyn*, **173**: 149–161.

Kredl, F. and I. Breyl, 1984. Rychlá provozní metoda na stanovení PCB v mase a masných. výrobćh. (Practical express method for PCB determination in meat and meat products.) *Acta hyg.epidem.-microbiol.*, **10**: 59–62.

Kredl, F., J. Svobodník, and Z. Svobodová, 1989. Rezidua chlorovaných pesticidů a polychlorovaných bifenylů v rybách pocházejících z různých lokalit ČSR. (Residues of chlorinated pesticides and polychlorinated biphenyls in fish coming from different localities in the Czech Socialist Republic.) *Vet.Med.(Praha)*, **34**: 239–250.

Mattheis, Th., M.Ch. Sommer and K. Grahl, l984. Datensammlung der Grenzkonzentrationen von Schadstoffen für die Fischproduktion. III. Polychlorierte Biphenyle. Berlin, Institut für Binnenfischerei. 58 pp.

Peneva, V., 1980. Ostatoni količestva chlororganični insekticidi i polichlorirani bifenili v njakoi vidove riba. *Vet.Med.Nauki (Sofia)*, **8**: 52–56.

Peters, G., 1986. Stress as a defense disturbing factor in aquaculture. International Symposium on Ichthyopathology in Aquaculture, Dubrovnik, 38–39.

Piskač, A., J. Ruprich and R. Halouzka, 1990. Účinek polychlorovaných bifenylů (PCB) na organismus kuřat: vliv krátkodobého příjmu vysokých dávek Deloru 103 na koncentraci thyroxinu, trijodthyroninu, sodíku, draslíku a vápníku v krevním séru. (Effects of polychlorinated biphenyls (PCB) on the chicken organism: effect of a short-term administration of high doses of Delor 103 on the concentrations of thyroxine, trijodthyronine, sodium, potassium and calcium in blood serum.) *Vet.Med.(Praha)*, **35**: 237–246.

Safe, S., *et al.*, 1987. Polychlorinated Biphenyls (PCBs): Mammalian and Environmental Toxicology. Envir. Toxin, Ser. 1. Berlin, Heidelberg, Springer-Verlag. 152 pp.

Schüler, W., H. Brunn, and D. Manz, 1985. Pesticides and PCBs in fish from the Lahn river. *Bull.Environ.Contam.Toxicol.*, **34**: 608–616.

Stechert, J. and A. Jantz, 1983. Zum Vorkommen von DDT und polychlorierten Biphenylen (PCB) in Fischen aus Seen des Bezirkes Schwerin. *Acta hydrobiol.hydrochim.*, **11**: 559–567.

Svobodová, Z. and M. Pečená, 1987. Changes in the red and white blood picture of carp after acute exposure to toxic substances. *Práce VÚRH Vodňany*, **17**: 116–128.

Svobodová, Z., D. Pravda and J. Paláčková, 1986. Jednotné metody hematologického vyšetřování ryb. (Unified methods of haematological examination of fish.) VÚRH Vodňany, Edice Metodik.

Svobodová, Z., F. Kredl and J. Svobodník, l989a. Rezidua PCB ve vodě a v rybách z řeky Vltavy v lokalitě nad a pod Prahou. (PCB residues in the fish and water of the Vltava river upstream and downstream of Prague.) *Bul.VÚRH Vodňany*, **25(3)**: 12–17.

Svobodová, Z., F. Kredl and J. Svobodník, l989b. Rezidua PCB ve složkách ekosystému vybraných vodárenských nádrží. (PCB residues in the individual components of the ecosystem of selected water reservoirs.) *Bul.VÚRH Vodňany*, **25(4)**: 7–13.

Wlasow, T., 1985. The leucocyte system in rainbow trout, *Salmo gairdneri* Rich., affected by prolonged subacute phenol intoxication. *Acta Ichthyol.Piscator.*, **15**: 83–94.

Chapter 9

The effects of low levels of 17α-ethynylestradiol upon plasma vitellogenin levels in male and female rainbow trout, *Oncorhynchus mykiss* held at two acclimation temperatures

D.A. SHEAHAN,[1] D. BUCKE,[2] P. MATTHIESSEN,[1] J.P. SUMPTER,[3]
M.F. KIRBY,[1] P. NEALL[1] and M. WALDOCK[1]

[1] *MAFF Fisheries Laboratory, Remembrance Avenue, Burnham-on-Crouch, Essex, CM0 8HA, UK*
[2] *MAFF Fish Diseases Laboratory, 33/33A Albany Road, Granby Industrial Estate, Weymouth, Dorset DT4 9TH, UK*
[3] *Brunel University, Department of Biology and Biochemistry, Uxbridge, Middlesex UB8 3PH, UK*

9.1   Introduction

Purdom *et al.* (1992) have demonstrated that exposure of male rainbow trout (*Oncorhynchus mykiss*) to the effluents of sewage treatment works can result in the induction of high plasma vitellogenin (VTG) levels. VTG is normally only induced in female trout in response to the production of 17β-estradiol, during the reproductive cycle (Bohemen *et al.*, 1981; Whitehead *et al.*, 1983). The vitellogenic response induced in trout exposed to sewage treatment effluents has been tentatively attributed to the presence of active oral contraceptive steroids, in particular 17α-ethynylestradiol (EE₂). Purdom *et al.* (1992) have shown that EE₂ administered in the water supply can induce vitellogenesis in carp (*Cyprinus carpio*) and in female and male rainbow trout. These studies indicated that 1 ng l⁻¹ EE₂ dosed into the water could induce the production of detectable levels of plasma vitellogenin after 10 days. The present study was intended to establish whether prolonged exposure of trout to low levels of EE₂, which might occur some distance downstream of sewage treatment works, can induce vitellogenesis. Two different holding temperatures were incorporated into the experimental design in order to assess the influence of season upon induced vitellogenesis.

9.2   Materials and methods

9.2.1   *Animals*

One hundred and twenty-eight one-year-old, mixed sex, rainbow trout were weighed, measured and tagged after anaesthetising with 2-phenoxyethanol (1 ml.l⁻¹). The fish had a mean body weight of 237 ±5 g and mean length of

264 ±20 mm. Each fish was allocated at random to one of eight 500 l light-proofed glass aquaria. A light:dark cycle of 12:12 hours was provided.

9.2.2   Test conditions

In one series of four tanks the water temperature was maintained at 11.4 ±0.3°C, dissolved oxygen saturation 84 ±1% and pH at 8.0 ±0.02. The temperature in the other four tanks was 17.4 ±1.1°C, dissolved oxygen saturation 80 ±1% and pH 8.0 ±0.02. The hardness of the test water was 50 mg.l^{-1} as $CaCO_3$ (range 30–78 mg.l^{-1}). A ration level of 0.8% body weight per day BP Nutrition Mainstream diet was fed throughout the study. All fish were acclimated to test conditions for a period of 4 weeks before the start of dosing.

9.2.3   17α-ethynylestradiol dosing

Three nominal concentrations of EE_2, 0.1, 0.3 and 1.0 ng.l^{-1}, were maintained in three aquaria under each temperature regime. A main stock solution was made up by adding EE_2 to 20 l of double distilled water which was agitated with a magnetic stirrer for three days. Aliquots of the main stock were further diluted to 5 l in distilled water to produce three appropriate stock solutions (1.6, 4.8 and 16 mg.l^{-1} EE_2). The nominal stock solutions were dosed into 2 l glass mixing chambers by a peristaltic pump at a rate of 0.25 ml.min^{-1}. Dilution water obtained from a borehole and reconstituted after reverse osmosis, was supplied to the mixing chamber at a rate of 4 l.min^{-1}.

17α-ethynylestradiol measurement

The nominal exposure concentrations of 17α-ethynylestradiol used were below the detection limit for standard liquid/liquid extraction techniques and were therefore difficult to verify analytically. On one occasion exposure concentrations were measured using a solid phase extraction system and gas chromatography/mass spectrometer detection (GC/MS). Twenty litre samples, spiked with 11.3 ng of a deuterated internal standard (17β-estradiol, D2) and 200 ml of methanol, were extracted using C18 Mega Bond Elut (Analytichem) columns. Sterols were eluted from the C18 columns using 20 ml ethyl-acetate. After evaporation to dryness in a stream of nitrogen, extracts were derivatised using a BIS-TMS-Acetamide and Trimethylchlorosilane ('TMCS') (Pierce) mixture to produce sterol silyl esters. The sterol esters were then analysed using GC/MS with multiple ion detection.

9.2.4   Blood sampling

At intervals throughout the study, fish from each tank were anaesthetised, weighed and measured. Blood was collected from the caudal sinus using a heparinised

(1000 IU) syringe before the fish were returned to their tank. The blood samples were centrifuged for 5 min at 10 000 g and the plasma obtained was stored deep frozen ($-20°C$) until needed. Plasma samples were assayed using a homologous rainbow trout VTG immunoassay (Sumpter, 1985) to determine the levels of plasma VTG.

9.2.5   *Gonadosomatic and hepatosomatic indices*

After 28 weeks, fish in each treatment were anaesthetised and then weighed and measured. They were then killed by severing the spinal cord and the liver and gonads from each were removed and weighed separately. The gonadosomatic index (GSI) was derived by calculating the total gonad weight as a percentage of body weight and the hepatosomatic index (HSI) as total liver weight as a percentage of body weight.

9.2.6   *Histology*

Small slices of liver and gonad (approximately 3 mm) were fixed in Bouins Fluid, which was changed after 24 hours for 70% alcohol. All samples were ultimately embedded in paraffin wax blocks, from which 5 μm sections were taken and subsequently stained with haematoxylin and eosin. The stained sections were examined with the aid of a light microscope. The liver sections were classified as stages 1 to 3 according to the cytoplasmic storage condition. The testes were also classified as stages 1 to 3 according to the stage of spermatogenesis. The ovaries were classified 1 to 6 dependent upon the stage of oogenesis. The 'histological score' for the gonads was based upon methods recommended in three reference works; Anderson and Mitchum (1974), Hibiya (1982) and Yasutake and Wales (1983).

9.2.7   *Statistics*

The results of the vitellogenin analyses and the GSI and HSI values were tested for significance by one-way analysis of variance on logarithmically transformed data. Vitellogenin levels were also compared in relation to temperature, maturity stage and concentration, using the general linear model procedure in the SAS Statistical Package.

9.3   **Results**

The data in Figures 9.1 and 9.2 show the plasma VTG levels sampled in individual trout during a 28-week period in the control and three EE_2 treatment levels at mean water temperatures of 11.4 and 17.4°C respectively.

VTG levels in the initial samples were not significantly different in any of the treatments in either temperature regime ($P > 0.05$). Retention of tags during the study was poor and made identification of individual fish difficult. Statistical comparisons of VTG levels in the different treatments are not valid without knowledge of the sex ratio of the fish sampled on each occasion. The general trend however is one of increasing VTG levels throughout the 28-week period. After 12 weeks 70% of the fish sampled in the 1 ng.l^{-1} treatments at both 11.4 and 17.4°C

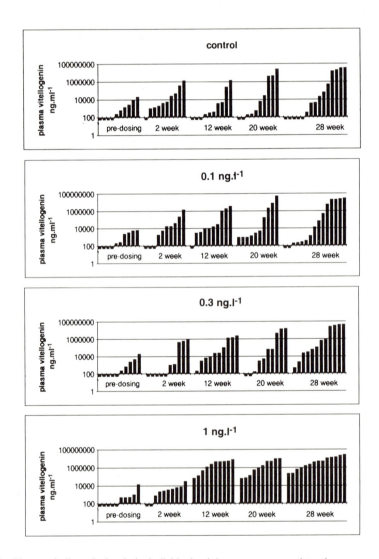

Fig. 9.1 Plasma vitellogenin levels in individual rainbow trout exposed to three concentrations of 17α-ethynylestradiol during a 28-week period, at a mean water temperature of 11.4°C.

Note: The detection limit between assays varied from 10 to 150 ng.ml^{-1}, therefore all values from below detection level up to 150 ng.ml^{-1} are represented as downward pointing bars.

exhibited VTG levels in excess of 1 mg.ml^{-1}. Only 20–30% of fish sampled in the other treatments and the controls exhibited similarly high levels.

Figures 9.3 and 9.4 show the plasma VTG levels present in male and female fish sampled in each treatment in both temperature regimes at the end of the study (28 weeks' dosing). The VTG levels in the females were not significantly different between the EE$_2$ treatments and the control within each temperature regime. However the plasma VTG levels in the males were significantly higher in the 1 ng.l^{-1} EE$_2$ treatments than in the controls in both temperature regimes and also

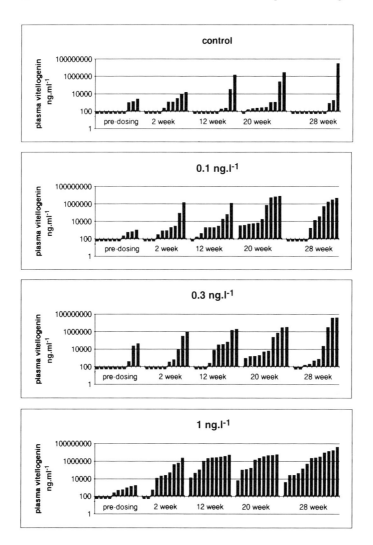

Fig. 9.2 Plasma vitellogenin levels in individual rainbow trout exposed to three concentrations of 17α-ethynylestradiol during a 28-week period, at a mean water temperature of 17.4°C.
Note: The detection limit between assays varied from 10 to 150 ng.ml^{-1}, therefore all values from below detection level up to 150 ng.ml^{-1} are represented as downward pointing bars.

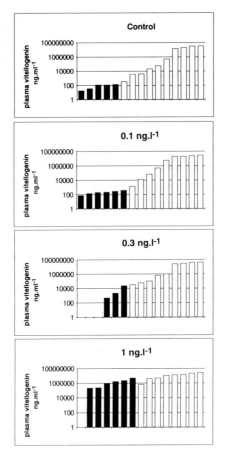

Fig. 9.3 Plasma vitellogenin levels (nanograms per ml) in male (black) and female (white) rainbow trout, exposed to three concentrations of 17α-ethynylestradiol for 28-weeks at a mean water temperature of 11.4°C.
Note: Spaces signify fish which died during the course of the study.

higher in the 0.3 ng.l^{-1} EE$_2$ treatment than in the control at 11.4°C (P <0.05). The mean vitellogenin level in the 0.3 ng.l^{-1} EE$_2$ treatment at 17.4°C was higher than that in the control but was not shown to be significantly different. In Figures 9.5 and 9.6 the levels of plasma VTG in the females in each treatment at 11.4 and 17.4°C, were plotted against maturation category (derived from Hibiya, 1982, and Anderson and Mitchum, 1974) based upon gonad histology. These plots indicate that higher VTG levels are present in more mature fish (categories 4 to 6) in both temperature regimes (P <0.001); however, there was a significant interaction between EE$_2$ concentration and the level of vitellogenin present (P <0.02) as can be seen in the 1 ng.l^{-1} EE$_2$ treatment at 11.4°C which resulted in similarly high VTG levels in categories 1 to 3.

The GSI values measured ranged between 0.02 and 17, and the HSI values ranged between 0.7 and 2.7 (Tables 9.1 and 9.2), neither index showing concentration related trends. There was a trend towards higher GSI and HSI values in females from all treatments held at a mean water temperature of 11.4°C compared with the 17.4°C treatments and this trend appears again in a plot showing the mean diameter of follicles measured in females in each treatment and temperature regime (Fig. 9.7). There was no apparent trend in follicle diameter related to EE$_2$ concentration.

The histological results are tabulated (Tables 9.3 and 9.4) with liver and gonads categorised according to their storage/maturation status. Decreased hepatocellular storage status was apparent in the high-dosed males and females held at 17.4°C

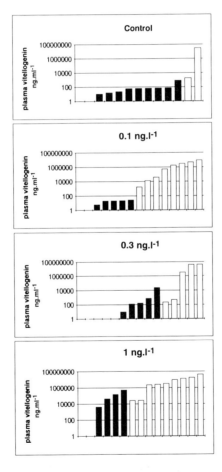

Fig. 9.4 Plasma vitellogenin levels (nanograms per ml) in male (black) and female (white) rainbow trout, exposed to three concentrations of 17α-ethynylestradiol for 28-weeks at a mean water temperature of 17.4°C.
Note: Spaces signify fish which died during the course of the study.

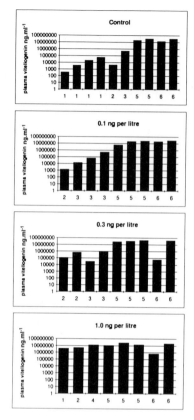

Fig. 9.5 Plasma vitellogenin levels (nanograms per ml) in female rainbow trout, plotted against the histological development of the gonad, when maintained in different levels of 17α-ethynylestradiol at a mean water temperature of 11.4°C.

Stages: 1. Germinal epithelium and small oogonia predominant
   2. Oocytes, dark blue cytoplasm predominant
   3. Oocytes and provitelline predominant
   4. Euvitelline nuclei and early cytoplasmic vacuolation
   5. Follicular cells with yolk globules (various sizes)
   6. Large follicular cells and atresic follicules (various sizes)

compared with those in the control group. At 11.4°C this difference was less marked but still apparent. The histological changes associated with the higher liver categories included thickened connective tissue layers around bile duct walls and enlarged blood vessels, which were prominent in the livers of 1 ng.l^{-1} EE$_2$ treated fish at both 11.4 and 17.4°C.

The results of the EE$_2$ concentration determinations are shown in Table 9.5. These results are tentative because samples were only analysed on one occasion, but the data do indicate that the dosed concentrations were unlikely to have been orders of magnitude different from the nominal concentrations.

9.4   Discussion

In the present study there were indications that plasma VTG levels were beginning to increase after two weeks in fish dosed with 1 ng.l^{-1} EE$_2$. After 28 weeks, immature females and males in the 1 ng.l^{-1} EE$_2$ treatment had VTG levels up to several mg.ml^{-1}. The VTG levels were also significantly elevated in male fish exposed to 0.3 ng.l^{-1} EE$_2$ for 28 weeks at 11.4°C. The 28-week no-observed-effect concentration for EE$_2$, with respect to increasing VTG levels was therefore 0.1 ng.l^{-1}.

The histological changes observed in the livers of fish exposed to 1 ng.l^{-1} EE$_2$ indicate that there was a depletion in the storage material present in the hepatocytes. This change is consistent with increased usage of storage materials in the liver for production of vitellogenin which would occur during natural vitellogenesis. Although there were indications that changes had occurred in the liver histology of

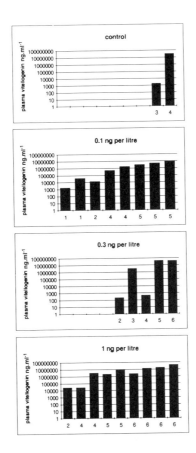

Fig. 9.6 Plasma vitellogenin levels (nanograms per ml) in female rainbow trout, plotted against the histological development of the gonad, when maintained in different levels of 17α-ethynylestradiol at a mean water temperature of 17.4°C. Stages as in Figure 9.5.

Table 9.1 Gonadosomatic and hepatosomatic indices of male and female rainbow trout exposed to different concentrations of 17α-ethynylestradiol at a mean water temperature of 11.4°C.

	Control			0.1 ng.l^{-1}			0.3 ng.l^{-1}			1 ng.l^{-1}	
Sex	GSI	HSI	Sex	GSI	HSI	Sex	GSI	HSI	Sex	GSI	HSI
m	1.79	1.41	m	0.05	1.46	m	0.19	1.33	m	0.03	1.02
m	2.16	1.22	m	0.07	1.55	m	0.91	1.14	m	1.15	0.88
m	2.40	1.36	m	2.29	1.35	m	1.72	1.13	m	1.89	1.34
m	2.44	1.15	m	3.32	1.43	m	5.30	1.55	m	2.57	1.00
m	3.99	0.95	m	3.47	0.87	f	0.14	1.48	m	3.35	1.26
f	0.11	0.96	m	5.14	1.07	f	0.15	2.66	m	5.15	1.09
f	0.11	1.40	f	0.15	1.36	f	0.16	2.16	m	8.42	1.68
f	0.14	1.29	f	0.16	1.17	f	0.18	1.17	f	0.04	1.64
f	0.15	1.12	f	0.20	1.02	f	2.28	1.72	f	0.27	1.84
f	0.20	1.21	f	2.00	0.96	f	5.68	1.56	f	1.67	1.46
f	0.27	1.10	f	3.49	1.59	f	16.93	1.84	f	2.01	1.62
f	4.62	1.84	f	5.81	1.54	f	17.05	1.92	f	3.15	1.40
f	5.58	1.92	f	8.15	1.98				f	4.81	1.80
f	6.09	1.45	f	9.68	1.89				f	12.56	1.94
f	12.12	1.45	f	14.48	1.28						

Table 9.2 Gonadosomatic and hepatosomatic indices of male and female rainbow trout exposed to different concentrations of 17α-ethynylestradiol at a mean water temperature of 17.4°C.

	Control			0.1 ng.l^{-1}			0.3 ng.l^{-1}			1 ng.l^{-1}	
Sex	GSI	HSI	Sex	GSI	HSI	Sex	GSI	HSI	Sex	GSI	HSI
m	0.02	1.17	m	0.47	1.17	m	0.14	1.17	m	0.50	0.91
m	0.03	1.16	m	1.11	0.74	m	0.68	1.24	m	0.66	1.32
m	2.15	1.06	m	1.56	0.99	m	2.59	0.88	m	1.38	1.12
m	2.28	1.18	m	2.48	0.79	m	4.89	1.13	m	2.69	0.74
m	2.29	1.77	m	4.62	0.95	m	5.40	1.22	f	0.20	1.52
m	2.41	1.31	f	0.15	1.01	f	0.15	1.04	f	0.36	0.96
m	2.51	1.01	f	0.15	1.13	f	0.17	1.71	f	1.38	0.74
m	3.44	1.23	f	0.16	1.20	f	1.15	1.41	f	3.32	1.02
m	3.95	1.20	f	0.64	1.13	f	3.82	0.90	f	3.58	0.82
f	0.40	0.92	f	2.14	1.00	f	5.45	0.92	f	3.58	1.26
f	3.78	1.04	f	3.37	1.00				f	4.91	1.34
			f	4.38	1.04				f	7.23	1.15
			f	7.72	0.89				f	7.98	1.22

fish in the highest EE$_2$ treatments, the HSI values were not as large as those reported for mature females during vitellogenesis (>12%, Bohemen *et al.*, 1981). The development of the female gonads was not significantly different between treatment groups as measured by the GSI values (P >0.4); the high values present in each treatment were probably due to the presence of fish that would have spawned later in the same year.

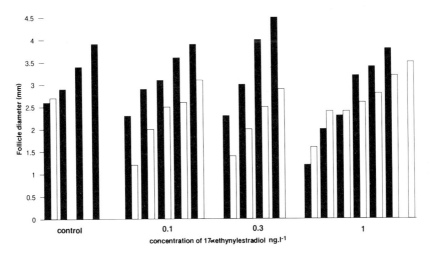

Fig. 9.7 Mean follicle diameter measured in gonads from female rainbow trout exposed to 17α-ethynylestradiol at two mean water temperatures: 11.4°C (black) and 17.4°C (white).

Purdom *et al.* (1992) found mean VTG levels of 33 mg.ml^{-1} in male trout exposed for one week to the treated effluents from sewage works. Based upon Purdom's findings and on those of the present study, EE$_2$ levels of between 1 and 10 ng.l^{-1} in the effluents could have produced similar results, providing the EE$_2$ was bioavailable. Aherne *et al.* (1984) predicted levels of 6 ng.l^{-1} EE$_2$ in rivers containing substantial quantities (>50%) of treated effluent. However, using radio-immunoassay procedures these authors were unable to measure EE$_2$ concentrations above their limit of detection (5 ng.l^{-1}) in samples taken from nine rivers (the distance downstream of sewage treatment works at which samples were taken was not reported).

Based upon the results of the present study, levels of 1 ng.l^{-1} EE$_2$ or more in a treated sewage effluent would be expected to increase plasma VTG to mg.ml^{-1} levels in immature female and male trout after 28 weeks' constant exposure. Such a situation might occur in the environment when direct exposure to a treated effluent was unavoidable (in settlement lagoons) or when an effluent forms a considerable percentage of a river's flow (e.g. during dry summers). In such extreme cases, deleterious effects upon the fish may also occur as a result of exposure to other components of the same effluent. However, induced vitellogenesis could represent a more long-term problem. In the present study, immature female and male trout exposed to 1 ng.l^{-1} EE$_2$ for 28 weeks produced up to 5 mg.ml^{-1} VTG. This represents a considerable metabolic expenditure on a non-essential protein. Synthesis of normal serum proteins may also be suppressed. Studies by Follett and Redshaw (1968) on *Xenopus laevis* (cited by Clemens, 1974) have indicated that during vitellogenesis, synthesis of albumin and globulins is suppressed *in vivo* after prolonged exposure to hormone treatment. A further possible consequence of

Table 9.3 Histology of the liver and gonads of female and male rainbow trout exposed to different concentrations of 17α-ethynylestradiol at a mean water temperature of 11.4°C.

	Control			0.1 ng.l^{-1}			0.3 ng.l^{-1}			1 ng.l^{-1}	
Sex	Liver category	Gonad category	Sex	Liver category	Gonad category	Sex	Liver category	Gonad category	Sex	Liver category	Gonad category
m	1	3	m	1	2	m	1	2	m	1	1
m	1	2	m	2	2	m	1	2	m	1	2
m	1	3	m	2	2	m	2	3	m	2	x
m	2	2	m	2	2	m	3	3	m	2	3
m	2	2	m	2	2	m	1	2	f	2	2
m	1	3	f	2	3	f	1	6	f	3	3
m	1	1	f	2	3	f	1	2	f	3	2
m	1	1	f	2	6	f	2	3	f	1	2
m	1	2	f	2	3	f	3	6	f	3	6
f	2	1	f	2	6	f	3	5	f	3	5
f	3	5	f	2	3	f	3	5	f	3	5.5
f	3	6	f	3	5	f	3	5	f	3	4
f	3	6	f	3	5				f	3	5
f	3	5	f	3	6				f	3	6
f	3	1	f	3	5						

Gonad categories males

1 = Mostly spermatogonia and spermatocytes present
2 = Secondary spermatocytes and spermatotids
3 = Spermatotids and spermatozoa
x = Posterior testis only observed

Liver categories

1 = Good overall cytoplasmic distension
2 = Patchy cytoplasmic distension
3 = Densely stained hepatocytes

Gonad categories females

1 = Germinal epithelium and small oogonia predominant
2 = Oocytes, dark blue cytoplasm predominant
3 = Oocytes and provitelline predominant
4 = Euvitelline nuclei and early cytoplasmic vacuolation
5 = Follicular cells with yolk globules (various sizes)
6 = Large follicular cells and atresic follicles (various sizes)

VTG induction has been described by Carragher and Sumpter (1991). VTG is a calcium-rich molecule (0.5–0.6% by weight; Bjornsson and Haux, 1985) and therefore calcium requirements will increase during vitellogenesis, leading to the mobilisation of calcium from all available sources, including calcified tissues. Injection of estradiol into immature female trout was shown to cause small but significant decreases in scale calcium (Carragher and Sumpter, 1991). Continuous exposure of fish to EE_2 may therefore result in loss of scale calcium and if this is coupled with increased production of non-essential protein (and possibly suppression of the manufacture of proteins active in the immune system) reduction in the disease resistance of affected fish may occur. Several mortalities occurred in the present study but these were not shown to be treatment related and comparisons of condition index of male trout between treatments showed no significant differences. Therefore in the 28-week exposure period employed in this study, levels of

Table 9.4 Histology of the liver and gonads of female and male rainbow trout exposed to different concentrations of 17α-ethynylestradiol at a mean water temperature of 17.4°C. Gonad and liver categories as in Table 9.3.

	Control			0.1 ng.l^{-1}			0.3 ng.l^{-1}			1 ng.l^{-1}	
Sex	Liver category	Gonad category	Sex	Liver category	Gonad category	Sex	Liver category	Gonad category	Sex	Liver category	Gonad category
m	1	1	m	1	2	m	1	1	m	2.5	2
m	1	1	m	1	2	m	1	1	m	3	1.5
m	1	2	m	1	2	m	1	2.5	m	3	2
m	1	2	m	2	2	m	2	2	m	3	2
m	1	2	m	3	2	m	3	1.5	f	3	2
m	1	2	f	1	1	f	2	3	f	3	4
m	1	2	f	1	1	f	3	2	f	3	4
m	1	2	f	1	2	f	3	4	f	3	5
m	1	2.5	f	1	4	f	3	5	f	3	5
f	1	3	f	1	4	f	3	6	f	3	6
f	1	4	f	2	5				f	3	6
			f	2	5				f	3	6
			f	2	5				f	3	6

Table 9.5 Results of ethynylestradiol determinations using C18 columns. The results are based on quantitation of the non-specific mass 73 which is characteristic of silylated products.

Treatment ng.l^{-1}	17 ethynylestradiol concentration ng.l^{-1}
Control	<0.1
0.1	<0.1
0.3	0.5
0.3	0.1
1	0.7
1	0.9

1 ng.l^{-1} EE$_2$ had no measured deleterious effect upon the trout in which VTG production was induced.

At predicted environmental concentrations of EE$_2$, effects on vitellogenesis in fish are likely to be confined to the immediate vicinity of a treated sewage effluent. However it should be noted that other, as yet unidentified, estrogenic chemicals may be partly or wholly responsible for the effects seen in the field. Future studies need to consider whether long-term exposure (over several years) to low concentrations of the estrogenic chemicals present in effluents, which may extend further downstream of a discharge, has any effects upon the disease resistance of exposed fish populations, or upon their overall productivity and survival.

Acknowledgements

The authors wish to thank Mr Michael Nicholson for advice on the statistical analysis of the data and Mrs Donna Murray and Mrs Amanda Mills for typing the paper.

References

Aherne, G.W., J. English and V. Marks, 1984. The role of immunoassay in the analysis of micro-contaminants in water samples. *Ecotoxicol.Environ.Safety*, **9**: 79–83.

Anderson, B.G. and D.L. Mitchum, 1974. Atlas of trout histology. Cheyenne, Wyoming. Wyoming Game and Fisheries Dept. publication, 110 pp.

Bjornsson B.T. and C. Haux, 1985. Distribution of calcium, magnesium and inorganic phosphate on plasma of 17 β-oestradiol treated rainbow trout. *J.Comp.Physiol.B*, **155**: 347–352.

Bohemen, van Ch.G., J.D.G. Lambert, H.J.Th. Goos and P.G.W.J. Van Oordt, 1981. Estrone and estradiol participation during exogenous vitellogenesis in the female rainbow trout, *Salmo gairdneri. Gen.Comp.Endocrinol.*, **46**: 81–92.

Carragher, J.F. and J.P. Sumpter, 1991. The mobilization of calcium from calcified tissues of rainbow trout (*Oncorhynchus mykiss*) induced to synthesize vitellogenin. *Comp.Biochem.Physiol.*, **99A**(1/2): 169–172.

Follett, B.K. and M.R. Redshaw, 1968. *J.Endocrinol.*, 40: 439, cited in Clemens, M.J., 1974. The regulation of egg yolk protein synthesis by steroid hormones. *Progr.Biophys.Mol.Biol.*, **28**: 71–107.

Hibiya, T. (Ed.), 1982. *An Atlas of Fish Histology: Normal and Pathological Features*. Tokyo, Stuttgart, New York, Kodansha, Gustav Fischer Verlag.

Purdom, C.E., V.J. Bye, P.A. Hardiman, N.C. Eno, C.R. Tyler and J.P. Sumpter, 1992. Estrogenic effects of effluents from sewage treatment works, in preparation.

Sumpter, J.P., 1985. The purification, radioimmunoassay and plasma levels of vitellogenin from the rainbow trout, *Salmo gairdneri*. In: Lofts, B. and W. N. Holmes (Eds) *Current Trends in Comparative Endocrinology*, pp. 355–357. Hong Kong, University Press.

Whitehead, C., N.R. Bromage and B. Breton, 1983. Changes in serum levels of gonadotropin, oestradiol 17 b and vitellogenin during the first and subsequent reproductive cycles of female rainbow trout. *Aquaculture*, **34**: 317–326.

Yasutake, W.T. and J.H. Wales, 1983. *Microscopic Anatomy of Salmonids: an Atlas*. US Dept. Interior. Washington DC, Fish and Wildlife Service, Res.Publ. 150, 190 pp.

Chapter 10
Prolonged exposure of rainbow trout (*Oncorhynchus mykiss*) to sublethal concentrations of bis(tri-n-butyltin)oxide: effects on leucocytes, lymphatic tissues and phagocytosis activity

J. SCHWAIGER,[1] H.F. FALK,[2] F. BUCHER,[3] G. ORTHUBER,[4] R. HOFFMANN[4] and R.-D. NEGELE[1]

[1] *Bavarian State Agency for Water Research, Experimental Station, D–8121 Wielenbach, Germany*
[2] *Max-Planck-Institute for Biochemistry, Martinsried, Germany*
[3] *Institute of Zoology, University of Innsbruck, Technikerstr. 25, A-6020 Innsbruck, Austria*
[4] *Institute of Zoology and Hydrobiology, University of Munich, Germany*

10.1   Introduction

Bis(tri-n-butyltin)oxide (TBTO) has been widely used as a biocide. In particular, its use as a component in antifouling paints for ships as well as for net cages has contributed to the occurrence of TBT species in the aquatic environment. Fresh and saline waters have been found to contain up to 5.85 $\mu g.l^{-1}$ TBT and 2.25 $\mu g.l^{-1}$ TBT, respectively (Maguire *et al.*, 1986). Acute toxicity data ($96hLC_{50}$) for TBT compounds found for various species of fresh water fish range between 6.0 and 24.0 $\mu g.l^{-1}$ (Cardwell and Sheldon, 1986). In rainbow trout however, the $48hLC_{50}$ has been reported to be about 30.0 $\mu g.l^{-1}$ (Plum, 1981).

In the present study a prolonged toxicity study (10 days, 28 days) following the OECD guideline 204 for testing chemicals (1984) has been carried out with rainbow trout (*Oncorhynchus mykiss*). The objective was to evaluate the toxic effects of sublethal TBTO concentrations in the range 0.6–6.0 $\mu g.l^{-1}$. Haematological, histopathological and histochemical investigations were carried out, with emphasis on leucocytes and lymphatic tissues. Furthermore, phagocytotic activity has been measured *in vitro* and the concentration of butyltin species within various tissues of test fish has been analysed.

10.2   Materials and methods

10.2.1   *Test substance*

Bis(tri-n-butyltin)oxide (TBTO) (purity of 98%) was obtained from Schering AG, Bergkamen, Germany. Stock solutions of the appropriate TBTO concentration

$(10.0 \ \mu g.l^{-1})$ were prepared under neutral pH conditions without the addition of solvent. Test solutions were prepared by dilution of the stock solution.

10.2.2   *Test fish*

Eighty-five 4-month-old rainbow trout (mean body length: 8.5 ±0.4 (SD) cm; mean body weight: 6.0 ±0.7 (SD) g) from the Institute's breeding stock were used as test animals. During the rearing period, parasitological and microbiological monitoring examinations were carried out. In parallel experiments, four groups of fish were exposed to TBTO concentrations of 0.6, 1.0, 2.0 and 4.0 $\mu g.l^{-1}$ for a 28-day period. In addition 10 test fish were exposed to 6.0 $\mu g.l^{-1}$ TBTO for 10 days. Two groups of fish (10 per group), not exposed to TBTO, served as controls (28 days and 10 days). Haematological and histopathological investigations were carried out on all the test fish and controls. Six fish from the groups exposed to 2.0, 4.0 (28 days) and 6.0 $\mu g.l^{-1}$ TBTO (10 days) were selected for histochemical analysis. *In vitro* evaluation of phagocytotic activity was carried out on isolated leucocytes from six fish per test group exposed to 0.6, 1.0, 2.0 and 4.0 $\mu g.l^{-1}$ TBTO (28 days). Three groups of test fish exposed to TBTO concentrations of 1.0, 4.0 and 6.0 $\mu g.l^{-1}$ (14 days) were used for the analysis of butyltin species in various tissues.

After the exposure periods, all test fish and controls were anaesthetised in chlorobutanole (Merck, Darmstadt, Germany; 1.5–2:1000), and then measured and weighed. Blood samples were collected by cardiac puncture into heparinised syringes. The fish were sacrificed under anaesthesia by decapitation.

10.2.3   *Test conditions*

The spring water used was regularly monitored for pH (7.7–7.8), dissolved oxygen saturation (90%), hardness (21.3°GH), conductivity (760 $\mu S.cm^{-1}$) and temperature (10 ±1.0°C). Photoperiod was maintained in a 12:12 hours light:dark regime. TBTO concentrations in the test waters were measured once a week throughout the exposure period by a method in which the butyltin compounds were extracted with n-hexane and the chelating agent tropolone. Following extraction, the cationic butyltin compounds were converted to non-polar n-pentyl derivatives with n-pentyl magnesium bromide via a Grignard reaction. The extract was cleaned up by liquid chromatography and the butyltins were quantified by gas chromatography with selected ion mass spectrometry (GC/MS). Measured actual concentrations of TBTO deviated by less than 20% from the nominal concentrations.

10.2.4   *Haematological examinations*

Haematological investigations included differential blood cell counts as well as the determination of the total number of leucocytes. Also, the packed cell volume (%), the haemoglobin concentration (mmol.l^{-1}) and the total number of erythrocytes were measured. The data were analysed by ANOVA (analysis of variance) and significance was determined using Duncan's multiple-range-test. A value of $P<0.05$ was considered to be statistically significant.

10.2.5   *Histopathological techniques*

A complete necropsy of all fish was performed and tissue specimens of the liver, spleen, kidney, heart, stomach, intestine, swim bladder, gills, pseudobranch, muscle and skin were fixed in buffered formalin (6%) and routinely processed for embedding in paraffin wax. Sections were cut at 5 μm and stained with hematoxylin and eosin (HE), Mallory's trichrome stain, periodic acid schiff reaction (PAS) and the Turnbull-blue reaction.

10.2.6   *Histochemical techniques*

Tissue specimens of the liver, kidney and gills were fixed in buffered formalin (5%), processed with 0.15 M cacodylate buffer (pH 7.4) and embedded in methacrylate. Sections, cut at 4 μm, were stained for the histochemical analysis of alkaline phosphatase (Burck, 1982), acid phosphatase (Lojda *et al.*, 1976), non-specific esterase (Mocikat, 1983), myeloperoxidase (Gerrits, 1983) and glutamyl-transferase (Lojda *et al.*, 1976). After the enzyme histochemical reactions the sections were embedded in glycerine gelatine.

The degree of histochemical reaction in liver and kidney was graded from 0 to 5 (0 = no activity, 5 = highest activity). In the gills, the number of acid phosphatase-positive cells (macrophages) and myeloperoxidase-positive cells (granulocytes) was counted. At least 50 randomly selected secondary lamellae (acid-phosphatase reaction) and three gill filaments (myeloperoxidase reaction) were analysed in each fish. Means ±SD were calculated for each group and the data were analysed for the significance of differences using Student's *t*-test.

10.2.7   *In vitro determination of phagocytotic activity*

Blood samples (ca. 100 μl) were centrifuged at 400 g for 10 min. at room temperature; the supernatant was then removed and the cells lysed in 1 ml erythrocyte lysis reagent (0.874 g NH_4Cl, 0.1 g $KHCO_3$, 3.67 mg EDTA in 100 ml distilled water and adjusted to pH 7.4 with 1 N NaOH) for 10 min and then washed once in 1.5 ml phosphate buffer saline (pH 7.4) and twice in complete RPMI 1640 tissue culture medium. The medium was supplemented with 5% foetal calf serum (Gibco, heat inactivated at 56°C, 20 min). 100 μl cell suspension and 25 μl of a 1:50 suspension of monodisperse fluorescent polystyrene beads (1 μm Fluoresbrite bright blue, Polyscience) were added to 2.0 ml of this medium and incubated at 4°C for 2 h. As a functional parameter the percentage of cells that had taken up more than one particle was measured by flow cytometry. The phagocytosis scores were presented as mean ±standard error of the mean. Significance was determined by one-way analysis of variance ($P<0.05$).

10.2.8   *Analysis of butyltin species in tissues*

The concentration of TBT (tributyltin), DBT (dibutyltin) and MBT (monobutyltin) in the kidney, spleen, liver, muscle and gills was measured by the same method as described for the analysis of TBT in water samples.

10.3   Results

10.3.1   *Haematological results*

Measurements of the differential blood cell count showed that TBTO had a marked influence on the percentage of various cell types within the leucocyte population. The absolute number of lymphocytes was significantly reduced in fish exposed to 2.0, 4.0 μg.l^{-1} TBTO (28 days) and 6.0 μg.l^{-1} TBTO (10 days), while the number of neutrophilic granulocytes and monocytes was elevated. Also, a significant increase in the packed cell volume and the haemoglobin concentration was observed, and this was correlated to both the duration of exposure and the test concentration of TBTO. Changes in the haematological parameters are shown in Figure 10.1.

10.3.2   *Histopathological results*

The most prominent histopathological change was a concentration-related lymphocytic depletion of the spleen in fish of all test groups. In addition, a proliferation and an increased phagocytotic activity of reticuloendothelial cells, including an increased erythrophagia, was observed (Fig. 10.2).

A degeneration and necrosis of epithelial cells and chloride cells was found in both the primary lamellae and secondary lamellae of the gills in all groups of fish exposed to TBTO. Similarly, in the epithelial cells of the pseudobranch tissue and in the surrounding oral mucosa, vacuolisation of cytoplasma, cell oedema and karyorrhexis were detected. Infiltration of neutrophilic granulocytes and macrophages was observed within the damaged areas of the gills and pseudobranch.

The incidence of histopathological alterations in spleen, gills and pseudobranch is shown in Figure 10.3. In all the other organs examined there were no pathological lesions found.

10.3.3   *Histochemical results*

In liver tissue, an increased activity of acid phosphatase and of non-specific esterase was observed in fish exposed to 4.0 and 6.0 μg.l^{-1} TBTO, which indicated an

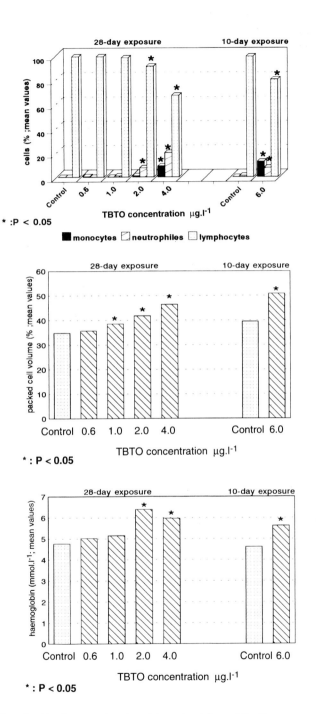

Fig. 10.1 Values for blood parameters in rainbow trout (n = 10) after exposure to 0.6, 1.0, 2.0, 4.0 μg.l^{-1} TBTO (28 days) and 6.0 μg.l^{-1} TBTO (10 days).

elevated lysosomal activity. Whereas the latter was detected only within hepato-cytes, an increase in acid phosphatase activity was observed within hepatocytes, biliary epithelial cells and macrophages.

In the gill epithelia of fish exposed to 6.0 μg.l^{-1} TBTO there was a significant increase in the number of myeloperoxidase-positive cells (3.7 $\pm$2.7 (SD); control: 0.40 $\pm$0.60) and acid phosphatase-positive cells (0.75 $\pm$0.23; control: 0.49 $\pm$0.13).

In the kidney, a marked increase in the activity of non-specific esterase in cells of the reticulohistiocytary system (histiocytes) was detected in fish from the 6.0 and 4.0 μg.l^{-1} test group. Fish exposed to 6.0 μg.l^{-1} TBTO showed an elevated lysosomal activity of non-specific esterase within the epithelial cells of the first proximal segments of the renal tubules.

10.3.4   *Determination of the phagocytotic activity*

Prolonged exposure to TBTO in the present study induced changes in phagocytotic activity. After exposure to 0.6 μg.l^{-1} TBTO a slight increase was detected in the percentage of phagocytotic cells, whereas in fish exposed to 1.0 μg.l^{-1} TBTO a suppressive effect was seen. An increase in phagocytotic activity was observed after exposure to 2.0 and 4.0 μg.l^{-1} TBTO, although only within the 4.0 μg.l^{-1} group

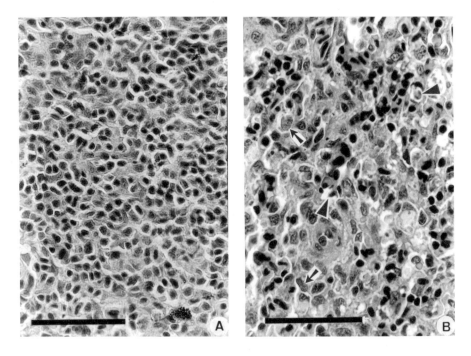

Fig. 10.2   Tissue from the spleen of rainbow trout. (A) Control, (B) after exposure to 4.0 μg.l^{-1} TBTO (28 days) showing lymphocytic depletion, proliferation of reticuloendothelial cells (arrow), and increased erythrophagia (arrowhead). Bar equal to 0.1 mm, HE stain.

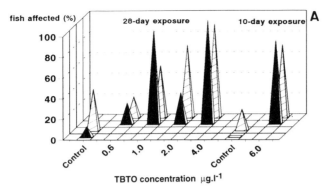

▲ lymphocytic depletion △ increased erythrophagia

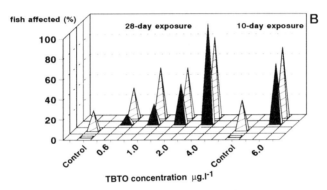

cell necrosis within: ▲ primary lamellae △ secondary lamellae

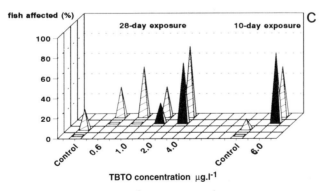

cell necrosis within : ▲ oral mucosa △ pseudobranchial tissue

Fig. 10.3 Incidence of pathological changes in (A) spleen, (B) gills and (C) pseudobranch of rainbow trout ($n = 10$) after exposure to 0.6, 1.0, 2.0, 4.0 µg.l^{-1} TBTO (28 days) and 6.0 µg.l^{-1} TBTO (10 days).

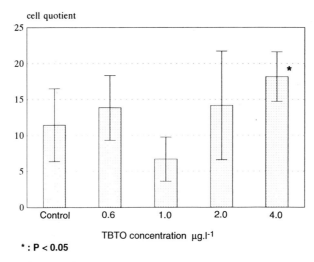

Fig. 10.4 Effects on phagocytotic activity of blood cells in rainbow trout (n = 6) after 28-day exposure to 0.6, 1.0, 2.0 and 4.0 μg.l^{-1} TBTO. Percentage of phagocytosing cells to total live cells 2 hours after exposure at 4°C.

was this difference considered to be statistically significant ($P<0.05$) compared to controls (Fig. 10.4).

10.3.5   *Concentrations of butyltin species within tissues*

An accumulation of TBT, DBT and MBT was found in all the organs analysed. The highest residue levels were in the kidney and spleen, and directly correlated with the TBTO test concentrations. The levels of butyltin species within the gills and muscle tissue were relatively low (Fig. 10.5).

10.4   **Discussion**

It has been shown in the present study that prolonged exposure to sublethal TBTO concentrations between 0.6 and 6.0 μg.l^{-1} cause severe lymphotoxic effects, characterised by a marked lymphocytic depletion of the spleen and a significant decrease in circulating lymphocytes. Published data on splenic changes in TBTO exposed fish are not available. However, the observations presented here are in agreement with those found for TBTO treated rats (Funahashi *et al.*, 1980; Krajnc *et al.*, 1984; Vos *et al.*, 1984) and mice (Ishaaja *et al.*, 1976) which exhibited immunological disorders. Short-term studies by Vos *et al.* (1984) with rats given low dietary levels of TBTO showed a TBTO induced direct cytotoxic effect on the thymus, resulting in a diminished influx of thymus-derived lymphocytes into the peripheral lymphoid tissue and a suppression of thymus-dependent immune responses.

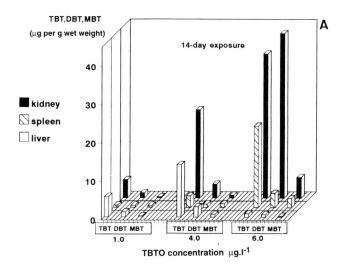

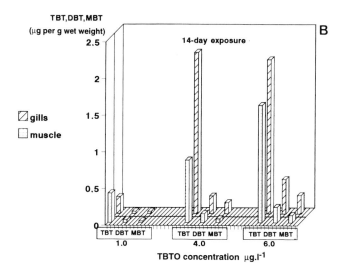

Fig. 10.5 Concentrations of tributyltin (TBT), dibutyltin (DBT) and monobutyltin (MBT) in (A) kidney, spleen, and liver, (B) gills and muscle tissue of rainbow trout after 14-day exposure to TBTO-concentrations of 1.0, 4.0 and 6.0 $\mu g.l^{-1}$ (mean values; $\mu g.g^{-1}$ wet weight).

Prolonged toxicity studies by Wester and Canton (1987) with guppies (*Poecilia reticulata*) showed that these fish developed a thymic atrophy after TBTO exposure, in contrast to Japanese medaka (*Oryzias latipes*) in which such changes could not be induced (Wester *et al.*, 1990). Although thymic alterations were not observed by Seinen *et al.* (1981) in rainbow trout yolk-sac fry after exposure to tributyltinchloride (TBTC), a primary thymotoxic effect as a cause of the marked splenic lymphocytic depletion cannot be excluded since thymic tissue was not examined in the present study.

Haematological findings, e.g. reduction in lymphocytes and total leucocytes have also been observed in mice after dietary uptake of TBTO (Ishaaya *et al.*, 1976).

Proliferation and increased phagocytotic activity of reticuloendothelial cells of the spleen, found in the present study, suggests an increased requirement for phagocytosing cells as shown for example by the increased erythrophagia noted in the spleen.

In both the hepatocytes and epithelial cells of the renal tubules, an increased non-specific esterase activity suggests an elevated lysosomal activity. In addition, an increased activity of the non-specific esterase in cells of the reticulohistiocytary system may indicate an increased phagocytic reaction by the histiocytes.

Also, a marked infiltration of macrophages and neutrophilic granulocytes into gill epithelia was detected by both histopathological and histochemical examinations. In the case of the severe histopathological lesions found in gill epithelia, it can be assumed that an increased phagocytosis took place to remove cell detritus.

The *in vitro* measurement of the phagocytotic activity showed that an increase occurred in fish from the lowest concentration group (0.6 μg.l^{-1} TBTO). However, a suppressive effect was observed in those fish exposed to 1.0 μg.l^{-1} TBTO. After exposure to the higher TBTO concentrations (2.0, 4.0 μg.l^{-1}) a concentration-related increase was found in the percentage of phagocytotic cells to total live cells. This effect was confirmed by haematological findings, in that a significant increase of monocytes and neutrophilic granulocytes was found in fish exposed to 2.0 and 4.0 μg.l^{-1} TBTO.

The present study has shown that sublethal TBTO concentrations can cause a reduction in the number of circulating lymphocytes and serious pathological changes in lymphatic tissue of the spleen as shown by a marked lymphocyte depletion. In contrast, an increase of phagocytotic cells and of the lysosomal activity has been observed in various tissues. In addition, damage to gill epithelia was found in fish from all the test groups. In all the organs affected, an accumulation of TBT and its dealkylated metabolites DBT and MBT was found. Since TBTO concentrations in natural aquatic systems may reach or even exceed the concentrations used in the present study (Maguire *et al.*, 1986) it can be assumed that they may result in immunological disorders and respiratory dysfunctions.

References

Burck, H.C., 1982. Histologische Technik, fifth edn, pp. 160–162. Stuttgart, Georg Thieme Verlag.

Cardwell, R.D. and A.W. Sheldon, 1986. A risk assessment concerning the fate and effects of tributyltins on the aquatic environment. Oceans '86 Conference Record, Vol. 4, pp. 1117–1129, Organotin Symposium, Washington D.C., September 23–25, Piscataway N.J., IEEE Service Center.

Funahashi, N., I. Iwasaki and G. Ide, 1980. Effects of bis(tri-n-butyltin)oxide on endocrine and lymphoid organs of male rats. *Acta Pathol.Jpn.*, **30**(6): 955–966.

Gerrits, P.O., 1983. Verfahren zur Färbung von Gewebe, das in 2-Hydroxyethyl-Methacrylat eingebettet wird, pp. 18–20. Sonderdruck f. Kulzer.

Ishaaya, I., J.L. Engel and J. E. Casida, 1976. Dietary triorganotins affect lymphatic tissues and blood composition of mice. *Pestic.Biochem.Physiol.*, **6**: 270–279.

Krajnc, E.I. *et al.*, 1984. Toxicity of bis(tri-n-butyltin)oxide in the rat. I. Short-term effects on general parameters and on endocrine and lymphoid systems. *Toxicol.Appl.Pharmacol.*, **75**: 363–386.

Lojda, Z., R. Gossrau and T.H. Schiebler, 1976. *Enzymhistochemische Methoden*, pp. 64–78. Berlin, Heidelberg, Springer Verlag.

Maguire, R.J. *et al.*, 1986. Occurrence of organotin compounds in water and sediment in Canada. *Chemosphere*, **15**(3): 253–274.

Mocikat, K.H., 1983. Haematologische Labormethoden, third edn, pp. 38–40. Diagnostika Merck, GIT-Verlag.

OECD, 1984. OECD Guideline for testing of chemicals; No. 204, fish, 'Prolonged toxicity study of at least 14 days'.

Plum, H., 1981. Organotin compounds and their influence on the environment. *Inf.Chim.*, **220**: 135–139.

Seinen, W. *et al.*, 1981. Short term toxicity of tri-n-butyltinchloride in rainbow trout (*Salmo gairdneri* Richardson) yolk sac fry. *Sci.Tot.Environ.*, **19**: 155–166.

Vos, J.G. *et al.*, 1984. Toxicity of bis(tri-n-butyltin)oxide in the rat. II. Suppression of thymus dependent immune response and of parameters of nonspecific resistance after short-term exposure. *Toxicol.Appl.Pharmacol.*, **75**: 387–408.

Wester, P.W. and J.H. Canton, 1987. Histopathological study of *Poecilia reticulata* (guppy) after long-term exposure to bis(tri-n-butyltin)oxide (TBTO) and di-n-butyltindichloride (DBTC). *Aquat.Toxicol.*, **10**: 143–165.

Wester, P.W. *et al.*, 1990. The toxicity of bis(tri-n-butyltin)oxide (TBTO) and di-n-butyltinchloride (DBTC) in the small fish species *Oryzias latipes* (medaka) and *Poecilia reticulata* (guppy). *Aquat.Toxicol.*, **16**: 53–72.

Chapter 11
Adaptation of freshwater fish to toxicants: stress mechanisms induced by branchial malfunctioning

R.A.C. LOCK, P.H.M. BALM and S.E. WENDELAAR BONGA

Department of Animal Physiology, University of Nijmegen, Toernooiveld,
6525 ED Nijmegen, The Netherlands

11.1   Introduction

Fish experiencing sudden physical or chemical changes in their environment become stressed. This condition could for example be brought about by abrupt pH or temperature changes in the water, by handling, capture, and confinement, or by aquatic toxicants (Pickering and Pottinger, 1989; Fu *et al.*, 1989b). These extrinsic stressors could influence branchial activities and jeopardise the homeostatic control of the body fluids (Wendelaar Bonga and Van der Meij, 1989; Wendelaar Bonga and Pang, 1989).

Although the fish's skin with its external secretions effectively protects the animal from its potentially hostile environment, there is now a general consensus that the gills represent the weak spot in this barrier (Eddy, 1981). In particular, the numerous gill lamellae comprising up to 90% of the total body surface and the ion-transporting cells (chloride cells) in the epithelial layer are vulnerable to aquatic toxicants. As a consequence, vital processes such as respiration, ion and water exchange, acid–base regulation and excretion of nitrogenous wastes are endangered (Heath, 1987; Evans, 1987).

At sublethal toxicant concentrations, fish are able to compensate for branchial malfunctioning via an increased hormonal response mediated by the pituitary–interrenal axis (Donaldson, 1981; Balm *et al.*, 1987). This general stress response of fish is considered crucial for its survival. Adrenalin, adrenocorticotropic hormone (ACTH) and cortisol act as the primary endocrine messengers in this process controlling the cardio-vascular system, water and ion balance, and energy mobilisation (Mazeaud and Mazeaud, 1981; Schreck, 1981, 1982; Pickering, 1989). In general, during successful adaptation to a stressor, the initially raised plasma cortisol levels gradually return to control values, despite the continued presence of the stressor (Pickering and Pottinger, 1989; Fu *et al.*, 1989b). This is important because chronically elevated cortisol levels also act as an immuno-suppressant in fish (Ellsaesser and Clem, 1986; Pickering and Pottinger, 1989), thus increasing their susceptibility to diseases.

In this chapter the effects of aquatic toxicants on the structure and function of

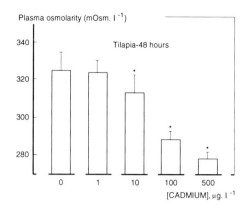

Fig. 11.1 Plasma osmolarity of tilapia after 48 hours of exposure to different concentrations of cadmium. $n = 12$; means $\pm$S.D.; * $P < 0.01$.

fish gills will briefly be analysed. The adaptational responses of a freshwater fish to a stressor will be illustrated in tilapia (*Oreochromis mossambicus*), exposed to acute and chronic concentrations of cadmium. Finally, we will consider to what extent additional stressors may interfere with the successful adaptation of fish to an environmental pollutant.

11.2   Effects of toxicants on the gills

Mallatt (1985) extensively reviewed the morphological changes taking place in fish gills in the presence of environmental pollutants. The most common changes, applicable to a wide range of pollutants, are: lifting of the epithelium covering the secondary lamellae, increased number of lymphatic spaces, changed blood flow patterns and appearance of granulocytes in the epithelium. Furthermore, hypertrophy and hyperplasia of epithelial cells including mucous and chloride cells are often observed. Loss of structural integrity of the gills may easily lead to a drop in the concentration of blood electrolytes, such as sodium, chloride and calcium. Electrolyte losses have been described, for example, after exposure of freshwater fish to pesticides (Mallatt and Stinson, 1990), mercury (Lock *et al.*, 1981); chromium (Van de Putte *et al.*, 1982); zinc (Spry and Wood, 1985); copper and cadmium (Reid and McDonald, 1988; Fu *et al.*, 1989a). In Figure 11.1 a concentration-dependent reduction of plasma osmolarity obtained in our studies on the effects of cadmium on tilapia, is shown.

The reduction in plasma electrolyte levels has two important causes. First, there is an elevated passive efflux of ions across the gills, due to a more or less non-selective increase in the branchial permeability to water and ions. This may lead to haemodilution by enhanced osmotic uptake of water across the gills, and to passive diffusional ion losses. Second, the inhibition of active ion uptake by the chloride cells of the gills may further contribute to the negative ion balance of the blood.

11.2.1   *Effects on gill permeability*

Although the routes via which water and ions passively cross the gill epithelium have not yet been clearly defined, both the paracellular and transcellular pathways are likely to be involved. The permeability of the paracellular pathway appears related to the characteristics of the tight junctions, interconnecting the apical parts of the lateral membranes of the superficial cell layer (Freda *et al.*, 1991). McDonald *et al.* (1991) showed an inverse correlation between the ionic permeability of the gills and the depth of the tight junctions in several freshwater fish species at low pH. Although the relative contribution of the transcellular route to the passive trans-epithelial water and ion flows has not been clearly established, it is likely to be important. The permeability of cellular membranes to water and ions is determined by, for example, their phospholipid composition and the amount of calcium bound to the negative groups of the membranes (Chase, 1984). Indeed, loss of bound calcium from the membranes and tight junctions of fish gills as a consequence of water acidification leads to an increased permeability to water and ions (McWilliams, 1983; McDonald *et al.*, 1991).

Heavy metals may also influence branchial permeability. Lock *et al.* (1981) demonstrated a dose-related increase of osmotic water uptake and lymphatic spaces in rainbow trout gills after exposure to mercury. We also found that exposure of carp (*Cyprinus carpio*) for 4 days to cadmium affects the tight junctions in their gills and so increases branchial permeability. Although the effects of toxic metals differ with respect to site and rapidity of action, their effects on gill permeability are generally attributed to displacement of Ca^{2+} from membrane stabilising sites on the gill (Laurén and McDonald, 1985). Indeed, high calcium levels in the water generally reduce heavy metal toxicity in fish (Pascoe *et al.*, 1986). Such antagonism between calcium and cadmium levels is shown in Figure 11.2.

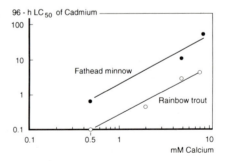

Fig. 11.2 Relationship between water calcium concentration (mM Ca) and mean acute toxicity (96hLC$_{50}$ value; mg.l^{-1} Cd) for cadmium in two freshwater fish. Source: Pickering and Gast (1972); Calamari *et al.* (1980).

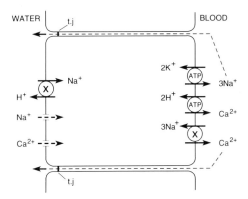

Fig. 11.3 Model for ion exchanges in chloride cells of freshwater fish. Broken arrow = pump; X = exchanger; t.j. = tight junction.

11.2.2 *Effects on active ion uptake*

The electrolyte concentrations of the body fluids in freshwater fish are considerably higher than those in the ambient water. Thus, freshwater fish are continuously faced with passive osmotic water uptake and diffusional ion losses via their gills. In response, freshwater fish produce a large quantity of dilute urine and take up ions actively from the water. The bulk of ion uptake occurs via the chloride cells, specialised transport cells equipped with an extensive tubular membrane system containing transport ATPases and exchangers (Fig. 11.3). Since mature chloride cells are in permanent contact with the surrounding water they form an obvious target for aquatic pollutants (Mallatt, 1985; Evans, 1987). Several studies have been carried out measuring the effect of toxicants on chloride cells, demonstrating heavy metal deposition (see Karlsson-Norrgren *et al.*, 1986). Based on this observation, the effects of toxic metals have been extensively studied on branchial or whole-body ion transport in fish. For example, inhibition of Na^+, and/or Ca^{2+} and Cl^- fluxes have been reported after, for example, exposure to copper (Laurén and McDonald, 1985), cadmium (Reid and McDonald, 1988; Verbost *et al.*, 1987, 1988). Figure 11.4 shows the cadmium-induced decrease of Ca^{2+}-influx in rainbow trout. The biochemical basis for such inhibition is among other possible mechanisms a direct interaction with Ca^{2+} channels and/or the transport ATPases and exchangers in the chloride cells (Fig. 11.3).

In addition, there have been many reports on the effects of toxicants on the density of chloride cells. In particular, chloride cell proliferation and hyperplasia have been observed (Mallatt, 1985). Increases in cell numbers were found after exposure to, for example, cadmium (Oronsaye and Brafield, 1984; Fu *et al.*, 1989b), zinc and copper (Crespo *et al.*, 1981), chromium (Temmink *et al.*, 1983), aluminium (Karlsson-Norrgren *et al.*, 1986) and organic toxicants (Mallatt, 1985). The increase in the number of chloride cells has been explained by most authors as a compensatory response of the fish to maintain or increase its capacity to take up ions from the water, although conclusive evidence is lacking for this possibility.

Recently, we have examined the chloride cells in tilapia during exposure to cadmium. Exposure of the fish to 10 μg.l^{-1} Cd^{2+}, which caused a slight reduction in plasma osmolarity, produced a transient increase in chloride cell density, with a maximum of double the control levels after four days (Fig. 11.5). Many chloride cells were degenerative or in an early stage of differentiation (Wendelaar Bonga and Van der Meij, 1989). At this early phase of cadmium exposure, the total number of mature chloride cells was in fact slightly below the control levels. Also, the activity of Na$^+$/K$^+$-ATPase, the marker enzyme of chloride cells, was initially reduced in cadmium exposed fish compared to that of the controls. These data indicate that under such conditions the initial increase in chloride cell density is mainly a reflection of accelerated turnover of immature chloride cells rather than an increase in mature, functional cells. Subsequently, at 35 days the chloride cells apparently become functional as indicated by the increased Na$^+$/K$^+$-ATPase activity (results not shown).

11.3   Tolerance to toxicants

With prolonged exposure, fish are able to develop a resistance to sublethal toxicant concentrations. Toxicant tolerance is typically assessed by performance of the animals in LC$_{50}$ trials, following pre-exposure to these toxicants. Increased tolerance of fish to copper, cadmium or zinc, following pre-exposure to sublethal concentrations of these metals, resulted in a 1.5 to 2.7-fold increase in the observed LC$_{50}$ (see Hodson, 1988). We assume that such increase in, for example, cadmium tolerance was linked to the induction of intracellular metal-binding proteins, including cysteine-rich metallothioneins in the gills (Fu *et al.*, 1989b). In other

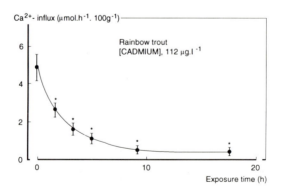

Fig. 11.4 Effect of cadmium exposure on whole-body calcium influx in rainbow trout. n = 6; means ±SD; *P <0.01.

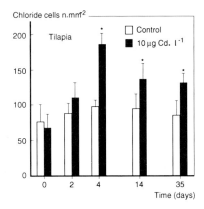

Fig. 11.5   Effect of cadmium exposure on opercular chloride cell density in tilapia. n = 6; means ±SD; *P <0.01.

cases, such as with copper, recovery occurred even without apparent induction of metal-binding proteins in these organs (Laurén and McDonald, 1987a, b).

Since toxic metals cause osmoregulatory disturbances via their action on the gills, it is reasonable to assume that the mechanism of acclimation occurs via functional modifications of these organs. Such modifying responses appear in part under the control of catecholamines and hormones. A negative effect of increased release of adrenalin and other vasoactive catecholamines in stressed fish will be the reduction of the vascular resistance of the lamellar blood flow, enhancing the number of lamellae that are perfused (Pärt *et al.*, 1982). Consequently, the passive diffusional losses of ions and osmotic water uptake will further increase. Modifying responses in metal-exposed fish also appear to be under the control of two principal hormones involved in teleost osmoregulation: prolactin and cortisol (for reviews see Hirano, 1986; Wendelaar Bonga and Pang, 1989). The pituitary hormone, prolactin, is considered to be the pivotal osmoregulatory hormone of freshwater fish, enhancing

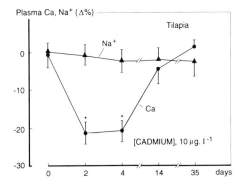

Fig. 11.6   Plasma total Ca and Na$^+$ in tilapia during prolonged exposure to cadmium. n = 8; means ±SD; *P <0.01.

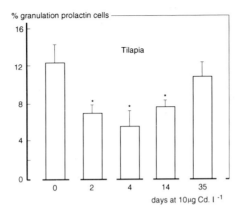

Fig. 11.7 Effect of cadmium exposure on granulation of pituitary prolactin cells in tilapia. n = 5; means ±SD; *P <0.01.

branchial Ca^{2+}-uptake and decreasing water and ion permeabilities of gill-, gut- and kidney epithelia (Hirano, 1986). It is expected therefore that decreased plasma ion levels and increased epithelial permeability in fish exposed to toxicants will trigger an increased release of prolactin. Indeed, this phenomenon has been shown in our laboratory with tilapia exposed to Cd^{2+}, where a transient hypocalcaemia (Fig. 11.6) is concurrent with degranulation of prolactin cells, indicating enhanced cellular activity (Fig. 11.7).

Cortisol, the major mineralo- and glucocorticoid of teleost fish, plays a crucial role in the primary response of these animals to environmental stressors. An initially elevated blood cortisol level is considered to be a non-specific response of fish to a stressful situation (Donaldson, 1981). Transient elevated levels of plasma

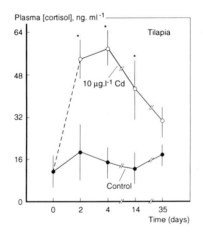

Fig. 11.8 Effect of cadmium exposure on plasma cortisol levels in tilapia. n = 6; means ±SD; *P <0.01.

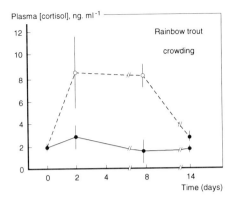

Fig. 11.9   Effect of crowding stress on plasma cortisol levels in rainbow trout. n = 10; means ±SEM; full line = control. (From: Pickering and Pottinger, 1989).

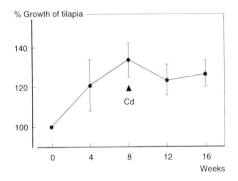

Fig. 11.10   Effect of cadmium (20 μg.l^{-1} Cd^{2+}) on the growth rate of tilapia. n = 10; means ±SD.

cortisol have been observed in tilapia exposed to cadmium (Fig. 11.8) as well as in rainbow trout subject to crowding (Fig. 11.9; Pickering and Pottinger, 1989). In both situations, blood cortisol concentrations eventually returned to basal levels, despite the continued presence of these stressors. This reduction in cortisol level appears to be crucial for the survival of fish. Pickering and Pottinger (1989) demonstrated that chronic elevation of plasma cortisol levels via intraperitoneal implantation of cortisol-releasing capsules caused a dose-dependent increase in the mortality rate of brown trout. Causes of death were severe bacterial fin-rot and furunculosis, both well known stress-related diseases. In contrast to these negative side-effects of elevated cortisol levels during toxicant stress, the animal benefits from the capacity of the hormone to promote active ion uptake mechanisms (Balm, 1986), especially in view of the increased ion losses. Contrary to the transient nature of the cortisol response, plasma glucose levels in fish lag behind during stressful conditions such as low pH environment (Balm, 1986), cadmium exposure

(Fu *et al.*, 1989b), or handling (Pickering and Pottinger, 1989). This hyperglycaemic response is mediated, depending on the species studied, by cortisol and/or by adrenergic stimulation of liver glycogenolysis (Mazeaud and Mazeaud, 1981). This reflects an increase in the metabolic costs required to maintain internal water and ion homeostasis, implying that any chronic disturbance of the homeostasis will have immediate and serious consequences for the energy balance, and thus for growth and survival of the fish. Indeed, as shown in our laboratory, the growth rate of tilapia exposed to a sublethal concentration of cadmium in the water is significantly affected (Fig. 11.10).

It is obvious from this finding and from the other toxicant-induced effects reviewed here that under these conditions, or in any other stressful situation, additional stress(ors) will put an extra metabolic burden on fish. As a result the energy costs, which under stress-free conditions in some fish are already 30% or more of their standard metabolic energy (Furspan *et al.*, 1984), may exceed the critical level. This will be aggravated further in a situation where synergism of toxicants occurs. For example, work carried out in our laboratory demonstrates that Cd^{2+} accumulation in tilapia is markedly affected by the presence of a second heavy metal, in this case, copper (Pelgrom *et al.*, 1994). In our opinion, sublethal concentrations of toxicants may become lethal for populations confronted with additional stressors. This should be taken into serious consideration when evaluating the effects of mixtures of toxicants on freshwater fish under natural conditions or in aquaculture.

References

Balm, P.H.M., 1986. Osmoregulation in teleosts by cortisol and prolactin, adaptation to low pH environments. Ph.D. thesis, University of Nijmegen, Nijmegen, The Netherlands.

Balm, P.H.M., A. Lamers and S.E. Wendelaar Bonga, 1987. Regulation of pituitary–interrenal axis activity in tilapia acclimating to low pH conditions. *Ann.Soc.Roy.Zool.Belg.*, **117**: 343–352.

Calamari, D., R. Marchetti and G. Vailati, 1980. Influence of water hardness on cadmium toxicity to *Salmo gairdneri* R. *Water Res.*, **14**: 1421–1426.

Chase, H.S. Jr, 1984. Does calcium couple the apical and basolateral membrane permeability in epithelia? *Am.J.Physiol.*, **16**: F869-F876.

Crespo, S., E. Soriano, C. Sampera and J. Balasch, 1981. Zinc and copper distribution in excretory organs of the dogfish *Scyliorhinus canicula* and chloride cell response following treatment with zinc sulphate. *Mar.Biol.*, **65**: 117–123.

Donaldson, E.M., 1981. The pituitary–interrenal axis as an indicator of stress in fish. In: Pickering, A.D. (Ed.) *Stress and Fish*, pp. 11–47. London, Academic Press.

Eddy, F.B., 1981. Effects of stress on osmotic and ionic regulation in fish. In: Pickering, A.D. (Ed.) *Stress and Fish*, pp. 77–102. London, Academic Press.

Ellsaesser, C.F. and L.W. Clem, 1986. Haematological and immunological changes in channel catfish stress by handling and transport. *J.Fish Biol.*, **28**: 511–521.

Evans, D.H., 1987. The fish gill: site of action and model for toxic effects of environmental pollutants. *Env.Health Perspect.*, **71**: 54–58.

Freda, J., D.A. Sanchez and H.L. Bergman, 1991. Shortening of branchial tight junctions in acid-exposed rainbow trout (*Oncorhynchus mykiss*). *Can.J.Fish.Aquat.Sci.*, **48**: 2028–2033.

Fu, H., R.A.C. Lock and S.E. Wendelaar Bonga, 1989a. Effect of cadmium on prolactin cell activity and plasma electrolytes in the freshwater teleost *Oreochromis mossambicus*. *Aquat.Toxicol.*, **14**: 295–306.

Fu, H., O.M. Steinebach, C.J.A. Van den Hamer, P.H.M. Balm and R.A.C. Lock, 1989b. Involvement of cortisol and metallothionein-like proteins in the physiological responses of tilapia (*Oreochromis mossambicus*) to sublethal cadmium stress. *Aquat.Toxicol.*, **16**: 257–270.

Furspan, P., H.D. Prange and L. Greenwald, 1984. Energetics and osmoregulation in the catfish, *Ictalurus nebulosus* and *I. punctatus*. *Comp.Biochem.Physiol.*, **77A**: 773–778.

Heath, A.G., 1987. *Water Pollution and Fish Physiology*. Boca Raton, Florida, CRC Press.

Hirano, T., 1986. The spectrum of prolactin action in teleosts. In: Ralph, C.L. (Ed.) *Comparative Endocrinology: Developments and Directions*, pp. 53–74. New York, A.R. Liss.

Hodson, P.V., 1988. The effect of metal metabolism on uptake, disposition and toxicity in fish. *Aquat.Toxicol.*, **11**: 3–18.

Karlsson-Norrgren, L., W. Dickson, O. Ljungberg and P. Runn, 1986. Acid water and aluminium exposure: gill lesions and aluminium accumulation in farmed brown trout, *Salmo trutta* L. *J.Fish Diseases*, 9: 1–9.

Laurén, D.J. and D.G. McDonald, 1985. Effects of copper on branchial ionoregulation in the rainbow trout, *Salmo gairdneri* Richardson. *J.Comp.Physiol.B*, **155**: 635–644.

Laurén, D.J. and D.G. McDonald, 1987a. Acclimation to copper by rainbow trout, *Salmo gairdneri*: physiology. *Can.J.Fish.Aquat.Sci.*, **44**: 99–104.

Laurén, D.J. and D.G. McDonald, 1987b. Acclimation to copper by rainbow trout, *Salmo gairdneri*: biochemistry. *Can.J.Fish.Aquat.Sci.*, **44**: 105–111.

Lock, R.A.C., P.M.J.M. Cruijsen and A.P. van Overbeeke, 1981. Effects of mercuric chloride and methylmercuric chloride on the osmoregulatory function of the gills in rainbow trout, *Salmo gairdneri* Richardson. *Comp.Biochem.Physiol.C*, **68**: 151–159.

McDonald, D.G., J. Freda, V. Cavdek, R. Gonzalez and S. Zia, 1991. Interspecific differences in gill morphology of freshwater fish in relation to tolerance of low-pH environments. *Physiol.Zool.*, **64**: 125–144.

McWilliams, P.G., 1983. An investigation of the loss of bound calcium from the gills of the brown trout, *Salmo trutta*, in acid media. *Comp.Biochem.Physiol.A*, **74**: 107–116.

Mallatt, J., 1985. Fish gill structural changes induced by toxicants and other irritants: a statistical review. *Can.J.Fish.Aquat.Sci.*, **42**: 630–648.

Mallatt, J. and C. Stinson, 1990. Toxicant extraction efficiency and branchial NaCl fluxes in lampreys exposed to Kepone. *Arch.Environ.Contam.Toxicol.*, 19: 307–313.

Mazeaud, M.M. and F. Mazeaud, 1981. Adrenergic responses to stress in fish. In: Pickering, A.D. (Ed.) *Stress and Fish*, pp.49–75. London, Academic Press.

Oronsaye, J.A.O. and A.E. Brafield, 1984. The effect of dissolved cadmium on the chloride cells of the gills of the stickleback, *Gasterosteus aculeatus* L. *J.Fish Biol.*, **25**: 253–258.

Pärt, P., H. Tuurala and A. Soivio, 1982. Oxygen transfer, gill resistance and structural changes in rainbow trout (*Salmo gairdneri*) gills perfused with vaso-active agents. *Comp.Biochem.Physiol.*, **71C**: 7–13.

Pascoe, D., S.A. Evans and J. Woodward, 1986. Heavy metal toxicity to fish and the influence of water hardness. *Arch.Environ.Contam.Toxicol.*, **15**: 481–487.

Pelgrom, S.M.G.J., L.P.M. Lamers, A. Haaijman, P.H.M. Balm, R.A.C. Lock and S.E. Wendelaar Bonga, 1994. Interactions between copper and cadmium during single or combined metal exposures in the teleost fish *Oreochromis mossambicus*. Heavy metal accumulation and endocrine events. (This volume).

Pickering, A.D., 1989. Environmental stress and the survival of brown trout, *Salmo trutta*. *Freshw.Biol.*, **21**: 47–55.

Pickering, Q.H. and M.H. Gast, 1972. Acute and chronic toxicity of cadmium to the fathead minnow (*Pimephales promelas*). *J.Fish.Res.Bd.Can.*, **29**: 1099–1106.

Pickering, A.D. and T.G. Pottinger, 1989. Stress responses and disease resistance in salmonid fish: effects of chronic elevation of plasma cortisol. *Fish Physiol.Biochem.*, **7**: 253–258.

Reid, S.D. and D.G. McDonald, 1988. Effects of cadmium, copper, and low pH on ion fluxes in the rainbow trout, *Salmo gairdneri*. *Can.J.Fish.Aquat.Sci.*, **45**: 244–253.

Schreck, C.B., 1981. Stress and compensation in teleostean fishes: responses to social and physical factors. In: Pickering, A.D. (Ed.) *Stress and Fish*, 295–321. London, Academic Press.

Schreck, C.B., 1982. Stress and rearing of salmonids. *Aquaculture*, **28**: 241–249.

Spry, D.J. and C.M. Wood, 1985. Ion flux rates, acid-base status, and blood gases in rainbow trout, *Salmo gairdneri*, exposed to toxic zinc in natural soft water. *Can.J.Fish.Aquat.Sci.*, **42**: 1332–1341.

Temmink, J.H.M., P.J. Bouwmeister, P. de Jong and J.H.J. van den Berg, 1983. An ultrastructural study of chromate-induced hyperplasia in the gill of rainbow trout (*Salmo gairdneri*). *Aquat.Toxicol.*, **4**: 165–179.

Van de Putte, I., M.B.H.M. Laurier and G.J.M. van Eijk, 1982. Respiration and osmoregulation in rainbow trout (*Salmo gairdneri*) exposed to hexavalent chromium at different pH values. *Aquat.Toxicol.*, **2**: 99–112.

Verbost, P.M., G. Flik, R.A.C. Lock and S.E. Wendelaar Bonga, 1987. Cadmium inhibition of Ca^{2+}-uptake in rainbow trout gills. *Am.J. Physiol.*, **253**: 216–221.

Verbost, P.M., G. Flik, R.A.C. Lock and S.E. Wendelaar Bonga, 1988. Cadmium inhibits plasma membrane calcium transport. *J.Membrane Biol.*, **102**: 97–104.

Wendelaar Bonga, S.E. and P.K.T. Pang, 1989. Pituitary hormones. In: Pang, P.K.T. and M.P. Schreibman (Eds.) *Vertebrate Endocrinology: Fundamentals and Biomedical Implications*, Vol. III, pp. 105–137. San Diego, California, Academic Press.

Wendelaar Bonga, S.E. and J.C.A. van der Meij, 1989. Degeneration and death, by apoptosis and necrosis, of the pavement and chloride cells in the gills of the teleost *Oreochromis mossambicus*. *Cell Tissue Res.*, **255**: 235–243.

Chapter 12
Sublethal effects of ammonia on freshwater fish

I. D. TWITCHEN and F. B. EDDY

Department of Biological Sciences, University of Dundee,
Dundee DD1 4HN, Scotland, UK

12.1   Introduction

Ammonia is a common pollutant of fresh waters originating from sources which include sewage effluent, industrial discharges, agricultural wastes, and as a natural end product of protein catabolism through intensive fish culture. It is highly poisonous to salmonids and symptoms of acute toxicity include hyperventilation, hyperexcitability, convulsions, loss of equilibrium, coma and death (World Health Organization, Environmental Health Criteria, 1986).

The chemistry of ammonia in freshwater has been extensively reviewed and ammonia toxicity to fish is usually expressed in terms of the NH_3 concentration (EIFAC, 1970; Alabaster and Lloyd, 1982; Erickson, 1985; WHO, 1986). Various water quality standards for ammonia have been proposed for salmonids (e.g. EIFAC, 1970; Seager *et al.*, 1988) based on lethal toxicity studies, or on sublethal effects such as reduced growth rate and gill damage. Based on a lowest lethal concentration of 200 $\mu g.l^{-1}$ NH_3 (EIFAC, 1970; Alabaster and Lloyd, 1982) healthy salmonid populations should occur where the 95 percentile concentration was below 25 $\mu g.l^{-1}$ NH_3 (EIFAC, 1970), a level where adverse effects were apparently absent. However concentrations lower than 200 $\mu g.l^{-1}$ NH_3 have been shown to be lethal to juvenile brown trout (*Salmo trutta*) (Taylor, 1973) and rainbow trout (*Oncorhynchus mykiss*) (Calamari *et al.*, 1981; Solbé and Shurben, 1989). Consequently the recommended water quality standards for ammonia are currently under review.

Gill studies suggest that NH_4^+ competes with Na^+ for entry to the fish (Maetz and Garcia-Romeu, 1964; Maetz, 1973), leading to ionic imbalance in the blood (Buckley *et al.*, 1979) and acid–base disturbances (Wright and Wood, 1985; Cameron and Heisler, 1983). In perturbing Na^+ balance it appears that the effects of NH_4^+ are similar to those of H^+ in acid rain studies (reviewed by Morris *et al.*, 1989). We therefore believe Na^+ balance status in fish to be a sensitive indicator of stress relating to the sublethal effects of ammonia. Our experiments were designed to provide a detailed study of sodium balance in juvenile salmonids and the way by which this is affected by ammonia. Results of such studies will be of help in recommending water quality standards.

Table 12.1   Composition of Dundee aquarium fresh water (mean values).

	mg.l^{-1}
Free CO_2	1.0
Alkalinity as $CaCO_3$	0.5
Total hardness as $CaCO_3$	31.2
Non-carbonate hardness as $CaCO_3$	10.6
Calcium as Ca	9.8
Magnesium as Mg	1.8
Chloride as Cl	10.7
Free ammonia as N	0.002
Sodium as Na	4.3
Potassium as K	0.7

12.2   Methods and materials

Rainbow trout of 10–30 g, fry and alevins, together with wild Atlantic salmon (*Salmo salar*) alevins, were obtained from Perthshire sources and maintained in flowing aerated Dundee aquarium fresh water (see Table 12.1 for composition) at 8–12°C, pH 7.4–9.3, 12:12 light/dark photoperiod and where relevant fed on ground up trout pellets.

For 10–30 g fish the flux measurement techniques of Wood *et al.* (1984) were used while for alevins and fry those of McWilliams and Potts (1978) were found to be more suitable. Both techniques use ^{22}Na to measure unidirectional Na$^+$ influx and efflux whose rates control Na$^+$ balance status. The fish are in net Na$^+$ loss when unidirectional Na$^+$ efflux rates are greater than Na$^+$ influx rates. The methods are non-invasive and measure perturbations in Na$^+$ balance of fish provoked by the presence of pollutants in the water.

Water sampling procedures, pH measurements and additions of NH$_4$Cl were arranged so that the fish were unaware of these operations, thus minimising disturbance stress. Water pH was measured using a Russell CTL/LCW electrode system specifically designed for measuring the pH of low ionic strength waters, even in the presence of ammonia. During experiments the pH was maintained at the required value by the addition of dilute H$_2$SO$_4$ or KOH. Total ammonia was determined by the phenol-hypochlorite method (Solorzano, 1969). Un-ionised and ionised concentrations of ammonia were calculated using pK$_a$ values and methods given by EIFAC (1970) and Alabaster and Lloyd (1982). The sodium concentration of the medium was determined by flame photometry. Table 12.1 shows the medium used in the experiments depicted in Figures 12.1, 12.2 and 12.3, and in Table 12.3, while Table 12.2 shows the medium used in the experiments depicted in Figures 12.4, 12.5 and 12.6, and in Table 12.4.

Table 12.2 Artificial river water medium (A) and sodium free artificial river water medium (B) for sodium uptake and efflux kinetic studies, made using appropriate salts added to deionised water. A range of external Na^+ concentrations were prepared by dilution of the artificial river water medium with Na^+ free medium or addition of NaCl.

	Medium A $(mg.l^{-1})$	Medium B $(mg.l^{-1})$
Na^+	4.6	0.0
Ca^{2+}	10.0	11.0
Cl^-	10.6	10.6
SO_4^{2-}	12.0	9.6
NO_3^-	12.4	6.2
CO_3^{2-}	4.5	4.5
Mg^{2+}	2.4	2.4
K^+	0.8	0.8
OH^-	0.3	0.3

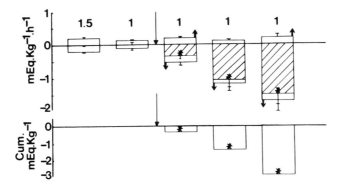

Fig. 12.1 Sodium fluxes for rainbow trout (10–30 g) in aquarium water (see Table 12.1) at 10°C, pH 7, during a control period (2.5 hours) followed by 3 hours ammonia exposure (long arrow) nominally 580 $\mu g.l^{-1}$ NH_3, showing a response within 1 hour. Fluxes are in $mEq.kg^{-1}.h^{-1}$. Values above the zero line are unidirectional influx while values below are unidirectional efflux. Net flux is indicated by the hatched column. The numbers above the columns indicate the period in hours over which the fluxes were measured. Mean and standard error are shown for n = 12. Also shown is the cumulative net loss or gain of sodium over the experimental period (below).
(*) within the hatched column indicates a significant difference between unidirectional Na^+ fluxes i.e. significant net Na^+ loss or gain.
Short arrow indicates a significant difference between control and test Na^+ fluxes. Student's t-test, paired or unpaired as appropriate, $P < 0.05$.

12.3 Results

For unexposed fish (pH 7) sodium efflux rates were balanced by influx rates, suggesting that the experimental protocol had no detectable disadvantageous effects upon this physiological parameter, and that the fish had settled in a 'relaxed' and stress-free way (e.g. first part of Fig. 12.1 and Table 12.3).

A potentially lethal concentration of 580 $\mu g.l^{-1}$ NH_3 (pH 7) (EIFAC, 1970;

Table 12.3 Effect of ammonia as NH_3 and as total ammonia (Tamm) on sodium loss and mortality for rainbow trout and wild salmon.

Treatment $NH_3 \mu g.l^{-1}$ (Tamm mg.l^{-1})	Mean body sodium lost or gained in 24 h mEq.kg^{-1}	% of body sodium lost or gained in 24 h	% mortality at 24 h
pH 7, 10–30 g trout			
Control	+0.259	+1.36	0
25 (14)	−0.175	−1.72	0
110 (64)	−0.338	−1.44	0
185 (105)	−2.564	−7.75	8.3
480 (273)	−7.35	−19.0	16.7
pH 8, 10–30 g trout			
control	+0.266	+0.6	0
540 (34)	−0.884	−4.55	9.1

Treatment $NH_3 \mu g.l^{-1}$ (Tamm mg.l^{-1})	Mean body sodium lost or gained in 48 h mEq.kg^{-1}	% of body sodium lost or gained in 48 h	% mortality at 48 h
pH 7, 0.13 g, Trout fry			
Control	+2.32	+4.65	0
100 (57)	−7.54	−15.0	8.3*
200 (114)	−21.6	−43.1	54.6*
pH 7, 0.58 g, Trout fry			
Control	+0.49	+0.97	0
25 (14)	+1.2	+2.4	0
50 (28.5)	−13.6	−27.1	0
100 (57)	−12.9	−25.9	30*
pH 7, Trout alevins			
Control	+5.504	+14.88	0
25 (14)	+8.621	+23.3	0
50 (28.5)	+10.67	+28.84	0*
100 (57)	−10.09	−27.3	0*
200 (114)	−20.18	−54.54	82*
pH 7, Salmon alevins			
Control	+3.73	+10.08	0
25 (14)	+3.015	+8.15	0
50 (28.5)	$+4.8 \times 10^{-3}$	+0.013	0*
100 (57)	−14.98	−40.5	68*
200 (114)	−	−	100* (within 24 h)

All experiments were carried out in aquarium water (see Table 12.1), at 10°C.

* indicates hyperexcitable behaviour

Alabaster and Lloyd, 1982; WHO, 1986), within an hour of exposure caused a strong net loss of Na^+ from 10–30 g trout, achieved by a significant stimulation of Na^+ efflux (Fig. 12.1), confirming that ammonia interferes with Na^+ balance.

Results from longer exposures (24 hours) to a range of ammonia concentrations at pH 7 are summarised in Table 12.3, which shows progressive mortalities and body Na^+ loss with increasing ammonia levels. Significant stimulation of Na^+ efflux and a net loss of Na^+ were observed at and above 110 $\mu g.l^{-1}$ NH_3 (pH 7), although Na^+ balance was re-established by the end of exposure at this concentration but not at higher concentrations (Table 12.3).

Unexposed fish showed virtually no change in Na^+ balance status at pH 8 compared to pH 7 (Table 12.3). However, ammonia effects were less pronounced, for example, at approximately 500 $\mu g.l^{-1}$ NH_3, the Na^+ imbalance was not as severe at pH 8 as at pH 7 (Table 12.3). This suggests that there is an ionised ammonia (NH_4^+) effect on Na^+ balance which agrees with the suggestion of Erickson (1985) that ammonia is unexpectedly less toxic at pH 8 compared to pH 7.

Rainbow trout fry showed similar ammonia responses to the 10–30 g fish, except they were much more sensitive (Table 12.3). After 48 hours' exposure to 200 $\mu g.l^{-1}$ NH_3 (pH 7) there was 43% body Na^+ loss with approximately 55% mortality. Similar though attenuated effects were evident at lower ammonia levels, and even at 50 $\mu g.l^{-1}$ NH_3 (pH 7) body Na^+ loss was 27% (Table 12.3). Transfer of fry between fresh water with no added ammonia and water containing 25 or 50 $\mu g.l^{-1}$ NH_3 (pH 7) showed elevated Na^+ efflux rates even at these low ammonia levels (Fig. 12.2). Fry showed ammonia-induced behavioural abnormalities, characterised by hyperexcitability at and above 100 $\mu g.l^{-1}$ NH_3 at pH 7 (Table 12.3).

The response of rainbow trout late alevins was similar to that of the fry, showing Na^+ imbalance at 100 $\mu g.l^{-1}$ NH_3 (pH 7) (Fig. 12.3, Table 12.3). Although late alevins were able to maintain a positive Na^+ balance at 25 and 50 $\mu g.l^{-1}$ NH_3

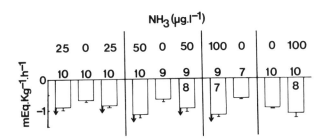

Fig. 12.2 Sodium efflux rates for rainbow trout fry (0.58 g) in aquarium water (Table 12.1) containing 0, 25, 50 or 100 $\mu g.l^{-1}$ NH_3 at 10°C, pH 7. Note that there are four separate experiments. The fry were exposed to 25 or 50 $\mu g.l^{-1}$ NH_3 for 24 hours then placed in ammonia free water for 24 hours before return to water with the original NH_3 level for a further 24 hours. In the case of 100 $\mu g.l^{-1}$ NH_3, the fry were exposed to this level initially for 24 hours then to ammonia free water for 24 hours, or vice versa. Numbers of fry starting the experiments are indicated above the columns, while numbers surviving the exposure, if different, are indicated within the columns.
Arrow indicates significant difference from the no-added-ammonia efflux value.

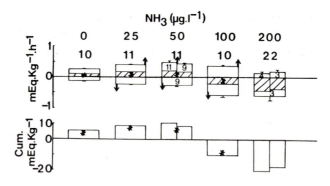

Fig. 12.3 Effect of increasing ammonia concentrations 0, 25, 50, 100 and 200 $\mu g.l^{-1}$ NH_3, on sodium fluxes for rainbow trout alevins (0.11 g) in aquarium water (Table 12.1) at 10°C, pH 7. Note that there are five separate experiments. Influx measurement for 24 hours followed by 24 hour efflux. At 200 $\mu g.l^{-1}$ NH_3 survivors were too few for statistical analysis of fluxes. Details as in Figure 12.1 except that the cumulative Na^+ loss or gain refers to the 48-hour flux period. Numbers of alevins starting the experiment are indicated above the columns while numbers surviving, if different, are indicated within the columns. Moribund alevins and hyperexcitable behaviour was observed at and above 50 $\mu g.l^{-1}$ NH_3.

(pH 7) they showed signs of stress. Sodium fluxes increased at both concentrations, while at 50 $\mu g.l^{-1}$ NH_3 (pH 7) hyperexcitability was observed with some late alevins entering a moribund state. Salmon late alevins were even more sensitive to ammonia than rainbow trout late alevins (Table 12.3).

For Atlantic salmon early alevins, Na^+ effluxes were significantly stimulated at and above 12.5 $\mu g.l^{-1}$ NH_3 (pH 7) and remained elevated upon return to ammonia-free water (Fig. 12.4). They were more tolerant to acute ammonia exposure than late alevins, however there were high mortalities during the post exposure period especially after exposure to 200 $\mu g.l^{-1}$ NH_3 (pH 7) (Fig. 12.4).

The hyperbolic relationship between Na^+ uptake and the external Na^+ concentration for rainbow trout (Fig. 12.5) is analogous to enzyme-substrate saturation kinetics and has been observed for many fish including brown trout (McWilliams, 1982), rainbow trout (Freda and McDonald, 1988) and Atlantic salmon (McWilliams and Shepherd, 1989). From the curve the kinetic parameters K_m and V_{max} were determined using the computational techniques of Wilkinson (1961) (Table 12.4). K_m is an indication of the relative affinity of the Na^+ transport system for Na^+ (the lower the K_m value the greater the affinity) while V_{max} is the maximum rate of Na^+ uptake at saturating external Na^+ concentrations. Relevant details of the kinetics of the Na^+ transport system are discussed by Twitchen (1990).

Using rainbow trout fry from the same population as above the effects of ammonia on the relationship between Na^+ uptake and the external Na^+ concentration were investigated and the results are summarised in Table 12.4. There was a progressive increase in K_m values with increased ammonia levels, resulting in a significant inhibition of Na^+ uptake at low external Na^+ concentrations (i.e. those normally found in fresh waters). Sodium uptake was reduced during three hours acute exposure by 10% at 50, 27% at 100 and 50% at 200 $\mu g.l^{-1}$ NH_3 (pH 7). Na^+ balance was achieved in ammonia exposed fish only at higher external Na^+ levels.

12.4 Discussion

The physiological effects of sublethal concentrations of ammonia have rarely been studied in relation to water quality, but in one of the few studies (Lloyd and Orr, 1969) a renal response was noted at about 100 $\mu g.l^{-1}$ NH_3 (pH 8), which was

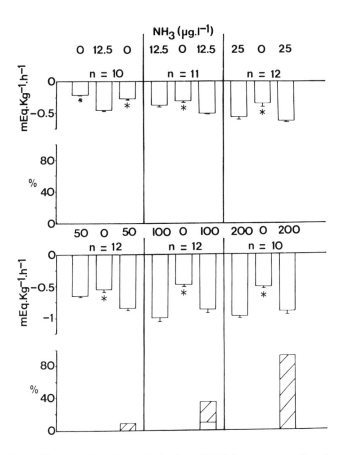

Fig. 12.4 Sodium efflux rates for salmon alevins in artificial river water medium (see Table 12.2) at 10°C containing 0, 12.5, 50, 100 and 200 $\mu g.l^{-1}$ NH_3 at pH 7. The alevins were exposed to ammonia for 24 hours then placed in ammonia-free water for 24 hours before return to water with the original NH_3 level for a further 24 hours. Note that one group was originally in ammonia-free water followed by transfer to 12.5 $\mu g.l^{-1}$ NH_3 before return to ammonia-free fresh water. Also shown is the percentage mortality during acute ammonia exposure and mortality three weeks post-exposure (hatched column). (*) significantly different from all other fluxes. (✳) significantly different from ammonia exposure fluxes. For other details see Figure 12.2. Hyperexcitable behaviour was observed at and above 50 $\mu g.l^{-1}$ NH_3.

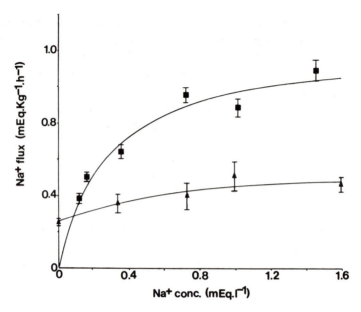

Fig. 12.5 The relationship between sodium fluxes and the external sodium concentration of the medium for rainbow trout fry in ammonia-free artificial river water (Table 12.2) at 10°C, pH 7. Each point represents the mean ±SE. For sodium influx (squares) and efflux (triangles) all data points n = 8. Sodium influx rates were measured for 2–3 hours and efflux rates for 12 hours at each external sodium concentration.

Table 12.4 The effect of ammonia at pH 7 on the kinetic parameters K_m and V_{max} for rainbow trout fry.

				K_m		V_{max}		Relative Aff Na$^+$ $1/K_m$
No added ammonia				0.263		1.214		3.8

$[NH_3]$ $\mu g.l^{-1}$	$[NH_4^+]$ $mEq.l^{-1}$	K_m^{app}	V_{max}^{app}	K_i	Aff NH$_4^+$ $1/K_i$	Relative Aff Na$^+$ Aff NH$_4^+$	% mortality during ammonia challenge
50	1.58	0.308	1.225	9.335	0.1071	35.5	12.5
100	3.16	0.398	1.222	6.154	0.1625	23.4	50
200	6.32	1.130	2.044	1.917	0.5218	7.3	100

Definition of terms

K_m is the Michaelis constant, the external Na$^+$ concentration at which Na$^+$ uptake is half the maximum.

V_{max} is the maximum rate of Na$^+$ uptake when the Na$^+$ transport system is operating at saturating external Na$^+$ concentrations.

$1/K_m$ is a measure of the affinity of the Na$^+$ transport system for Na$^+$.

K_m^{app} and V_{max}^{app} are the values of K_m and V_{max} in the presence of external ammonia.

K_i is the dissociation constant for the carrier/channel–ammonium ion complex.

$1/K_i$ is the affinity of the Na$^+$ transport system for NH$_4^+$.

stronger at higher ammonia levels. While a number of studies have used ammonia to explore the mechanisms of branchial ionic exchanges and ammonia excretion (Maetz and Garcia-Romeu, 1964; Maetz, 1973; McDonald and Prior, 1988; Avella and Bornancin, 1989), this is the first attempt to quantify sublethal ammonia effects using Na^+ balance as an indicator.

In agreement with previous work (Calamari *et al.*, 1981; Meade, 1985; WHO, 1986; Solbé and Shurben, 1989), rainbow trout alevins and fry were much more sensitive to ammonia compared with 10–30 g fish (Table 12.3). In terms of mortality, late alevins of rainbow trout and especially of salmon were even more sensitive to ammonia than fry (Table 12.3). Although Na^+ balance was maintained by alevins at 25 and 50 $\mu g.l^{-1}$ NH_3 (pH 7), it was at the expense of increased Na^+ fluxes (Fig. 12.3). Na^+ efflux rates are elevated in the presence of ammonia and the fish have to increase the Na^+ influx if they are to remain in Na^+ balance. This has profound implications for the fish during exposure to sublethal ammonia levels because more energy will be required for maintaining Na^+ balance, thus reducing the energy available for other important aspects of metabolism, possibly explaining the reduced growth rate observed during chronic exposures (reviewed by Meade, 1985; WHO, 1986).

Elevated Na^+ efflux shown by early salmon alevins during acute exposure, continued after return to ammonia-free water which may be linked to their post-exposure mortality (Fig. 12.4).

Ionised ammonia has been considered to be much less toxic than NH_3; however, its potential for perturbing Na^+ uptake and Na^+ balance is worth consideration, especially as an added stress to the effects of NH_3. Meade (1985) and WHO (1986) noted several studies where NH_4^+ toxicity was implicated. Such effects will be important in neutral and moderately acidic waters where relatively low and mildly toxic levels of NH_3 are accompanied by high levels of NH_4^+, sometimes up to several hundred ppm, far exceeding the concentration of existing cations particularly in soft and medium hardness waters, presumably partly explaining why ammonia effects at pH 8 are less severe than at pH 7 (Table 12.3).

Perturbation of Na^+ fluxes by NH_4^+ have been shown in goldfish (*Carassius auratus*) (Maetz and Garcia-Romeu, 1964; Maetz, 1973), crayfish (*Astacus pallipes*) (Shaw, 1960) and chironomid larvae (Wright, 1975) which support the present findings that increased external NH_4^+ interferes with Na^+ balance.

The increase in K_m with increased external ammonia (Table 12.4) is characteristic of competitive inhibition. The Dixon plot (Dixon and Webb, 1979; Fig. 12.6) demonstrates for the first time that the inhibition of Na^+ uptake by NH_4^+ in fish is competitive in nature. It should be noted that unionised ammonia (NH_3) cannot be a competitive inhibitor in this system.

The relative affinity of the Na^+ transport system for Na^+ ($1/K_m$) can be compared with its affinity for NH_4^+ ($1/K_i$) (Table 12.4). The dissociation constant for the carrier/channel–ammonium ion complex (K_i) can be calculated from the relationship:

$$K_i = \frac{[I]}{[(K_m^{app}/K_m) - 1]}$$

where

K_m^{app} is the value of K_m observed in the presence of the ammonium ion

$[I]$ is the concentration of NH_4^+

The relative affinity of the Na^+ transport system for NH_4^+ ($1/K_i$) increases with increasing external ammonia concentrations (Table 12.4), which is also reflected in the ratio of relative affinities of the Na^+ transport system for Na^+ and NH_4^+. These changes may indicate NH_4^+ induced variations in the existing Na^+ transport system which would have far reaching consequences in the study of ammonia toxicity.

The increase in V_{max} at 200 µg.l^{-1} NH_3 (pH 7) (Table 12.4) is characteristic of an ion depletion response (Maetz, 1973; Avella *et al.*, 1987; Twitchen, 1990) and is attributed to increased Na^+ carrier/channel activity (Stobbart, 1974; Maetz, 1973; Wright, 1975; Avella *et al.*, 1987; Twitchen, 1990) through Na^+ depletion and/or increased availability of intracellular counter ions, most probably NH_4^+.

On initial exposure of the fish to ammonia, Na^+ efflux is stimulated once external NH_3 has diffused into the body and ionised to NH_4^+, while external NH_4^+ competes with Na^+ for access to the branchial uptake sites and NH_4^+ entry to the fish will further stimulate Na^+ efflux. Thus while NH_3 is believed to be the more toxic species in the water, within the fish toxicity is related to the NH_4^+ concentration (WHO, 1986). There is a strong relationship between body Na^+ loss and mortality

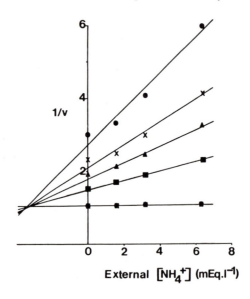

Fig. 12.6 A Dixon plot of the data derived from Table 12.4, to demonstrate the competitive nature of sodium uptake inhibition by ammonium ions in rainbow trout fry. The rate of sodium uptake is indicated by v. Note that the intersection of the lines for varying external Na^+ (denoted by different symbols) is indicative of competitive inhibition, see Dixon and Webb (1979).

for fish exposed to low pH, death usually occurring when about 50% of the body Na^+ is lost (e.g. Freda and McDonald, 1988). Therefore it is likely that the body Na^+ loss observed during ammonia exposure, especially for alevins and fry, is a major factor contributing to mortalities (Table 12.3).

In conjunction with Na^+ depletion, the body tissues will become loaded with NH_4^+, these effects resulting in increased activity of the Na^+ transport carriers/channels which have two major functions: (a) to replace lost Na^+ and (b) to remove internal NH_4^+ via Na^+/NH_4^+ exchange. Na^+ uptake via Na^+ channels is believed to be driven by an electrogenic proton pump (Avella and Bornancin, 1989; Lin and Randall, 1991) which predominates during normal physiological conditions but during ammonia exposure Na^+/NH_4^+ exchange increases (Cameron and Heisler, 1983; Wilson and Taylor, 1992). Although increased carrier/channel activity will stimulate Na^+ uptake (e.g. Fig. 12.3) it may have detrimental effects, for example, the uptake of NH_4^+ will also increase in proportion to Na^+ uptake, contributing to tissue ammonia loading which in severe cases leads to hyperexcitability, convulsions, coma and death.

This pattern of events is evident at all stages of the life history but early stages such as alevins and fry are the most sensitive. Alevins show hyperexcitability and fry are in significant Na^+ net loss at external NH_3 levels as low as 50 $\mu g.l^{-1}$ at pH 7 (Table 12.3). Sublethal effects of ammonia were evident even at 12.5 $\mu g.l^{-1}$ NH_3 (pH 7) where Na^+ efflux was significantly stimulated for early salmon alevins, indicating a physiological sensitivity to this low level (Fig. 12.4). If stimulation of Na^+ efflux is taken as an indication of sublethal ammonia effects, then these early stages of the life history are much more sensitive than had previously been believed.

Atlantic salmon alevins from a wild population were more sensitive than cultured rainbow trout alevins (Table 12.3). It is important, therefore, that future research should be directed at wild populations of endemic species such as Atlantic salmon and brown trout, so that realistic maximal environmental ammonia levels can be recommended which take into consideration their greater sensitivity.

In establishing recommendations for ammonia levels in fresh water the NH_4^+ fraction cannot be neglected, especially in neutral and acidic waters where the vast majority of the ammonia is in the ionised form. As suggested by Szumski *et al.* (1982) we believe that water quality standards for ammonia should be based not solely on the NH_3 concentration, but also on the total ammonia concentration. It has been suggested that ammonia levels should not exceed 25 $\mu g.l^{-1}$ NH_3 and total ammonia 1 $mg.l^{-1}$. However our study suggests that even these levels may be too high to prevent sublethal effects on salmonids, particularly wild populations.

Acknowledgement

This work was funded by the Department of the Environment, London.

References

Alabaster, J.S. and R. Lloyd, 1982. *Water Quality Criteria for Freshwater Fish*. 2nd edn, London, Butterworth.

Avella, M. and M. Bornancin, 1989. A new analysis of ammonia and sodium transport through the gills of the freshwater rainbow trout (*Salmo gairdneri*). *J.Exp.Biol.*, **142**: 155–175.

Avella, M. *et al.*, 1987. Gill morphology and sodium influx in the rainbow trout (*Salmo gairdneri*) acclimated to artificial freshwater environments. *J.Exp.Biol.*, **141**: 159–169.

Buckley, J.A., C.M. Whitmore and B.D. Liming, 1979. Effects of prolonged exposure to ammonia on the blood and liver glycogen of coho salmon (*Oncorhynchus kisutch*). *Comp.Biochem.Physiol.*, **63C**: 297–303.

Calamari, D., R. Marchetti and G. Vailati, 1981. Effects of long term exposure to ammonia in the developmental stages of rainbow trout (*Salmo gairdneri* Richardson). *Rapp.P.-v.Reun., Cons.Int.Explor.Mer*, **178**: 81–86.

Cameron, J.N. and N. Heisler, 1983. Studies of ammonia in the rainbow trout: physico-chemical parameters, acid–base behaviour and respiratory clearance. *J.Exp.Biol.*, **105**: 107–125.

Dixon, M and E.C. Webb, 1979. Enzymes. 3rd edn. London, Longman Green and Co., Academic Press.

EIFAC (European Inland Fisheries Advisory Commission), 1970. Water quality criteria for European freshwater fish. Report on ammonia and inland fisheries. *EIFAC Tech.Paper*, **11**, 12 pp.

Erickson, R.J., 1985. An evaluation of mathematical models for the effects of pH and temperature on ammonia toxicity to aquatic organisms. *Water Res.*, **19**: 1047–1058.

Freda, J. and D.G. McDonald, 1988. Physiological correlates of interspecific variation in acid tolerance to fish. *J.Exp.Biol.*, **136**: 243–258.

Lin, H. and D. Randall, 1991. Evidence for the presence of an electrogenic proton pump on the trout gill epithelium. *J.Exp.Biol.*, **161**: 119–134.

Lloyd, R. and L.D. Orr, 1969. The diuretic response by rainbow trout to sublethal concentrations of ammonia. *Wat.Res.*, **3**: 335–344.

Maetz, J., 1973. Na^+/NH_4^+, Na^+/H^+ exchanges and NH_3 movements across the gill of *Carassius auratus*. *J.Exp.Biol.*, **58**: 255–275.

Maetz, J. and F. Garcia-Romeu, 1964. The mechanism of sodium and chloride uptake by the gills of a freshwater fish *Carassius auratus*. Evidence for NH_4^+/Na^+ and HCO_3^-/Cl^- exchanges. *J.Gen.Physiol.*, **47**: 1209–1227.

McDonald, D.G. and E.T. Prior, 1988. Branchial mechanisms of ion and acid–base regulation in freshwater rainbow trout, *Salmo gairdneri*. *Can.J.Zool.*, **66**: 2699–2708.

McWilliams, P.G., 1982. A comparison of physiological characteristics in normal and acid exposed populations of the brown trout *Salmo trutta*. *Comp.Biochem.Physiol.*, **72A**: 515–522.

McWilliams, P.G. and W.T.W. Potts, 1978. The effects of pH and calcium concentrations on gill potentials in the brown trout *Salmo trutta*. *J.Comp.Physiol.*, **126**: 277–286.

McWilliams, P.G. and K.L. Shepherd, 1989. Kinetic characteristics of the sodium uptake mechanism during the development of embryos and fry of Atlantic salmon *Salmo salar* L., in an improved water quality. *J.Fish Biol.*, **35**: 855–868.

Meade, T.L., 1985. Allowable ammonia for fish culture. *Progr.Fish-Cult.*, **47**: 135–145.

Morris, R. *et al.*, 1989. *Acid toxicity and aquatic animals*. Cambridge, Cambridge University Press.

Seager, J., E. Wolff and V.A. Cooper, 1988. Proposed environmental quality standards for List II substances in water. – Ammonia, 260. WRC Technical Report TR.

Shaw, J., 1960. The absorption of sodium ions by the crayfish *Astacus pallipes* Lereboullet. III. The effect of other cations in the external solution. *J.Exp.Biol.*, **37**: 548–556.

Solorzano, L., 1969. Determination of ammonia in natural water by the phenol hypochlorite method. *Limnol.Oceanogr.*, **14**: 799–801.

Solbé, J.F. de L.G. and D.G. Shurben, 1989. Toxicity of ammonia to early life stages of rainbow trout (*Salmo gairdneri*). *Wat.Res.*, **23**: 127–129.

Stobbart, R.H., 1974. Electrical potential differences and ionic transport in the larvae of the mosquito *Aedes aegypti* (L.). *J.Exp.Biol.*, **60**: 493–533.

Szumski, D.S. *et al.*, 1982. Evaluation of EPA. Un-ionised ammonia toxicity criteria. *J.Wat.Poll.Contr.Fed.*, **54**: 281–291.

Taylor, J.E., 1973. Water quality and bioassay study from Crawford National Fish Hatchery. *Trans.Nebr.Acad.Sci.*, **2**: 176–181.

Twitchen, I.D., 1990. The physiological bases of resistance to low pH among aquatic insect larvae, pp. 413–419. In: Mason, B.J. (Ed.) *The Surface Waters Acidification Programme*. Cambridge, Cambridge University Press.

WHO (World Health Organization) 1986. Environmental Health Criteria 54. Ammonia. Geneva. 210 pp.

Wilkinson, G.N., 1961. Statistical estimations in enzyme kinetics. *Biochem.J.*, **80**: 324–332.

Wilson, R.W. and E.W. Taylor, 1992. Transbranchial ammonia gradients and acid–base responses to high external ammonia concentrations in rainbow trout (*Oncorhynchus mykiss*) acclimated to different salinities. *J.Exp.Biol.*, **166**: 95–112.

Wood, C.M., M.G. Wheatley and H. Hobe, 1984. The mechanisms of acid–base and ionoregulation in the freshwater rainbow trout during environmental hyperoxia and subsequent normoxia. III. Branchial exchanges. *Respir.Physiol.*, **55**: 175–192.

Wright, D.A., 1975. The effect of external sodium concentrations upon sodium fluxes in *Chironomus dorsalis* (Meig.) and *Camptochironomus tentans* (Fabr.), and the effect of other ions on sodium influx in *C. tentans*. *J.Exp Biol.*, **62**: 141–155.

Wright, P.A. and C.M. Wood, 1985. An analysis of branchial ammonia excretion in the freshwater rainbow trout: effects of environmental pH change and sodium uptake blockade. *J.Exp.Biol.*, **114**: 329–353.

Chapter 13
Stimulation of nonspecific immunity after immunosuppression induced by chemical stress in carp (*Cyprinus carpio*)

A.K. SIWICKI and M. STUDNICKA

Inland Fisheries Institute in Olsztyn, Ichthyopathology and Immunology Research Laboratory, Zabieniec near Warsaw, 05–500 Piasecno, Poland

13.1   Introduction

Investigations on the effects of environmental contamination on fish health have increased in recent years. In particular, chronic exposure to sublethal concentrations of heavy metals, pesticides or other chemicals has been suspected of increasing the sensitivity of fish to infectious diseases. Therefore, the study of sublethal and chronic effects of pollutants on the immune system in fish has become important.

Organophosphorus insecticides are widely used in agriculture, and are used in fisheries management for the control of populations of planktonic invertebrates and for the treatment and prevention of parasite infestation. Previous studies on the effects of organophosphorus compounds on fish health have concentrated on factors affecting their toxicity to fish, and the kinetics of elimination from the fish and the determination of withdrawal periods (Studnicka, 1970; Studnicka and Sopinska, 1983; Jeney and Jeney, 1986; Demael *et al.*, 1990). These organophosphorus insecticides are known to cause a specific inhibition of acetylcholinesterase, which in some cases is accompanied by the inhibition of neuro target esterase (Studnicka, 1970; Repetto *et al.*, 1988).

Trichlorfon and dichlorvos are the organophosphates most frequently used in aquaculture to eliminate ectoparasites on finfish. Trichlorfon is also used on crops and fields as an insecticide under the name Neguvon.

Many studies have been made on the effects of trichlorfon on the non-specific and specific immune system of carp (Cossarini-Dunier *et al.*, 1990; Siwicki *et al.*, 1990a). Trichlorfon depressed the nonspecific immune response of carp: a leucopenia was observed and also a decrease in the phagocytic activity of neutrophils and macrophages, as well as a decrease in lysozyme activity and an increase in the ceruloplasmin activity in serum (Siwicki *et al.*, 1990a). *In vitro* effects of trichlorfon on lymphocyte proliferation and phagocytic activity of macrophages showed a strong inhibition at concentrations greater than 12.5 ppm but there was no effect at 1 to 0.001 ppm (Cossarini-Dunier *et al.*, 1991).

Studies on humans and animals have demonstrated the effect of levamisole on the activity of immune cells, mainly during impaired immune function. Levamisole, an *in vivo* immunostimulator, has a potential use in the treatment and prophylaxis of fish diseases; the immune response was enhanced in fish injected intraperitoneally with levamisole (Siwicki, 1987). Application of levamisole in food or by immersion (in a bath) enhances the phagocytic activity of neutrophils and macrophages in fish (Siwicki, 1989; Siwicki *et al.*, 1989; Anderson *et al.*, 1989). An *in vitro* study showed an immunostimulatory effect of levamisole on the lymphocyte proliferation and macrophage activity in carp and rainbow trout (Siwicki and Cossarini-Dunier, 1990; Siwicki *et al.*, 1990b).

This study was performed to examine the immunomodulation effect of levamisole on the non-specific immunity in carp after immunosuppression induced by trichlorfon.

13.2   Materials and methods

13.2.1   *Fish*

Carp (*Cyprinus carpio*) weighing 100–120 g were purchased from the Inland Fisheries Institute in Zabieniec. They were maintained at 22°C. Fish were fed daily with carp commercial pellets at 3% of body weight.

13.2.2   *Experimental design*

Fish were distributed into three groups of 100 carp each. Carp from group I and II were kept in 1% solution of trichlorfon (95%, Bayer) for 30 min and fish from group III acted as the control. On day 5 after exposure, blood samples were collected from 10 fish of each group and non-specific defence mechanisms were examined. Fish from group I were then given levamisole (Polfa) in their food, at dose of 5 mg.kg^{-1} body weight, three times every 3 days. Blood samples were collected from 10 fish of each group at 9, 14, 21 and 28 days after the first application of levamisole.

13.2.3   *Assays of nonspecific defences*

Total leucocyte numbers, phagocytic ability of neutrophils (NBT index), percentage of NBT (Nitro Blue Tetrazolium) positive PMN cells, phagocytic index, myeloperoxidase (MPO) activity in neutrophils and lysozyme level in serum were determined.

The phagocytic ability of neutrophils (NBT index) was determined by a spectrophotometric method (Siwicki, 1989) and the percentage of NBT positive PMN cells was determined using the method of Sigma as modified by Siwicki (1989).

The phagocytic activity of macrophages (phagocytic index) was determined by a cytochemistry method (Siwicki, 1989) and lysozyme levels in serum were measured using the turbidimetric assay (Studnicka *et al.*, 1986).

The myeloperoxidase (MPO) activity in neutrophils was determined by the cytochemistry method of Sankowska *et al.* (1986).

Results are presented as mean values with their standard deviations. Statistical analysis was performed by Student's *t*-test. Mean differences compared to the control group were considered statistically significant at $P<0.05$.

13.3   Results

On day 5 after the trichlorfon exposure, fish from groups I and II showed a leucopenia (Fig. 13.1a) and decreases in the percentage of PMN cells NBT positive (Fig. 13.1b), in the phagocytic ability of neutrophils (Fig. 13.1c) and in the phagocytic index (Fig. 13.1d), as well as a decrease in myeloperoxidase activity in neutrophils (Fig. 13.1e) and in lysozyme levels in serum (Fig. 13.1f). The suppression of some non-specific defence parameters in fish from group II continued to the end of the experiment.

On day 9, four days after the application of levamisole to group I all immunological parameters were significantly increased in those fish, compared to the fish from group II. At days 14, 21 and 28, immunostimulation effects were observed in group I, compared to the control and group II.

13.4   Discussion

The addition of levamisole to the food of fish enhances their non-specific defence mechanisms after an immunosuppression induced by trichlorfon. This observation is important especially in view of the possibility that this treatment could be used to eliminate the depressive effects of sublethal and chronic pollutants on the immune responses of fish.

Similar immunomodulatory effects of levamisole have been observed in humans and animals (Simoens and Rosenthal, 1977). The drug eliminates a depressive effect of corticosteroids on the migration of peripheral blood leucocytes *in vivo* and *in vitro*. The spontaneous movement of PMN cells and monocytes from healthy humans was increased in the presence of levamisole (Schmidt and Douglas, 1976).

The results show that levamisole may be applied in practice for the enhancement of immune functions after an exposure of fish to trichlorfon.

Acknowledgement

Part of this work was financed by Project MR/USDA-91–66.

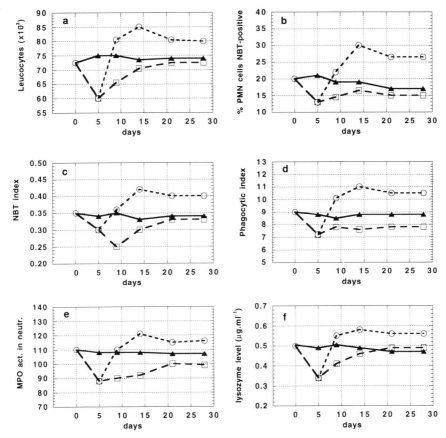

Fig. 13.1 Effect of levamisole administered at 5 mg.kg^{-1} to Group 1 (circles) on day 5 on selected blood parameters after immunosuppression induced by trichlorfon.
Squares: Group II exposed to trichlorfon, no levamisole treatment.
Triangles: Group III (control). Mean values of 10 fish in each group.

References

Anderson, D.P. *et al.*, 1989. Immunostimulation by levamisole in rainbow trout (*Salmo gairdneri*) *in vivo*. In: Ahne, W. and E. Kurstak (Eds.) *Viruses of Lower Vertebrates*, pp. 469–478. New York, Springer.

Cossarini-Dunier, M., A. Demael and A.K. Siwicki, 1990. *In vivo* effect of an organophosphorus insecticide: trichlorfon on immune response of carp (*Cyprinus carpio*). I. Effect of contamination on antibody production in relation with residue levels in organs. *Ecotoxicol.Environ.Safety*, **19**: 93–99.

Cossarini-Dunier, M., A.K. Siwicki and A. Demael, 1991. Effect of organophosphorus insecticides: trichlorfon and dichlorvos on immune response of carp (*Cyprinus carpio*). III. *In vitro* effect on lymphocyte proliferation and phagocytosis and *in vivo* effect on humoral response. *Ecotoxicol.Environ.Safety*, **22**: 79–87.

Demael, A., M. Dunier and A.K. Siwicki, 1990. Some effects of dichlorvos on carp metabolism. *Comp.Biochem.Physiol.*, **93**: 237–240.

Jeney, Z. and G. Jeney, 1986. Studies on the effect of trichlorfon on different biochemical and physiological parameters of common carp (*Cyprinus carpio*). *Aquacult.Hungarica*, **5**: 79–89.

Repetto, G., P. Sanz and M. Repetto, 1988. *In vivo* and *in vitro* effect of trichlorfon on esterases of the red crayfish *Procambarus clarkii. Bull.Contam.Toxicol.*, **41**: 16–22.

Sankowska, E., E. Chomiak and G. Turowski, 1986. Aktywnosc mieloperoksydazy (MPO) granulocytow obojetnochlonnych krwi obwodowej u dzieci i doroslych osob zdrowych. *Diagn.Lab.*, **1**: 49–56.

Schmidt, M.E. and S.D. Douglas, 1976. Effects of levamisole on human monocyte function and immunoprotein receptors. *Clin.Immunol.Immunopathol.*, **6**: 299.

Simoens, J. and M. Rosenthal, 1977. Levamisole in the modulation of the immune response: the current experimental and clinical state. *J.Reticuloendothel.Soc.*, **3**: 175–215.

Siwicki, A.K., 1987. Immunomodulating activity of levamisole in carp spawners, *Cyprinus carpio. J.Fish Biol., Suppl. A*, **31**: 245–246.

Siwicki, A.K., 1989. Immunostimulating influence of levamisole on non-specific immunity in carp (*Cyprinus carpio*). *Dev.Comp.Immunol.*, **13**: 87–91.

Siwicki, A.K. and M. Cossarini-Dunier, 1990. Effect of levamisole on the lymphocyte and macrophage activity in carp (*Cyprinus carpio*). *Ann.Rech.Vet.*, **21**: 95.

Siwicki, A.K., D.P. Anderson and O.W. Dixon, 1989. Comparisons of non-specific and specific immunomodulation by oxolinic acid, oxytetracycline and levamisole in salmonids. *Vet.Immunol. Immunopathol.*, **23**: 195–200.

Siwicki, A.K. *et al.*, 1990a. *In vitro* effect of an organophosphorus insecticide: trichlorfon on immune response of carp (*Cyprinus carpio*). II. Effect of trichlorfon on nonspecific immune response in carp (*Cyprinus carpio*). *Ecotoxicol.Environ.Safety*, **19**: 98–105.

Siwicki, A.K. *et al.*, 1990b. *In vitro* immunostimulation of rainbow trout (*Oncorhynchus mykiss*) spleen cells with levamisole. *Dev.Comp.Immunol.*, **14**: 231–237.

Studnicka, M., 1970. Investigation on the remnants of the phospho-organic compound Foschlor in tissues of fishes subjected to the treatment with this preparation. *Pol.Arch.Weterynaryjne*, **13**: 107–121.

Studnicka, M., and A. Sopinska, 1983. Toxicity of technical Foschlor for fish. *Rocznik Nauk Rol.*, **2**: 111–116.

Studnicka, M., A.K. Siwicki and B. Ryka, 1986. Lysozyme level in carp (*Cyprinus carpio*). *Bamidgeh*, **38**: 22.

SECTION B
LIFE CYCLE AND POPULATION
EFFECTS

Laboratory methods for the study of toxic effects of environmental pollutants to fish and other organisms are being discussed within the OECD as well as the EC. Five papers presented at the Symposium addressed this issue. As the results obtained by these laboratory methods will be used for environmental hazard and risk assessments of new chemicals which may be introduced into the environment, as well as for chemicals that are already in use, the methods must be selected with great care. Not only is the sensitivity of the methods important but also the cost because of the relatively large number of chemicals that have to be investigated; more than 100,000 industrial chemicals are presently on the market and for most of these our knowledge of their ecotoxicity is very limited. It should be noted that data on toxicity to fish are not only used for estimating toxic thresholds to natural fish communities but, combined with physical/chemical data and other toxicity data (especially on crustaceans and micro-algae), to estimate the chronic threshold concentrations for relevant ecosystem compartments.

Studies on 3,4-dichloroaniline and atrazine (substances having a specific mechanism of toxicity), as well as on chemicals with a more general, narcotic mode of action, indicate that the early life stages (especially larvae and early juveniles) are the most sensitive of those in the life cycle of fish. Only a very few exceptions to this general rule have been reported in the literature. At present, however, we have very little knowledge on effects of chemicals on end-points relevant to the population level and to fish species other than those commonly used for laboratory studies (zebrafish, guppy, fathead minnow and rainbow trout). Until more comprehensive knowledge is available, however, we are forced to evaluate the potential effects of chemicals on aquatic life by applying all available data, including that derived from the test methods in current use.

Applying test methods which incorporate fewer life stages than the full life cycle of fish will, for most chemicals, lead to a reduction in sensitivity. In all reported studies the egg stage has been shown to be the least sensitive of the different life stages. The sensitivity depends, however, on the duration of the egg stage, because eggs from cold-water species such as the rainbow trout have a relatively higher vulnerability to chemicals than the more commonly tested warm-water species such as the zebrafish and fathead minnow. The specific ecology of a species may however change this general picture of embryo sensitivity, as illustrated by the effects of ochre on the sediment-buried eggs of brown trout. Although a short-term version of the fish early life stage (FELS) test (the exposure of eggs and sac-fry) is nearly (within a factor of 3) as sensitive as the FELS test for most chemicals, the exposure period should be sufficient to allow chemicals (especially lipophilic ones) to reach a steady state in the test organism within the period of exposure. The possibility of obtaining (sub)chronic toxicity data after a six-day exposure period of egg and sac-fry of zebrafish by raising the temperature by 2–3°C should therefore be attempted only for low-lipophilic substances.

The ecological relevance of the laboratory toxicity testing methods, and of the end-points applied, is presently under considerable debate in international fora, and there is an urgent need for studies to compare the data obtained in the laboratory with field or semi-field studies, and with end-points identified by ecologists as being of higher relevance for the protection of natural populations. Contributions which highlight this issue include observations that effects which prove to be significant in the laboratory may not be ecologically significant if the fish then recover from the intoxication; also, a low percentage of mortality observed in the laboratory may not be significant for the survival of *r*-strategist fish populations.

Methods for identifying sources of pollution which are harmful to fish populations were suggested. One method includes an integrated chemical and ecotoxicological approach including short-term acute toxicity tests with *Daphnia magna* and histopathological, physiological and biochemical studies on fish (a biomarker approach). This is similar to the validated methods for the identification of pollutants in complex mixtures by integrating chemical analysis and short-term toxicity tests using early life stages of fathead minnow and *Ceriodaphnia*, which have been recently developed by the US Environmental Protection Agency. Combined approaches for the monitoring and identification of complex mixtures of chemicals are promising new tools which in future are expected to be superior to a reliance only on the traditional chemical analytical approach.

P. Kristensen, Session Chairman
J.Paláčková, Session Vice-Chairperson

Chapter 14
Sensitivity of embryos and larvae in relation to other stages in the life cycle of fish: a literature review

P. KRISTENSEN

Water Quality Institute, 11 Agern Alle, DK-2970 Hørsholm, Denmark

14.1   Introduction

According to the OECD, more than 100 000 organic chemicals are now being manufactured and used in the modern industrial society. For most of these chemicals, information on their potential hazard to aquatic life is lacking or is only insufficiently known. In order to prevent new hazardous substances from being introduced into the environment, most countries as well as international organisations have enacted legislation for regulating the release of these new chemicals, based on data for their environmental fate and toxicity to man and environment. The methods to be used for collecting information on toxicity to aquatic life are presently being discussed in the OECD, the EC and other international fora. In addition to physical/chemical information on the substance, the minimum amount of data required for an initial environmental hazard assessment includes data on the acute toxicity to algae, crustaceans and fish after short-term exposures. For substances which might be of risk to the environment, long-term studies are required to evaluate the chronic toxicity to the same taxonomic groups of organisms.

The primary objective of environmental hazard and risk assessments is to obtain concentration levels which will protect environmental life (ecosystems) even after long-term exposure. The acute and chronic toxicity data are therefore used to extrapolate to those concentration levels which not only protect algae, crustaceans and fish, but also other inhabitants of the various environmental compartments, as well as other endpoints of toxicity at higher levels of organisation: the population level (fecundity, age-structure, adaptation, etc.) and the community and ecosystem level (structure and function). Although a number of comparative studies on the toxicity of chemicals to single species and to ecological communities (mesocosms) have shown insignificant differences in toxicity threshold values, the present knowledge is far from sufficient with regard to 'safe' extrapolation from the acute and chronic no-effect levels for single species to the no-effect levels for entire ecosystems.

For fish, methods for estimating long-term toxicity are presently under debate, and as the primary objective for these methods is to estimate the *level* of no-observed-effect-concentrations (NOECs) for the entire life cycle of fish, the focus is on methods by which the NOEC may be most cost-effectively approached.

From life cycle studies on fish reported in the literature since 1967, it has been shown that the early life stages (embryo, sac fry and juveniles) of the fish are almost always the most sensitive to the impact of chemicals (McKim, 1977, 1985; Macek and Sleight, 1977; Woltering, 1984). McKim concluded that in 82% of the tests reported up to 1985, the lowest observed effect concentrations (LOECs) for the early life stages (embryos, sac fry and juveniles) were identical to the LOECs obtained for the complete life cycle of fish. For tests in which other stages were the most sensitive (reproduction, F_1-generation), the difference in sensitivity to the early life stages was within a factor of two. This conclusion was drawn by comparing the effects on offspring from non-exposed parental fish with the effects on the complete life cycle. The most sensitive endpoints for the early life stages were mortality and growth of larvae and juveniles followed by hatchability, chorion fragility and malformations of fry. Macek and Sleight (1977) concluded that, for substances without cumulative toxicity and having a single mode of action, the early life stages were identical or very similar in sensitivity when compared to other stages in the life cycle of fish.

Based on these two publications, fish early life stage tests (FELS tests) were accepted as a good predictor of effects on the complete life cycle of fish, and thereafter life cycle tests became very rare (Stephan, 1989).

The present review was carried out to evaluate the relative sensitivity of the early life stages of fish in particular to organic chemicals, and focuses on the possibility of estimating chronic NOECs within reasonable limits from results of so-called short-term FELS tests, where the embryo and yolk-sac stages are exposed without feeding for a duration which does not affect the nutrition of the larvae. Compared to FELS tests, where embryo, sac fry and part of the juvenile stages are exposed, the short-term version has the advantage of a short test duration (for warm water species 7–10 days compared to 28 days for the FELS test), that no external feeding is needed thus avoiding this often critical stage in laboratory-held fish, and that the relatively simple test technique will allow a number of laboratories other than fish specialists to generate data on chronic toxicity to fish, leading to a relatively high level of reproducibility and precision of the calculated toxicity.

14.2   Sources and treatment of data

The present literature review is based on data published in the period 1969–89. Of the more than 100 references obtained, those reporting data for separate fish early life stages (non-exposure of parental fish) were selected, comprising 134 FELS tests on 24 inorganic and 112 organic chemicals. The data base covers 4 marine and 11 freshwater fish species.

For the early life stages covered, the following definitions have been used:

Embryo   The period from fertilisation to time of hatch.

Sac fry   The free embryo stage (eleuthero embryo) in which the larva is nourished endogenously by the yolk sac, involving the period from the time of hatching to the time of complete absorption of the yolk sac.

Juvenile   The free (exogenous) feeding stage from yolk sac absorption until maturity.

The transition between the sac fry and juvenile stages is particularly difficult to define exactly, because free feeding is initiated before the yolk sac has been completely absorbed, and also the sac fry of a number of coldwater species (e.g. Salmonids) are able to survive without feeding for days after the swim-up stage of larval development.

14.3   Contribution of the embryonic stage to the susceptibility of early life stages

Table 14.1 shows the LOEC values obtained from comparative studies including and excluding, respectively, the embryonic stages. The LOECs are, as far as possible, based on the same endpoints. For seven of the nine compounds for which comparable data were available, the difference in LOEC values was within a factor of 2.

Only in studies with rainbow trout and pentachlorophenol, ammonia and nickel chloride did the embryonic stage contribute significantly to the overall LOEC. The relatively long egg developmental period for the cold-water species rainbow trout may facilitate a higher total uptake of toxicants through the permeable egg membrane as compared to warm-water species, thus resulting in a higher 'susceptibility' for coldwater eggs.

In none of the results referred to in Table 14.1 were malformations of the larvae reported. For substances which readily penetrate the egg membrane, the reason to include the egg stage would be to observe effects on early embryogenesis such as mortality (possibly in later stages), hatching and especially malformations or other developmental effects. As the uptake of toxicants might be facilitated during the period from fertilisation to water hardening of the egg, it would be very important to initiate the exposure to toxicants as quickly as possible after fertilisation. In ELS tests with copper, teratogenic effects were only seen when the experiment was started with eggs before they were water hardened (Blaxter, 1977, ref. in Van Leeuwen *et al.*, 1985).

In studies with fathead minnow and hydrazine, where newly fertilised eggs were exposed for 2 days, the hatched larvae showed reduced growth (length) and also malformations (Henderson *et al.*, 1981). Studies with pike and rainbow trout (Helder, 1980, 1981) also showed effects on the hatched larvae (deformations,

Table 14.1 Comparison between LOECs ($\mu g.l^{-1}$) derived from FELS tests including and excluding the embryo stage, respectively.

Species	Substance	Termination stage	End-point	LOEC excl emb (1)	LOEC incl emb (2)	Ratio $LOEC_1/LOEC_2$	Reference
Fathead minnow	Carbaryl	SacF.	W	810–1640	1890	0.4–1	Norberg-King (1989)
Fathead minnow	Diazinon	SacF.	W	172–347	>285	<≈1	Norberg-King (1989)
Fathead minnow	Chromium VI	SacF.	W	5560–5840	5490	≈1	Norberg-King (1989)
Fathead minnow	Dodecyl sulphate	SacF.	Surv	9200	4600	2	Pickering (1988)
Fathead minnow	Pentachlorophenol	SacF.	Surv	512	256–512	1–2	Pickering (1988)
Sheepshead minnow	Pentachlorophenol	SacF./Juv	Surv	45	66	≈1	Hughes et al. (1989)
Sheepshead minnow	Copper	SacF./Juv	W/Surv	249	253	≈1	Hughes et al. (1989)
Californian grunion	Chlorpyrifos	Juv	W	0.6	0.3	2	Goodman et al. (1985)
Rainbow trout	Pentachlorophenol	Juv	W	80	25	≈3	Hodson & Blunt (1981)
Rainbow trout	Ammonia	Juv	Surv	130*	<22	>6	Solbé & Shurben (1989)
Rainbow trout	Nickel chloride	Juv	W	700	35–431	≈2–20	Nebeker et al. (1985)
Rainbow trout	Nickel chloride	Juv	W	431**	35–431	1–12	Nebeker et al. (1985)

*   test initiated with 24-day-old embryos
**   test initiated with 25-day-old embryos
W   Weight
Surv   Survival
SacF. Sac fry
Juv   Juvenile

survival and growth) at very low concentrations (ng.l^{-1}) after exposing newly fertilised eggs for 4 days to 2,3,7,8-TCDD.

In none of the studies referred to were effects on embryos (mortality, hatching success, and hatching time) reported as the most sensitive endpoint. On the contrary, in most studies this endpoint stands out as the least sensitive of the endpoints observed in the ELS tests.

14.4   Contribution of the juvenile stage to the susceptibility of early life stages

Data from 33 experiments (27 substances and 5 species) were available for a comparison between the relative susceptibility of sac fry and juvenile endpoints within the same study (Table 14.2). All these data included were derived from studies initiated with fertilised eggs except for the study by DeFoe *et al.* (1978) on Aroclor, initiated with sac fry shortly after hatch. In Table 14.2, the relative sensitivity of the embryo–sac fry and embryo–sac fry–juvenile stages for these studies are shown. Also, the most and second most sensitive endpoint for each life stage are shown.

For 25% of the studies, identical LOECs were observed for the most sensitive endpoints for juvenile and sac fry respectively. By comparing the same endpoint for the two stages the same LOECs were observed for another 22% of the studies. Thus, in 47% of the studies the inclusion of the juvenile stage in FELS tests did not produce a lower LOEC than that derived from FELS experiments terminated at the end of the sac fry stage.

Accepting an arbitrary factor of 3 as a 'significance' level, the juvenile stage contributed significantly to the sensitivity of the FELS test for Diazinon, pentachlorophenol, aniline and chloroanilines, representing 4 out of the 24 chemical compounds or chemical groups (17%).

Aniline and chloroanilines have recently been studied by Van Leeuwen *et al.* (1990). These compounds have been classified as substances having a specific mode of toxic action, probably exerted by metabolic activation. Thus it might be expected that toxic effects will increase with the development/increase of enzymatic activity and probably with the gradual change from endogenic (sac fry) to exogenic (juvenile) nutrition. Also for Diazinon and pentachlorophenol (uncoupler of oxidative phosphorylation) a specific mode of action is probably involved (Macek and Sleight, 1977; Hodson and Blunt, 1981).

From the data referred to in Table 14.2, it may be concluded that for most of the chemicals tested, the inclusion of the juvenile stage enhances the sensitivity of the FELS test. The reduction in sensitivity by omitting the juvenile stage was within a factor of 3, however, of the sensitivity of sac fry endpoints for all bar those substances which have a specific mode of toxic action.

Table 14.2 Relative sensitivities of sac fry and juvenile stages in FELS tests. The ratio of LOECs for the second most and the most sensitive endpoint is given. Comparable endpoint: the ratio of LOECs for the same endpoints in sac fry and juveniles.

Species	Substance	Most sensitive stage and endpoint	Second most sensitive stage and endpoint	Comparable endpoint	Reference
Fathead minnow	2,4-DCP	S: Surv J: Surv	–		Holcombe et al. (1982)
Fathead minnow	Diazinon	J: Growth	S: Growth ≈7.5X	≈7.5X	Norberg-King (1989)
Fathead minnow	Carbaryl	J: Growth, Surv	S: Growth 1.2X	1.2X	
Fathead minnow	Propanil	J: Growth	S: Devel 4X	–	Call et al. (1983)
Fathead minnow	Aroclor 1248	J: Growth S: Surv	–		Defoe et al. (1978)
Fathead minnow	Aroclor 1260	J: Growth	S: Surv 3X	1X	Spehar et al. (1983)
Fathead minnow	Permetrin	J: Surv S: Surv	–		
	AC 222.705	J: Growth S: Devel	–		
Sheepshead minnow	Permetrin	J: Surv S: Surv	–		Hansen et al. (1983)
	AC 222.705	J: Surv, Growth S: Surv	–		
Rainbow trout	Fenvalerat	J: Growth	S: Surv 1.8X	–	Curtis et al. (1985)
Rainbow trout	Fenvalerat	J: Growth	S: Growth, Surv 1.7X	1.7X	Mayes et al. (1987)
Rainbow trout	Picloram	J: Growth	S: Surv >2.2X	–	Hodson & Blunt (1981)
Rainbow trout	Pentachlorophenol	J: Growth	S: Growth 3.2X	3.2X	Norberg-King (1989)
Fathead minnow	Cr (VI)	J: Growth	S: Growth 1.8X	1.8X	Macek & Sleight (1977)
Rainbow trout	Cr (VI)	J: Weight	S: Length 8X	2 X	Davies et al. (1978)
Rainbow trout	Silver	J: Growth, Surv S. Devel	–		

Table 14.2 Continued.

Species	Substance	Most sensitive stage and endpoint	Second most sensitive stage and endpoint	Comparable endpoint	Reference
Rainbow trout	Nickel	J: Growth	S: Devel 1–6.8X	–	Nebeker *et al.* (1985)
Rainbow trout	Ammonia	J: Surv S: Surv	–		Solbé & Shurben (1989)
Green sunfish	Ammonia	J: Growth, Surv	S: Surv, Devel <1.8X	<1.8X	McCormick *et al.* (1984)
Fathead minnow	Methylene chloride	J: Growth	S: Surv 2.3X	1.5X	Dill *et al.* (1987)
Zebrafish	Aniline	J: Length	S: Surv 10X	3.2X	Van Leeuwen *et al.* (1990)
Zebrafish	3-Chloro-A	J:Length	S:Surv 10X	1.8X	Van Leeuwen *et al.* (1990)
Zebrafish	2,3,4,5-Tetrachloro-A	J: Length	S: Surv >10X	5.7X	Van Leeuwen *et al.* (1990)
Zebrafish	2,4,5-Trichloro-A	J: Length, Surv	S: Surv >10X	>10X	Van Leeuwen *et al.* (1990)
Zebrafish	3,5-Dichloro-A	J: Length	S: Surv 17.5X	5.6X	Van Leeuwen *et al.* (1990)
Zebrafish	Pentachloro-A	J: Length, Surv	S: Surv 5.6X	5.6X	Van Leeuwen *et al.* (1990)
Zebrafish	Chlorobenzene	J: Length	S: Surv 1.8X	1X	Van Leeuwen *et al.* (1990)
Zebrafish	1,4-Dichlorobenzene	J: Length	S: Surv 3.2X	1X	Van Leeuwen *et al.* (1990)
Zebrafish	1,2,3-Trichlorobenzene	J: Length	S: Surv 1.8X	1X	Van Leeuwen *et al.* (1990)
Zebrafish	1,2,3,4-Tetrachlorobenzene	J: Length	S: Surv 2.8X	1X	Van Leeuwen *et al.* (1990)
Zebrafish	Pentachlorobenzene	J: Length	S: Surv 3.2X	1X	Van Leeuwen *et al.* (1990)
Zebrafish	4-Chlorotoluene	J: Length	S: Surv 3.2X	1.8X	Van Leeuwen *et al.* (1990)

S: sac fry. J: juvenile

		RELATIVE SENSITIVITY OF ENDPOINTS	
		SAC FRY STAGE	JUVENILE STAGE
	NO. OF EXPERIM.	24 exp.	74 exp.
	"Growth" Single most sensitive	42% (10 exp.)	70% (52 exp.)
Two (or more) endpoints recorded	Next most sensitive: ENDPOINT	SURVIVAL (100%) 60 % : ≤3x 20 % : 3-6 20 % : >6	SURVIVAL (100%) 65%: ≤3x 22%: 3-6x 13%: >6x
	SURVIVAL and/or DEVELOPMENT Single most sensitive	16% (4 exp.) 1 exp: SURV. + DEV. 3 exp: DEVELOPMENT	11% (8 exp.) 8 exp: SURVIVAL
	Next most sensitive: ENDPOINT	Growth (1): 1.8x Surv.(3):>20x,2x,4x	Growth: 7 exp: ≤3x 1 exp: 4x
	Survival and growth equally sensitive	42% (10 exp.)	19% (14 exp.)
	NO. OF EXPERIM.	55 exp.:	9 exp.:
One endpoint recorded only	Frequency of endpoints applied	SURVIVAL: 80% GROWTH: 18% OTHER: 2%	SURVIVAL: 44% GROWTH: 56%

Fig. 14.1 Relative sensitivity of endpoints in sac fry and juveniles, respectively. The per cent values given refer to the number of experiments included. In the boxes a relative distribution (% values) are given together with the factor of differences between the second most and the most sensitive endpoint.

14.5   Relative sensitivity of endpoints of toxicity

Woltering concluded in his review (1984) that 'survival' was as sensitive (or insignificantly less sensitive) as 'growth', and since then a considerable emphasis has been placed on the question of whether or not the growth response in particular should be included in FELS tests as a 'cost-effective' endpoint.

In Figure 14.1 the relative sensitivity of the endpoint 'growth' (measured as either length or weight) is compared to 'survival' for the sac fry and juvenile stage, respectively.

For the experiments in which the toxicity to sac fry was reported, two or more endpoints were measured in only 20% of the studies; growth was the single most sensitive endpoint in 42% of these, and was as sensitive as survival in another 42%. Thus, in more than 80% of the experiments reporting the effects on two or more endpoints (20 out of 24 experiments), growth was significantly affected at LOEC level for the study.

For experiments covering the exposure of embryo to juveniles, 74 experiments (89%) reported the toxicity for two or more endpoints. Growth was the single most sensitive in 70%, survival the single most sensitive in 11%, and the two endpoints were equally sensitive in 19% of these experiments. Thus in nearly 90% of the tests, effects on growth were recorded at the LOEC for the juvenile stage.

For the juvenile stage, the next most sensitive endpoint to growth was survival, and in 35% of the experiments having growth as the single most sensitive endpoint, survival was more than a factor of 3 less sensitive. For 11% of the experiments having survival as the single most sensitive endpoint, growth was less sensitive by a factor of 3 in only one of the eight experiments.

Thus growth (weight or length) was very important in determining the LOEC, since more than 98% of the reported experiments showed growth to be within a factor of 3 of the lowest LOEC recorded for the different endpoints, the corresponding value for survival being 75%.

14.6   Discussion

For the hazard assessment of chemicals, cost-effective screening methods are needed to obtain data which can predict chronic toxicity to fish. A full life cycle test on populations of fish is the ultimate choice for obtaining the required data, but such tests are very time-consuming and therefore costly. It is therefore important at an early stage of testing to have alternative methods available which are more cost-effective, i.e. which can, for the majority of compounds, predict their chronic toxicity to fish within an acceptable range, and at low cost.

The data published up to 1989 indicate that for narcotic industrial chemicals, a short-term FELS test with survival of larvae, developmental effects and growth as endpoints will have a predictive capacity within relatively narrow limits for estimating the chronic effect threshold for fish. Narcosis is considered to be a non-specific and reversible physiological effect independent of chemical structure. The primary effects are expected to be a decreased nervous response and reduced respiratory activity (Call *et al.*, 1985). The following chemical groups have all been characterised as acting by narcosis (Veith and Call, 1984): aliphatic and aromatic hydrocarbons, chlorinated hydrocarbons, alcohols, ethers, ketones, aldehydes and some of the aliphatic nitrocompounds.

A comparison between the LOECs obtained from the embryo–sac fry portion of 33 FELS tests and the LOECs for the entire FELS test showed that the inclusion of the juvenile stage reduced the observed LOEC value by more than the usual factor between test concentration intervals (3.2) for diazinon (7.5×), propanile (4×) and chlorinated anilines (5.6–10×). For these substances, it has been shown that either there are specific effect mechanisms at work via a specific mode of action, or the toxic effects are dependent on metabolic conversion and thus depend on the presence of specific enzymatic activities in the target organisms (Van Leeuwen *et al.*, 1990; Call *et al.*, 1983; Norberg-King, 1989).

It has been shown by Van Leeuwen *et al.* (1985) that substantial changes may take place in enzymatic activities during the transition between internal and external nutrition of the larvae. The question is therefore whether toxic effects of compounds with specific effect mechanisms will show up in the sac fry stage, or whether the target sites/necessary enzymatic systems will have to be developed as the larvae progress from yolk sac feeding to an external food source. Thus, to pick up toxic effects exerted by non-narcotic substances in the short-term FELS method, it is essential to focus not only on lethality but also on sublethal effects (growth, effects on development), and to extend the test duration as close to the free-feeding stage as possible without affecting survival due to lack of food. Increased mortality due to starvation for sac fry of zebrafish will be initiated 11–12 days after fertilisation (at 25–27°C) according to Dave *et al.* (1987).

The observation that growth is an important endpoint is not surprising as sublethal effects (reduced growth, retarded yolk absorption, malformations, etc.) would be expected at concentrations below those causing mortality. LOECs for sublethal effects would thus be expected at or below the LOEC for survival. Failure to find sublethal effects at concentration levels below the LOEC for survival might be due particularly to a high variability in these endpoints within the test population.

In addition to the conclusion by Woltering (1984) that survival as an endpoint was a cost-effective replacement for growth, several authors have questioned the utility of using growth as an endpoint at the juvenile stage, especially as feeding of the larvae is one of the complicating variables which might impair the reproducibility of the growth parameter. Increased growth at concentrations which cause partial mortality is often seen for sheepshead minnow due to increased food and space for the remaining individuals (Hansen *et al.*, 1983). Also, variability in the quality of food and the feeding regimes may influence growth rates (Woltering, 1984). These concerns call for a more precise description of feeding regimes than are now seen in the various guidelines for FELS tests, as well as in other methods used for chronic toxicity studies with fish.

Thus, a short-term FELS test with zebrafish might be a favourable choice to obtain an initial estimate of chronic toxicity levels of chemicals for hazard assessment purposes or at a relatively early stage of environmental risk assessment. The applicability of this type of method for the regulation of chemicals should however be linked to a firm strategy for passing substances on from an initial level of testing (acute toxicity to fish) to higher levels including more advanced testing (FELS and/or other chronic tests). Accumulated effects which do not reach equilibrium within the test period, or effects observed late in the sac fry stage (increased mortality, abnormalities of larvae), would indicate a non-narcotic action of substances, thus triggering the requirement for additional information at the next level of testing. In addition to obtaining knowledge about the effect mechanisms, this information might include data on the toxic effects to other stages of the fish life cycle (e.g. reproduction).

Acknowledgements

The review was performed under contract with the Commission of the European Communities.

References

Call, D.J., L.T. Brooke, R.J. Kent, M.L. Knuth, C. Anderson and C. Moriarity, 1983. Toxicity, bioconcentration, and metabolism of the herbicide propanil (3', 4'- dichloropropionanilide) in freshwater fish. *Arch.Environ.Contam.Toxicol.*, **12**: 175–182.

Call, D.J., L.T. Brooke, M.L. Knuth, S.H. Poirier and M.D. Hoglund, 1985. Fish subchronic toxicity prediction model for industrial organic chemicals that produce narcosis. *Environ.Toxicol.Chem.* **4**: 335–341.

Curtis, L.R., W.K. Seim and G.A. Chapman, 1985. Toxicity of fenvalerate to developing steelhead trout following continuous or intermittent exposure. *J.Toxicol.Environ.Health*, **15**: 445–457.

Dave, G., B. Damgaard, M. Grande, J.E. Martilin, B. Rosander and T. Viktor, 1987. Ring test of an embryo-larval toxicity test with zebrafish (*Brachydanio rerio*) using chromium and zinc as toxicants. *Environ.Toxicol.Chem.*, **6**: 61–71.

Davies, P.H., J.P. Goettl, Jr. and J.R. Sinley, 1978. Toxicity of silver to rainbow trout (*Salmo gairdneri*). *Water Res.*, **12**: 113–117.

DeFoe, D.L., G.D. Veith and R.W. Carlson, 1978. Effects of aroclor 1248 and 1260 on the fathead minnow (*Pimephales promelas*). *J.Fish.Res.Board Can.*, **35**: 997–1002.

Dill, D.C., P.G. Murphy and M.A. Mayes, 1987. Toxicity of methylene chloride to life stages of the fathead minnow *Pimephales promelas* Rafinesque. *Bull.Environm.Toxicol.*, **39**: 869–876.

Goodman, L.R., D.J. Hansen, G.M. Cripe, D.P. Middaugh, and J.C. Moore, 1985. A new early life-stage toxicity test using the California grunion (*Leuresthes tenuis*) and results with chlorpyrifos. *Ecotoxicol.Environ.Safety*, **10**: 12–21.

Hansen, D.J., L.R. Goodman, J.C. Moore and P.K. Higdon, 1983. Effects of the synthetic pyrethroids AC 222,705, permethrin and fenvalerate on sheepshead minnows in early life stage toxicity tests. *Environ.Toxicol.Chem.*, **2**: 251–258.

Helder, T., 1980. Effects of 2,3,7,8-tetrachlorodibenzo-p-dioxin (TCDD) on early life stages of the pike (*Esox lucius* L.). *The Science of the Total Environment*, **14**: 255–264.

Helder, T., 1981. Effects of 2,3,7,8-tetrachlorodibenzo-p-dioxin (TCDD) on early life stages of rainbow trout (*Salmo gairdneri*, Richardson). *Toxicology*, **19**: 101–112.

Henderson, V., J.W. Fisher and R. D'Allessandris, 1981. Toxic and teratogenic effects of hydrazine on fathead minnow (*Pimephales promelas*) embryos. *Bull.Environm.Contam.Toxicol.*, **26**: 807–812.

Hodson, P.V. and B.R. Blunt, 1981. Temperature-induced changes in pentachlorophenol chronic toxicity to early life stages of rainbow trout. *Aquat.Toxicol.*, **1**: 113–127.

Holcombe, G.W., G.L. Phipps and J.T. Fiandt, 1982. Effects of phenol, 2,4-dimethylphenol, 2,4-dichlorophenol, and pentachlorophenol on embryo, larval, and early-juvenile fathead minnows (*Pimephales promelas*). *Arch.Environ.Contam.Toxicol.*, **11**: 73–78.

Hughes, M.M., M.A. Heber, G.E. Morrison, S.C. Schimmel and W.J. Berry, 1989. An evaluation of a short-term chronic effluent toxicity test using sheepshead minnow (*Cyprinodon variegatus*) larvae. *Environ.Pollution*, **60**: 1–14.

McCormick, J.H., S.J. Broderius and J.T. Fiandt, 1984. Toxicity of ammonia to early life stages of the green sunfish *Lepomis cyanellus*. *Environm.Poll.(Series A)*, **36**: 147–163.

Macek, K.J. and B.H. Sleight, III, 1977. Utility of toxicity tests with embryos and fry of fish in evaluating hazards associated with the chronic toxicity of chemicals to fishes. In: Mayer, F.L. and J.L. Hamelink (Eds.) *Aquatic Toxicology and Hazard Evaluation*, pp. 137–146. ASTM STP 634. Philadelphia, American Society for Testing and Materials.

McKim, J.M., 1977. Evaluation of tests with early life stages of fish for predicting long-term toxicity. *J.Fish.Res.Board Can.*, **34**: 1148–1154.

McKim, J.M., 1985. Early life stage toxicity tests. In: Rand, G.M. and S.R. Petrocelli (Eds.) *Fundamentals of Aquatic Toxicology*, pp. 58–94. Washington DC, Hemisphere Publishing.

Mayes, M.A., D.L. Hopkins and D.C. Dill, 1987. Toxicity of picloram (4-amino-3,5,6-trichloropicolinic acid) to life stages of the rainbow trout. *Bull.Environ.Contam.Toxicol.*, **38**: 653–660.

Nebeker, A.V., C. Savonen and D.G. Stevens, 1985. Sensitivity of rainbow trout early life stages to nickel chloride. *Environ.Toxicol.Chem.*, **4**: 233–239.

Norberg-King, T.J., 1989. An evaluation of the fathead minnow seven-day subchronic test for estimating chronic toxicity. *Environ.Toxicol.Chem.*, **8**: 1075–1089.

Pickering, Q.H., 1988. Evaluation and comparison of two short-term fathead minnow tests for estimating chronic toxicity. *Water Res.*, **22**: 883–893.

Solbé, J.F. de L.G. and D.G. Shurben, 1989. Toxicity of ammonia to early life stages of rainbow trout (*Salmo gairdneri*). *Water Res.*, **23** (1): 127–129.

Spehar, R.L., D.K. Tanner and B.R. Nording, 1983. Toxicity of the synthetic pyrethroids, permethrin and AC 222,705 and their accumulation in early life stages of fathead minnows and snails. *Aquat.Toxicol.*, **3**: 171–182.

Stephan, C.E., 1989. Topics on expressing and predicting results of life-cycle tests. *Aquat.Toxicol.Environm.Fate*, **11**: 263–272. ASTM STP 1007. Suter II, G.W. and M.A. Lewis (Eds.). Philadelphia, American Society for Testing and Materials.

Van Leeuwen, C.J., P.S. Griffioen, W.H.A. Vergouw and J.L. Maas-Diepeveen, 1985. Differences in susceptibility of early life stages of rainbow trout (*Salmo gairdneri*) to environmental pollutants. *Aquat.Toxicol.*, **7**: 59–78.

Van Leeuwen, C.J., D.M.M. Adema and J. Hermens, 1990. Quantitative structure-activity relationships for fish early life stage toxicity. *Aquat.Toxicol.*, **16**: 321–334.

Veith, G.D. and D.J. Call, 1984. Estimating the acute toxicity of narcotic industrial chemicals to fathead minnow. US Environmental Protection Agency, EPA 600/D-84-190.

Woltering, D.M., 1984. The growth response in fish chronic and early life stage toxicity tests: A critical review. *Aquat.Toxicol.*, **5**: 1–21.

Chapter 15
The embryo-larval test with zebrafish (*Brachydanio rerio*): validity, limits and perspectives

T. MEINELT and G. STAAKS

Institute of Freshwater Ecology and Inland Fisheries, Aquaculture and Fish Pathology Section, Müggelseedamm 310, D-12587 Berlin-Friedrichshagen, Germany

15.1   Introduction

Pollution of aquatic ecosystems is increasingly recognised as being caused by numerous chemicals which have not only acute but also chronic or subchronic harmful effects on fish populations. Tests for determining the acute toxicity of xenobiotics with adult life forms in order to compile classification schemes are no longer up-to-date and useful for environmental management; these should be replaced by tests with eggs and sensitive early developmental stages. Therefore, early-life-stage (ELS) tests and embryo-larval tests (ELT) are considered to be suitable methods for the determination of acute and subchronic toxicity of xenobiotics, and a substitute for acute tests. The growing number of chemicals that need to be tested requires cheap and rapid test methods, coupled with a high quantity and quality of data, if possible.

Due to seasonal limitations, and the associated long generation intervals and substantial test durations of ELT and ELS tests, the use of local commercial fish cannot provide quick, comprehensive and comparable data on the acute or subchronic potential harm of environment chemicals. Among alternative species of internationally approved test fish, preference should be given to the zebrafish (*Brachydanio rerio*) (as approved by ISO and other institutions) which seems to be suitable for ELT and ELS tests.

15.2   Methods

15.2.1   *Test animals*

The fish used in toxicity tests was the zebrafish (*Brachydanio rerio*), family Cyprinidae, sub-family Rasborinae.

15.2.2   *Pretest conditions*

The parental fish were stored in vessels of a sufficient volume. These holding vessels were equipped with continuous water supply, filtration, aeration, and

Table 15.1   Characteristics of tap water and reconstituted water used in the ELT.

	Tap water	Reconstituted water
oxygen concentr. $mg.l^{-1}$	>5 <8	>5 <8
pH value	7.3	6.75
hardness as $CaCO_3$ $mg.l^{-1}$	308.8	62.5
alkalinity as $CaCO_3$ $mg.l^{-1}$	169.6	33.9
NO_3^- $mg.l^{-1}$	4.3	0.2
NO_2^- $mg.l^{-1}$	<0.02	<0.02
NH_4^+ $mg.l^{-1}$	<0.1	<0.05
temperature °C	26–27	26–27

temperature control facilities. Oxygen concentrations up to 8 $mg.l^{-1}$ and temperatures between 24 and 26°C were maintained, and pH values were between 7.3 and 7.8. Because of the flow-through conditions, NO_2^- and NH_4^+ levels were maintained at close to detectable limits. Fish diet was important; nutrition of the parental fish influences the quality and quantity of fish eggs. Providing high quality eggs is necessary for securing a good reproducibility of the experimental results. High percentages of oocytes and unfertilised eggs affect the experimental data and complicate handling. The quality and accuracy of results from the ELT depend on the age and nutritional state of parents used for reproduction. To secure favourable spawning conditions, fish were fed with commercial trout food, newly hatched brine shrimp, tubifex worms and copepods.

Two main methods were used to obtain zebrafish eggs. Method I was carried out in the holding tanks, using egg traps. Flat PE chambers covered with nylon net were placed in the holding tanks; the spawning ground was established by applying *Vesicularia* sp. to the nylon net. To carry out method II, groups of two males and one female were allocated to darkened spawning aquaria in the evening. In both methods, the temperature was raised by 2°C and fish were fed intensively with natural live food. Spawning occurred after daybreak. The parental age was between 20 and 50 weeks; younger and older fish usually provide insufficient test material. After spawning, the eggs were removed with special care and rinsed with temperature controlled dilution water to remove uneaten food and excrement. To examine the influence of water composition, two dilution waters were used (Table 15.1).

Toxicity tests were performed with several reference chemicals, e.g., phenol, pentachlorophenol, dinitrophenol and copper, of reagent grade quality. Because of local requests, some chemicals used in inland fisheries management were also examined.

15.2.3   *Test procedure*

Each compound was tested at six concentrations using hard and soft water. Exposure began when the eggs reached the four-cell stage or the flat-blastula stage.

Table 15.2 LOEC and NOEC of reference chemicals against zebrafish in dependence of water composition and developmental stage of the eggs (all concentrations in mg.l^{-1}).

Substance	Dilution water			
	Tap water		Reconstituted water	
	Four-cell stage	Blastula	Four-cell stage	Blastula
Copper				
LOEC	0.150	0.100	0.050	0.050
NOEC	0.100	0.050	<0.050	<0.050
Phenol				
LOEC	20.0	20.0	80.0	80.0
NOEC	<20.0	<20.0	40.0	40.0
Pentachlorophenol				
LOEC	0.005	0.005	0.005	0.005
NOEC	<0.005	<0.005	<0.005	<0.005
2,4-Dinitrophenol				
LOEC	–	–	1.0	1.0
NOEC	>16.0	>16.0	<1.0	<1.0

This meant that the experiments began 30 minutes or two hours after fertilisation. The tests were terminated 6 days later, when the larvae still contain yolk, and swim free. Control eggs were cultured simultaneously with the experimental eggs under identical conditions. Each test vessel contained 20 eggs. Four vessels were used at each concentration. To secure a high reproducibility, all experiments were repeated three times. Thus, the sample size consisted of 240 eggs at each test concentration.

After transferring the eggs, the glass vessels were filled with 50 ml dilution water. The vessels were covered to minimise evaporation. Percentage survival was recorded daily over a period of 144 hours. The number of live and dead eggs and larvae, retardations and endpoints of development, as well as deformations, were continually monitored.

The statistical analyses of experimental data were made using the spreadsheet program Quattro pro 2.0.

15.3   Results

The lowest-observed-effect concentrations (LOECs) and no-observed-effect concentrations (NOECs) of the reference chemicals for zebrafish are shown in Table 15.2. No significant difference could be observed between the results from the four-cell stage and flat-blastula stage of initial exposure.

15.4   Discussion

15.4.1   *Copper*

The subchronic copper values with zebrafish confirm the correlation between water hardness and toxicity reported by Howarth and Sprague (1978), Miller and Mackay (1980) and Hutchinson and Sprague (1987). Compared with the acute $96hLC_{50}$ data for zebrafish, the sensitivity of the ELT is greater. Meinelt (1990) obtained a $96hLC_{50}$ of 0.53 mg.l^{-1} Cu for zebrafish. Copper LC_{50} values reported by Pant *et al.* (1980), Gupta and Rajbanshi (1981) and Blaylock *et al.* (1985) range from 0.571 mg.l^{-1} to 2.3 mg.l^{-1}.

Only data obtained for salmonids in dynamic $96hLC_{50}$ tests are comparable with the subchronic zebrafish values (Chapman and Stevens, 1978). By comparison with chronic data (Horning and Neiheisel, 1979) the zebrafish larvae are as sensitive as other Cyprinidae.

15.4.2   *Phenol*

Compared with other authors' data the zebrafish values for phenol obtained here are higher. Acute $96hLC_{50}s$ obtained for zebrafish by Fogels and Sprague (1977) and Razani *et al.* (1986) are 29 mg.l^{-1} and 24.9 mg.l^{-1} respectively. Birge *et al.* (1979) emphasise the higher toxicity of phenol in hard water and this was confirmed by our investigations. But compared to other species, there seems to be a high tolerance of zebrafish larvae to phenol.

15.4.3   *Pentachlorophenol (PCP)*

The third reference chemical is of special importance because of its environmental persistence and high toxicity. PCP was the most toxic substance tested. The LOECs obtained were independent of water composition and time of exposure, at 0.005 mg.l^{-1} PCP. Compared with acute values obtained by Fogels and Sprague (1977), Gupta (1983), and Khangarot *et al.* (1985) for cyprinids, the subchronic zebrafish data are very low. Basing upon chronic studies, Holcombe *et al.* (1982) obtained MATCs from 0.0459 to 0.079 mg.l^{-1} PCP. For this reason zebrafish larvae can be considered as highly sensitive to PCP.

15.4.4   *2,4-Dinitrophenol (DNP)*

DNP was the second toxic phenolic compound tested. The toxicity of this substance depends to a considerable extent on the water hardness. Although in hard tap water DNP at up to 16 mg.l^{-1} exerts no significant toxicity, in synthetic soft water 1 mg.l^{-1} DNP causes almost a 100% mortality of eggs and larvae. This dependence of DNP-toxicity on water hardness is confirmed by other authors (Verma *et al.*, 1980, 1981; Dalela *et al.*, 1980 and Gupta *et al.*, 1983). The subchronic zebrafish values in hard water are comparable with other DNP data obtained under similar conditions. In soft synthetic water zebrafish has a higher sensitivity to DNP.

15.4.5   *Deformations*

The transparent and uncoloured zebrafish eggs are ideal for embryo toxicological and teratological studies (Abedi and McKinley, 1968; Abedi and Scott, 1969). Another advantage is the rapid developmental rate of the zebrafish. For these reasons, zebrafish eggs have an established use in developmental investigations. In our investigations, the deformations observed in embryo-larval-studies with zebrafish could be divided into two main groups.

(1) Pronounced oedema
- cranial oedema
- abdominal oedema (ascites)
- cardiac oedema
- abdominal and cardiac oedema

(2) Skeletal deformations
- spine deformation
- tail/spine deformations
- tail deformation

These observed anomalies were not confined to certain substances; some degree of these anomalies could be found at all concentrations of almost all of the substances tested. We were surprised that along with malachite green, sodium chloride caused most of the deformations. Damage can be detected even in early stages of embryonic development, for example irregular cell division, spine distortions and the early elevation of head and tail from the yolk. Exposure at the four-cell stage and blastula stage leads to the same type and quantity of deformations. We agree with Hisaoka (1958), that the use of earlier stages, higher concentrations and longer exposure contribute to a greater teratogenic effect of teratogenic substances. But furthermore, the more important damage may be a retardation of development, and the inability of embryos to break through the chorion as was seen, for example, in the case of phenol.

15.5   Conclusions

The ELT with zebrafish, based on a proposal made by Besch *et al.* (1987), proved to be highly practicable. Compared with $96hLC_{50}s$ obtained with zebrafish and other cyprinids, and with values obtained from prolonged acute tests (28 days), this ELT seems to be very sensitive. Therefore, the death of the individual is not a necessary endpoint. Retardation in development and reduced hatchability are parameters which are able to show subchronic potentials of xenobiotics. Exposure at the four-cell stage or blastula stage allows the chemical to have an influence on the complete embryonic development. Subchronic and teratogenic effects may be observed directly because of the highly transparent chorion. Exposure at either the four-cell stage or the blastula stage yields almost similar results. However, an advantage of using eggs at the blastula stage is that it is possible to determine the state of fertilisation.

To obtain eggs in high quantity and quality it is necessary to pay special care to the parents' age and nutritional state. Moreover, the eggs themselves have to be treated with special care.

At temperatures of 26 to 27°C the larvae reach the swim-up stage in 144 hours. If the temperature is raised by 2 or 3°C, this stage will be reached after 120 hours. For this reason it is possible to obtain acute and subchronic results after 120 hours, that is, only 24 hours longer than the acute 96-hour test.

The ELT was carried out as a static procedure. This simulates a 'die-away' situation, which could happen if a chemical, substance or effluent enters a lake. To simulate other situations it is necessary to adapt this procedure, because static conditions can lead to a reduction of chemical concentrations of up to 80% within the exposure period.

The use of different types of dilution water can produce different LOECs; therefore, the dilution water should be standardised.

By comparison with ELTs carried out at the Institute with commercial species of fish, e.g., *Oncorhynchus mykiss*, *Cyprinus carpio* and *Silurus glanis* the zebrafish test has shown that it has several advantages:

(1) Zebrafish need little laboratory space for rearing and breeding. The ELT can be carried out under normal laboratory conditions.
(2) Only small amounts of dilution water and chemical are necessary. Tests are of short duration (zebrafish 5 days, compared with rainbow trout 45 days).
(3) Zebrafish eggs can be obtained throughout the year, and daily. Therefore, there are no seasonal difficulties and supply problems with local breeders. The handling of zebrafish is simple.
(4) The test is based on a defined parental stock, whose age, nutrition and health are known. Therefore, data obtained from such zebrafish are of a better reproducibility (repeatability) than those from commercial fish.
(5) The embryonic development can be easily observed because of the high transparency of the chorion. Compared with most commercial fish eggs, the fertilisation state of zebrafish eggs can easily be defined after spawning.
(6) Environmental chemicals are able to affect most sensitive developmental stages.
(7) Parameters such as retardation of development, reduced hatchability, end-points in development, and number of deformations, are additional factors for use in risk assessments of xenobiotics on fish.
(8) This test is an alternative to the controversial acute lethal test with fish.

It yields more information useful for risk analysis. For this reason, the zebrafish embryo-larval test should be considered as a substitute for the acute fish test.

Acknowledgements

We thank the Stifterverband für die Deutsche Wissenschaft for their financial support.

References

Abedi, Z.H. and W.P. McKinley, 1968. Mycotoxins – Zebra fish eggs and larvae as aflatoxin bioassay test organisms. *J.A.O.A.C.*, **4**: 902–910.

Abedi, Z.H. and P.M. Scott, 1969. Mycotoxins - Detection of toxicity of aflatoxins, sterigmatocystin, and other fungal toxins by lethal action on zebra fish larvae. *J.A.O.A.C.*, **5**: 963–969.

Besch, W.K., B.W. Scharf and E. Mayer, 1987. Toxizitätstests mit Goldorfe und Zebrabärbling, Vorschläge zur Durchführung und Bemühungen zur Ausssagekraft von Toxizitätstesten mit der Goldorfe (*Leuciscus idus*) und dem Zebrabärbling (*Brachydanio rerio*). Roth, *Wassergefährdende Stoffe*, 2. Aufl. 1985, 5. Erg. Liefrg. Landsberg.

Birge, W.J., J.A. Black, J.E. Hudson and D.M. Bruser, 1979. Embryo-larval-toxicity-test with organic compounds. In: Marking, L. and U.R.A. Kunerk (Eds.) *AquaticToxicology*, pp. 131–147. ASTM STP 667. Philadelphia, American Society for Testing and Materials..

Blaylock, B.G., M.L. Frank and J.F. McCarthy, 1985. Comparative toxicity of copper and Acridine to fish, daphnia and algae. *Environ.Toxicol.Chem.*, **4**: 63–71.

Chapman, G.A. and D.G. Stevens, 1978. Acutely lethal levels of cadmium, copper and zinc to adult male coho salmon and steelhead. *Trans.Am.Fish.Soc.*, **6**: 837–840.

Dalela, R.C., S. Rani, Sarita Rani and S.R. Verma, 1980. Influence of pH on the toxicity of phenol and its two derivatives pentachlorophenol and dinitrophenol to some fresh water teleosts. *Acta hydrochim.hydrobiol.*, **6**: 623–629.

Fogels, A. and J.B. Sprague, 1977. Comparative short-term tolerance of zebrafish, flagfish and rainbow trout to five poisons including potential reference toxicants. *Water Res.*, **11**: 811–817.

Gupta, P.K., 1983. Acute toxicity of pentachlorophenol to a freshwater teleost, *Rasbora daniconius neilgeriensis* (Hamilton). *Arch.Hydrobiol.*, **98**: 127–132.

Gupta, A.K. and V.K. Rajbanshi, 1981. Measurement of acute toxicity of copper to the freshwater teleost, *Mystus bleekeri* (Day) using bioassay, statistical and histopathological methods. *Arch.Hydrobiol.*, **4**: 427–434.

Gupta, P.K., R.C. Dalela and P.K. Saxena, 1983. Influence of temperature on the toxicity of phenol and its chloro- and nitroderivates to the fish *Notopterus notopterus* (Pallas). *Acta hydrochim.hydrobiol.*, **2**: 187–192.

Hisaoka, K.K., 1958. The effects of 2-acetylaminofluorence on the embryonic development of the zebrafish. *Cancer Res.*, **18**: 527–535.

Holcombe, G.W., G.L. Phipps and J.T. Fiandt, 1982. Effects of phenol, 2,4-dimethylphenol, 2,4-dichlorophenol, and pentachlorophenol on embryo, larval, and early-juvenile fathead minnows (*Pimephales promelas*). *Arch.Environ.Contam.Toxicol.*, **11**: 73–78.

Horning, W.B. and T.W. Neiheisel, 1979. Chronic effect of copper on the bluntnose minnow, *Pimephales notatus* (Rafinesque). *Arch.Environ.Contam.Toxicol.*, **8**: 545–552.

Howarth, R.S. and J.B. Sprague, 1978. Copper lethality to rainbow trout in waters of various hardness and pH. *Water Res.*, **12**: 455–462.

Hutchinson, N.J. and J.B. Sprague, 1987. Reduced lethality of Al, Zn and Cu mixtures to American flagfish by complexation with humic substances in acidified soft waters. *Environ.Toxicol.Chem.*, **10**: 755–765.

Khangarot, B.S., Atam Sehgal and M.K. Bhasin, 1985. Effect of pH on toxicity of sodium pentachloro-phenate to fry of common carp in softwater. *Arch.Hydrobiol.*, **3**: 375–379.

Meinelt, T., 1990. Untersuchungen zur Klassifizierung der akuten Fischtoxizität ausgewählter Therapeutika und Wasserschadstoffe. *Z.Binnenfischerei*, **4**: 118–125.

Miller, T.G. and W.C. Mackay, 1980. The effect of hardness, alkalinity and pH of test water on the toxicity to rainbow trout (*Salmo gairdneri*). *Water Res.*, **2**: 129–133.

Pant, S.C., S. Kumar and S. S. Khanna, 1980. Toxicity of copper sulphate and zinc sulphate to the fresh water teleost *Puntius conchonius* (Ham.) in hard water. *Comp.Physiol.Ecol.*, **3**: 146–149.

Razani, H., K. Nanba and S. Murachi, 1986. Acute toxic effect of phenol on zebrafish *Brachydanio rerio*. *Bull.Jap.Soc.Sci.Fish.*, **52**: 1547–1553.

Verma, S.R., S. Rani, A.K. Tyagi and R.C. Dalela, 1980. Evaluation of acute toxicity of phenol and its chloro- and nitroderivatives to certain teleosts. *Water Air Soil Pollut.*, 95–102.

Verma, S.R., I.P. Tonk and R.C. Dalela, 1981. Determination of the maximum acceptable toxicant concentration (MATC) and the safe concentration for certain aquatic pollutants. *Acta hydrochim.-hydrobiol.*, **3**: 247–254.

Chapter 16
Assessment of the value of including recovery periods in chronic toxicity test guidelines for rainbow trout (*Oncorhynchus mykiss*)

G. F. WHALE,[1] D. A. SHEAHAN[2] and M. F. KIRBY[2]

[1] *Shell Research Ltd, Sittingbourne, Kent ME9 8AG, UK*
[2] *MAFF Fisheries Laboratory, Remembrance Avenue, Burnham-on-Crouch, Essex CM0 8HA, UK*

16.1   Introduction

In a review of 56 life cycle toxicity experiments on 34 organic and inorganic chemicals to four species of fish, McKim (1977) found that embryo larval and early juvenile life stages were among the most sensitive. These tests also demonstrated that fish early life stages could be used to estimate the maximum acceptable toxicant concentrations (MATCs) within a factor of 2 in nearly all of the tests. In 82% of the tests reviewed, McKim also found that those using embryo-larval or early juvenile stages produced estimates of the MATC which were very similar to those determined from complete life cycle studies. Therefore, the combination of a fish early life stage (ELS) test and juvenile growth test would be expected to give confidence in predicting MATCs for chemicals. Such tests also present fewer technical difficulties and are less expensive to conduct.

Under the sixth amendment of the EC's 'Dangerous substances' directive, chronic fish toxicity data are required as part of the ecotoxicity information for Level 1 chemicals (i.e. chemicals manufactured and marketed at >10 tonnes per annum or 50 tonnes in total within the EC). Most of these chronic toxicity studies are conducted with continuous exposure of the fish to a fixed concentration of test chemical and do not assess how rapidly, if at all, the exposed fish can recover from any adverse toxicant effects. In this chapter two Level 1 chronic toxicity tests, an ELS and a 28-day juvenile growth test with the rainbow trout (*Onchorhynchus mykiss*) have been conducted using the triazine herbicide atrazine. Both of these studies were extended beyond their commonly accepted endpoints to assess whether fish adversely affected by exposure to atrazine during these studies were capable of recovery when returned to clean flowing water. Atrazine was chosen as a reference chemical for these studies since it has been proven to be persistent in fresh waters. For example, atrazine has been found above the EC limits for single pesticides in potable water supplies in the UK and its frequency of occurrence and persistence in natural watercourses has resulted in it becoming a provisional candidate on the UK Department of the Environment Red List (Chemical and Industry, 1988).

16.2　　Methods

16.2.1　　*Dosing system*

A continuous-flow dosing system was used for both the ELS and growth experiments. This system has already been validated for a poorly soluble compound (Whale *et al.*, 1988). A range of concentrations of technical grade atrazine (supplied by Schering Agrochemicals) were made up in dimethylsulphoxide (BDH Chemicals Ltd. Analar grade DMSO). The test system consisted of five atrazine concentrations (mean measured concentrations 0.036, 0.13, 0.41, 1.1 and 3.8 mg.l^{-1}), a solvent control (concentration 0.08 ml.l^{-1}) and a water control. The atrazine stock concentrations and the solvent control were dosed into mixing chambers (2.5 l glass aspirators) at a rate of 0.04 ml.min^{-1} and the diluent water flow rate was maintained at 500 ml.min^{-1}. The water and the toxicant were added to the vortex created by a magnetic stirrer in each mixing chamber; the diluted stock then passed through a glass over-flow tube into a 5 l glass tank and then via the over-flow of this tank into 35 l glass aquaria.

Because of the sensitivity of fish early life stages to light, the tanks were covered with dark plastic and minimal lighting was maintained in the constant temperature room. When the fish reached the swim-up stage the dark covers were removed from the top of the tanks and they were maintained under an artificial low light, 16:8 hours light:dark cycle. The water used in the trout acclimation tanks and the tests was a reconstituted borehole water with hardness of 50 ±15 mg.l^{-1} as calcium carbonate. Dissolved oxygen, temperature and pH were measured in each tank at least three times a week during the tests.

16.2.2　　*28-day juvenile trout growth test*

The 28-day growth test followed the guidelines recommended by Crossland (1988). Fingerling rainbow trout used in this test were supplied from Otford Fish Farm, Otford, Kent. Seven sets of 16 fish varying in weight 4.5–5.5 g were selected for this experiment. Individual fish in each treatment were identified by numbers freeze-branded onto their sides. Throughout the test the fish were fed twice daily on a trout food ration based on 2% of their body weight. This ration was adjusted on days 14 and 28 after the fish had been measured. Any fish which died during the course of the test were replaced with unbranded fish of similar size and weight. Subsequent to the 28-day exposure test the fish were placed into tanks supplied with clean flowing water and their lengths and weights recorded after a 14-day recovery period.

16.2.3　　*Early life stage (ELS) test*

This test was conducted in general accordance with draft OECD (1987) guidelines for fish ELS tests. Trout eggs from three females and milt from seven males were stripped from ripe fish from the Otford Fish Farm, Kent. The eggs were then well mixed by hand with the milt and 50 ml of 10 g.l^{-1} sodium bicarbonate solution in a 2 l glass crystallising dish. To minimise disturbance, a nominal egg volume of 30 ml (approximately 200 eggs) was added to each set of three replicate sections within stainless-steel egg trays suspended in each of seven tanks. Throughout this test the tanks were inspected daily and any dead eggs/fry, faecal material and uneaten food (if fed) were removed using a modified wide bore glass pipette.

The ELS test was divided into three main stages:

(1)   Immediately post-fertilisation to hatching (30 days' duration)
(2)   Post-hatch to swim up (28 days' duration)
(3)   Post-swim up to 3 months old (28 days' duration)

Details of these stages, the various procedures undertaken and a summary of the main observations recorded are shown in Table 16.1.

Stage 3 of the ELS test was conducted following the same basic principles as the juvenile trout growth test. For example they were fed a 2% body weight per day ration (Fry food No. 00, BP Nutrition Ltd) and were not fed during the day prior to measurement. The main differences in the procedure were that the rations were based on wet weights of subsampled fry rather than actual fish used and that these rations were adjusted to compensate for mortalities.

In stage 3 the growth of fry previously exposed during stages 1 and 2 was assessed in conditions of (a) continuous exposure (fry returned to their appropriate tanks in the dosing system) and (b) recovery conditions (fry placed into clean flowing water). All fish sampled throughout this stage were preserved in formalin. At the end of the experiment these were rinsed in clean tap-water and placed in a drying oven at 60°C for 24 hours. Their dry weights were then measured.

16.3   Results

16.3.1   *Water quality*

The dissolved oxygen concentrations recorded in the test vessels throughout this study were >60% of the air saturation value. The pH values recorded were 7.7 ±0.4 units. During the growth test the mean water temperatures recorded in all aquaria were within the acceptable limits of 12–15°C (OECD, 1987) for juvenile rainbow trout tests. Differences in water temperatures between tanks during the ELS tests were within the 1.5°C limit given in the draft OECD (1987) guidelines.

16.3.2   *Chemical analysis*

The results of the chemical analyses made throughout both tests (atrazine analysis technique based upon UK standard methods; DOE, 1985) indicated that the mean

Table 16.1 Summary of observations and procedures during the atrazine ELS study.

Day from start of test	Observation/comments	Action taken
0 (Start Stage 1)	Start of ELS test	Eggs fertilised, added to 3 replicates in each tank
26	Eggs start to hatch, retardation of hatching in higher atrazine concentrations	
30 (Start Stage 2)	Most eggs hatched with fish larvae escaping through mesh in some treatments	Egg holding trays removed, replication ended.
47	Most fry (except those exposed to 3.8.mg l^{-1} atrazine) at swim-up stage	Dark covers removed from tank tops. Feeding commences (all tanks fed same ration)
57	Yolk sacs of fry in control and low atrazine concentrations appear to be absorbed	Fry not fed
58 (Start Stage 3)	Fry in 3.8 mg.l^{-1} atrazine vessel still retarded in their development (not all at swim-up stage)	All fry removed. 50 fry subsampled from each treatment, weighed, measured and preserved in formalin. Two sets of 250 fry from each treatment* also taken, one set to test system and the others into recovery tanks
59	Fry appear to be unaffected by previous day's handling	Fry fed 2% per day ration (estimated on the wet weight of subsampled fry)
71		Fish not fed
72	No recovery of fry previously exposed to 3.8 mg.l^{-1} of atrazine	50 fry subsampled from all tanks, weighed, measured and preserved in formalin
73		Fry fed newly calculated rations
85		Fry not fed
86	End of test	Fry subsampled and measured as previously described

* Owing to slow development and mortalities two sets of 75 swim-up fry used for 3.8 mg.l^{-1} treatment

measured concentrations were close to the nominal concentrations although the recorded variability between measurements was large (Table 16.2). Mean measured concentrations rather than the nominal values have therefore been used in this report.

16.3.3   *Juvenile trout growth test*

In this test method, the individual growth rates for each fish are determined but the results are expressed in terms of the mean exponential growth rate 'r' of each set of trout tested. The exponential growth rate is calculated as a percentage per day figure (Crossland, 1988).

Table 16.2 Mean measured concentrations of atrazine determined throughout the study.

Nominal concentration (mg.l^{-1})	Mean measured concentration (mg.l^{-1})	SD (σ.n^{-1})
4	3.8	2.2
1.3	1.1	0.66
0.4	0.41	0.17
0.13	0.13	0.05
0.04	0.036	0.012
Solvent control	< 0.01	–
Water control	< 0.01	–

The growth rates of the trout over the 28-day exposure to atrazine and subsequent recovery period are presented graphically in Figure 16.1. Differences between the mean exponential growth rates in each treatment and the solvent control which were shown to be significant in a Dunnett's test (see Zar, 1974) are indicated by asterisks.

The results of this statistical analysis show that the growth of rainbow trout was significantly reduced in the three highest atrazine concentrations ($P<0.01$ for 3.8 and 1.1 mg.l^{-1} and $P<0.05$ for 0.41 mg.l^{-1}) over the initial 0–14-day exposure period. During the subsequent 14-day period, the growth rates of the trout were only significantly reduced ($P<0.01$) in the two highest exposure concentrations. When the growth rates are examined over the whole test period (i.e. 0–28 days) there was only a significant reduction ($P<0.01$) in growth rates of juvenile trout exposed to 3.8 and 1.1 mg.l^{-1} of atrazine. Although not statistically significant, a graduated reduction in growth rates of the trout was seen in all of the atrazine exposed fish and even in the solvent control compared to the water control. In the 14-day recovery period significant increases in growth rate ($P<0.05$) were seen in the trout which had been previously exposed to the three highest atrazine concentrations. Increases in growth rates were also recorded in all of the previously exposed fish relative to the controls although these were not statistically significant.

16.3.4 Early life stage tests

Stage 1 and 2

The mortalities which occurred during stages 1 and 2 of the ELS test are shown as percentage mortality (ignoring day 1 mortalities) in Table 16.3. The highest day 1 egg mortality was observed in replicate 1 which was the last to receive eggs at the start of the test, and was probably due to the prolonged handling which they received. Since these initial mortalities were not thought to be related to toxicant exposure they were not included in the results and the test mortalities were only recorded from the second day of exposure. The actual numbers of embryos which

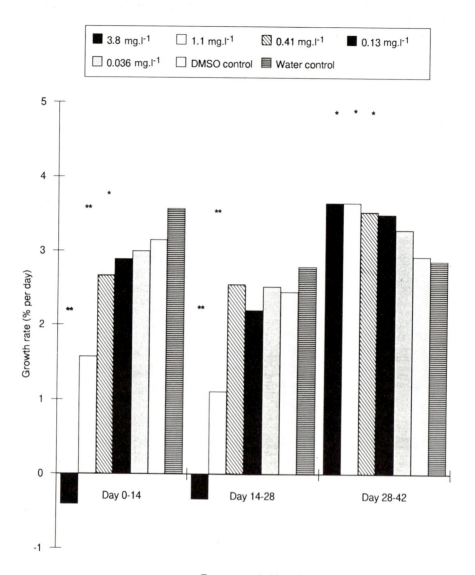

Fig. 16.1 Growth rate (% per day) based upon mean wet weights of juvenile rainbow trout exposed to five concentrations of atrazine and a solvent and water control during a 28-day growth test and a subsequent 14-day recovery period in clean water.

* Significantly different from the solvent control al *P* <0.05

** Significantly different from the solvent control al *P* <0.01

Table 16.3 Percentage mortality of rainbow trout from just after fertilisation to swim-up stage in an atrazine ELS test.

Concentration (mg.l^{-1})	Day 1 mortalities (1) replicate number			Mortalities (2) after 31 days	Mortalities (2) at swim-up
	1	2	3		
3.8	3.6	0.5	0	6.2	58.8
1.1	2.2	0.4	0.5	5.7	8.5
0.41	2.8	0.8	0.1	5.3	10.2
0.13	1.8	0.8	0.1	5.0	11.1
0.036	10	1.6	0.6	4.7	12.3
Solvent control	0.4	1.9	0.1	4.1	11.8
Water control	0.7	2.1	0.1	4.6	10.4

Notes: (1) Based on total egg numbers at start
       (2) Percentage mortalities excluding mortalities recorded on Day 1

were present in each exposure concentration after day 1 varied from 591 to 739 (mean = 693, SD ($\sigma.n^{-1}$) = 53).

Throughout the remainder of stage 1 of the ELS test, egg mortalities per treatment varied between 4.1 and 6.2% with no significant difference between either replicates or test concentrations. The size of the perforations in the stainless steel mesh were too large to restrain all of the newly hatched embryos from escaping to the bottom of the exposure tank, and it was decided then to remove the stainless steel chambers. The second phase of the test started from this time although not all of the eggs had hatched. This delay was particularly apparent in the two highest exposure concentrations of 1.1 and 3.8 mg.l^{-1} of atrazine. From the results shown in Table 16.3 it can be seen that significant mortalities (58.8%) occurred in the 3.8 mg.l^{-1} atrazine exposure during stage 1 and 2 of the ELS test although no other dose response relationships could be defined. Total mortalities in all the other treatments and controls varied between 8.5 and 12%. The mean wet and dry weights of the rainbow trout fry at the end of stage 2 are shown in Table 16.4. The results of a Dunnett's test applied to the mean wet weights of fish at the end of this phase of the ELS test show that there was a significant weight decrease ($P<0.01$) in concentrations of 1.1 and 3.8 mg.l^{-1} of atrazine compared to the solvent control.

However, Dunnett's test analysis of the dry weights of the same fish samples showed that a significant decrease in weight ($P<0.01$) occurred only in fish exposed to the highest atrazine concentration compared to the solvent control.

Stage 3 (fry growth test)

During this stage of the test, mortalities continued to occur in the highest exposure concentration of 3.8 mg.l^{-1} atrazine. Mortalities were also recorded in the recovery tank which held the trout embryos previously exposed to this high concentration.

Table 16.4   Mean wet and dry weights of trout at swim-up stage of the atrazine ELS test.

Concentration $(mg.l^{-1})$	Wet weight (g)	Dry weight (g)
3.8	0.111**	0.017**
1.1	0.139**	0.020
0.41	0.156	0.022
0.13	0.169	0.025
0.036	0.153	0.022
Solvent control	0.164	0.024
Water control	0.181	0.026

Note: ** = significantly different at $P<0.01$

Although a few mortalities did occur in some of the other test tanks these were neither significant nor dose-related.

Mean exponential growth rates (calculated using the mean and not individual fish weights at each sampling occasion) are shown in Figures 16.2 and 16.3. These results indicate that no recovery of growth was seen in ELS fish previously exposed to 3.8 $mg.l^{-1}$ atrazine. However good recovery in terms of increased growth rates was seen in ELS fish previously exposed to 1.1 $mg.l^{-1}$ atrazine. Although fry continuously exposed to 1.1 $mg.l^{-1}$ of atrazine had poor growth rates during the first 14-day period of stage 3, these doubled (but were still lower than the controls) in the following 14-day period.

16.4   Discussion

16.4.1   *Juvenile trout growth test*

The 28-day fish growth test has been demonstrated by Crossland (1988) to be a useful and robust test for assessing the chronic toxicity of chemicals to rainbow trout and has recently been validated by an EC ring test (Ashley *et al.*, 1990) . The results of the juvenile trout growth study, in which significant adverse effects on growth were detected at 0.41 $mg.l^{-1}$ of atrazine, are in good agreement with those obtained with brook trout (*Salvelinus fontinalis*) by Macek *et al.* (1976) who found that growth was adversely affected at 0.12 $mg.l^{-1}$ of atrazine and was the most sensitive species response to chronic exposure to this herbicide. In the report by Ashley *et al.*(1990) the results of the EC ring test did not demonstrate any difference in sensitivity if the EC_{50} (chemical concentration having an observed effect on 50% of the exposed fish) or the NOEC (no-observed-effect concentration) values were based on the mean fish weights or the instantaneous growth rates.

However, the value of using the instantaneous growth rate can be seen in studies which incorporate recovery periods. In these studies the use of a variable which is

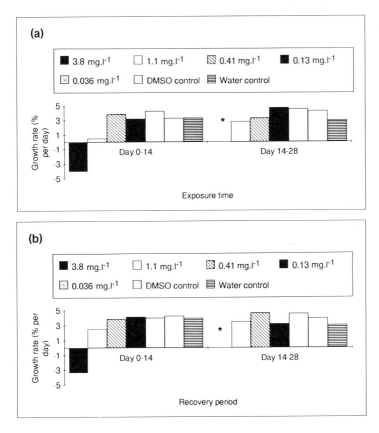

Fig. 16.2 Growth rate (% per day, dry weight) of trout fry (a) continuously exposed to atrazine and to a solvent and water control in a 28-day growth test and (b) in clean water for a 28-day recovery period (in each case following previous exposure to atrazine and solvent and water controls from just after fertilisation to swim-up stage).

* Insufficient fish remained at this concentration to allow a representative sample to be taken after 28 days' exposure/recovery.

independent of the initial size of the fish gives a better indication of recovery of previously growth-inhibited fish than comparisons based on mean weight data alone. The statistically significant increase in growth rates of previously exposed trout relative to the controls during the 14-day recovery period suggests that these fish have the ability to compensate for reduced growth due to toxic effects of atrazine exposure. The fish loading rates compared to the water flow rate per aquaria should not have been limiting since, even after 42 days, the water flow rate in all aquaria was greater than the value of 2 l.g^{-1} wet fish weight per day as recommended by Alabaster and Lloyd (1980). It appears unlikely that other physical factors reduced the control fish growth rates since these were higher during the final 14-day period when the fish were larger and any physical constraints would have been likely to be accentuated.

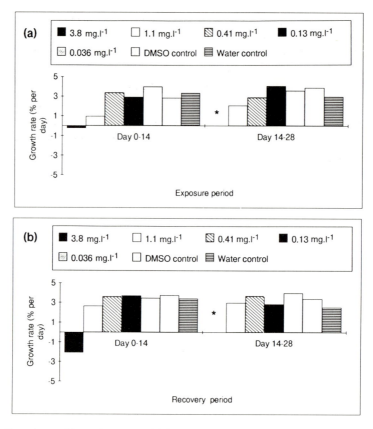

Fig. 16.3 Growth rate (% per day, wet weight) of trout fry (a) continuously exposed to atrazine and to a solvent and water control in a 28-day growth test and (b) in clean water for a 28-day recovery period (in each case following previous exposure to atrazine and solvent and water controls from just after fertilisation to swim-up stage).
* Insufficient fish remained at this concentration to allow a representative sample to be taken after 28 days' exposure/recovery.

Therefore, the results of the recovery period in the growth test indicate that the previously exposed trout were compensating for impaired growth. These findings imply that the trout allocate more of their energy budget to growth following atrazine exposure than trout held under control conditions. Reduced activity in trout which had been previously exposed to high atrazine concentrations could have contributed to such an effect; however, no measurements were made in this study which would confirm this. This type of compensatory response has been seen, although not statistically verified, in other previous exposure and recovery growth experiments (Sheahan and Whale, unpublished data). Compensatory growth of rainbow trout has also been reported to occur after periods of starvation by Dobson and Holmes (1984). In their studies, four out of five groups of rainbow trout which had been starved for three weeks and then fed for three weeks showed a weight gain equivalent to or greater than fish fed normally for the total six-week period. These findings suggest that concentrations of atrazine which adversely affected the growth of trout in our study had a similar effect to periods of starvation. Inclusion of a recovery period in such growth tests allows these transient effects to be discriminated from effects which may be of a longer term and more deleterious nature (e.g. discriminating between the effects of chemical tainting of fish food leading to starvation and of irreversible destruction or long-term impairment of specific fish enzyme systems).

16.4.2   *Early life stage tests*

Post fertilisation to swim up (stages 1 and 2, Table 16.1)

The observation that even short delays in assigning groups of newly fertilised eggs to their relevant exposure vessels appear to influence the degree of mortality occuring during the first day of the test highlights the need for this process to be both rapid and randomised.

   The low mortalities in the highest dose of atrazine which occurred in stage 1 compared to stage 2 indicate that rainbow trout eggs are less sensitive to this chemical than the newly hatched fry. The lack of sensitivity of salmonid eggs to pollutants has been reported previously (Eddy and Talbot, 1985; Peterson *et al.*, 1980; Brown and Lyman, 1981). These authors considered that the chorion and perivitelline fluid offer protection from toxicants although the mechanisms are not well defined or clearly understood. Van Leeuwen *et al.* (1985) thought that the increased sensitivity of the fry stage was due to the accumulation of toxicants in the yolk sac which then become available to the fish when the yolk-sac is utilized. However, atrazine is not known to bioconcentrate in fish tissues. For example, Cossarini-Dunier *et al.* (1988) reported that carp orally dosed with atrazine did not show any significant accumulation of atrazine, and Gunkel and Streit (1980) reported low bioconcentration factors of between 1.3 to 2.6 and 7.4 to 8 for the whole fish and liver of *Coregonus fera* following an atrazine pollution incident. Another possible explanation for the increasing effect of exposure to 3.8 mg.l^{-1} of atrazine which began immediately prior to and after hatching (Fig. 16.1) is that the chorion (zona radiata) is relatively resistant to toxicants as suggested by Williams and Eddy (1989).

Exposed and 'recovery' trout fry growth (stage 3)

One anomaly seen when comparing the growth rates calculated from mean wet weights is that fry previously continuously exposed to 3.8 mg.l^{-1} of atrazine had higher growth rates than their counterparts in the recovery aquaria. However, this is not reflected in growth rates based on dry weight and may be an indication that the continuously exposed fish at this concentration had begun to lose their osmoregulatory control and therefore had a greater water content. Studies carried out by Fischer-Scherl *et al.* (1991) indicated that atrazine concentrations greater than 80 mg.l^{-1} caused necrosis of renal haemopoietic tissue and this may explain the results obtained in the present study.

The calculated trout fry growth rates appear to be more variable than those for juvenile trout. There are several possible explanations for this variability. These include inaccuracies due to measuring population mean rather than individual fish growth rates, difficulties associated with feeding the fry (fry feed tends to float and can be lost via overflows), fry feeding rates based on an estimated weight of the population as opposed to individually identified weights in the growth test, and the ease and accuracy of measurement of juveniles compared to fry. This variability makes interpretation of the results from the fry stage more difficult, although it is clear that no recovery occurred with fry previously exposed to 3.8 mg.l^{-1} of atrazine whereas those exposed to 1.1 mg.l^{-1} recovered.

16.5   Conclusions

The chronic fish toxicity studies reported here produced similar results in terms of MATC values to those found in other salmonid fish studies reported in the literature. However, our studies revealed that valuable information can be gained by the inclusion of a recovery period. For example, although juvenile rainbow trout growth rates are sensitive to atrazine exposure, affected fish are capable of recovery and show compensatory growth rates even after 28 days exposure to 3.8 mg.l^{-1} of atrazine. On the other hand, ELS trout which had been continuously exposed to 3.8 mg.l^{-1} atrazine for 86 days after fertilisation were not capable of recovery although ELS fish exposed to 1.1 mg.l^{-1} for the same period were capable of recovery at growth rates similar to those of control fish. Inclusion of a recovery period will allow those chemicals (or concentrations of chemicals) which produce permanent adverse chronic effects to be separated from those producing transient effects. This will improve confidence in predictions of direct effects of either chemical spills or seasonally high levels of specific chemicals such as herbicides, on natural fish populations with only a minimal addition to existing chronic toxicity test procedures.

Acknowledgements

The authors wish to thank Mr Colin Allchin for his analytical support during this study and Dr Peter Matthiessen for his comments on the draft. The typing of the paper by Mrs Donna Murray is also gratefully acknowledged.

References

Alabaster, J.S. and R. Lloyd, 1980. *Water Quality Criteria for Freshwater Fish*. London, Butterworth.

Ashley, S., M.J. Mallett and N.J. Grandy, 1990. EEC ring test of a method for determining the effects of chemicals on the growth rate of fish. Final Report to the Commission of the European Communities. WRc Report No. EEC 2600-M.

Brown, D.J.A. and S. Lyman, 1981. The effect of sodium and calcium concentrations on the hatching of eggs and the survival of yolk sac fry of brown trout *Salmo trutta* L. at low pH. *J.Fish Biol.*, **19**: 205–211.

Chemical and Industry, 1988. Red list for water pollutants. Chemical and Industry, 15th August 1988, p. 504.

Cossarni-Dunier, M. *et al.*, 1988. Effects of oral doses of the herbicide atrazine on carp (*Cyprinus carpio*). *Ambio*, **17**(6): 401–405.

Crossland, N.O., 1988. A method for evaluating effects of toxic chemicals on fish growth rates. In: Adams, W.J., G.A. Chapman and W.G. Landis (Eds.) *Aquatic Toxicology and Hazard Assessment*, ASTM STP 971, 10th vol, pp. 463–467. Philadelphia, American Society for Testing and Materials.

Dobson, S.H. and R.M. Holmes, 1984. Compensatory growth in the rainbow trout, *Salmo gairdneri* Richardson. *J.Fish Biol.*, **25**: 649–656.

DOE Standing Committee of Analysts, 1985. Methods for the examination of waters and associated materials. Chlorophenoxy acidic herbicides, trichlorobenzoic acid, chlorophenols, triazines and glyphosate in water. London, HMSO.

Eddy, F.B. and C. Talbot, 1985. Sodium balance in eggs and dechorionated embryos of the Atlantic salmon *Salmo salar* L. exposed to zinc, aluminium and acid waters. *Comp.Biochem.Physiol.*, **81**c: 259–266.

Fischer Scherl, T., A. Veesier, R.W. Hoffmann, C. Kühnhausser, R. Negele and T. Erwingmann, 1991. Morphological effects of acute and chronic atrazine exposure in rainbow trout (*Oncorhynchus mykiss*). *Arch.Environ.Contam.Toxicol.*, **20**: 454–461.

Gunkel, G. and B. Streit, 1980. Mechanisms of bioaccumulation of a herbicide (atrazine, s-triazene) in a freshwater mollusc (*Ancylus fluviatilis*) and a fish (*Coregonus fera*). *Wat.Res.*, **14**: 1573–1584.

Macek, K.J. *et al.*, 1976. Chronic toxicity of atrazine to selected aquatic invertebrates and fishes. US Environmental Protection Agency, EPA 600/3–76–047.

McKim, J.M., 1977. Evaluation of tests with early life stages of fish for predicting long-term toxicity. *J.Fish.Res.Bd.Can.*, **34**: 1148–1154.

OECD, 1987. OECD guideline for testing of chemicals. Fish, early life stage toxicity test full OECD ECO 87.2 (Draft).

Peterson, R.H., P.G. Daye and J.L. Metcalfe, 1980. Inhibition of Atlantic salmon (*Salmo salar*) hatching at low pH. *Can.J.Fish.Aquat.Sci.*, **37**: 770-774.

Van Leeuwan, C.J. *et al.*, 1985. Differences in the susceptibility of early life stages of rainbow trout (*Salmo gairdneri*) to environmental pollutants. *Aquat.Toxicol.*, **7**: 59–78.

Whale, G., D. Sheahan and P. Matthiessen, 1988. The toxicity of Tecnazene, a potato sprouting inhibitor, to freshwater fauna. *Chemosphere*, **17**: 1205–1217.

Williams, E.M. and F.B. Eddy, 1989. Effect of nitrite on the embryonic development of Atlantic salmon (*Salmo salar*). *Can.J.Fish.Aquat.Sci.*, **46**: 1726–1729.

Zar, J.H., 1974. *Biostatistical Analysis*. pp. 167–168, Englewood Cliffs, Prentice Hall.

Chapter 17
Complete life cycle tests with zebrafish – a critical assessment of the results

R. NAGEL

Institut für Zoologie, AG Ökotoxikologie, Johannes Gutenberg– Universität Mainz,
Saarstraße 21, D-6500 Mainz, Germany

17.1   Introduction

The publications of Mount and Stephan (1967, fathead minnow, *Pimephales promelas*), Eaton (1970, bluegill, *Lepomis macrochirus*) and McKim and Benoit (1971, brook trout, *Salvelinus fontinalis*) were among the first published results of life cycle toxicity tests with fish. A life cycle test with trout and bluegill requires 30 months, while the fathead minnow requires only 12 months.

In order to reduce time and expense, a partial life cycle toxicity test starting with yearlings just prior to gonad development was created; this requires 12 months with brook trout and bluegill. For several heavy metals, a similarity in sensitivity was shown between the partial life cycle test and the complete life cycle test (McKim and Benoit, 1971, 1974; McKim *et al.*, 1976; Holcombe *et al.*, 1976).

In 1977, McKim published a summary of data based on 56 partial life cycle and complete life cycle tests with 34 organic and inorganic chemicals and four species of fish. In all tests the embryo-larval or early juvenile estimate of the MATC was within a factor of 2 of the actual MATC. In 82% of the tests the embryo-larval or early juvenile estimate of the MATC was essentially identical to the actual MATC. Therefore the use of embryo-larval fish toxicity tests would make possible the rapid screening of large numbers of chemicals at a far lower cost per test than for a partial or complete life cycle toxicity test.

In 1985, McKim presented an updated evaluation based on 72 partial and complete life cycle tests with four freshwater species and 37 organic and inorganic chemicals, and one saltwater fish exposed to 11 organic chemicals. In 83% of the tests the early life stage (ELS) portion of the life cycle gave the same MATC as the full life cycle, while the remaining 17% of the ELS tests showed a greater or lesser sensitivity than the life cycle tests within a factor of 2. It was emphasised that a variation by a factor of 2 is almost meaningless, since the MATCs for toxicants with different species and water quality combinations can easily vary by the same factor. In both evaluations, the sensitivity of ELS tests was usually the same when parent exposed embryos (Pe) and parent unexposed embryos (Pue) were compared. In practice, four of the 11 saltwater studies showed no differences in sensitivity between Pe and Pue embryos, two studies showed Pue embryos to be more sensitive, and five studies showed Pe embryos to be more sensitive. Only in six of the 72 tests was reproduction the critical life stage endpoint.

In 1984, Woltering reviewed a total of 173 tests including exposure to metals, pesticides and other xenobiotics. The data were summarised for 24 species of fish (12 warm freshwater, nine cold freshwater and three marine species) according to the 'most sensitive' response(s) which provided the LOEC. In these tests, fry survival was the most sensitive response, a reduction being significant in 57% of the tests. Fry growth was reduced in 36% and hatchability in 19%. Based on the 100 partial and complete life cycle tests evaluated, reproduction was reduced significantly in 30% of the tests. Adult survival and growth were reduced in only 13% and 5% respectively. Two-thirds of the 173 tests had a single most sensitive response at the LOEC. Fry survival was the single most sensitive indicator of toxicity in 32% of the cases. Reproduction (15%), and fry growth (14%) were the single most sensitive responses to an equal extent. Egg hatchability (8%), adult survival (4%) and adult growth (2%) were seldom the single most sensitive response. The conclusion was that the growth response could be deleted from routine toxicity tests.

The first publication by McKim (1977) in particular has contributed to a decrease in the number of life cycle tests in favour of ELS tests. For example, of the 72 life cycle tests evaluated in 1985 by McKim, only 20% were carried out in 1978 or later. In contrast, of the 69 ELS tests reviewed by Woltering (1984), 74% were performed in 1978 or later.

Level 2 tests according to the EC 6th Amendment and the German Chemical Act provide for a long-term investigation with fish, including a study of effects on reproduction. A working group under the auspices of the German Standard Institute (DIN) was established in order to develop a suitable method (Bresch *et al.*, 1986). The working group rejected the concept of a complete life cycle test and favoured a partial life cycle test with zebrafish developed by Bresch (1982). However, recent results with 4-nitrophenol show that the partial life cycle test is not as sensitive as a complete life cycle test starting with eggs and followed by an investigation of embryonic and larval development in the FII-generation (Nagel, 1988). In order to seek further proof, three additional experiments were carried out with atrazine, lindane and 3,4-dichloroaniline, using the complete life cycle test with zebrafish.

17.2   Materials and method

17.2.1   *Test fish*

In Europe, the zebrafish (*Brachydanio rerio*) is increasingly used in toxicological studies. This fish, well known to breeders, measures 3–5 cm in the adult state. It thrives both in soft and hard waters, grows quickly at temperatures around 26°C and reaches sexual maturity within three months. Zebrafish produce gametes

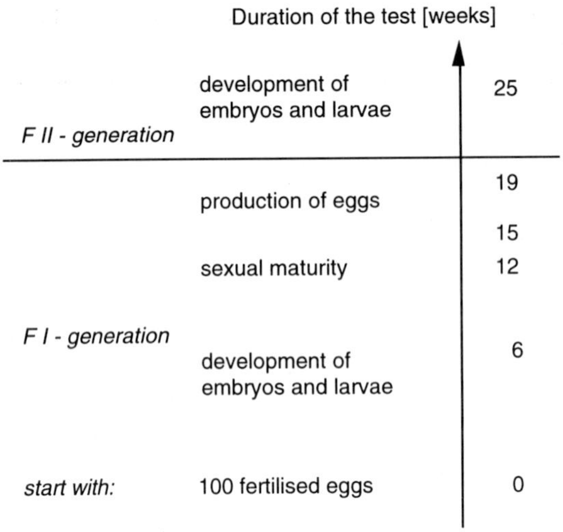

Duration of the test [weeks]

F II - generation	development of embryos and larvae	25
	production of eggs	19
		15
	sexual maturity	12
F I - generation	development of embryos and larvae	6
start with:	100 fertilised eggs	0

Fig. 17.1   Test scheme of a complete life cycle test with zebrafish.

throughout the year and are not particularly demanding of special conditions. Because of these characteristics, and in view of the fact that the zebrafish is already used as a test fish in the two lower tiers of the German Chemical Act, the DIN working group chose this species.

17.2.2   *Principle of the complete life cycle test*

The test begins with fertilised eggs and follows the development of fish until their sexual maturity. After an investigation of gamete production, the test is continued with the development of fish in the FII-generation for a period of six weeks. The complete life cycle test takes about 25 weeks to complete (Fig. 17.1). For technical details see Nagel (1986, 1988).

17.3   **Results and discussion**

Table 17.1 summarises the most important results of the complete life cycle test with zebrafish.

Atrazine

In the case of atrazine, survival (an endpoint of a normal early life stage test in the FI-generation) was a sensitive parameter (NOEC–LOEC, 0.1–1.0 mg.l^{-1}). Comparing the NOEC–LOEC based on survival of early life stages of zebrafish and brook trout (0.06–0.12 mg.l^{-1}; Macek *et al.*, 1976a) it is evident that the zebrafish is

Table 17.1   The most important results from four complete life cycle tests with zebrafish. The data represent NOEC–LOEC (mg.l^{-1}).

Substance (test concentrations)	FI-generation ELS	FI-generation Juveniles	FI-generation Adults	FII-generation ELS
Atrazine (0.1, 1.0, 10.0)	0.1 – 1.0 (SR)		1.0 – / (R) / – 0.1 (G) / – 0.1 (H)	1.0 – / (SR)
4-Nitrophenol (0.1, 1.0, 5.0)	5.0 – / (SR)		5.0 – / (R) / – 0.1 (H)	/ – 0.1 (SR)
3,4-Dichloroaniline (0.002, 0.02, 0.2)	0.02 – 0.2 (SR)		0.02 – / (R) / – 0.002 (H)	0.002 – 0.02 (SR)
Lindane (0.04, 0.08, 0.11, 0.13, 0.15)	0.11 – 0.13 (SR) / – 0.04 (G)	0.08 – 0.11 (SR) / – 0.04 (B)	0.04 – 0.08 (R) / – 0.04 (B) / – 0.04 (H)	0.08 – / (SR)

SR: survival rate
G: growth
B: behaviour
R: reproduction
H: histopathological changes of the liver (in cooperation with T. Braunbeck)
/ = no NOEC or LOEC could be established within the concentrations tested.

about ten times less sensitive than brook trout. The growth of adults was affected at 0.1 mg.l^{-1}, but there was a difference in loading caused by death of the early life stages and therefore a statistically based statement is difficult to obtain.

4-Nitrophenol

There are no results available from partial or complete life cycle tests with other species and 4-nitrophenol. With zebrafish the survival of the early life stages of the FII-generation was the most sensitive parameter, and within the concentrations tested no NOEC could be established.

3,4-dichloroaniline

There are no results published from partial or complete life cycle tests with other species and 3,4-dichloroaniline. In this study survival of the early life stages of the FII-generation was the most sensitive endpoint. A comparative laboratory study with zebrafish and 3,4-dichloroaniline has shown that an ELS test with this species can be conducted and produce meaningful results. Since the ELS test encompasses the most difficult experimental phase in the zebrafish life cycle, a complete life cycle test could probably also be performed by experienced laboratories (Nagel *et al.*, 1991).

Lindane

Reproduction was only affected by lindane, but this was caused by 0.08 mg.l^{-1}, a concentration close the LC$_{50}$ for adult zebrafish. Macek *et al.* (1976b) have carried out partial life cycle tests with bluegill, fathead minnow and brook trout and lindane. According to the opinion of Chorus (1987) these results are not conclusive. McKim included merely the results with fathead minnow in his review and stated the growth of adults as the most sensitive parameter. Based on the data of Macek *et al.* (1976b), both Chorus (1987) and Suter *et al.* (1987) came to the conclusion that growth is the most sensitive parameter for brook trout. Suter *et al.* (1987) stated additionally that reproduction was a comparably sensitive endpoint.

The significant effect found for growth of the ELS FI-generation was no longer significant when the fish had reached sexual maturity. This phenomenon shows that the endpoint of growth should be examined further. Swimming behaviour of juveniles and adults was influenced by lindane (0.004 mg.l^{-1}), but a correlation with population relevant parameters was not possible because of the small database.

In general, morphological alterations of hepatocytes were the most sensitive reactions of fish. In all cases no NOEC could be established. A correlation with population-relevant parameters was not possible. Nevertheless, such investigations are necessary in order to identify the mode of action of chemicals. The results are published and discussed in Braunbeck *et al.* (1989a), Braunbeck *et al.* (1989b), Braunbeck *et al.* (1990), and Braunbeck *et al.* (1992).

These various effects need to be assessed at the population level. Based on investigations of zebrafish populations in complex laboratory systems (Schäfers *et al.*, 1989), Oertel *et al.* (1991) have created a stochastic model named 'zebrafish'. The model can be used for an extrapolation of the effects occurring in life cycle tests to the level of a mean laboratory population. The general experience with zebrafish tests and the use of this model leads to the following evaluation of the various endpoints.

For the maintenance of zebrafish populations, the survival of the older larval and young juvenile stages is vital. Fitness of larvae is also important; however, there is as yet no method for testing the parameter 'fitness'. In the author's opinion, reproduction is not as important as survival. For example, a 20% reduction in egg production is not as dramatic for the population as would be the same percentage reduction in survival of older larvae.

The results with the four compounds show that complete life cycle tests with zebrafish can be carried out and that they provide meaningful results. It was interesting to find that in the case of 4-nitrophenol and 3,4-dichloroaniline the early life stages of the FII-generation were more sensitive than those of the FI-generation. These results show that McKim's opinion (1977, 1985) that ELS tests can replace complete life cycle tests is worthy of further discussion. This point of

Table 17.2 Acute to chronic ratio (ACR)[*].

	LC50 (mg.l^{-1})	ACR	Endpoint	
Atrazine	37	370	FI	ELS survival
4-Nitrophenol	14	no NOEC	FII	Survival
		140	FII	Survival (LOEC)
3,4-Dichloroaniline	8	4000	FII	ELS survival
Lindane	0.09	1	FII	ELS survival
		2	FI	Reproduction
		2	FI	ELS growth (LOEC)
		2	FI	adults' behaviour (LOEC)

[*] LC$_{50}$ (96 h)/NOEC life cycle test

view is supported by the results of Bresch *et al.* (1990) and by a literature review of Chorus (1987).

It is clear that complete life cycle tests are the only way to demonstrate the chronic toxicity of chemicals to fish. An extrapolation from acute to chronic effects is not possible, and the acute to chronic ratio can be considerable (Table 17.2). Therefore, a complete life cycle test should be recommended for level 2. A feasible test framework with zebrafish for the base level and level 1 and 2 has been discussed in Nagel (1991).

It was hoped that complete life cycle tests with zebrafish could be shown to be useful tools in fish toxicology. But there are still some remaining problems. Assuming that there has been an observed effect within a life cycle test, we are now able to assess the consequences of this effect on a population of test fish. But can we extrapolate the results to other species or to the situation in the environment? These questions are under investigation in the author's working group and some aspects and a concept to solve some problems are discussed in Schäfers and Nagel (1991, 1994).

Acknowledgements

This study was supported by a grant from the Federal Minister of Science and Technology, BMFT. The author wishes to thank Michael Leonhard for reading the manuscript.

References

Braunbeck, T., H. Bresch, H. and R. Nagel, 1989a. Stoffspezifische Reaktionen der Ultrastruktur der Leber des Zebrabärblings (*Brachydanio rerio*) auf Chemikalien. *Verh.Dtsch.Zool.Ges.*, **82**: 183.

Braunbeck, T., V. Storch and R. Nagel, 1989b. Sex-specific reaction of liver ultrastructure in zebrafish (*Brachydanio rerio*) after prolonged sublethal exposure to 4-nitrophenol. *Aquat.Toxicol.*, **14**: 185–202.

Braunbeck, T., G. Görge, V. Storch and R. Nagel, 1990. Hepatic steatosis in zebrafish (*Brachydanio rerio*) induced by long-term exposure to γ-hexachlorocyclohexane. *Ecotox.Environ.Safety*, **19**: 355–374.

Braunbeck, T., P. Burkhardt-Holm, G. Görge, R. Nagel, R.D. Negele and V. Storch, 1993. Regenbogenforelle und Zebrabärbling, zwei Modelle für verlängerte Toxizitätstests: relative Empfindlichkeit, Art- und Organspezifität in der cytopathologischen Reaktion von Leber und Darm auf Atrazin. *Schriftenr.Ver.Wasser-, Boden-, Lufthygiene*, in press.

Bresch, H., 1982. Investigation of long-term action of xenobiotics on fish with special regard to reproduction. *Ecotoxicol.Environ.Safety*, **6**: 102–112.

Bresch, H., P. Gode, B. Hamburger, P.-D. Hansen, I. Juhnke, F. Krebs, K. Lillelund, M. Markert, R. Munk, R. Nagel, E.A. Nusch, J. Scheubel and O.H. Spieser, 1986. Deliberations and investigations of the DIN working group 'fish test' on a long-term test according to the German Chemicals Act. *Z.Wasser-Abwasser-Forsch.*, **19**: 47–49.

Bresch, H., H. Beck, D. Ehlermann, H. Schlaszus and M. Urbanek, 1990. A long-term toxicity test comprising reproduction and growth of zebrafish with 4-chloroaniline. *Arch.Environ.Contam. Toxicol.*, **19**: 419–427.

Chorus, I., 1987. Literaturrecherche und Auswertung zur Notwendigkeit chronischer Tests – insbesondere des Reproduktionstests – am Fisch für die Stufe II nach dem Chemikaliengesetz, Berlin, Umweltbundesamt.

Eaton, J.G., 1970. Chronic malathion toxicity to the bluegill (*Lepomis macrochirus* Rafinesque). *Water. Res.*, **4**: 673–684.

Holcombe, G.W., D.A. Benoit, E.N. Leonard and J.M. McKim, 1976. Long-term effects of lead exposure on three generations of brook trout (*Salvelinus fontinalis*). *J.Fish.Res.Bd.Can.*, **33**: 1731–1741.

Macek, K.J., K.S. Buxton, S. Sauter, S. Gnilka and J.W. Dean, 1976a. Chronic toxicity of atrazine to selected aquatic invertebrates and fishes. US Environmental Protection Agency, EPA-600/3–76–047.

Macek, K.J., K.S. Buxton, S.K. Derr, J.W. Dean and S. Sauter, 1976b. Chronic toxicity of lindane to selected aquatic invertebrates and fishes. US Environmental Protection Agency, EPA-600/3–76–046.

McKim, J.M., 1977. Evaluation of tests with early life stages of fish for predicting long term toxicity. *J.Fish.Res.Bd.Can.*, **34**: 1148–1154.

McKim, J.M., 1985. Early life stage toxicity tests. In: Rand, G.M. and S.R. Petrocelli (Eds.) *Fundamentals of Aquatic Toxicology*, pp. 58–95. Washington, Hemisphere Publishing.

McKim, J.M. and D.A. Benoit, 1971. Effects of long-term exposures to copper on the survival, growth, and reproduction of brook trout. *J.Fish.Res.Bd.Can.*, **28**: 655–662.

McKim, J.M. and D.A. Benoit, 1974. Duration of toxicity tests for establishing 'no effect' concentrations for copper with brook trout. *J.Fish.Res.Bd.Can.*, **31**: 449–452.

McKim, J.M., G.W. Holcombe, G.F. Olson and E.P. Hunt, 1976. Long-term effects of methylmercuric chloride on three generations of brook trout: toxicity, accumulation, distribution and elimination. *J.Fish.Res.Bd.Can.*, **33**: 2726–2739.

Mount, D.I. and C.E. Stephan, 1967. A method for establishing acceptable limits for fish – Malathion and the butoxyethanol ester of 2,4-D. *Trans.Am.Fish.Soc.*, **96**: 185–193.

Nagel, R., 1986. Untersuchungen zur Eiproduktion beim Zebrabärbling (*Brachydanio rerio*, Ham.-Buch.). *J.Appl.Ichthyol.*, **2**: 173–181.

Nagel, R., 1988. Fische und Umweltchemikalien – Beiträge zu einer Bewertung. Dissertation, University of Mainz.

Nagel, R., 1993. Fish and environmental chemicals – a critical evaluation of tests. In: Braunbeck, T., W. Hanke and H. Segner (Eds.) *Fish in Ecotoxicology and Ecophysiology*, pp. 147–156. Weinheim, VCH.

Nagel, R., H. Bresch, N. Caspers, P.-D. Hansen, M. Markert, R. Munk, N. Scholz and B.B. ter Höfte, 1991. Effect of 3,4-dichloroaniline on the early life stages of the zebrafish (*Brachydanio rerio*): results of a comparative laboratory study. *Ecotoxicol.Environ.Safety*, **21**: 157–164.

Oertel, D., C. Schäfers, H.J. Poethke, R. Nagel and A. Seitz, 1991. Simulation of the population dynamics of zebrafish in a complex experimental system. *Verh.Ges.Ökologie*, **20**(2): 865–869.

Schäfers, C. and R. Nagel, 1991. Effect of 3,4-dichloroaniline on fish populations. Comparison of r- and K-strategists. A complete life cycle test with guppy (*Poecilia reticulata*). *Arch.Environ.Contam. Toxicol.*, **21**: 297–302.

Schäfers, C. and R. Nagel, 1994. Fish toxicity and population dynamics - effects of 3,4-dichloroaniline and the problems of extrapolation. Chapter 20, this volume..

Schäfers, C., R. Nagel and A. Seitz, 1989. Behaviour, reproduction, and population dynamics of zebrafish (*Brachydanio rerio*) in a complex experimental system. *Fischökologie*, **1**(2): 45–59.

Suter, G.W., A.E. Rosen, E. Linder and D.V. Parkhurst, 1987. Endpoints for responses of fish to chronic toxic exposures. *Environ.Toxicol.Chem.*, **6**: 793–809.

Woltering, D.M., 1984. The growth response in fish chronic and early life stage toxicity tests: a critical review. *Aquat.Toxicol.*, **5**: 1–21.

Chapter 18
Influence of ochre and acidification on the survival and hatching of brown trout eggs (*Salmo trutta*)

P. GEERTZ-HANSEN and G. RASMUSSEN

Inland Fisheries Laboratory, Lysbrogade 52, DK-8600 Silkeborg, Denmark

18.1   Introduction

Denmark (excluding Bornholm) is a low lying country with a terrain formed during the second-last and last glacial period. Deposits from the Cretaceous and Tertiary period are found just below the moraine and the fluvial deposits from the two glacial periods. From the Tertiary period, lignite containing pyrite (FeS_2) is found in West Jutland where intensive mining took place up to the 1960s. In other swampy areas with anaerobic degradation, deposits containing pyrite and siderite ($FeCO_3$) were established. When intensive cultivation was developed from the middle of the last century thousands of small streams and bogs were either channelled or drained.

Pyrite and siderite are nearly insoluble, and when they remain in the soil without access to air they will remain unchanged. When exposed to the atmosphere on the surface of a lignite strip mine, by drainage of peat bogs, or by other measures that lower the groundwater level, the pyrite or siderite is oxidised, causing the formation of sulphur or carbonic acid and iron salts, predominantly ferric sulphate or ferric carbonate. During the last ten years, acidification of soil and groundwater by large amounts of farmyard manure spread over the fields has also been responsible for some ochre pollution. The buffering capacity of the streams will then control the time taken for the soluble iron (Fe^{2+} and/or Fe^{3+}) to be transformed into ferric hydroxide (ochre), which is insoluble and thus precipitates. These processes may also be facilitated by the presence of iron bacteria (e.g. *Thiobacillus* sp.). Where the pH has been reduced to below 3–4 by sulphuric acid and ferric sulphate, fish will be rapidly killed by the action of the acid alone (Alabaster and Lloyd, 1980) but under conditions where hydrolysis of the soluble iron is initiated, possibly accelerated by bacteria, the fish may be killed by the precipitation of ferric hydroxide.

Trout (migratory and non-migratory *Salmo trutta*) is the most common fish species in small shallow Danish streams of up to 5–6 m wide (Larsen, 1955). If these trout populations are to be maintained without stocking, it is necessary for all the phases in the life cycle to be protected, including reproduction and survival of the fry.

In Denmark, the spawning of trout takes place in November and December. The fertilised eggs develop in the protection of the stream gravel. Water-flow through the gravel provides oxygen for respiration and removes carbon dioxide and ammonia. The fry emerge from the gravel in April after having spent up to 5 months there. Deposits (e.g., clay, sand and suspended iron complexes) can impede the water flow through the spawning redds with adverse consequences.

The potentially detrimental effects of iron on the fish populations in streams and in trout ponds were recognised in the 1930s (Otterstrøm, 1938; Larsen and Olsen, 1950; Dahl, 1963).

The combination of acid water and iron on the development of trout eggs and larvae might have the following effects. Soluble iron (Fe^{2+}) might be precipitated on and between the stones of the gravel (Scullion and Edwards, 1980) and/or upon the low alkaline surfaces of fish eggs (Smith *et al.*, 1978) and the gill epithelium of developing sac-fry larvae. Also, there may be a direct toxic effect of the iron on the eggs and larvae.

This chapter describes part of a field and laboratory study (Geertz-Hansen *et al.*, 1984) on the relationship between iron, aluminium, acid water and the survival of several fish species in Denmark. The study took place in the period 1982–84 but some earlier data (Geertz-Hansen and Mortensen, 1983) from a single stream are included.

18.2   Study areas

The river systems and field sites where the study took place are shown in Figure 18.1. Brief descriptions of the field sites are as follows.

Goldbæk, station 1A, 1B, 1C

The stream is about 6.5 km from source to outlet into the Skjern Å river system which drains to the North Sea. The stream arises as drainage channels which are the main source of iron. Most of the stream length is channelled. The bed consists of sand and gravel. The content of iron varies considerably throughout the year. Some eels (*Anguilla anguilla*) and minnows (*Phoxinus phoxinus*) are found at station 1A, and some single trout that have migrated upstream from the lower stretches can be found at station 1B.

Risbjærg Bæk, station 2A, 2B, 2C

The stream is about 8 km from source to outlet into the Skjern Å river system. Most of the stream has been channelled. The bed consists of sand and gravel. The first 6 km of the water course receives water containing iron from channels and drains arising from areas with bogs. Self-sustaining populations of rainbow trout (*Oncorhynchus mykiss*), pike (*Esox lucius*), eel and scorpion fish (*Cottus poecilopus*) are found.

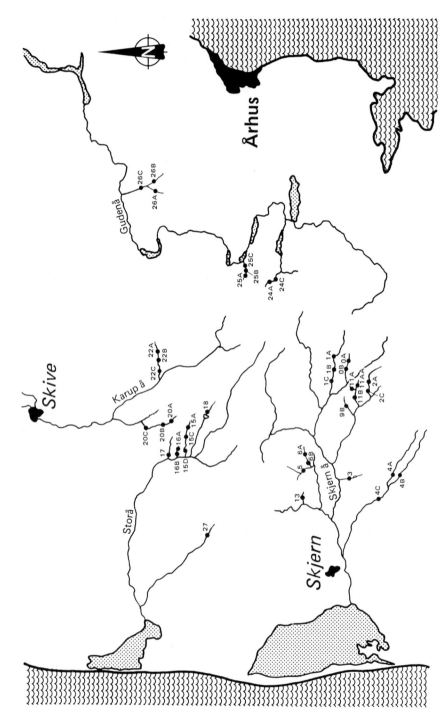

Fig. 18.1   River systems and field sites. Details of the individual sites are described in the text.

Sigbæk 3

The stream is about 6 km from source to outlet into the Skjern Å river system. Most of the stream has been channelled and the stream receives water containing iron from drains and old lignite mining areas. Sometimes trout, eel and dace (*Leuciscus leuciscus*) are present.

Birkholt Bæk 4A and Engmose Bæk 4B

These streams run almost parallel and are both about 2.5 km from source to outlet into Hårkær Bæk (about 9 km) which then goes into the Skjern Å river system. The streams are channelled and station 4A receives water containing iron. The bed consists of sand and gravel. Both streams have some sparse self-reproducing trout populations; some pike and eel are also found.

Blindbæk 5

The stream is about 5 km from source to outlet into the Von Å which then goes into the Skjern Å river system. The stream arises from old lignite mining areas with acid water and the stream receives an effluent containing iron. The bed consists of sand and gravel. No fish species are found.

Følpøt Bæk 6A, 6AA, 6B

The stream is about 2 km from source to outlet into the Von Å which then goes into the Skjern Å river system. The bed consists of sand and gravel. The upper half arises as channels containing acid water and iron. The lower half of the stream is much less channelled and contains a self-reproducing trout population. Station 6AA is situated in a little inlet with a self-reproducing trout population.

Tarp Bæk 9A, 9AB, 9B

The stream is about 3 km from source to outlet into the Karstofte Å which then goes into the Skjern Å river system. The stream has been channelled to some extent and about 1 km below the source and between station 9A and 9AB the stream receives an effluent containing iron. The bed consists of sand and gravel. Besides self-reproducing trout the stream has a small population of brook trout (*Salvelinus fontinalis*).

Brogaard Bæk 11B

The stream is about 5 km from source to outlet into the Karstofte Å which then goes into the Skjern Å river system. The stream has been channelled and it receives water with a low iron content. The bed consists of sand and gravel with larger stones. Besides self-reproducing trout, three-spined stickleback (*Gasterosteus aculeatus*) and brook lampreys (*Lampetra fluviatilis*) are found.

Lille Skærbæk 13

The stream is about 2.5 km from source to outlet into the Vorgod Å which then goes into the Skjern Å river system. The stream is a natural watercourse. The bed consists of sand and gravel. The water is slightly acidic but with very low content of iron. Self-reproducing trout are found.

Hallund Bæk 17

The stream is about 6 km from source to outlet into the Storå river system which drains to the North Sea. The stream has been channelled and receives water containing iron from several drains. The iron content of the water varies considerably during the year. The bed consists of sand and gravel. No fish species are found in the stream.

Sunds Møllebæk 18

The stream is about 8 km from source to outlet into the Lake Sunds which then goes into the Storå river system. The stream has been channelled and receives water and iron from several drains. The water flow and iron content of the water varies considerably during the year. The bed consists of sand and gravel. Besides eel, dace and gudgeon (*Gobio gobio*) are found.

Ginderskov Bæk 20A, 20B, 20C

The stream is about 10 km from source to outlet into the Karup Å river system which then goes into the Limfjord. The first 3.5 km of the stream has been heavily channelled and receives acid water with a high iron content. The bed consists of sand and turf. The lower part of the stream is much less channelled but receives water containing iron from several drains and the bed consists of sand and gravel. At station 20A there are no fish present. At station 20B a few large trout and pike are found. At station 20C a small self-reproducing trout population is present.

Åresvad Å 22A, 22B

The stream is about 8 km from source to outlet into the Karup Å river system. The upper part of the stream has been channelled and it receives water containing iron from bogs and drained cultivated areas. The bed consists of sand and gravel. The stream has a sparse trout population that has immigrated from the lower stretches.

Skærbækken 24A, 24B, 24C, 24Ø, 24M, 24N, 24K

The stream is about 4.5 km from source to outlet into Salten Å which then goes into the Gudenå river system which drains to the Kattegat. The stream is almost completely channelled and receives water containing iron from siderite deposits. The bed consists of sand and gravel. Self-reproducing trout and also lampreys are found.

Lysbro Møllebæk 25A, 25B, 25C

The stream is about 1.5 km from source to outlet into the Lake Silkeborg Langsø which then goes into the Gudenå river system. The stream has been channelled and the lower part of the stream receives water containing iron. The bed consists of sand and gravel. No fish species are found at the sampling stations.

Tjærbæk 26A, 26B, 26C

The stream is about 7 km from source to outlet into the Gudenå river system. The upper part of the stream (26A) is a natural watercourse and with water containing iron and with some individual trout. Downstream of the confluence the stream is a natural watercourse and contains a self-reproducing trout population. The bed consists of sand and gravel.

Fuglkær Å 27

The stream is about 7 km from source to outlet into Råsted- Lilleå which then goes into the Storå river system. The upper part of the stream is channelled but free of iron. The lower part of the stream receives water containing iron from bogs and drains. The bed consists of sand and gravel. The stream has a self-reproducing trout population.

18.3   Material and methods

The localities were visited at one- or two-weekly intervals. Acidity (pH) was measured at the sites at ambient water temperature, using a Radiometer PHM 80 pH-meter.

Soluble iron (Fe^{2+}) was measured on site by the bipyridyl method using a Corning 252 field-colorimeter (Danish Agency of Environmental Protection, 1981). The water sample was filtered through a 145 μ millipore filter before the determination of iron.

Total iron ($Fe^{2+}+Fe^{3+}$) was measured using the bipyridyl method. The water samples were acidified with 0.5% HCl on site and analysed in the laboratory (Danish Agency of Environmental Protection, 1981).

Eggs from a commercial trout strain from a local hatchery were used in the experiments. Green eggs were stripped at the hatchery, fertilised and transported in plastic containers to the different stations. A certain volume of eggs (containing 374 to 418 depending of the age of the mature fish) were measured in a cylinder and placed in a Vibert box. Each box had previously been filled with gravel from the same stream in order to prevent silting of the box. From three to five Vibert boxes were tied together and buried about 10 cm down in the gravel of an artificially made spawning ground made of the local stream gravel. In some streams only one spawning ground was made but in other streams up to five spawning grounds were made. The eggs were placed out between 25 and 28 January 1983. Minimum–maximum thermometers made it possible to calculate the date when all the eggs would have hatched under normal circumstances. After about 13 weeks the boxes were dug up (between 19 April and 3 May 1983) and brought to the laboratory where the number of dead and live eggs and larvae were counted. A total of 193 Vibert boxes were distributed between the 27 different stations in 15 different streams.

Eyed eggs had been kept as green eggs at the hatchery and when at the eyed stage they were transported to the different stations. 250 or 326 eggs were placed in Vibert boxes and spawning grounds using the same method as that for green eggs. The eggs were placed out during 8–11 January 1983. After about 5–6 weeks the boxes were dug up during 8–30 March 1983 and brought to the laboratory where the number of dead and live eggs and larvae were counted. A total of 207 Vibert boxes were distributed between 30 different stations in 14 different streams, all of which included those streams used for green eggs.

Eyed eggs (about 150 eggs in each dish) were placed in petri dishes with holes and placed in the over-lying water from 8–11 February 1983 and recovered after about four weeks (8–11 March 1983). A total of 32 boxes were distributed between 16 different stations in 10 different streams, all of which except for two included those streams used for green and eyed eggs.

During the period when the eggs were being incubated in the streams, pH and concentration of soluble iron (Fe^{2+}) and total iron ($Fe^{2+}+Fe^{3+}$) in the water were measured.

From the count of dead and live eggs and larvae, the following data were calculated:

Percentage egg hatch

$$= \frac{\text{Number of incubated eggs} - \text{Number of dead eggs}}{\text{Number of incubated eggs}} \times 100$$

Percentage maximal larval survival

$$= \frac{\text{Number of incubated eggs} - \text{Number of dead eggs} + \text{larvae}}{\text{Number of incubated eggs}} \times 100$$

Kendall's rank correlation coefficient Tau and Pearson's correlation coefficient r (Siegel, 1956) were used to examine the relationship between maximal larval survival and the variables pH, Fe^{2+} and $Fe^{2+}+Fe^{3+}$). These comparisons were used to calculate the levels of acidity and iron which would allow a reasonable development of eggs and larvae in Danish trout spawning streams. The criterion for the precise derivation of a 'safety limit' is that no correlation between the variables exists *below* this value and a significant correlation exists *above* this figure. The exact procedure used was to begin the calculation with data including high values of the independent variables of pH and iron and then progress to lower values until the 'safety limit' was determined.

18.4   Results

The mean values of pH, Fe^{2+} and $Fe^{2+}+Fe^{3+}$ and percentage egg hatch and maximal larval survival from the different stations and streams are given in Tables 18.1, 18.2 and 18.3. The mean values of water chemistry calculated for the period when the green eggs were being incubated were also used for the eyed eggs. This might introduce some bias in the data but the extent of this bias is less than the variation of the mean of the measurements.

An example of the variations found in the ferrous iron content during the year at one of the stations is shown in Figure 18.2.

In the tables, negative values for hatching and larval survival are given. This is because the number of eggs in the Vibert boxes were only estimated from their volume in the syringe and number of eggs per unit volume varied. When 100% of eggs and larvae are dead (and this happened especially with the green eggs) there may have been cases where the total dead eggs and larvae exceeded the estimated number incubated.

From the data in Table 18.1 the summary in Table 18.4 can be made for green eggs in Vibert boxes.

Table 18.5 shows the statistical analysis where

Y:	% maximal larval survival	*ns*:	$P \geqslant 0.05$
$x1$:	Fe^{2+} mg.l^{-1}	*s*:	$P < 0.05$

The relationship between percentage maximal larval survival and Fe^{2+} (>0.8 mg.l^{-1}) gives the following:

$$Y\% = 14.1\ (\pm 5.4) - 7.4\ (\pm 4.0) \times Fe^{2+}\ (\text{mg.l}^{-1}), \quad r = -0.46\ (s)$$

Similarly, Table 18.6 shows the summary data for eyed eggs in Vibert boxes (from Table 18.2) and the statistical analysis is shown in Table 18.7, where

Y:	% maximal larval survival	*ns*:	$P \geqslant 0.05$
$x1$:	Fe^{2+} mg.l^{-1}	*s*:	$P < 0.05$
$x2$:	$Fe^{2+} + Fe^{3+}$ mg.l^{-1}		
$x3$:	pH		

Table 18.1 Physico-chemical characteristics of the field sites, and the hatching success and maximal larval survival of green eggs in the Vibert boxes.

Locality	pH	Fe^{2+} mg.l^{-1}	$Fe^{2+}+Fe^{3+}$ mg.l^{-1}	Hatching success %	Maximal larval survival %	Number of Vibert boxes
1A	6.68	1.70	3.79	4.9	4.9	4
1B	6.78	0.58	2.81	5.1	5.1	5
2A	6.66	1.13	2.26	6.0	5.9	5
2C	6.53	0.89	2.58	4.9	4.5	10
4A	5.87	0.55	0.84	7.2	7.2	8
4B	6.00	0.12	0.31	6.6	6.6	8
5	5.37	1.90	2.26	0.2	0.2	8
6A	5.98	0.80	1.33	−5.0	−5.0	5
6B	6.38	0.47	0.73	4.5	1.3	10
9A	6.25	0.11	0.30	2.9	2.7	6
9AB	6.22	0.50	0.65	14.5	11.1	6
9B	6.35	0.38	0.79	−3.0	−3.9	3
11B	6.44	0.53	1.02	6.4	5.7	10
17	6.51	1.66	3.25	1.7	1.4	5
13	6.00	0.18	0.19	−5.1	−5.1	8
18	6.64	1.60	3.50	−0.6	−0.6	5
22A	6.70	0.51	0.62	20.7	20.7	6
22B	6.81	0.89	1.15	10.9	9.6	15
24A	6.95	0.19	0.37	22.7	20.6	15
24B	6.99	0.29	0.47	24.3	24.3	8
24C	7.00	0.67	0.89	16.7	16.7	8
25A	7.00	0.22	0.33	25.7	19.2	6
25B	7.00	0.40	2.13	18.7	18.5	6
26A	7.41	0.17	0.50	23.9	19.1	6
26B	7.18	0.76	1.71	18.2	18.2	6
26C	7.23	0.53	1.43	15.5	14.5	5
27	6.17	0.17	0.47	27.2	27.1	6

The relationship between % maximal larval survival and Fe^{2+} (>0.65 mg.l^{-1}) gives the following:

$$Y\% = 42.4 \ (\pm18.2) - 18.95 \ (\pm14.8) \times Fe^{2+} \ (mg.l^{-1}), \quad r = -0.27 \ (s)$$

Figure 18.3 shows the relationship between maximal larval survival from eyed eggs in Vibert boxes and concentrations of ferrous iron. The relatively low 'maximal larval survival' (i.e. 61.2%) in the boxes at the lowest iron concentrations (0–0.25 mg.l^{-1}) reflects the bias due to the use of Vibert boxes. Much of the reduction in survival rates is possibly due to the suffocation of the eyed eggs by siltation.

The correlations $r \ (Y,x1)$, $r \ (Y,x2)$ and $r \ (Y,x3)$ between % maximal larval survival and different concentrations of Fe^{2+} and $Fe^{2+} + Fe^{3+}$ and pH, and partial correlations $r \ (Yx1.x2)$ and $r \ (Yx1.x3)$ excluding the effects of acidity or total iron gives the values shown in Table 18.8. These results show that there are no significant ($P<0.05$) correlations between the survival of eggs and larvae, and total

Table 18.2 Physico-chemical characteristics of the field sites, and the hatching success and maximal larval survival of eyed eggs in the Vibert boxes.

Locality	pH	Fe^{2+} mg.l^{-1}	$Fe^{2+}+Fe^{3+}$ mg.l^{-1}	Hatching success %	Maximal larval survival %	Number of Vibert boxes
1A	6.68	1.70	3.79	57.2	19.8	5
1B	6.78	0.58	2.81	77.5	32.2	5
2A	6.66	1.13	2.26	53.2	36.7	10
2B	6.53	1.27	2.73	9.0	7.3	10
2C	6.53	0.89	2.58	54.0	29.5	10
4B	6.00	0.12	0.31	60.1	50.6	5
5	5.37	1.90	2.26	35.7	2.6	8
6A	5.98	0.80	1.33	70.9	4.1	5
6AA	6.47	0.35	0.47	25.6	24.5	6
6B	6.38	0.47	0.73	64.1	50.9	8
9A	6.25	0.11	0.30	56.7	24.9	6
9AB	6.22	0.50	0.65	76.7	65.4	6
9B	6.35	0.38	0.79	100.0	96.2	3
11B	6.44	0.53	1.02	95.8	71.7	10
17	6.51	1.66	3.25	2.9	2.9	5
18	6.64	1.60	3.50	1.5	1.5	5
22A	6.70	0.51	0.62	−0.2	−0.2	6
22B	6.81	0.89	1.15	65.0	55.9	12
24A	6.95	0.19	0.37	67.2	49.4	15
24B	6.99	0.29	0.47	31.0	29.9	8
24C	7.00	0.67	0.89	3.9	3.8	8
24Ø	6.76	0.06	0.31	90.3	76.8	5
24M	7.05	0.23	0.46	100.0	100.0	4
24N	7.05	0.51	0.82	56.7	54.5	4
25A	7.00	0.22	0.33	86.9	82.3	6
25B	7.00	0.40	2.13	62.6	42.2	6
26A	7.41	0.17	0.50	74.6	69.3	6
26B	7.18	0.76	1.71	29.3	18.0	5
26C	7.23	0.53	1.43	31.7	24.4	9
27	6.17	0.17	0.47	76.0	67.3	6

iron ($Fe^{2+} + Fe^{3+}$) and pH within the range found for this study. But it can also be seen that even if pH and total iron have no direct effect on eggs and larvae, excluding their effects ($r\,(Yx1.x2)$ or $r\,(Yx1.x3)$) lowers the toxicity (effect) of Fe^{2+} from about 0.65 mg.l^{-1} to about 0.5 mg.l^{-1}.

Although the data for eyed eggs in petri-dishes (Table 18.3) are limited, the information in Table 18.9 can be derived from them.

18.5   Discussion

In this study the very sensitive green eggs and the much more resistant eyed eggs were incubated in Vibert boxes in artificially made spawning grounds. The former were kept in the gravel and were exposed to iron and acid water for up to about 13 weeks, whereas the eyed eggs were incubated for only about 5–6 weeks. Although the hatching success and larval survival varied considerably within the two groups

Table 18.3 Physico-chemical characteristics of the field sites, and the hatching success and maximal larval survival of eyed eggs in the petri dishes.

Locality	pH	Fe^{2+} $mg.l^{-1}$	$Fe^{2+}+Fe^{3+}$ $mg.l^{-1}$	Hatching success %	Maximal larval survival %	Number of petri dishes
1A	6.68	1.70	3.79	98.7	96.9	1
1B	6.78	0.58	2.81	97.0	93.4	2
3	5.93	1.08	2.86	62.7	57.0	2
4B	6.00	0.12	0.31	100.0	99.3	2
5	5.37	1.90	2.26	16.7	1.7	2
6A	5.98	0.80	1.33	97.0	88.0	2
17	6.51	1.66	3.25	62.0	26.1	1
18	6.64	1.60	3.50	71.3	20.7	2
20A	6.43	5.90	7.83	5.7	0.3	2
20B	6.58	2.50	5.91	52.3	18.0	2
20C	6.66	0.98	4.36	92.7	92.6	1
24Ø	6.76	0.06	0.31	95.3	56.0	2
24N	7.05	0.51	0.82	98.5	53.3	4
24K	6.97	2.08	3.02	97.0	20.7	2
25Ø	6.55	2.91	5.17	50.7	11.7	2
25C	6.67	4.97	8.79	11.3	3.8	2

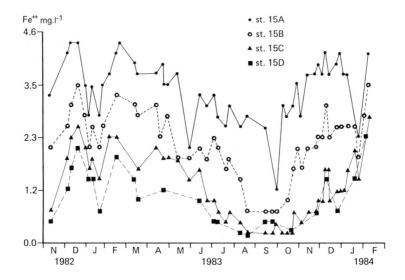

Fig. 18.2 Variation in the ferrous iron concentration during the year, at four stations (15A, 15B, 15C, 15D) in Røjen bæk. The distance between the stations is about 2 km. Station 15A is situated furthest upstream. The ferrous iron concentration is declining downstream due to oxidation and dilution of ferrous iron. Yearly variation in concentration of ferrous iron is typical for the localities involved.

Table 18.4 Green eggs in Vibert boxes

Fe^{2+} (mg.l^{-1})	Egg hatching % (±95% CL)	Maximal larval survival % (±95% CL)	Number of Vibert boxes
$Fe^{2+} \leq 0.25$	14.6% ±4.6%	13.0% ±4.4%	55
$0.25 < Fe^{2+} \leq 0.50$	11.8% ±5.0%	11.1% ±4.7%	33
$0.50 < Fe^{2+} \leq 0.75$	1.7% ±2.6%	11.2% ±2.3%	42
$0.75 < Fe^{2+} \leq 1.00$	8.2% ±3.3%	7.6% ±3.3%	36
$1.00 < Fe^{2+}$	2.0% ±1.7%	2.0% ±1.7%	27

Table 18.5 Statistical analysis of the data in Table 18.1

	r ($Yx1$)	Tau ($Yx1$)	Number of Vibert boxes
for x1 ≤ 0.8	−0.12 (*ns*)	−0.04 (*ns*)	141
for x1 > 0.8	−0.46 (*s*)	−0.33 (*s*)	52

Table 18.6 Eyed eggs in Vibert boxes

Fe^{2+} (mg.l^{-1})	Egg hatching % (±95% CL)	Maximal larval survival % (±95% CL)	Number of Vibert boxes
$Fe^{2+} \leq 0.25$	73.6% ± 6.7%	61.2% ± 8.8%	53
$0.25 < Fe^{2+} \leq 0.50$	53.3% ±11.8%	46.7% ±11.8%	37
$0.50 < Fe^{2+} \leq 0.75$	49.9% ±13.4%	32.0% ±11.6%	42
$0.75 < Fe^{2+} \leq 1.00$	56.9% ±11.5%	33.7% ±11.3%	32
$1.00 < Fe^{2+}$	24.2% ±11.2%	13.5% ± 6.8%	43

Table 18.7 Statistical analysis of the data in Table 18.2

	r ($Yx1$)	Tau ($Yx1$)	Number of Vibert boxes
for x1 ≤ 0.65	−0.19 (*ns*)	−0.08 (*ns*)	124
for x1 > 0.65	−0.27 (*s*)	−0.18 (*s*)	83

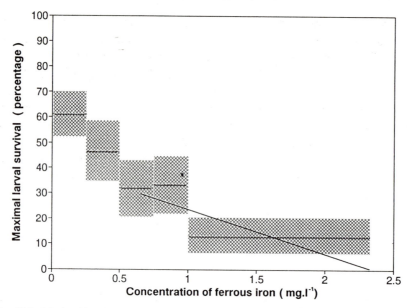

Fig. 18.3   Maximal larval survival from the eyed eggs in Vibert boxes. The broken horizontal lines show the mean maximal survival in four different concentrations regimes of ferrous iron. Shaded areas show the 95% confidence limits. The heavy line gives the relationship between the maximal larval survival and the ferrous iron concentration for eyed eggs in Vibert boxes exposed to ferrous iron concentrations higher than 0.65 mg.l^{-1}.

Table 18.8   Multiple correlation analysis (see text)

	$r (Yx1)$	$r (Yx2)$	$r (Yx3)$	$r (Yx1.x2)$	$r (Yx1.x3)$	Number of Vibert boxes
$x1 \leq 0.5$	−0.03 (*ns*)	−0.04 (*ns*)	−0.01 (*ns*)	0.01 (*ns*)	−0.03 (*ns*)	90
$x1 > 0.5$	−0.28 (*ns*)	−0.05 (*ns*)	−0.06 (*ns*)	−0.39 (*s*)	−0.49 (*s*)	117
$x1 \leq 0.6$	−0.19 (*ns*)	−0.06 (*ns*)	−0.04 (*ns*)	−0.14 (*ns*)	−0.18 (*ns*)	124
$x1 > 0.6$	−0.21 (*s*)	−0.07 (*ns*)	0.13 (*ns*)	−0.25 (*s*)	−0.25 (*s*)	83
$x1 \leq 0.7$	−0.30 (*s*)	0.03 (*ns*)	−0.07 (*ns*)	−0.42 (*s*)	−0.29 (*s*)	132
$x1 > 0.7$	−0.28 (*s*)	−0.22 (*ns*)	0.17 (*ns*)	−0.15 (*ns*)	−0.26 (*s*)	75
$x1 > 1.0$	−0.41 (*s*)	−0.11 (*ns*)	−0.04 (*ns*)	−0.37 (*s*)	−0.64 (*s*)	43

Table 18.9   Eyed eggs in petri dishes

Fe^{2+} (mg.l^{-1})	Egg hatching % (±95% CL)	Maximal larval survival % (±95% CL)	Number of petri-dishes
$Fe^{2+} \leq 1.00$	97.3% ± 1.4%	75.3% ±12.8%	13
$1.00 < Fe^{2+} \leq 2.00$	58.2% ±20.6%	34.2% ± 4.3%	9
$2.00 < Fe^{2+}$	43.4% ±25.1%	10.9% ± 6.7%	10

(doubtless reflecting the influence of iron), the mean percentages were 10.2% ±3.8% and 9.3% ±3.6% for the green eggs and 53.9% ±11.1% and 39.8% ±10.8% for the eyed eggs respectively. For the eyed eggs held in petri dishes the corresponding figures were 69.3% ±17.7% and 46.2% ±19.8%, respectively. The low figures given above and in Table 18.1 for the green eggs must reflect the effect of a much longer incubation time than the eyed eggs, but it is most probable that there was a weakness in the chosen method of incubation, because the Vibert boxes were designed for the hatching of eyed eggs (Vibert, 1977). During incubation, the buried eggs would be more affected by silting and sand (the box acts as a silt-trap) than would naturally spawned eggs, especially in Danish lowland streams.

On the other hand, it is necessary to evaluate the development of trout eggs throughout the whole incubation period, especially if the effect of ochre is not a direct toxicity, but is caused by precipitation and/or siltation. In this case, the eyed eggs held in petri dishes were not so influenced by silting although precipitated iron was found in the dishes. It seems that an increasing mortality occurred when the concentration of iron rose to above 1 mg.l^{-1}. It is possible that there is a toxic effect occurring in combination with a precipitation of iron on the eggs.

The eyed eggs in the Vibert boxes were supposed to represent the normal situation for trout eggs in streams with an increased content of iron in the water. When the concentration of iron was less than about 0.25 mg.l^{-1}, the larval survival was about 61%. This is a rather low value and would normally have been expected to be about 90–95% (Hobbs, 1937). The difference between the expected and observed values (about 30–35%) might represent the 'mortality of the method used', that is an increased mortality from siltation. Nevertheless, it can be seen from the results that when soluble iron is above about 0.5 mg.l^{-1} there is a significant decrease in larval survival. It is therefore reasonable to suppose that in those streams where the normal egg and larval development of salmonids are required to take place, the content of Fe^{2+} should not increase above 0.5 mg.l^{-1}.

The difference in hatching success between the eyed eggs incubated in the Vibert boxes and in petri dishes respectively, shows the very great importance of simulating the natural circumstances as far as possible in this type of study, if the goal is to set limits for water quality.

References

Alabaster, J. S. and R. Lloyd, 1980. *Water Quality Criteria for Freshwater Fish*. London, Boston, Butterworth.

Dahl, J., 1963. Transformation of iron and sulphur compounds in soil and its relation to Danish inland fisheries. *Trans.Am.Fish.Soc.*, **90**: 469–474.

Danish Agency of Environmental Protection, 1981. Notat vedrørende bestemmelse af jern. (Determination of iron). (In Danish). Miljøstyrelsens Ferskvandslaboratorium (Freshwater Laboratory).

Geertz-Hansen, P. and E. Mortensen, 1983. Okkers virkning på reproduktionen hos ørred (*Salmo trutta* L.). (The influence from ochre on the reproduction of trout). (In Danish). *Vatten*, **39**: 55–62.

Geertz-Hansen, P., G. Nielsen and G. Rasmussen, 1984. Fiskebiologiske okkerundersøgelser. (Fishery biological studies on ochre) (in Danish). Report Miljøstyrelsen. Okkerredegørelsen.

Hobbs, D. F., 1937. Natural reproduction of quinnat salmon, brown and rainbow trout. *New Zealand Mar.Dep.Fish.Bull.*, **6**: 1–104.

Larsen, K., 1955. Fish population analysis in some small Danish trout streams by means of d.c. electrofishing. *Meddelelser fra Danmarks Fiskeri- og Havundersøgelser, Ny Serie. Bind 1.*, **10**: 1–63.

Larsen, K. and S. Olsen, 1950. Ochre suffocation of fish in the River Tim Å. *Rept.Danish Biol.Sta.*, **50**: 1–47.

Otterstrøm, C. V., 1938. Svovlsyreforgiftningen af vandløb fra udgrøftet eng. Katastrofen ved Lysbro. (The poisoning from sulphurous acid on streams coming from drained meadow. The catastrophe at Lysbro) (in Danish). *Ferskvandsfiskeribladet*, **36**: 2–14.

Scullion, J. and R.W. Edwards, 1980. The effect of pollutants from the coal industries on the fish fauna of a small river in the South Wales coalfield. *Environ.Poll.Ser. A*, **14**: 141–153.

Siegel, S., 1956. *Nonparametric Statistics for the Behavioural Sciences*. New York, McGraw-Hill.

Smith, E.J. *et al.*, 1978. Effects of lime neutralized iron hydroxide suspensions on survival, growth and reproduction of the fathead minnow (*Pimephales promelas*). *J.Fish.Res.Bd.Can.*, **30**: 1147–1153.

Vibert, R., 1977. Boîtes Vibert – Nouvelles précisions sur leur utilisation et leurs résultats. *Piscicult.Française*, **50**: 24–32.

Chapter 19
Effects of ammonia on the early life stages of carp (*Cyprinus carpio*) and roach (*Rutilus rutilus*)

M.J. MALLETT and I. SIMS

WRc plc, Henley Road, Medmenham, Buckinghamshire, SL7 2HD, England, UK

19.1   Introduction

Ammonia is one of the most common pollutants in British fresh waters. The main sources of ammonia in rivers are from sewage, including storm sewer overflows, and agriculture which includes drainage from silage, livestock wastes and sludge spread on land. Under the EC Dangerous Substances Directive (76/464/EC) member states are required to reduce the pollution of both fresh and salt waters which results from the discharge of List II substances, including ammonia, by the environmental quality objective (EQO) approach. In the UK the single mandatory standard of 0.025 mg.l^{-1} as NH_3 as a 95 percentile, specified under the EC Directive on Water Quality for Freshwater Fish (Council of the European Communities, 1978), has been adopted. The purpose of the work reported here was to determine whether that standard would provide adequate protection for species of freshwater fish common in UK waters.

In the development of standards for the protection of fish and other aquatic life it is important to ensure that all life stages are protected. Since previous work had shown that the early life stages (ELS) of rainbow trout (*Oncorhynchus mykiss*) were considerably more sensitive to ammonia than older stages (Solbé and Shurben, 1989) it was considered important to examine the sensitivity of equivalent stages of representative species. The species chosen were common carp (*Cyprinus carpio*) and roach (*Rutilus rutilus*). Studies were conducted on two stages of development for both species – fertilised eggs and newly hatched larvae; in both cases the studies lasted sufficiently long to include the free-feeding fry stage. The effect of ammonia on the fertilisation of roach eggs was also assessed.

19.2.   Methods and materials

19.2.1   *Source and use of ova*

(a)   *Roach*

Mature adult roach were obtained by electrofishing ponds situated at the WRc laboratory in March 1988. They were allowed to recover in stock tanks for several days before ovulation was induced by hypophysation using a 5 g.l^{-1} suspension of carp pituitary extract. This technique has been described for roach by Worthington (1983). A priming dose, equivalent to 0.5 mg pituitary extract per kilogram of wet body weight, followed 12 hours later by a resolving dose (5 mg.kg^{-1}) were given by intraperitoneal injection close to the ovaries. Twelve hours after the resolving dose, eggs were hand stripped and fertilised immediately.

Seven spawnings were carried out, and four resulted in the production of fertile eggs. These will subsequently be referred to in the text as spawnings 1 to 4. Deviations from the above procedures are described below.

Spawning 1   Occurred spontaneously in the stock tank without hypophysation. Some of these eggs were removed and placed in 125 ml crystallising dishes (50 per dish) and subsequently placed into the test vessels (one dish per vessel).

Spawning 2   Hypophysation and hand stripping were used. Eggs were removed from one female fish into a fertilisation solution consisting of 2 g.l^{-1} sodium chloride and 1.5 g.l^{-1} urea. They were immediately fertilised by mixing with milt obtained from a single male, with a goose wing feather. The eggs were then placed in trays (200–250 per tray) containing dilution water and one tray was added to each test vessel.

Spawning 3   As above but half the eggs were stripped into 125 ml crystallising dishes containing the test concentrations (about 150 eggs per dish). Two drops of milt were added to each dish and the dish swirled to distribute the eggs evenly over the bottom. Two dishes were placed into each of 10 test vessels. The remaining eggs were fertilised before being placed into a further 10 test vessels. By comparing the hatching success and survival of these two batches of eggs any effect on fertilisation success could be ascertained.

Eggs from the spawnings 1–3 described above were held in dishes or trays in the test vessels until hatching. On hatching, but before swim-up (11–15 days after fertilisation) the larvae from spawnings 1 and 2 were discarded. Exposure of spawning 3 was continued to post swim-up stage (130 days total exposure).

Spawning 4   Eggs were stripped from a fish, which had ovulated naturally, into a beaker containing 2 l of fertilisation solution. Milt was added and mixed by swirling. A gentle flow of groundwater was maintained over the eggs until hatching. The toxicity of ammonia to the hatched larvae from this spawning was examined.

(b)   Carp

Fertilised eggs were obtained from a commercial hatchery, Munton Fisons plc, Stowmarket, Suffolk in November 1987. After hypophysation, using the techniques described for roach above, spawning took place naturally over an artificial spawning media consisting of strips of plastic netting. The eggs were distributed among the test vessels by cutting out and adding sections of mesh to which they had adhered. Exposure started approximately 6 hours after fertilisation, and continued for a total of 28 days.

A test starting with larvae was conducted from a sample of those eggs hatched in clean water.

19.2.2   Apparatus

Flow-through tests were carried out using single-axis siphon dosers as shown in Figure 19.1. Analytical grade ammonium chloride was delivered in aqueous stock

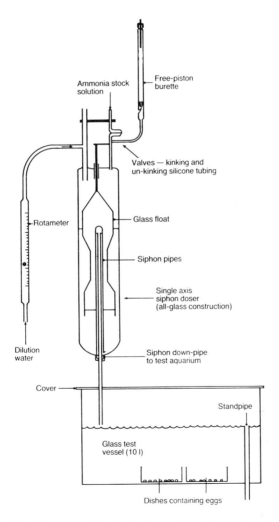

Fig. 19.1 Apparatus for dosing ammonia solutions to early life stages of roach and carp.

solution via free piston burettes to the dosers where it was mixed with dilution water, the flow of which was regulated by rotameters. The doser operation was cyclical, with a volume of 1 litre delivered to the test vessel each time the doser siphoned. One doser was used per vessel.

The test vessels consisted of all-glass tanks with volumes regulated to 10 l by standpipes set in their bases. Close fitting, semi-transparent plastic lids covered each vessel. For the tests starting with eggs, four replicate test vessels were used for the control and each test concentration. Only one vessel per concentration was used for the tests starting with larvae.

19.2.3   *Dilution water*

(a)   Dilution water characteristics for the tests with roach

For the tests with roach the dilution water consisted of a natural, hard, un-chlorinated groundwater, supplied to each vessel at the rate of 200 ml.min^{-1}. This gave a volume replacement rate of 29 volumes per day.

The pH, temperature and DO (as a percentage of the air saturation value) were measured daily in each vessel throughout the test; hardness was measured on four occasions and alkalinity twice in each vessel. The ranges of the means of the above parameters for the replicate vessels at each concentration are given in Table 19.1.

Samples from four of the test vessels were taken for analytical determinations of a range of metals and nitrite and nitrate. The results are summarised in Table 19.2.

Table 19.1   Dilution water quality for tests with roach.

	Tests beginning with ova	Tests beginning with larvae
pH	7.77–7.81	7.77–7.85
Temperature °C	14.8–15.9	15.1–15.5
Dissolved oxygen (% ASV)	98–99	98–99
Alkalinity mg.l^{-1} as CaCO$_3$	245–258	240–255
Hardness mg.l^{-1} as CaCO$_3$	278–290	282–290

Table 19.2   Concentrations of metals, nitrite, and nitrate (mg.l^{-1})

Major cations	Heavy metals	Nitrite	Nitrate
Ca 107–110	Cu <0.004	<0.01–0.08	4.58–4.84
Na 6.73–6.81	Pb <0.05		
Mg 1.72–1.74	Zn <0.003		
K 1.13–1.35	Hg <0.0001		
	Cd <0.004		
	Ni <0.008		
	Al <0.04		
	Cr 0.007–0.009		

All metal concentrations were significantly below toxic levels, the nitrite and nitrate levels indicated that nitrification had not occurred in the test vessels containing ammonia.

(b)   Dilution water characteristics for the tests with carp

For the tests with carp, which required warmer water for the development of the embryos, the same water as that described for roach above was blended with water having all dissolved salts removed by reverse-osmosis treatment. Approximately equal proportions of each were used since previous experience had shown that heating the groundwater resulted in a considerable amount of limescale forming in the tanks and dosing equipment.

The flow rates through each vessel were regulated to $150 \, ml.min^{-1}$ giving volume replacement rates of 22 volumes per day respectively.

Measurements of the dilution water quality are summarised in Table 19.3.

Table 19.3 Dilution water quality for tests with carp

	Tests beginning with ova	Tests beginning with larvae
pH	7.66–7.93	7.72–7.88
Temperature °C	22.5–23.0	22.5–22.9
Dissolved oxygen (% ASV)	94–97	94–96
Alkalinity mg.l^{-1} as CaCO$_3$	105–122	105–110
Hardness mg.l^{-1} as CaCO$_3$	115–128	110–134

19.2.4   Procedure

To start the tests, eggs and larvae of roach and carp were added to the test vessels already containing the exposure concentrations of ammonia.

(a)   Carp test starting with eggs

Approximately 100 eggs were added to vessels containing the following nominal concentrations of total ammonia:

   0 (control), 3.0, 9.6, 16.7, 29.9 and 38.9 mg.l^{-1} total N

These corresponded to the following concentrations of un-ionised ammonia under the test conditions (pH 7.85 and temperature of 23°C):

   0 (control), 0.10, 0.32, 0.56, 1.0 and 1.3 mg.l^{-1} NH$_3$–N

Since four replicate vessels were used at each treatment, the total number of eggs exposed at each treatment was approximately 400.

The test was ended after 31 days of exposure. The data collected from this test comprised daily counts of live and dead eggs, larvae and fry to assess hatching success and survival of hatched fry. Measurements of wet weights of individual surviving fry were made at the end of the test.

The data for hatching, fry survival and wet weights of fry were analysed using analysis of variance (ANOVA) and Dunnett's (1955) multiple comparison test. Where necessary, the hatching success and survival data were converted to a form suitable for the above analysis using arc-sine transformation of the proportions hatching and surviving in each vessel. Regression analysis was performed on the wet weight data.

(b)   Carp test starting with larvae

One hundred larvae were placed into vessels containing the following nominal concentrations of un-ionised ammonia:

0 (control), 0.56, 1.0, 1.3 and 1.8 mg.l^{-1} NH$_3$-N

The test was ended after 28 days of exposure. The numbers alive and dead were counted daily. An LC$_{50}$ was calculated, using the probit method of Finney (1971), at the end of the test.

(c)   Roach test starting with eggs

The test was started with varying numbers of roach eggs from spawnings 1, 2 and 3 by addition to the test vessels containing the test solutions. The following nominal concentrations of total ammonia were used:

0 (control), 1.5, 3.0, 5.9 and 18.9 mg.l^{-1} total N

These corresponded to the following concentrations of un-ionised ammonia under the test conditions (pH 7.8 and temperature of 15°C):

0 (control), 0.025, 0.05, 0.10 and 0.32 mg.l^{-1} NH$_3$-N

The actual numbers of eggs used are shown below:

Eggs from spawning 1: 326, 254, 292, 218, 313
Eggs from spawning 2: 1002, 1015, 922, 929, 929
Eggs from spawning 3: 801, 989, 891, 1048, 1129

The numbers of eggs shown are the combined numbers from all of the four replicate vessels for each concentration.

Eggs from the different spawnings were kept separate in trays in the test vessels. Approximately half of the eggs from spawning 3 were fertilised in the test solutions, the other half were mixed with milt before addition to the test solutions. For this spawning, effects of ammonia on fertilisation success could therefore be ascertained. Exposure of the eggs from spawning 3 was continued for a total of 130 days; exposure of eggs from spawnings 1 and 2 was stopped soon after hatching for the reason given in section 19.3.2a below.

Data from all three spawnings were examined to determine effects on hatching success as described in section 19.2.4a above. Data on fry survival from spawning 3, and the individual wet weights and fork lengths measured at the end of the test were also obtained. These data were analysed using analysis of variance followed by Dunnett's (1955) multiple comparison procedure.

(d)   Roach test starting with larvae

Twenty larvae from spawning 4 (see section 19.2.1a above) were added to vessels containing the ammonia solutions. The following nominal concentrations of un-ionised ammonia were used:

0 (control), 0.025, 0.05, 0.10, 0.18, 0.32 and 0.57 mg.l^{-1} NH$_3$−N

The test was ended after 111 days of exposure.

Numbers of live and dead larvae and fry were counted each day. At the end of the test the median periods of survival at each ammonia concentration were calculated using the method of Litchfield (1949).

19.2.5   *Analysis of exposure concentrations*

For the tests with carp, samples for the analytical determination of ammonia were taken from each vessel once per week, and every other week for the tests with roach. The indophenol blue spectrophotometric method was used (Nield, 1977). Concentrations of un-ionised ammonia were calculated from the measured total ammonia concentrations using the formula of Emerson *et al.* (1975). All results shown in Figures 19.2 to 19.9 are expressed in terms of mean measured concentrations of un-ionised ammonia.

It was found that conductivity of the test solutions was related to the ammonia concentration present, and this measurement was made daily in each vessel for tests with carp and roach to check the doser operation. This was found to be satisfactory throughout both studies.

19.2.6   *Feeding during the tests*

Roach were fed daily starting three days after the onset of hatching. Initially, the food consisted mainly of rotifers filtered from pond water through 60 μm mesh. From day 20, newly-hatched San-Francisco brine shrimp nauplii were given. From day 25 this was supplemented with a dried food (Ewos Larvastart sizes 0 and 00 and finely ground BP Fry 02 Trout Food); as the fry increased in size the particle size offered was increased.

For carp, feeding was started two days after hatching and consisted of brine shrimp nauplii as above. Eight days after hatching this was supplemented with Ewos Larvastart sizes 0 and 1, again the particle size was increased as the fry grew.

For both species, food was given *ad libitum* two or three times per day, uneaten food being removed each morning before the first feed.

19.3   Results

19.3.1   *Effects of ammonia on carp*

(a)   Exposure starting with eggs

Figure 19.2 shows the percentage hatching of eggs, the percentage survival of the fry which hatched, and the overall survival of the egg and fry stage combined for each replicate vessel at each concentration of ammonia.

Ammonia had no effect on hatching success even at the highest concentration tested (0.66 mg.l^{-1} NH$_3$−N), although hatching success appeared to be very variable between the replicates at each concentration. Survival of the post-hatch stages was significantly reduced at 0.66 mg.l^{-1} NH$_3$−N compared with the control group ($P<0.01$). The overall effect, therefore, was an increased mortality of the post-hatch stages.

(b)   Exposure starting with larvae

Figure 19.3 shows the numbers of surviving carp during the test with larvae for each concentration of ammonia over the 28-day exposure period. Survival at 0.32 mg.l^{-1} NH$_3$−N was slightly better than the control group. Mortality at 0.63 mg.l^{-1} NH$_3$−N was significantly greater ($P = 0.05$) than the controls.

A 28-day LC$_{50}$ value of 0.5 mg.l^{-1} NH$_3$−N with 95% confidence limits of 0.46–0.54 was calculated from these data using the method of Finney (1971). This was not corrected for control mortality.

(c)   Effects on growth of carp

After 31 days' exposure, the surviving fry from the test starting with eggs were weighed and measured. The mean wet weights of each exposure group are shown (together with 95% confidence limits) in Figure 19.4. Comparison of the confidence intervals showed that ammonia inhibited growth significantly at concentrations at and above 0.35 mg.l^{-1} NH$_3$−N. A similar result was found on analysing the fork length data.

The assessment of growth inhibition was complicated by the effect of stocking density (defined as the numbers of fish in the vessel), on growth. Unlike the roach test, the numbers of larvae in each vessel were not made uniform on hatching. At the time this was not considered important since the loading rate, in terms of wet weight of fish per litre was low (less than one gram of fish per litre at the end of the test for all vessels). However, it was found that the growth of carp decreased with increasing stocking density. This can be seen by inspection of Figure 19.4, where the numbers of fry at the end of the test are indicated. It is likely that the effect was due to an interaction between individual fish rather than loading rate because there was no correlation between loading rate, in terms of grams of fish per litre, and growth.

It was also apparent that the influence of stocking density on growth of the individual fish diminished as the concentration of ammonia increased. This can also

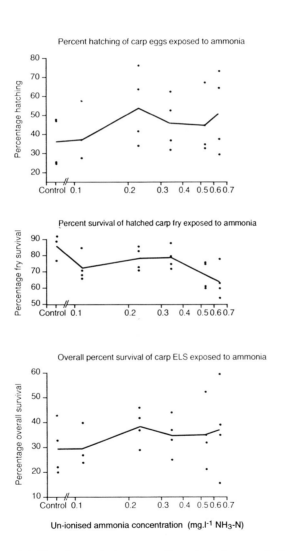

Fig. 19.2 Percentage hatching, fry survival and overall survival of carp early life stages exposed to ammonia (dots indicate individual vessels, lines are means).

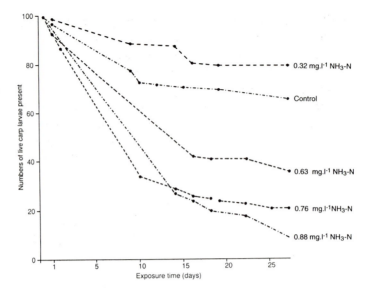

Fig. 19.3 Survival of carp in test starting with larvae. (Mean observed concentrations of un-ionised ammonia are given.)

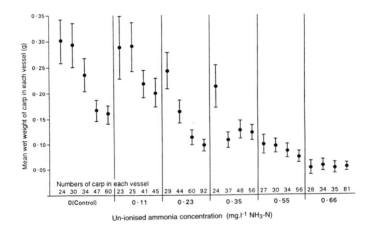

Fig. 19.4 Mean wet weight, with 95% confidence limits, of carp after the 31-day exposure period (test started with eggs) in each test vessel. The relationship between the numbers of carp present in each vessel (stocking density) and mean wet weight can also be seen.

be seen from Figure 19.4, the effect of ammonia on growth appearing to overcome the effect of stocking density at the higher concentrations.

Expressing growth in terms of total weight of each exposure group at the end of the test provided a simple relationship with ammonia concentration and stocking density. This relationship is shown in Figure 19.5. These data were analysed using regression analysis as described below, and the lines fitted to the relationship between numbers of fish (stocking density) and total weight of each exposure group, for each concentration of ammonia, are shown in the figure.

Regression analysis of the total weight data indicated that ammonia concen-

Key:

✕——✕ 0 (control)
●------● 0.11 mg.l⁻¹ NH₃-N
▲——▲ 0.23 mg.l⁻¹ NH₃-N
■—·—■ 0.35 mg.l⁻¹ NH₃-N
▼----▼ 0.55 mg.l⁻¹ NH₃-N
✚——✚ 0.66 mg.l⁻¹ NH₃-N

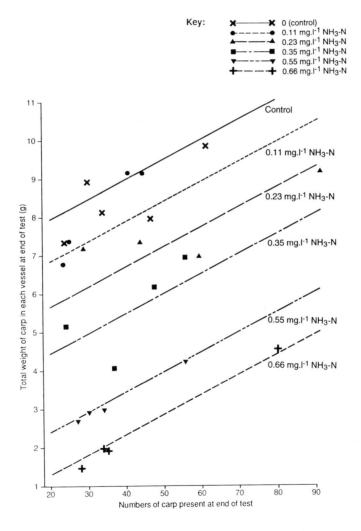

Fig. 19.5 Relationship between stocking density and total weight of carp remaining at the end of the 31-day exposure period. Symbols represent actual observed values, lines are fitted using the model given in section 19.3.1c.

tration accounted for 80% of the variability seen. This was improved to 93% when a factor accounting for stocking density was included. The model describing the relationship between ammonia concentration, stocking density and growth found for this experiment is shown below;

$$W = 6.912 - 9.981(c) + 0.05034(n)$$

where   W = total weight of fish in exposure group (grams)
          c = un-ionised ammonia concentration (mg.l^{-1} $NH_3$$-$N)
          n = stocking density (number of fish per litre)

The model predicts that concentrations of ammonia resulting in 10 and 25% reductions in growth (EC_{10} and EC_{25}) would be 0.08 and 0.20 mg.l^{-1} $NH_3$$-$N respectively for a stocking density of 20 fish per litre. Extrapolation to one fish per litre gives values of 0.07 and 0.18 mg.l^{-1} $NH_3$$-$N respectively.

19.3.2   *Effects of ammonia on roach*

(a)   Exposure starting with eggs

The degree of variation between replicates for each spawning, and the effect of ammonia on hatching success, is shown in Figure 19.6. Spawning 3 proved to be most successful, with a mean hatching success across all treatments of approximately 60–70%. Spawning 2 proved to be least successful with a hatching success of just 15%. Hatching for spawning 1 was slightly lower than spawning 3.

No dose-related effect was seen for hatching success up to the maximum concentration tested (0.31 mg.l^{-1} $NH_3$$-$N) as determined from ANOVA of the data combined from all the spawnings.

On hatching, the larvae from spawnings 1 and 2 were discarded. Exposure of the larvae from spawning 3 was continued for a total of 130 days but the numbers exposed were reduced to about 50 in each vessel on hatching. This was done to reduce the influence of variation in stocking density which had been seen in the test with carp (section 19.3.1c above).

The percentages of surviving fry for each replicate are shown in Figure 19.7. Although a slight decrease in survival of hatched fry was seen at 0.31 mg.l^{-1} $NH_3$$-$N, ANOVA of the arc/sine transformed data revealed no significant differences between any of the treatments and the control group. Also, there was no difference, in terms of hatching success and subsequent survival, between those eggs which were fertilised in the presence of ammonia and those fertilised in clean water.

The swim-up fry proved to be particularly sensitive to external disturbance. Removal of faeces and uneaten food by siphoning, and even visual inspection, occasionally resulted in one or more fry overturning; however, these overturned fry usually recovered. The fish in the controls and lower concentrations of ammonia exhibited this response to the greatest degree, while those exposed to the highest concentration of ammonia appeared to be more subdued and were less excited by external disturbance.

(b) Exposure starting with larvae

Figure 19.8 shows the numbers of larvae surviving over the 111-day exposure period. It can be seen that mortality occurred rapidly among the roach exposed to 0.72 mg.l^{-1} NH$_3$−N. Mortality occurred considerably less rapidly for the other groups, but by the end of the test it was high for all groups, including the unexposed control. Survival at the lowest ammonia concentration (0.03 mg.l^{-1} NH$_3$−N) was slightly greater than the control group.

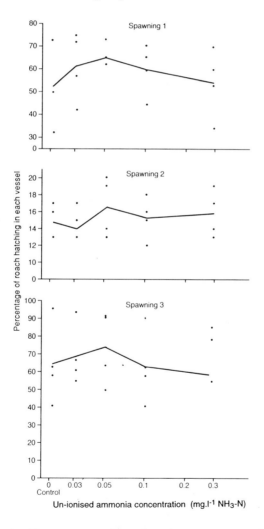

Fig. 19.6   Percentage hatching amongst roach eggs from three separate spawnings exposed to ammonia (dots indicate individual vessels, lines are means).

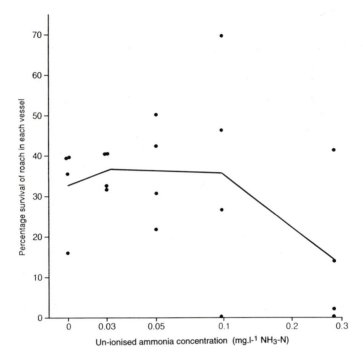

Fig. 19.7   Percentage survival of roach larvae from spawning 3 (test started with eggs) after 130 days' exposure (dots indicate individual replicas, line indicates position of mean values).

It was not possible to estimate an LC_{50} value from these data because of the high control mortality. Instead median periods of survival (the time at which half the test population had died) were calculated for each exposure group, using the method of Litchfield (1949). Survival of each group was then compared with the control. The median periods of survival of the groups exposed to 0.54 and 0.72 mg.l^{-1} NH$_3$–N were significantly shorter than that for the control group, whereas those exposed to 0.36 mg.l^{-1} NH$_3$–N and below were not significantly different ($P = 0.05$).

(c)   *Effects on growth of roach*

The weights and lengths of surviving fry from spawning 3, after 130 days of exposure, are shown in Figure 19.9. Hierarchical analysis of variance, separating between-concentration and between-replicate effects was carried out on these data. Where this indicated significant differences, Dunnett's (1959) test was applied. This revealed a significant growth inhibition only at the highest concentration tested (0.31 mg.l^{-1} NH$_3$–N).

Unlike the test with carp (see section 19.3.1c above) the stocking density at the end of the test had no effect on growth. The range of stocking densities was lower, however, due to the reduction in numbers to 50 on hatching.

19.4   Discussion

The test with roach early life stages has demonstrated that they are not significantly more susceptible to ammonia intoxication than their older stages. In studies carried out under similar water quality conditions, Solbé *et al.* (1988) reported an incipient LC_{50} for older stages of roach of 0.25 mg.l^{-1} NH_3-N, and a 4-day LC_{50} of 0.35 mg.l^{-1} NH_3-N was reported by Ball (1967). Mortality of the roach early life stages was not affected by ammonia concentrations up to and including 0.31 mg.l^{-1} NH_3-N when exposure was commenced either immediately before, or after, fertilisation. However, this must be viewed against a rather high background mortality rate of over 60%. Their relatively low sensitivity to ammonia is confirmed by examining the effects on growth; only at 0.31 mg.l^{-1} NH_3-N (the highest concentration tested) were adverse effects seen.

Some disadvantages were identified in the use of roach ELS as test organisms. Obtaining viable eggs proved to be difficult, and the fry were very sensitive to disturbances such as taking water quality measurements. The latter may have contributed to the high rate of background mortality seen. Since the controls and lower concentration groups appeared to be particularly sensitive to this disturbance, the overall sensitivity of the test may have been reduced.

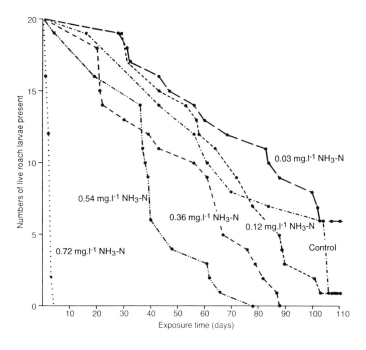

Fig. 19.8 Survival of roach in test starting with larvae. (Mean observed concentrations of un-ionised ammonia are given).

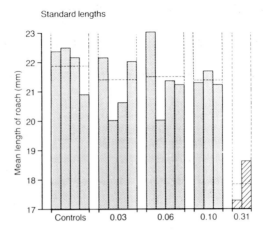

Standard lengths

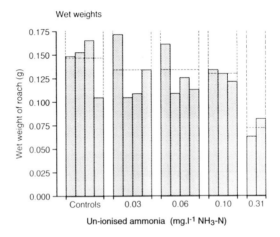

Wet weights

Un-ionised ammonia (mg.l⁻¹ NH₃-N)

Significantly different from controls at p = 0.05

Mean of replicates

Fig. 19.9 Mean lengths and wet weights of roach from spawning 3 after 130 days' exposure to ammonia.

Early life stage carp, on the other hand, appeared to show no adverse reaction to routine observations and measurements. Survival of the post hatch fry, but not hatching success, was adversely affected only at the highest concentration tested, 0.66 mg.l^{-1} NH$_3$–N, when exposure was commenced six hours post-fertilisation and continued for 31 days.

Sensitivity of carp to ammonia appears to decrease with age of fry. For older fry (9.9 g wet weight) 21-day LC$_{50}$ values of 1.20 mg.l^{-1} NH$_3$-N (95% confidence limit 1.05–1.41) to 1.64 mg.l^{-1} NH$_3$–N (95% confidence limit 1.45–1.85) were found in tests carried out over a range of pH values from 7.5 to 8.4 in water of similar alkalinity and temperature (Mallett and Sims, unpublished data). The larvae and swim-up fry used in the present test were more sensitive, having a 28-day LC_{50} value of 0.5 mg.l^{-1} NH_3-N. Hasan and MacIntosh (1986) found young fry (0.2 g) to be more resistant, with a 4-day LC_{50} of 1.84 mg.l^{-1} NH_3-N (95% confidence limit 1.78–1.91). This may have been because the test was carried out in softer water with an alkalinity of 43 mg.l^{-1} as $CaCO_3$, since a similar reduction in ammonia toxicity in waters of lower alkalinity has been found for rainbow trout (Lloyd, 1961).

In contrast with the results of studies with trout ELS reported by Solbé and Shurben (1989) and Calamari *et al.* (1981), the early life stages of carp and roach were not markedly more sensitive than their older stages. Also contrary to that found for trout, exposure as pre- or post-fertilisation eggs did not result in measurably increased sensitivity compared with starting exposure with newly-hatched larvae. The most sensitive stages appeared to be the hatched larvae and early fry.

Ammonia inhibited the growth of carp at concentrations below those having adverse effects on survival. An unexpectedly large effect of stocking density on growth was also found. A model describing the growth response surface predicts values for the EC_{10} and EC_{25} for growth reduction of 0.08 and 0.20 mg.l^{-1} NH_3-N respectively. Although the data for the growth of roach were analysed in a different way, similar concentrations of ammonia resulted in similar levels of growth inhibition to those seen for carp, with effects on growth being seen at concentrations below those causing mortality. For both species, therefore, adverse effects would only be likely at concentrations three to four times greater than the current standard specified under the relevant EC Directive (Council of the European Communities, 1978) of 0.025 mg.l^{-1} NH_3-N. This suggests that the standard would be adequate to protect populations of carp and roach.

19.5   Conclusions

(1)   The early life stages of carp and roach were found to be considerably less sensitive to ammonia than the equivalent stages of trout reported by other workers.

(2)   No difference was seen between sensitivities of fry exposed to ammonia from the egg or from the later larval stage.

(3)   Newly-hatched larvae and early fry were more sensitive to ammonia than either eggs or older fish.

(4)   The current standard specified under the EC Directive on Water Quality for Freshwater Fish (Council of the European Communities, 1978) of 0.025 mg.l^{-1} NH_3-N should be adequate to protect populations of carp and roach, and provide a reasonable margin of safety.

Acknowledgements

The work was funded by the UK Department of the Environment (DoE); we would like to thank the DoE for allowing its publication. The authors wish to acknowledge the advice and effort given by Dr Andrew Worthington of Cypri Culture in spawning the roach, and Dr Ian Dolben of Yorkshire NRA for advice concerning the breeding of carp and roach; technical assistance from Dr Nicola Grandy, Peter Waxman and Kate Horn of the Ecotoxicology section of WRc; statistical advice from Peter VanDijk of WRc; and analysis of ammonia samples by Alex Blair of Thames NRA. The work was carried out under project licence PPL 30/00095.

References

Ball, I.R., 1967. The relative susceptibilities of some species of freshwater fish to poisons – I. Ammonia. *Water Res.*, **1**: 767–775.

Calamari, D., R. Marchetti and G. Vailati, 1981. Effect of long-term exposure to ammonia on the developmental stages of rainbow trout (*Salmo gairdneri* Richardson). *Rapp.P.-v.Reun.Cons. int.Explor.Mer*, **178**: 81–86.

Council of the European Communities, 1978. Directive on the quality of freshwaters needing protection or improvement in order to support fish life, 18 July 1978 (78/659/EC). Official Journal L222, 14 August 1978.

Dunnett, C.W., 1955. A multiple comparison procedure for comparing several treatments with a control. *Am.Statist.Assoc.J.*, December: 1096–1120.

Emerson, K., R.C. Russo, R.E. Lund and R.V. Thurston, 1975. Aqueous ammonia equilibrium calculations: effect of pH and temperature. *J.Fish.Res.Bd.Can.*, **32**: 2379–2383.

Finney, D.J., 1971. *Probit Analysis*. 3rd edn. Cambridge, Cambridge University Press.

Hasan, M.R. and D.J. MacIntosh, 1986. Acute toxicity of ammonia to common carp fry. *Aquaculture*, **54**: 97–107.

Litchfield, J.T., 1949. A method for rapid graphical solution of time/percent-effect curves. *J.Pharmacol.Exp.Therapeut.*, **96**: 399–408.

Lloyd, R., 1961. The toxicity of ammonia to rainbow trout (*Salmo gairdneri* Richardson). *Water and Waste Treatment J.*, March/April: 278–279.

Nield, A.H., 1977. Automatic determination of ammonia in raw and drinking waters using the Technicon Auto-analyser II. Water Research Centre, Report ER 471.

Solbé, J.F. de L.G. and D.G. Shurben, 1989. Toxicity of ammonia to early life stages of rainbow trout (*Salmo gairdneri*). *Water Res.*, **23**(1): 127–129.

Solbé, J.F. de L.G., V.A. Cooper, C.A. Willis and M.J. Mallett, 1988. Effects of pollutants in fresh waters on European non-salmonid fish: Non-metals. FSBI Symposium, Cardiff, Wales 23–26 July 1985. *J.Fish Biol.*, **27**, Suppl. A (ISSN 0022–1112): 197–208.

Worthington, A.D., 1983. Studies on the reproduction and culture of the roach (*Rutilus rutilus*). PhD thesis, Department of Life Sciences, Trent Polytechnic, Nottingham.

Chapter 20
Fish toxicity and population dynamics: effects of 3,4-dichloroaniline and the problems of extrapolation

C. SCHÄFERS and R. NAGEL

Institut für Zoologie, AG Ökotoxikologie, Johannes Gutenberg-Universität Mainz, Saarstraße 21, D-6500 Mainz, Germany

20.1 Introduction

20.1.1 *Extrapolation from individual data to populations*

At present, the level of population seems to be the highest tier of organisation for which a reliable predictive evaluation of xenobiotic effects may be possible (Rudolph and Boje, 1986). Exposure experiments with age-structured populations of European fish species, however, are mostly too complex and lengthy. Therefore, the maximum amount of information on effects on those individual properties which are relevant for populations of the test species has to be gathered as a basis for extrapolation to that level. But the two questions that need to be answered are: which individual properties are relevant for populations; are possible relevant properties included in the toxicological tests that are now being carried out.

Complete life cycle tests provide the most comprehensive coverage of toxicological responses and include interactions beyond those at the individual level by providing data on reproductive effects. However, the data are not obtained in the context of age-structured populations, but only by successively exposing life stages of the same age. Therefore, these investigations are not yet population-related. Furthermore, life cycle tests with European fish species can be difficult to conduct.

One of the commonest test fish in Europe is the zebrafish (*Brachydanio rerio*). Some life cycle tests have already been conducted with this species (Nagel 1994, Bresch *et al.*, 1990). Behaviour, reproduction and the population dynamics of zebrafish have been investigated in a complex laboratory system (Schäfers *et al.*, 1989). Based on these investigations, a stochastic model named 'zebrafish' (Oertel *et al.*, 1991) was created to provide a simulation of the population dynamics. This model can be used to extrapolate from effects occurring in life cycle tests to the level of the average laboratory population. Also, it can reveal new endpoints for toxicological testing which are more relevant for estimating effects on the population (Schäfers, 1991; Oertel, 1992).

The reference chemical used was 3,4-dichloroaniline (3,4-DCA), an intermediate and degradation product of pesticides. Call *et al.* (1987) and Schäfers and Nagel

(1991) have pointed out its unusual high acute–chronic toxicity ratio (ACR) in fish of >1000. For a review of fate and toxicity of 3,4-DCA, see Crossland (1990).

20.1.2   *Extrapolation from zebrafish to other species*

When choosing the zebrafish as a 'model species', the question of the extrapolation of individual responses to populations of zebrafish is also accompanied by the problems of extrapolation to other fish species. The strategy of reproduction may differ enormously between species. Two aspects are the difference between seasonal and all-year reproduction depending on climate, and the differentiation in those characteristics of population dynamics which can be summarised as *r*- and *K*-strategy (MacArthur and Wilson, 1967). The *r*-strategists have a relatively high rate of reproduction, with low investment of energy in the individual offspring; in contrast, *K*-strategists invest more in the individual offspring, are better competitors and utilise the resources more extensively and consequently they can reach higher *K*-values (specific environmental capacity).

   To provide a comparison with as much data as possible, a second species reproducing throughout the year was used: the zebrafish as an egg-laying *r*-strategist was compared to the live-bearing guppy (*Poecilia reticulata*), a *K*-strategist. Investigations of the reproduction and dynamics of laboratory populations were conducted, and the simulation model 'zebrafish' was fitted to the guppy data (Schäfers and Nagel, 1992). A life cycle test with the guppy and 3,4-DCA extending to two generations (Schäfers and Nagel, 1991) and the validation of the model by a population exposure experiment (Schäfers and Nagel, in press) completed the comparison. Also, the European *r*-strategists roach (*Rutilus rutilus*) and perch (*Perca fluviatilis*) were compared with zebrafish by early life stage tests (Schäfers, 1991).

20.2   **Toxicity data for 3,4-dichloroaniline to fish**

20.2.1   *Acute toxicity*

A comparison of the sensitivity of different fish species in acute toxicity tests (Table 20.1) shows that the small species tested at 25 to 26°C (zebrafish, guppy, fathead minnow) form a cluster. The larger species tested at lower temperatures (rainbow trout and perch) form another cluster showing a threefold higher sensitivity after 96 hours.

20.2.2   *Chronic toxicity*

(a)   *Complete life cycle tests with zebrafish and guppies*

Although in terms of acute toxicity the sensitivity of zebrafish and guppies is similar – in both cases the 96hLC$_{50}$ is between 8 and 9 mg.l^{-1} 3,4-DCA (Table 20.1) –

Table 20.1   Acute toxicity of 3,4-dichloroaniline in fish.

Species	96hLC$_{50}$ mg.l^{-1}	LC$_{50}$ n n	mg.l^{-1}	Temperature °C
Zebrafish	8.5[1]			26
Guppy	8.7–9.0[2]	14	6.8[3]	26
Fathead minnow	7.0–8.1[4] (ft)			25
Rainbow trout	2.7[5] (ft)			
Perch	3.1[6]	6	1.5[6]	19

[1] Becker *et al.* (1990). [2] Adema and Vink (1981) (differing origins). [3] Hermens *et al.* (1984). [4] Call *et al.* (1987) (differing water qualities). [5] Crossland (1990). [6] Schäfers (1991)

n = number of days; ft = flow-through experiment.

there are differing responses to chronic toxicity at lower concentrations (2, 20, 200 μg.l^{-1}). Zebrafish larvae died within two weeks at 200 μg.l^{-1} and the survival of larvae was reduced at 20 μg.l^{-1} in the following generation (Nagel, 1994a); reproduction was not affected by six weeks' exposure to 200 μg.l^{-1} (Schäfers, 1991), whereas after eight weeks, reproduction was reversibly disabled (Ensenbach, 1991). Thus, the larval stages are the most sensitive ones for evaluating the effects of 3,4-DCA on zebrafish.

The survival of new-born guppies was not affected at 200 μg.l^{-1}. Mean growth of the females, and therefore also mean reproduction, decreased significantly at 2 and 20 μg.l^{-1}. In spite of these effects, there still was a 57% production of offspring even at 200 μg.l^{-1}. In guppies, therefore, reproduction is the most sensitive parameter with 3,4-DCA (Schäfers and Nagel, 1991).

(b)   Early life stage tests with other species

The early life stage tests showed no decrease of hatching or survival of early yolk sac fry with exposure to 3,4-DCA at 2 to 200 μg.l^{-1}, for all species tested (Table 20.2). Increased mortality occurred at the effect concentrations when larvae switched to an external food supply. The larvae of all the egg-laying species compared were in the same range of sensitivity, despite differences in water temperature (NOEC–LOEC = 15–200 μg.l^{-1} 3,4-DCA); they also had similar body lengths. In this special case and on the individual level, zebrafish provide a good model to evaluate the toxicity of a chemical to fish with a similar strategy of reproduction.

20.3   Extrapolation from effects found in life cycle tests to laboratory populations

In order to construct hypotheses on the consequences of 3,4-DCA to laboratory populations of zebrafish and guppies, the effects derived from the life cycle tests

Table 20.2   Effects of 3,4-dichloroaniline (μg.l^{-1}) on the early life stages of fish.

Species	Survival 28 days		
	NOEC	LOEC	0 %
Zebrafish (ft)[1]	20	100	200
Guppy (ft)[2]	200	?	?
Fathead minnow (ft)[3]	15/26	23/45	157
Roach (ss)[4]	20	200	?
Perch (ss)[*4]	20	200	?

[1] Nagel *et al.* (1991), [2] Schäfers and Nagel (1991), [3] Call *et al.* (1987) (dechlorinated tap water/water from Lake Superior), [4] Schäfers (1991)
NOEC = no, LOEC = lowest observed effect concentration in μg.l^{-1}
ft = flow-through experiment, ss = semi-static experiment
[*] valid experimental time: 18 days

with both species were extrapolated to the level of the populations by using the simulation program (Schäfers *et al.*, 1992).

In zebrafish populations, the most crucial stages for the population dynamics and the most sensitive ones to 3,4-DCA are almost the same, i.e. the older larvae and the young juvenile stages.

A concentration of 2 μg.l^{-1} 3,4-DCA does not affect the endpoints used in the zebrafish life cycle tests; consequently, no effect of this value can be calculated for populations. For a long-term exposure to 20 μg.l^{-1}, the longevity of the populations is predicted to be severely reduced; and 200 μg.l^{-1} 3,4-DCA would lead to the extinction of all populations within a year. The NOECs and LOECs that were derived from the life cycle test are thus confirmed also at the population level.

Observations and simulations provide evidence that changes in the constitution or in the behaviour of feeding larvae or juvenile fish, leading to a reduced predator avoidance, are at least as important than a selective mortality of weak fish at the same stages. A quantifiable endpoint of 'larval fitness' or 'larval swimming behaviour' is not yet part of the life cycle tests. The sensitivity of zebrafish populations, therefore, may be much higher than that calculated from actual life cycle test data.

In guppy populations, there are no such crucial life stages because of the different reproduction strategy, which guarantees shelter for the offspring during their most critical stages. Thus, the number of offspring, which is the most sensitive parameter for 3,4-DCA toxicity, should also be the most effective one to predict effects at the population level.

Even the observed reduction of surviving offspring by 43% at 200 μg.l^{-1}, combined with an increase of 2.5 days in the brood intervals (Schäfers and Nagel, 1991), would cause a reduction in mean abundance of only 22%. This estimate was confirmed in a population exposure experiment with three replications per concentration, starting with two pairs of fish per replication; the mean abundances were reduced at 20 and 200 μg.l^{-1}, but not to a significant extent (Schäfers and Nagel, 1992).

In 20 and 200 $\mu g.l^{-1}$, variances in abundance occurred which far surpassed the extent of the simulated variability; for example, the abundance was reduced by 80% in one population at 200 $\mu g.l^{-1}$. These variations can be explained by unexpected individual differences in the reactions to the stressor 3,4-DCA, in addition to the stress of high population densities, such as an extra mortality or active resorption of embryos (Schäfers, 1991; Schäfers and Nagel, 1992). In natural populations sensitive individuals would be affected, thus favouring more tolerant ones. A concentration of 200 $\mu g.l^{-1}$ 3,4-DCA would then lead to an impoverishment in the genetic diversity of guppy populations rather than a reduction of abundance.

These results provide evidence that xenobiotic effects on endpoints of the life cycle test, or on populations of zebrafish, cannot simply be used to extrapolate to fish populations with other reproductive strategies. Even within the same species, a simple extrapolation of NOECs and LOECs gained with life cycle tests to the population level is not admissible; the effect concentrations may differ by orders of magnitude.

20.4   Relevance of the simulation model 'zebrafish' for populations in the field

The objective of using a complex laboratory system and the derived model 'zebrafish' as a means to evaluate those xenobiotic effects which will have possible consequences at the natural population level needs to be critically assessed.

First, it is unclear whether the assumed method for the regulation of the laboratory populations is quantitatively correct. In particular, the values used for the predation parameters, which are sensitive within narrow limits, are more estimated than measured. They may be plausible and lead to satisfying results, but they cannot be proved.

Second, even in the case of an exact quantitative estimation, it may be questioned whether the type of regulation is in any way relevant for natural populations of zebrafish.

Third, the evidence for populations of other fish species is limited, even when the natural situation of the zebrafish is modelled adequately. However, if some properties of the complex system are proved to be of general significance, the model is worthwhile for the evaluation of xenobiotics.

Bailey and Houde (1989) reviewed the consequences of predation on the eggs and larvae of mainly marine fish. The general statements coincide well with the information that has been derived from the complex zebrafish system including the results of the simulations (Schäfers, 1991). Crucial interactions are modelled by the simulation parameters. However, the model can only be used when describing populations in which cannibalism plays a decisive role in their regulation. This is the case with the laboratory populations of zebrafish and guppy which have been described. In the field this kind of regulation is observed more rarely.

20.4.1   *Extrapolation to the perch*

An example of cannibalistic self-regulation is given by perch and other percid populations in many natural lakes (Le Cren, 1965; Craig, 1987; Rask and Raitaniemi, 1988; Treasurer, 1989). Thus, the simulation model 'zebrafish' can be used to provide information on the crucial stages for regulation of perch populations. As yet, the entering of data into the simulation model cannot be carried out, because the field data for perch are still incomplete. Because of the more significant *r*-strategy of perch and their slower development, it can be assumed that the regulative importance of juvenile fish will be more pronounced than in zebrafish populations; additional mortalities and inhibited growth will cause a decrease of abundance particularly when this stage is involved.

The toxicity data obtained are insufficient for a derivation of population effects, because endpoints of growth, time of maturation and reproduction are not included. By analogy with zebrafish, whose larvae were the most sensitive stages towards 3,4-DCA and were also the most relevant for the calculation of population effects, a cautious estimate of population effects based on the early life stage tests can be attempted. Since data about the toxicity to the larvae of the filial generation are unavailable (compare Nagel, 1994), this estimate must be restricted to medium scale effects.

An additional mortality of 40% at 200 µg.l^{-1} 3,4-DCA, with no visible effects on the survivors, will not result in severe population effects when only the perch themselves are considered. When effects on zooplankton and secondary effects on perch larvae (starvation, increase of cannibalism), are included, 200 µg.l^{-1} 3,4-DCA may cause significant losses in perch populations; this is because the chemical has a higher acute and chronic toxicity for potential prey organisms such as crustaceans than in fish. For example, the reproduction of *Daphnia magna* was decreased at 10 µg.l^{-1} (EC$_{50}$), and the 96hLC$_{50}$ is 100 µg.l^{-1} (Adema and Vink, 1981); an extinction of such populations could be expected at slightly higher concentrations than 100 µg.l^{-1} (Seitz and Ratte, 1991). Populations of *Ceriodaphnia quadrangula* were significantly impaired even at 5 µg.l^{-1} and became extinct at 10 µg.l^{-1} (Seitz and Ratte, 1991). These concentrations are of the same magnitude as those measured in the field: in 1979, mean concentrations of 3,4-DCA of 0.29 µg.l^{-1} were detected in the River Maas with maxima at 2.1 µg.l^{-1} (Wegman and deKorte, 1981). In the River Rhine the chemical was found in all samples in the same year (mean 0.39 µg.l^{-1}, maximum 1.2 µg.l^{-1}).

Low temperatures, or the consequences of competition by other fish species, may also lead to losses of age classes; roach larvae are better swimmers and planktivorous predators than are perch larvae. High population densities of roach can cause perch to switch to fish prey and cannibalism at an earlier life stage (Persson and

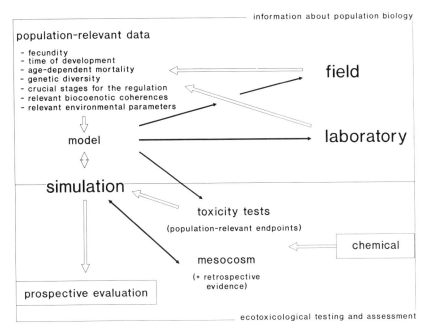

Fig. 20.1 Necessary sources and flows of information for the prospective evaluation of the effects of environmental chemicals on fish populations. Open arrows: flow of data and information; thin arrows: conceptional hints and validation. Further explanations are given in the text.

Greenberg, 1990). Additional mortalities of 70–95% and significant harmful effects in surviving larval roach at 200 μg.l^{-1} 3,4-DCA (Schäfers, 1991) could result in the complete breakdown of the year class and a decrease in the abundance of the exposed population.

20.5   A concept for a predictive evaluation

Based on the investigations presented here, a concept for a predictive evaluation can be proposed as follows (see also Figure 20.1):

(1) To enable a predictive evaluation of toxic effects on fish populations, the primary regulative interactions within the populations must be known. Therefore, the first step is to obtain relevant field data.

(2) From this field data, hypotheses on the regulative interactions should be made. Gaps in the information should be filled by additional and specific investigations.

(3) If such field data cannot be obtained, investigations must be conducted in the laboratory based on the hypotheses. Such investigations may also help to confirm or reject a hypothesis based on field data.

(4) The total information available should be condensed into a simulation model

of the population dynamics, based on the hypotheses. Critical life stages or properties for the regulation of the model population can then be calculated by analyses of sensitivity.

(5)   Long-term toxicity tests should be developed to include endpoints which are related to the critical stages or properties.

(6)   The results of the toxicity tests with the chemical to be evaluated can be extrapolated to the population level by using the simulation program. Biocoenotic coherences such as the breakdown of populations of prey or competitors caused by the chemical can be integrated, if adequate toxicity data are available.

(7)   The evaluation should be validated by population exposure tests in the laboratory or in controlled field systems. Depending on the dominant regulative coherence, mono- and/or relevant multi-species tests in mesocosms should be conducted.

(8)   In the case of hazard analysis, retrospective evaluations are helpful not only to detect real effects, but also to validate and modify the hypotheses and models.

(9)   This procedure is only possible when using a very limited number of fish species. Therefore, the test species should be chosen to be representative of the regulatory properties and the resulting sensitivity of the populations, and not based solely on the sensitivity of individuals in routine toxicity tests. The choice of the test species and the resulting simulation model has to be a compromise between the relevance of extreme variants within the ecological species cluster (specificity) and the width of that cluster itself (generality).

20.6   Preliminary conclusions

The concept presented here enables predictions to be made on the effects of chemicals on certain target populations under standardised conditions. Synergistic or antagonistic effects, caused by temperature or interspecific interactions, depend on structural, functional and temporal properties of the single ecosystem and cannot generally be predicted.

As there is still a lack of relevant population data, a routine method which enables a reasonable predictive evaluation of the effects of xenobiotics on fish populations will not be available for some time. Until then, such evaluations should be confined to the level of individuals and reproductive capacity.

The problems of extrapolations based on insufficient data are described by Barnthouse *et al.* (1990), who developed simulation models of two marine fish populations with differing life strategies (*Brevoortia patronus* and *Morone saxatilis*) and then fitted available toxicity data to the models. They then extrapolated from specific toxicity data to other fish species by using regression analyses, based on systematic and not ecological relationships. Furthermore, they calculated sublethal effects at the population level partly from the acute toxicity data or even the physicochemical properties of the chemicals, which in fact is not possible (Rudolph and Boje, 1986; Nagel, 1992). Therefore, the results of Barnthouse *et al.* (1990) are not surprising; in each case the extrapolation errors easily surpassed the simulated differences between the two species, when no life cycle data for the two target species were available. It is clear the even sophisticated mathematical procedures cannot replace either precise data on population ecology or the toxicity testing of endpoints which are relevant for the regulation of the population.

Acknowledgements

This study was supported by a grant from the Federal Ministry of Science and Technology (BMFT, N° 0339200D). The authors wish to thank Susan Nink for reading the manuscript.

References

Adema, D.M.M. and G.J. Vink, 1981. A comparative study of the toxicity of 1,1,2-trichloroethane, dieldrin, pentachlorophenol and 3,4-dichloroaniline for marine and freshwater organisms. *Chemosphere*, **10**: 533–554.

Bailey, K.M., and E.D. Houde, 1989. Predation on eggs and larvae of marine fishes and the recruitment problem. *Advances in Marine Biology*, **25**: 1–83.

Barnthouse, L.W., G.W. Suter II and A.E. Rosen, 1990. Risks of toxic contaminants to exploited fish populations: influence of life history, data uncertainty and exploitation intensity. *Environ. Toxicol.Chem.*, **9**: 297–311.

Becker, B., G. Görge, W. Kalsch, S. Zok and R. Nagel, 1990. Aufnahme, Metabolismus, Elimination und Toxizität von aromatischen Aminen beim Zebrabärbling *Brachydanio rerio* (Ham.-Buch., 1822). Forschungsbericht 106 03 053/02. Berlin, Umweltbundesamt.

Bresch, H., H. Beck, D. Ehlermann, H. Schlaszus and M. Urbanek, 1990. A long-term toxicity test comprising reproduction and growth of zebrafish with 4-chloroaniline. *Arch.Environ. Contam.Toxicol.*, **19**: 419–427.

Call, D.J., S.H. Poirier, M.L. Knuth, S.L. Harting and C.A. Lindberg, 1987. Toxicity of 3,4-dichloroaniline to fathead minnows, *Pimephales promelas*, in acute and early life-stage exposures. *Bull.Environ.Contam.Toxicol.*, **38**: 352–358.

Craig, J.F., 1987. *The Biology of Perch and Related Fish*. London, Croom Helm. 333 pp.

Crossland, N.O., 1990. A review of the fate and toxicity of 3,4-dichloroaniline in aquatic environments. *Chemosphere*, **21**(12): 1489–1497.

Ensenbach, U., 1991. Kinetik und Dynamik von Fremdstoffgemischen beim Zebrabärbling (*Brachydanio rerio*). Dissertation thesis, Johannes Gutenberg-Universität Mainz, Germany.

Hermens, J.L.M., P. Leeuwangh and A. Musch, 1984. Quantitative structure-activity relationships and mixture toxicity studies of chloro- and alkylanilines at an acute lethal toxicity level to the guppy (*Poecilia reticulata*). *Ecotoxicol.Environ.Safety*, **8**: 388–394.

Le Cren, E.D., 1965. Some factors regulating the size of populations of freshwater fish. *Mitt.Internat. Verein.Limnol.*, **13**: 88–105.

MacArthur, R.H. and E.O. Wilson, 1967. *The Theory of Island Biogeography*. Princeton, New Jersey, Princeton University Press. 203 pp.

Nagel, R., 1992. Fish and environmental chemicals – a critical evaluation of tests. In: Braunbeck, T., W. Hanke and H. Segner (Eds.) *Fish in Ecotoxicology and Ecophysiology*, pp. 147–156. Weinheim, VCH.

Nagel, R., 1994. Complete life cycle tests with zebrafish – a critical assessment of the results. Chapter 17, this volume.

Nagel, R., H. Bresch, N. Caspers, P.D. Hansen, M. Markert, R. Munk, N. Scholz and B.B. ter Höfte, 1991. Effect of 3,4-dichloroaniline on the early life stages of the zebrafish (*Brachydanio rerio*): results of a comparative laboratory study. *Ecotoxicol.Environ.Safety*, **21**: 157–164.

Oertel, D., 1992. Beiträge zu Methoden, Möglichkeiten und Grenzen der Simulation von Schadstoffauswirkungen in aquatischen Ökosystemen. Dissertation thesis, Johannes Gutenberg-Universität Mainz, 159 pp.

Oertel, D., C. Schäfers, H.J. Poethke, R. Nagel and A. Seitz, 1991. Simulation of the population dynamics of zebrafish in a complex experimental system. *Verh.Ges.Ökologie*, **20**(2): 865–869.

Persson, L. and L.A. Greenberg, 1990. Juvenile competitive bottlenecks: the perch *Perca fluviatilis* – roach *Rutilus rutilus* interactions. *Ecology*, **71**(1): 44–56.

Rask, M. and J. Raitaniemi, 1988. The growth of perch, *Perca fluviatilis* L., in recently acidified lakes of Southern Finland – a comparison with unaffected waters. *Arch.Hydrobiol.*, **112**(3): 387–397.

Rudolph, P. and R. Boje, 1986. *Ökotoxikologie. Grundlagen für die ökotoxikologische Bewertung von Umweltchemikalien nach dem Chemikaliengesetz*. Landsberg, Ecomed Verlagsgesellschaft. 105 pp.

Schäfers, C., 1991. Toxizität und Populationsökologie – Wirkungen von 3,4-Dichloranilin auf Fische mit unterschiedlichen Reproduktionsstrategien. Dissertation thesis, Johannes Gutenberg-Universität Mainz. 174 pp.

Schäfers, C. and R. Nagel, 1991. Effects of 3,4-dichloroaniline on fish populations. Comparison between r- and K-strategists: a complete life cycle test with the guppy *(Poecilia reticulata)*. *Arch.Environ.Contam.Toxicol.*, **21**(2): 297–302.

Schäfers C. and R. Nagel, in press. Consequences of 3,4-dichloroaniline on guppy populations (*Poecilia reticulata*): computer simulation and experimental validation. *The Science of the Total Environment*.

Schäfers, C., R. Nagel and A. Seitz, 1989. Behaviour, reproduction, and population dynamics of zebrafish (*Brachydanio rerio*) in a complex experimental system. *Fischökologie*, **1**(2): 45–59.

Schäfers, C., D. Oertel and R. Nagel, 1992. Effects of 3,4-dichloroaniline on fish populations with differing strategies of reproduction. In: Braunbeck, T., W. Hanke and H. Segner (Eds.) *Fish in Ecotoxicology and Ecophysiology*, pp. 133–146. Weinheim, VCH.

Seitz, A. and H.T. Ratte, 1991. Aquatic ecotoxicology: on the problems of extrapolation from laboratory experiments with individuals and populations to community effects in the field. *Comp. Biochem.Physiol.*, **100**C(1/2): 301–304.

Treasurer, J.W., 1989. Mortality and production of 0+ perch, *Perca fluviatilis* L., in two Scottish lakes. *J.Fish Biol.*, **34**: 913–928.

Wegman, R.C.C. and G.A.L. deKorte, 1981. Aromatic amines in surface waters of the Netherlands. *Water Res.*, **15**: 391–394.

Chapter 21
A holistic concept for toxicological diagnosis of sublethal processes in aquatic environments

M.J. MUÑOZ,[1] A. CASTAÑO,[2] J.A. ORTIZ,[1] G. CARBONELL,[1]
T. BLAZQUEZ,[1] M. VEGA[1] and J.V. TARAZONA[1]

[1] *Animal Health Department, Instituto Nacional de Investigaciones Agrarias (CIT-INIA),
E-28130 Valdeolmos (Madrid), Spain*
[2] *Toxicology Group, Centro Nacional de Sanidad Ambiental, Instituto Carlos III,
Majadahonda (Madrid), Spain*

21.1   Introduction

Toxicological assessments have become important in the investigation of sublethal and chronic effects in freshwater populations, requiring a considerable effort on the part of the people involved in making the diagnoses. Two aspects have become important in this context: the synergistic effects of some pollutants, which can be very common in the components of urban, industrial and agricultural discharges, and the wide variety of pathways involved in predicting the ultimate effects of such toxicological action, including the impact on the different levels of biological organisation (e.g. cellular, organ, individual, and population). Because of this wide context, toxicological diagnosis needs to be discussed within a holistic framework.

The tools employed in a toxicological diagnosis are those aimed at detecting the chemical(s) responsible for the toxic action, together with those that can assess the biological effects on the organisms exposed to them.

Since a wide variety of effects can be expected to occur in the aquatic biota of many types of water, numerous analytical methods are required in order to obtain a comprehensive body of information on the different biological aspects of the toxic damage. This holistic concept for the toxicological diagnosis of sublethal processes incorporates the following methodologies:

(a) *In vivo* acute toxicity tests with *Daphnia magna*, commonly employed to obtain acute toxicity data for different compounds (EEC, 1984), and used as a rapid method to determine the toxicity of substances as well as to indicate the toxic action of groups of compounds.

(b) *In vitro* cytotoxicity tests using the fish cell line RTG-2 (Tarazona *et al.*, 1990), which is a very useful alternative because of the very low sample volume requirement which allows its use as a biological detector within an HPLC analytical system.

(c) The study of stress parameters, including plasma cortisol which is one of the corticosteroid hormones considered to be an indicator of primary stress in fish, and used to detect the onset of environmental pollution by various chemicals (Muñoz *et al.*, 1991).

(d) The study of alterations in those physiological and biochemical parameters commonly used in mammalian diagnostics (Stewart and Stolman, 1960).

(e) Anatomo-pathological and histopathological techniques, of special value for the final diagnosis (Tarazona *et al.*, 1987), of special importance in bioassays, and used in combination with other methods of specific value.

Each technique has been used to a different extent in the diagnosis of sublethal effects. Their selection has depended on the specific situation and on the information provided by the preceding stages of the investigation. These different methodologies contained within the 'holistic concept' are appropriate to a variety of field situations, within which different approaches are necessary to provide a final diagnosis.

21.2   Material and methods

In all the field situations which required a diagnosis on the cause of harmful effects, a complete clinical history was obtained and evaluated prior to the study in the field. When the field study was implemented, specific sampling areas were selected and water samples collected upstream and downstream of the suspect effluent or of the area where damage had occurred. At each sampling station, *in situ* physico-chemical parameters were measured in addition to up to 30 physical and chemical parameters which were analysed according to standard methods (APHA, 1980).

Specific pretreatments were used to preserve water samples before analysis (APHA, 1980).

Biological damage was investigated using toxicity tests. Because acute tests were used, concentrated solutions were prepared by pumping the water samples through Sep-Pak C18 cartridges using a TRIS peristaltic pump; alternatively liquid–liquid extraction with methylene chloride was used. The toxicity of these concentrates was then tested using *Daphnia magna* (EEC, 1984) and RTG-2 cells (Castaño *et al.*, 1994). The inorganic fraction was also tested after evaporation and ashing of water samples, in order to determine the toxicity of the non-volatile inorganic compounds. If toxicity was detected in the organic fraction, the concentrate was injected into a HPLC system (Waters) in order to sequentially separate some of the organic compounds; toxic compounds could be identified by the different chromatographic pattern obtained for the different peaks and their toxicity as measured by the two tests (Tarazona *et al.*, 1990).

Stress conditions were studied by measuring the plasma cortisol, using an immunological kit (Sibar, Italy).

Infectious diseases were diagnosed by the use of CHSE, BF-2 and RTG-1 cell cultures for viral diseases, by the general methods of isolation used for bacterial

Table 21.1 Distribution of the cases studied by the Division of Environmental Toxicology of the INIA (percentages of the total).

	Acute	Subacute	Chronic	Total
Rivers and estuaries	9.7	6.5	6.4	22.6
Ponds and reservoirs	12.9	12.9	3.2	29.0
Fish farms	19.3	12.9	16.2	48.4
Total	41.9	32.3	25.8	100.0

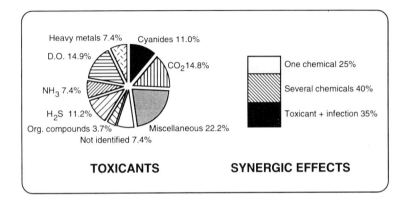

Fig. 21.1 Causative aetiological agents.

diseases, and by the presence and growth of fungi in body and mucus samples for fungal diseases.

Macroscopic and microscopic lesions were examined using general protocols based on haematoxylin and eosin staining methods in order to obtain histopathological information.

Biochemical parameters were analysed in organ and blood samples using the methods recommended by Stewart and Stolman (1960).

Measurements of the chemical concentration of toxicants in a number of biological samples were made using standard procedures (APHA, 1980).

21.3   Results

Of the cases shown in Table 21.1, 58% of the cases studied were diagnosed as having subacute and chronic problems; 29.1% were associated with fish farms, 16.1% with ponds and reservoirs and 12.9% with rivers and estuaries. In all of these cases, the effects found in marine and freshwater fish were related to different pollutants.

Figure 21.1 shows the more significant aetiological agents responsible for the sublethal and chronic cases found in freshwater systems. It can be seen that numerous causes were responsible for the pathological effects, although carbon dioxide, low dissolved oxygen, cyanides and sulphide appear to be the more frequent, followed by ammonia and heavy metals (iron, cadmium and lead). Other chemicals included in the miscellaneous group include fluoride, anionic detergents, nitrite, chloride, pH, and some specific instances referred to as anaerobic conditions, in which hydrogen sulphide and ammonia were found to be present. Some organic compounds (e.g. polycyclic aromatic hydrocarbons) were found at low concentrations. In a small percentage of the cases studied the specific causative chemicals could be not identified because the toxicological effects were related more to a generally poor environmental quality.

In all the toxicological investigations, the water analyses played a very important role, allowing a diagnosis to be made when sufficient information was available. However, in some studies, e.g. the River Cifuentes, considerable effects were observed in the stream biota, and water analyses alone were not sufficient to determine the cause, and thus some modelling was required to solve the problem. In this particular case, large quantities of organic matter were discharged in the form of an industrial sewage, and degradation products (e.g. ammonia and nitrite) were appearing a few kilometres downstream from the source. Toxic concentrations of these chemicals downstream could be predicted by applying the model, and a biochemical parameter, methaemoglobin, was used to confirm that nitrite was having a toxic effect on fish.

Sometimes, the causative aetiological agents could not be identified from a physicochemical analysis of the water, and investigations including histological examinations, plasma cortisol concentrations as a measure of stress level, and toxic chemical concentrations in biological samples were needed to make a final diagnosis.

Where the specific causative agents remained unknown, as was the case in a situation on the River Tajo where sublethal effects were found, further tests were required. In this particular case, the affected area was separated from the source in time and space; tests were made on the toxicity of the water samples, and sample fractions and concentration peaks obtained by HPLC separation were subjected to the standard acute toxicity test with *Daphnia magna* and the *in vitro* cytotoxicity test with the RTG-2 cell line. As a result, a fraction or peak with a demonstrable toxicity could be chemically identified using sophisticated instrumental techniques.

21.4   Discussion

Ecotoxicology is one of the essential disciplines which provide the scientific basis for an environmental protection policy, and the precautionary principle states that the harmlessness of chemicals should be established before they can be released into the environment. However, in reality the present condition of fresh waters in Europe, and in most developed countries, shows a very different picture. Toxicological problems in fish are not merely anecdotal but are commonly found in natural populations. Therefore, the study of sublethal and chronic toxic effects of aquatic pollutants includes not only an assessment of their potential risks under experimental conditions, but also a diagnosis of the cause of damage to fish in the field.

The ability to diagnose the cause of toxic effects is one of the basic functions of toxicology (Bartik and Piskac, 1981), but it is not the easiest to be carried out. As Stewart and Stolman (1960) have stated:

'Life would be much simpler for the toxicologist if his task ended when he was able to report that in the material submitted to him he had found such-and-such a poison and that the concentration was so-and-so. But he must go further than that and must interpret his results in such a way that the maximal amount of information may be derived from them.'

The diagnosis of the cause of sublethal and chronic effects differs from that used for acute mortalities; in general the effects are more difficult to observe and quantify. In our opinion, this would explain why most cases of sublethal and chronic effects studied in our laboratory have came from fish farms, where the fish are observed and monitored daily. However, sublethal and chronic pathologies have an important advantage in relation to making a diagnosis; sampling can be carried out over a period of time, and each new sample can be examined by protocols determined by the results previously obtained. This advantage has allowed us to construct a step-wise holistic procedure to diagnose the cause of these kinds of harmful effects. There are two main elements in this procedure:

(a) The collection of different kinds of samples which will allow the study of all the ecotoxicological aspects which may be needed, and
(b) The reduction, as far as possible, of the cost and time of the study by using a step-wise protocol in which each decision for further testing depends on the previous results.

Figure 21.2 shows a schematic representation of this protocol with its different steps. The first step is to assess all the available information, including not only the sources of pollution etc., but also the clinical findings and the basic condition of the water. The latter can be very useful, e.g. heavy metal toxicity is rarely encountered in very hard waters, and ammonia poisoning is unlikely to be found at acid pH values. This step ends with the selection of suspected chemicals and their analysis.

The second steps involve those decisions that must be made if toxic concentrations are found, in which case a toxicological assessment must be made. If there is not sufficient evidence to identify a cause, some specific biochemical parameters should be measured in the fish, e.g. methaemoglobin for nitrite toxicity (Huey *et al.*, 1984; Paláčková and Adámek, 1994), d-aminolevulinic acid dehydratase for lead (Canovas and Mas, 1987) or acetylcholinesterase for organophosphorus and carbamate insecticides (Cunha Bastos *et al.*, 1991). If such a biochemical study cannot be used, then a specific confirmatory bioassay must be carried out.

The third step covers those cases in which toxic concentrations are not found; therefore, additional information must be obtained using three different methods:

(a) Histopathological studies (Bucke, 1972; Ingersoll *et al.*, 1990; Narain *et al.*, 1990);
(b) Toxicity tests on concentrated samples (Tarazona *et al.*, 1991; Lippincott *et al.*, 1990; Andersson and Ingri, 1991), and chromatographic separation with additional toxicity tests of each chromatographic peak (Tarazona *et al.*, 1990);
(c) The study of the physiological status of the fish population, using biochemical parameters for specific groups of chemicals, e.g. metallothionein for heavy metals (Carpene and Vasak, 1989), acetylcholinesterase for organophosphorus and carbamate insecticides (Cunha Bastos *et al.*, 1991), or P450 for some priority planar organic pollutants (Gorksoyr and Larsen, 1991; Gorksoyr *et al.*, 1991).

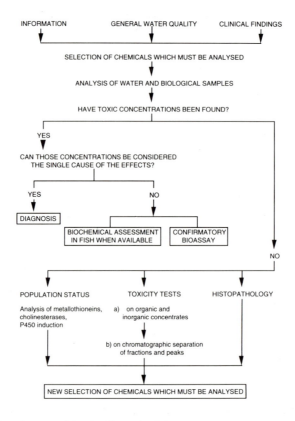

Fig. 21.2 Step-wise scheme used for the diagnosis of the cause of harmful effects in fish.

Finally, it must be recognised that toxic pollutants can increase the susceptibility of fish to infectious diseases (Carballo and Muñoz, 1991) and therefore their diagnosis must be considered within the general framework of the scheme.

References

APHA (American Public Health Association), 1980. Standard methods for the examination of water and waste-water, 15th edn. Washington, DC, American Public Health Association.

Andersson, P. and J. Ingri, 1991. A rapid preconcentration method for multielement analysis of natural freshwaters. *Wat.Res.*, **25**(5): 617–620.

Bartik, M. and A. Piskac, 1981. *Veterinary Toxicology*. Amsterdam, Elsevier Scientific Publications. 346 pp.

Bucke, D., 1972. Some histological techniques applicable to fish tissues. *Symp.Zool.Soc.London*, **30**: 153–189.

Canovas, M. and J. Mas, 1987. Efecto del ion Cd^{+2} sobre el enzima d-aminolevulinato deshidratasa de higado y bazo de alevin de mujol, *Liza aurata* (Risso). *Bol.Inst.Esp.Oceanogr.*, **4**(1): 29–32.

Carballo, M. and M.J. Muñoz, 1991. Effect of sublethal concentrations of four chemicals on susceptibility of juvenile rainbow trout (*Oncorhynchus mykiss*) to saprolegniosis. *Appl.Environ.Microbiol.*, **57**(6): 1813–1816.

Carpene, E. and M. Vasak, 1989. Hepatic metallothioneins from goldfish (*Carassius auratus* (L.)). *Comp.Biochem.Physiol.*, **92B**: 463–468.

Castaño, A., M.M. Vega, T. Blazquez and J.V. Tarazona, 1994. Biological alternatives to chemical identification for the ecotoxical assessment of industrial effluents: the RTG-2 in vitro cytotoxicity test. *Environm.Toxicol.Chem.* (in press).

Cunha Bastos, V.L.F., J. Cunha Bastos, J.S. Lima and M.V. Castro Faria, 1991. Brain acetylcholinesterase as in vitro detector of organophosphorous and carbamate insecticides in water. *Wat.Res.*, **25**(7): 835–840.

EEC, 1984. EEC Directive 84/449.

Goksoyr, A. and H. Larsen, 1991. The cytochrome P450 system of atlantic salmon (*Salmo salar*): I. Basal properties and induction of immature and mature fish. *Fish Physiol.Biochem.*, **9**(4): 339–349.

Goksoyr, A., A. Husoy, J. Larsen, S. Wilhelmsen, A. Maage, E.M. Brevik, T. Andersson, M. Celander, M. Pesonen and L. Förlin, 1991. Environmental contaminants and biochemical responses from the Hvaler archipelago in Norway. *Arch.Environ.Contam.Toxicol.*, **21**: 486–496.

Huey, D.W., T.L. Beitinger and M.C. Wooten, 1984. Nitrite-induced methemoglobin formation and recovery in channel catfish (*Ictalurus punctatus*) at three acclimation temperatures. *Bull.Environ. Contam.Toxicol.*, **32**: 674–681.

Ingersoll, C.G., D.A. Sanchez, J.S. Meyer, D.D. Gulley and J.E. Tietge, 1990. Epidermal response to pH, aluminum, and calcium exposure in brook trout (*Salvelinus fontinalis*) fry. *Can.J.Fish. Aquat.Sci.*, **47**: 1616–1642.

Lippincott, R.L., E.A. Ibrahim, J.B. Louis, T.B. Atherholt and I.H. Suffet, 1990. Continous liquid–liquid extraction for the preparation of chlorinated water samples for the Ames bioassay. *Wat.Res.*, **6**: 709–716.

Muñoz, M.J., M. Carballo and J.V. Tarazona, 1991. The effect of sublethal levels of copper and cyanide on some biochemical parameters of rainbow trout along subacute exposition. *Comp.Biochem. Physiol.*, **100C**(3): 577–582.

Narain, A.S., A.K. Srivastava and B.B. Singh, 1990. Gill lesions in the perch, *Anabas testudines*, subjected to sewage toxicity. *Bull.Environ.Contam.Toxicol.*, **45**: 235–242.

Paláčková, J. and Z. Adámek, 1994. The use of methaemoglobin concentration to measure sublethal effects in fish. Chapter 31, this volume.

Stewart, C.P. and A. Stolman, 1960. *Toxicology. Mechanisms and Analytical Methods*. London, Academic Press. 774 pp.

Tarazona, J.V., M.J. Muñoz, J.A. Ortiz, G. Carbonell, A. Rueda, M. Carballo, M.O. Nuñez, P. Nuñez and J.A. Camargo, 1987. Estudio toxicologico del proceso de mortalidad ocurrido en la piscifactoria del rio Duraton, de Vivar de Fuentidueña (Segovia). II.- Informe histopatologico, diagnostico y conclusiones. *Cuadernos Marisqueros Publicacion Tecnica*, **8**: 175–182.

Tarazona, J.V., A. Castaño and B. Gallego, 1990. Detection of organic toxic pollutants in water and waste-water by liquid chromatography and in vitro cytotoxicity tests. *Analytica Chimica Acta*, **234**: 193–197.

Tarazona, J.V., M.J. Muñoz, G. Carbonell, J.A. Ortiz and A. Castaño, 1991. A toxicological assessment of water pollution and its relationship to aquaculture development in Algeciras Bay, Cadiz, Spain. *Arch.Environ.Contam.*, **20**: 480–487.

SECTION C
ALUMINIUM TOXICITY AND ACID
WATERS

Surface water acidification is associated with the transfer of acidity from the catchment and from atmospheric deposition, with consequent mobilisation of aluminium, iron and trace metals, often at potentially toxic concentrations. Physical and chemical conditions in lakes and streams are diverse, reflecting the heterogeneity of catchment areas and the availability of sources of alkalinity and base cations. Acidification is observed in headwaters with limited catchment alkalinity but some effects are also observed downstream, such as in low salinity estuaries in the Gulf of Bothnia (Finland). Acid–base chemistry of surface waters is greatly influenced also by in-lake processes, including alkalinity and base cation production, sulphur and nitrogen retention, and adsorption/desorption of metals (such as aluminium). More of the acid neutralising capacity is derived from in-lake processes, principally within sediments, than from the catchment.

Biological effects are found in all ecosystem components, but EIFAC interests are focused on fish and fisheries, especially to applied considerations, including conservation of rare species and the genetic resource. However, it should also be remembered that fish do not live in isolation and that changes in other fauna, e.g. food chains, predation, habitat availability, are affected in acid systems even though ecosystem processes are reasonably robust even in some waters with a pH <5.0.

Physiological effects of acid exposure are primarily located at the gill membrane. Acid exposure displaces calcium held at the gill membrane, in turn affecting the ion regulatory pump and increasing the leakage of ions; in turn this leads to the progressive depletion of tissue ion concentrations. With high aluminium concentrations present, aluminium may precipitate at the gill surface (at moderate pH), provoking mucus production and inflammation, reducing oxygen/carbon dioxide exchange and respiratory stress. At more extreme pH levels, aluminium binds to the gill surface, displacing calcium ions and causing additional membrane disruption. If sufficient calcium is present, sodium and chloride loss is reduced, but respiratory stress is not eased. Acute exposure to acid and high aluminium conditions is usually responsible for mass fish kills, whereas chronic exposure leads to adverse interactions at the ecosystem level and the decline of populations.

The sensitivity of several non-salmonid fish to acidity and aluminium has been demonstrated by both field and laboratory observations. In particular, perch and pike are now known to be relatively tolerant to waters with a pH as low as 4.0 to

4.5. A whitefish species is also tolerant. In contrast, roach is sensitive at the egg/fry stage to pH <5. In general, aluminium enhances the effects of acidity; however, in many acid waters at low pH, acid is the major toxicant, whereas at pH >5 aluminium is the dominant factor.

Research studies suggest that there may be some acclimation to acid exposure, but that there is clearly genetically determined strain tolerance. Selection of tolerant strains, for example to match conditions for successful spawning, may have practical value.

More studies should be made of temperature effects in the field, related to year-by-year fluctuations in populations (especially significant for spawning); this has implications for the design of monitoring programmes which should integrate temperature and fry abundance.

The difference between strains and between a wider range of species (including those in estuaries) should be explored by laboratory exposures. The provenance of test fish and their pre-test conditions and stress should be recorded. Some important economic species have been neglected. Some guidance may be needed on the design of experiments, for instance on the use of natural vs. make-up media, natural vs. hatchery stocks, and the range of histological responses. The complex interactions between metal exposures and target organisms necessitate a better interpretation ('finding a pathway through a jungle'), seeking for convergent and consistent responses from a variety of approaches, including field observation of populations, bioassays, histology and physiology. Practical monitoring schemes of relevance to fisheries and conservation considerations should be an aim of further work.

G. Howells, Session Chairperson
R. Hudd, Session Vice-Chairman

Chapter 22
Anti-oxidant enzyme activity as biomarkers of acid stress in natural aquatic systems

R.A. STRIPP[1] and L.D. TROMBETTA[2]

[1] *U.S. Department of Energy, Environmental Measurements Laboratory, 376 Hudson Street, New York, NY 10014–3621, USA*
[2] *Toxicology Program, St John's University, Jamaica, New York 11439, USA*

22.1   Introduction

Acid rain and its associated affects on organisms inhabiting areas sensitive to acidic deposition has been the focus of a considerable amount of research (Schofield, 1976; Driscoll and Newton, 1985; Goldstein *et al.*, 1987; Stripp *et al.*, 1990). Much of this work has examined the acidification process and the associated affects on fish due to the mobilisation of toxic metals from sediments and soils (see review by Spry and Wiener, 1991). Several lakes and streams in the Adirondack Park in New York State have become acidified and certain populations of fish have been lost due to this process (Baker and Schofield, 1982; Schofield and Driscoll, 1987). Although rare, documented fish kills have occurred in response to episodes of acidic runoff (see review by Reader and Dempsey, 1989). Aluminium has received the most attention with reference to its toxicity at low pH. Aluminium toxicity in fish is strongly dependent upon the pH conditions (Wood, 1989; Baker and Schofield, 1982). The fact that aluminium is more bioavailable and toxic at low pH has led several investigators to examine this problem (see review by Spry and Wiener, 1991). Many morphological and physiological effects caused by acidic waters and aluminium on fish have been investigated (Jagoe and Haines, 1983; Chevalier *et al.*, 1985; Karlsson-Norrgren *et al.*, 1986; Ingersoll *et al.*, 1990; Wood, 1989); however, there is still a need for studies addressing the subcellular and biochemical mechanisms associated with this problem. These are particularly important because they may be sensitive indicators of acid stress and can be used to further elucidate the mechanisms by which acidity and/or metals, such as aluminium, causes toxicity to fish in acidified ecosystems.

Gills, the site of respiration and osmotic regulation, are the main targets of acid toxicity in fish (Wood, 1989). The respiratory system is the most important interface of fish with the surrounding environment and is very often the first target of a potential toxicant. The gills of fish are very vulnerable to pollutants and lethality is usually due to alterations in respiratory homeostasis. The gills are a multipurpose organ directly involved in a variety of functions including: respiratory gas exchange, osmoregulation, acid–base balance, and nitrogenous waste excretion.

Since respiratory gases must pass through the lamellar epithelium by diffusion, this surface is quite delicate compared to the rest of the surface of the fish. Moreover, there is a large flow of water over the lamellae even in a resting fish (approximately 70 ml.min^{-1} in a 0.5 kg trout), therefore, there is ample opportunity for dissolved or suspended materials to come into contact with the lamellae and cause injury to the respiratory tissues (Heath, 1987). At low pH, death is due to ionic and osmotic regulatory disturbances and reduced oxygen uptake (Wood, 1989). Such effects are enhanced by the presence of potentially toxic metals because the gills are also the most likely target for metal ion toxicity (McDonald *et al.*, 1989). This problem is further complicated by the fact that the chemical species of most metals in acidic aquatic systems are altered, very often enhancing their bioavailability and toxicity.

There is some uncertainty as to whether aluminium toxicity alone is the only influencing factor involved in the cause of acute mortality in fish during episodes of acidic runoff. The chemistry of other metals would also be influenced by the water pH and may have a detrimental effect on fish. Andersson and Nyberg (1984) exposed caged brown trout (*Salmo trutta*) to periods of snow melt and reported increased mortality even at low concentrations of aluminium. They found that the gills were enriched in iron, aluminium and manganese and suggested that iron may have been involved in the mortality. Many metals such as iron are known to produce oxidative injury. Aluminium itself does not stimulate peroxidation of lipids, but greatly accelerates the peroxidation induced by iron at acidic pH values and has also been shown to increase the peroxidation caused by H_2O_2 in erythrocyte membranes (Gutteridge *et al.*, 1985). The impairment of the cellular antioxidant defence or increases in the production of highly reactive free radical species may be the primary cause of cellular injury. Enhanced lipid peroxidation, alterations in antioxidant enzyme activity, or imbalance in the cellular redox system may be used as early 'markers' of oxidative stress. In this regard, we measured the activity of the antioxidant enzyme glutathione peroxidase in fish exposed to acidic natural waters containing elevated aluminium and iron. We also examined the fish for subcellular alterations to determine if oxidative injury was present.

22.2   Methodology

22.2.1   *Study sites and field preparations*

Fingerling brook trout (*Salvelinus fontinalis*) were obtained from the Cornell University, Little Moose Hatchery located in Old Forge, New York. A total of 120 fish were placed in four lakes during early spring snow melt. Equal numbers of trout from the hatchery were retained as baseline controls. The study sites selected and the pH values measured during the experiment were as follows: Squash Pond Outlet, 4.3; Dart's Lake, 5.0; Big Moose Lake, 5.0; and Moss Lake, 6.8. Moss

Lake is a circumneutral lake which was used as a reference site. The lakes are all located in Herkimer County in close proximity to each other. The elevation (525–585 m above sea level) is similar and the water temperature (4°C) was the same at all four sites. They are clear, soft-water lakes with low concentrations of dissolved organic carbon.

The fish were monitored at regular intervals over the entire exposure period of 72 hours. Lack of opercular movement was the criterion used to determine mortality. The surviving fish were removed after 72 hours and the left second gill arches were immediately removed and fixed for electron microscopy or frozen in liquid nitrogen for biochemistry. The samples were then transported to the laboratory for study. Only those fish surviving the exposure were processed for electron microscopy and biochemistry. Water samples were also collected for metal analysis.

22.2.2   *Glutathione peroxidase activity*

Glutathione peroxidase (EC 1.11.1.9) activity was determined by a modification of the methods of Paglia and Valentine (1967) and Germain and Arneson (1977) as described in Kromidas *et al.* (1990).

22.2.3   *Graphite furnace atomic absorption spectrophotometry (GFAAS)*

Analysis of filterable water fraction and gill tissue samples for trace metal content was performed by graphite furnace atomic absorption spectrophotometry. The techniques used are described elsewhere (Stripp *et al.*, 1990).

22.2.4   *Microscopy*

Mayer's mucicarmine stain (Luna, 1968) for mucus was used on paraffin embedded sections using appropriate controls. For electron microscopy, gill tissues from various groups of fish were fixed in cold Sorenson's phosphate buffered (pH 7.4) 3.0% glutaraldehyde for 3 hours, washed overnight with buffer and post-fixed in 1% osmium tetroxide. Tissue was washed in buffer, dehydrated in a water/acetone series and then embedded in LX112-Araldite. Ten tissue blocks from each of four different fish were sectioned on a LKB NOVA ultramicrotome. Sections were stained with lead citrate and uranyl acetate and viewed at 75 kV on a Hitachi HU11E electron microscope.

22.2.5   *Statistics*

Significance was tested among groups using the one-way analysis of variance (ANOVA) followed by the LSD post hoc analysis to test for difference among several means. Differences between values with $P<0.05$ were considered to be significant.

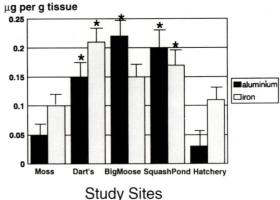

Study Sites

Fig. 22.1 Mean aluminum and iron concentrations in brook trout gill tissues. n = 10 fish per group. Values expressed as mean of three replicate analyses. *$P < 0.05$.

22.3   Results

22.3.1   *Metal analysis*

The chemical characteristics of the lake water are given in Table 22.1. The concentrations of aluminium and iron in the fish gills are shown in Figure 22.1. The gill tissues of the fish held in the acidic sites contained elevated aluminium and iron concentrations when compared to the fish from circumneutral Moss Lake. Iron, manganese and aluminium were significantly higher in the lake water samples collected from the acidic sites than from Moss Lake.

22.3.2   *Glutathione peroxidase activity*

Glutathione peroxidase activity (GSH-Px) was significantly ($P < 0.05$) higher in the tissues of the fish held in the acidic sites (Fig. 22.2). Trout held in all the acidic sites had GSH-Px activities that were significantly higher ($P < 0.05$) when compared to the fish from Moss Lake. The activity of GSH-Px in the fish from the hatchery was not significantly different from the fish from the reference lake.

22.3.3   *Microscopy*

Histopathological and ultrastructural examination of brook trout exposed to low pH water and elevated metals in the natural environment showed alterations to the chloride cells. Light microscopic examination showed that the chloride cells were swollen, vacuolated, and contained granular material in the cytoplasm (Fig. 22.4–22.5). All of the fish examined from the acidic locations had anomalies associated with the degeneration of the primary and secondary lamellae. 'Clubbing' and fusion of the lamellae was seen. Transmission electron microscopy showed that the

Table 22.1 Physical and chemical characteristics and trace metals in lake water samples from Herkimer County.

	Moss Lake	Dart's Lake	Big Moose	Squash Pond Outlet
Elevation	525 m	536 m	524 m	580 m
pH	6.8	4.9	5.0	4.3
Cond.	30	28	42	38
ANC	66	6	8	5
Ca^{2+} (μmol.l^{-1})	73	48	57	41
DOC	310	312	307	305
Trace metals (μg.l^{-1} $\pm$SD)				
Al*	67 $\pm$6	221 $\pm$12	295 $\pm$37	340 $\pm$23
Cd	0.6 $\pm$0.3	0.7 $\pm$0.3	1.0 $\pm$0.9	0.6 $\pm$0.5
Cu	1.8 $\pm$0.1	2.0 $\pm$0.1	4.1 $\pm$1.7	2.9 $\pm$0.9
Fe*	33 $\pm$7	56 $\pm$12	112 $\pm$24	131 $\pm$29
Mn*	39 $\pm$5	115 $\pm$11	121 $\pm$12	117 $\pm$16
Pb	2.5 $\pm$0.4	3.0 $\pm$0.1	2.7 $\pm$0.5	3.6 $\pm$0.3
Zn	187 $\pm$22	141 $\pm$13	199 $\pm$9	157 $\pm$19

Notes: * $P<0.05$
ANC = acid neutralising capacity (μeq.l^{-1})
DOC = dissolved organic carbon (μmol.l^{-1})
Cond. = specific conductance (μmho.cm^{-1})

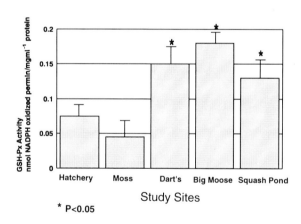

Fig. 22.2 GSH-Px activity in brook trout gills. n = 6 fish per group. Values expressed as the mean of 6 replicate analyses.

chloride cells of the fish exposed to low pH waters contained swollen mitochondria indicative of high amplitude swelling and a loss of cristae (Fig. 22.7, cf. Fig. 22.6). There was also a discontinuity of the membranes. Lipid deposits and myelin whorls were seen in the cytoplasm and the endoplasmic reticulum was dilated (Fig. 22.7, cf. Fig. 22.6). Paraffin sections stained with mucicarmine and electron microscopic observation did not show the presence of excessive mucus in fish placed in acidic waters. The gills from the hatchery fish appeared normal (Fig. 22.6) and the gills removed from the fish held in the reference lake (Fig. 22.3 and 22.6) were similar in appearance to those removed from the hatchery.

22.4   Discussion

Understanding the toxic action of contaminants is fundamental to predicting the important sublethal effects. This leads to the design of meaningful bioassays, screening procedures, and a knowledge of indices of fish health in the wild. Metal ion concentrations, which are generally the most bioavailable forms of elements, increase as the pH decreases. This leads to an enrichment of these potentially toxic elements in low alkalinity aquatic systems (Stripp *et al.*, 1990). At a pH of 5.0, $Al(OH)^{2+}$ and Al^{3+} proportions increase. The mono, di and trivalent cations of aluminium are only stable at acidic pH, and this has profound effects on toxicity. A decrease in one pH unit below 5.6 results in a thousandfold increase in aluminium solubility. These ions are effective in inhibiting influxes of ions and the harmful effects of aluminium ions are related to interactions with the enzyme ATPase (Potts and McWilliams, 1989). As the enzyme is believed to be situated on the baso-lateral membranes the Al ions must cross the apical membrane, or penetrate the intracellular junctions, more readily at low pH. This is consistent with the fact that Fe^{2+} will affect membrane permeability by oxidative injury.

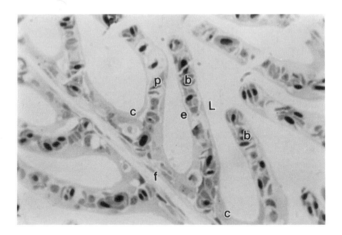

Fig. 22.3 Basal and branchial respiratory lamellae. Photomicrograph of a longitudinal section of the gill of a brook trout collected from circumneutral Moss Lake, illustrating the junctions of the gill lamellae (L) and the gill filament or primary lamellae (f), and showing the supporting pilaster cells (p), epithelial cells (e), chloride cells (c), and blood spaces. Note the uniformity and regular spacing of the lamellae and the normal cellular structure of the junction between the primary and the secondary lamellae. There is a minimal diffusion distance between the respiratory surface and the blood spaces. The epithelium extends from the basement membrane to the surface. Gill sections from the hatchery fish appeared essentially the same.

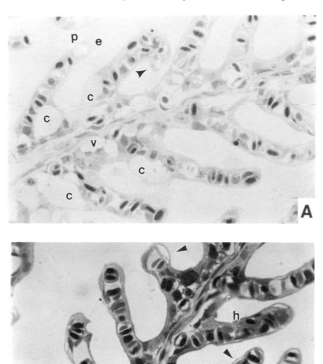

Fig. 22.4   A. Basal and branchial respiratory lamellae. Photomicrograph of a longitudinal section of the gill of a brook trout collected from Big Moose Lake (pH 4.9). Note the clubbing like distortion of the lamellae (arrowhead), vacuoles (v), lifting of the epithelium (e), fluid in the space between epithelial and pilaster cells (p) (suggestive of an impairment of cell membrane permeability), cell vacuolisation and a proliferation and swelling of the chloride cells (c).

B. Basal and branchial respiratory lamellae. Photomicrograph of a longitudinal section of the gill of a brook trout collected from Dart's Lake (pH 4.9). Note the epithelial hyperplasia (h), the lifting of the epithelium from the basement membrane causing an increase in diffusion distance (arrowheads); the chloride cells (c) appear swollen and necrotic.

Increases in aluminium concentration and alterations in its chemical species at low pH has also been shown to affect the survival and growth of fish (Baker and Schofield, 1982). It has also been shown that aluminium accumulates in the gill tissue of wild fish collected from acidic lakes (Stripp *et al.*, 1990). Acidity alone can be toxic to fish; however, with the exception of Squash Pond (pH 4.3), the pH of the lakes are within the tolerance level for brook trout (generally toxic below pH 5.0). Calcium also reduces the toxicity of aluminium at low pH; however, the lakes used in this study contain clear, soft water with relatively low concentrations of Ca^{2+} (Table 22.1).

There is also evidence that the Al ion follows Fe^{3+} pathways *in vivo*. Aluminum binds to the iron transport protein transferrin and there is evidence of a concomitant lysosomal storage and deposition of iron and aluminium. The function of transferrin is to transport iron into cells which have transferrin receptors on the plasma membrane and may provide a mechanism for aluminium transport into

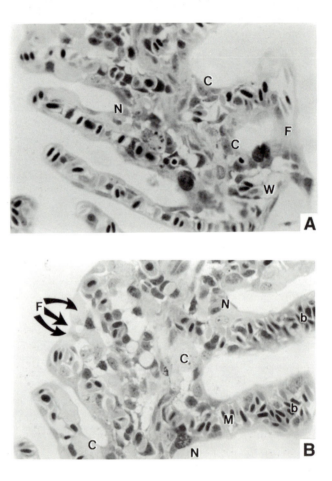

Fig. 22.5   A. Basal and branchial respiratory lamellae. Photomicrograph of a longitudinal section of the gill of a brook trout collected from Squash Pond Outlet (pH 4.3). Note the fusion of two neighbouring lamellae (F), the dilation of the lamellar blood sinus with infiltration of white blood cells (w), and the presence of granules within some of the severely degenerate chloride cells (c). Some chloride cells appear necrotic (N).

B. Basal and branchial respiratory lamellae. Photomicrograph of a longitudinal section of the gill of a brook trout collected from Squash Pond Outlet (pH 4.3). Note the swelling and the total fusion of three adjacent lamellae (F) and the congestion of the blood spaces (b) and marginal blood channel (M). The chloride cells appear very swollen (c) and cellular vacuolisation can be seen in necrotic cells with picnotic masses present (N).

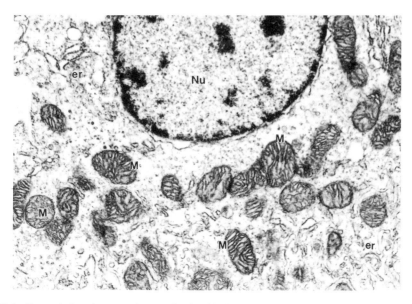

Fig. 22.6 Transmission electron micrograph of a chloride cell from a section of brook trout gill. Note the endoplasmic reticulum (er) and numerous mitochondria (M) in the cytoplasm and their well-defined cristae and membranes. This cell exhibits a normal ultrastructure. This sample was taken from fish placed in circumneutral Moss Lake (pH 6.8) for 72 hours. Samples from the hatchery appeared similar. Nu, nucleus.

cells. This raises the question of competitive binding of aluminium and iron to ligands and a mechanism for amplification of the toxicity of both ions and their effects on membrane permeability (there are more free ions available to promote oxidative stress).

The molecular mechanisms responsible for cell injury are complex. Injury to cells may have many causes, and probably there is no common pathway to cell death. There are, however, a number of considerations that are useful when examining the effect of chemicals on intact tissues. Although it is not always possible to determine the precise biochemical lesion caused by a chemical, four intracellular systems are particularly vulnerable: (1) the maintenance of the cell membranes, upon which the ionic and osmotic homeostasis of the cell is dependent; (2) aerobic respiration and the production of ATP; (3) protein synthesis; and (4) preservation of the genetic apparatus of the cell.

However, the structural and biochemical elements of the cell are so closely related that whatever the precise point of initial attack by the damaging agent, injury at one locus leads to a variety of secondary effects. For example, impairment of aerobic respiration or membrane integrity can disrupt the energy-dependent sodium pump that maintains the ionic fluid balance of the cell, resulting in altered intracellular content of ions and water. Morphologic changes only become apparent after some critical biochemical system within the cell becomes deranged.

The physical state of biological membranes is very important for the regulation of many processes. Alterations in the integrity of the membrane due to lipid peroxidation is a common event in cellular injury. This may be characteristic of aluminium toxicity at acidic pH. Using electromagnetic paramagnetic resonance spectroscopy, Vierstra and Haug (1978), showed that Al^{3+} produces a dramatic decrease in membrane fluidity at acidic pH. One of the major causes of a loss of membrane fluidity, increasing membrane permeability to ions and a loss of membrane integrity, is lipid peroxidation. Membrane bound enzymes are also inactivated by peroxidative injury. The aldehydes produced by lipid peroxidation are cytotoxic, and an intracellular pigment known as lipofuscin is an end product of the oxidative degradation of lipids. These pigments form in the lysosomes where aluminium accumulates intracellularly. The finding of electron dense material in the gill tissue of the fish held in acidic natural waters may be indicative of aluminium accumulation. Aluminium has been detected in electron-dense material in the chloride cells of fish exposed to these conditions (Karlsson-Norrgren *et al.*, 1986).

While aluminium itself does not produce lipid peroxidation, the toxic action of Al^{3+} is characterised by the formation of intracellular occlusions which are the result of lipid peroxidation. Interestingly, Al^{3+} stimulates the peroxidation of phospholipids induced by iron salts to the extent that desferrioxamine, an inhibitor

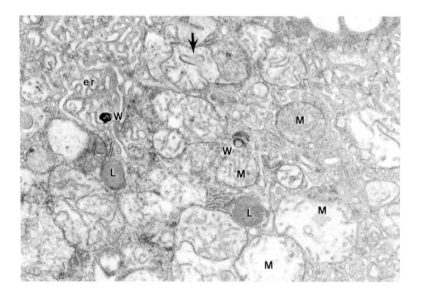

Fig. 22.7 Transmission electron micrograph of a chloride cell from a section of brook trout gill placed in acidic Squash Pond Outlet (pH 4.3). Mitochondria appeared swollen (M). Loss of cristae and the disruption of their internal matrix was seen. Note the presence of myelin whorls (W) and the continuation of a myelin whorl with the mitochondrial membrane (arrow). Lipid droplets are also seen in the cytoplasm (L) and the endoplasmic reticulum (er) appeared swollen. These degenerative changes can be associated with lipid peroxidation. This was representative of all the samples collected from the acidic sites.

of iron-dependent peroxidation, has been used to decrease the lipid peroxidation stimulated by aluminium (Gutteridge *et al.*, 1985). One of the most damaging species of oxygen derived radicals is the hydroxyl radical (OH·). Hydroxyl radicals are generated by interactions with transition metals in the Fenton reaction. Iron is particularly important in oxidative injury. Most iron is in ferric (Fe^{3+}) form and has to be reduced to the ferrous (Fe^{2+}) form to be active in the Fenton reaction. At the acidic pH ranges of the low alkalinity lakes, much of the iron present is in the ferrous form enhancing the production of hydroxyl radicals capable of inducing oxidative stress.

Subcellular alterations such as abnormal mitochondria, scattered areas of electron dense material, discontinuous membranes, lipid deposits, myelin whorls, and dilated endoplasmic reticulum are all indications of advanced degeneration associated with oxidative injury. Our results also indicated that the antioxidant enzyme glutathione peroxidase activity was higher in the fish placed in the acidic sites. This fact, supported by the subcellular evidence of peroxidative injury, indicates that oxidative stress may be a contributing factor in the loss of ion regulation associated with aluminium toxicity at low pH. Aluminum is most toxic in a pH range of 5.0 to 5.5 and enhances the peroxidation of membrane lipids caused by transition metals such as iron, thereby altering the integrity of the membrane. Changes in the fluctuation of ions, or the direct action of metals, cause further intracellular damage by poisoning the mitochondria. This leads to alterations in energy metabolism and a decreased synthesis of ATP. Loss of cellular energy then affects energy requiring activities such as ion pumps, membrane maintenance and protein synthesis which leads to further losses in membrane integrity. Ultimately the cell will reach a point of no return and the cytological effects are irreversible and the cell enters the stages of necrosis as demonstrated in this study.

From the results of these studies, it is probable that death in fish exposed to low pH waters containing metals is associated with the accumulation of aluminium in the respiratory epithelium of the gills resulting in branchial oedema and lamellar fusion. A present working hypothesis is that gill aluminium concentration increases due to alterations in the permeability of the plasma membrane by peroxidative injury (the GSH-Px activity supports this) which is enhanced by the presence of transition metals. Alterations and injury to the plasma membrane induce an influx of metals that interact with the mitochondria and cause further harm to the cell because of an altered energy metabolism. The branchial epithelium thickens and distorts causing a decrease in transcellular permeability to oxygen and carbon dioxide, while increasing the loss of intracellular ions such as sodium and chloride. The alteration in ion flux causes changes in the plasma volume and eventual circulatory collapse.

These biochemical changes, together with the histopathology, have a use as a potential monitoring tool. Because many environmental pollutants are capable of inducing oxidative stress, such information could be used as a method of determining exposure to, and the effects of, these stressors on aquatic organisms. We are currently continuing studies examining other anti-oxidant enzymes, lipid peroxidation, and reduced and oxidised glutathione levels as potential biomarkers of environmental stress.

References

Andersson, P. and P. Nyberg, 1984. Experiments with brown trout (*Salmo trutta* L.) during spring in mountain streams at low pH and elevated levels of iron, manganese and aluminum. *Rept.Inst.Freshwater Res.Drottningholm*, **61**: 34–47.

Baker, J.P. and C.L. Schofield, 1982. Aluminum toxicity to fish in acidic waters. *Water Air and Soil Pollut.*, **18**: 289–309.

Chevalier, G., L. Gauthier and G. Moreau, 1985. Histopathological and electron microscopic studies of gills of brook trout, *Salvelinus fontinalis*, from acidified lakes. *Can.J.Zool.*, **63**: 2062–2070.

Driscoll, C.Y. and R.M. Newton, 1985. Chemical characteristics of Adirondack lakes. *Envir.Sci. Technol.*, **19**: 11.

Germain, G.S. and R.M. Arneson, 1977. Selenium induced glutathione peroxidase activity in mouse neuroblastoma cells. *Biochem.Biophys.Res.Commun.*, **79**: 119–123.

Goldstein, R.A., S.A. Gherini, C. Driscoll, R. April, C.L. Schofield and C.W. Chen, 1987. Lake-watershed acidification in the North Branch of the Moose River. *Biogeochem.*, **3**: 5.

Gutteridge, J.M.C., G.J. Quinlan, I.Clark and B. Halliwell, 1985. Aluminum salts accelerate peroxidation of membrane lipids stimulated by iron salts. *Biochem.Biophs.Acta*, **835**: 441–447.

Heath, A.G., 1987. *Water Pollution and Fish Physiology*, 1st edn. Boca Raton, Florida, CRC Press.

Ingersoll, C.G., D.D. Gully, D.R. Mount, M.E. Mueller, J.D. Fernandez, J.R. Hockett and H.L. Begman, 1990. Aluminum and acid toxicity to two strains of brook trout (*Salvelinus fontinalis*). *Can.J.Fish.Aquat.Sci.*, **47**: 1641–1648.

Jagoe, C.H. and T.A. Haines, 1983. Alterations in gill epithelial morphology of yearling sunapee trout exposed to acute acid stress. *Trans.Am.Fish.Soc.*, **112**: 689–695.

Karlsson-Norrgren, L., I. Bjorklund, O. Ljungberg and P. Runn, 1986. Acid water and aluminium exposure: experimentally induced gill lesions in brown trout, *Salmo trutta* L. *J.Fish Diseases*, **9**: 11–25.

Kromidas, L., L.D. Trombetta and I.J. Jamal, 1990. The protective effects of glutathione against methylmercury cytotoxicity. *Tox.Lett.*, **51**: 67–80.

Luna, L.G., 1968. In: *Manual of Histological Staining Methods of the Armed Forces Institute of Pathology*, 3rd edn. New York, McGraw-Hill.

McDonald, D.G., J.P. Reader and T.R.K. Dalziel, 1989. The combined effects of pH and trace metals on fish ionoregulation. In: Morris, R. *et al. Acid Toxicity and Aquatic Animals*. pp. 221–242, Cambridge, Cambridge University Press.

Paglia, D.E. and W.N. Valentine, 1967. Studies on the qualitative and quantitative characterization of erythrocyte glutathione peroxidase. *J.Lab.Clin.Med.*, **70**: 158–169.

Potts, W.T.W. and P.G. McWilliams, 1989. *Acid Toxicity and Aquatic Animals*, Cambridge, Cambridge University Press, 217 pp.

Reader, J.P. and C.H. Dempsey, 1989. Episodic changes in water quality and their effects on fish. In: Morris, R. *et al. Acid Toxicity and Aquatic Animals*. pp. 67–83, Cambridge, Cambridge University Press.

Schofield, C.L., 1976. Acid precipitation: effects on fish. *Ambio*, **5**: 228.

Schofield, C.L. and C.T. Driscoll, 1987. Fish species distribution in relation to water-quality gradients in the North Branch of the Moose River. *Biogeochem.*, **3**: 63.

Spry, D.J. and J.G. Wiener, 1991. Metal bioavailability and toxicity to fish in low alkalinity lakes: a critical review. *Environ.Poll.*, **71**: 243–304.

Stripp, R.A., M. Heit, D.C. Bogen, J. Bidanset and L. Trombetta, 1990. Trace element accumulation in the tissues of two species of fish from three lakes with different pH values. *Water Air and Soil Pollut.*, **51**: 75–87.

Vierstra, R. and A. Haug, 1978. The effect of Al^{+3} on the physical properties of membrane lipids in *Theroplasma acidophilum. Biochem.Biophys.Res.Commun.*, **84**(1): 138–143.

Wood, C.M., 1989. The physiological problems of fish in acid waters. In: Morris, R. *et al. Acid Toxicity and Aquatic Animals*. pp. 125–152. Cambridge, Cambridge University Press.

Chapter 23
Effects of calcium and magnesium in acid water on the ion balance of eggs and alevins of rainbow trout (*Oncorhynchus mykiss*)

M. LAITINEN and M. KARTTUNEN

University of Jyväskylä, Department of Biology, Yliopistonkatu 9,
SF-40100 Jyväskylä, Finland

23.1   Introduction

The main effect of acidification on fish populations is on reproduction, and can be exerted at various stages of the cycle, from reduction in gamete production and quality to mortality of the developing eggs and alevins (Lee and Gerking, 1980; Valtonen and Laitinen, 1987), the nature of the change varying with the developmental stage of fish (Rask, 1984; Ingersoll *et al.*, 1990). The calcium concentration of the water has a protective effect on the response of fish to acid stress (Brown and Lynam, 1981; Brown, 1982; Wood *et al.*, 1990b), and a correlation has also been found between water conductivity and egg survival (Rask, 1984). Little is known about the possible role of magnesium during acid stress, although it is well established that this divalent intracellular cation catalyses or activates hundreds of enzymes and also plays an important role in the breeding of both aquatic and terrestrial animals (Wacker, 1969; Cutchberson, 1977; Stolkowski, 1977). Magnesium may also play a role in the wintering of fish (Valtonen and Laitinen, 1987), but the combined effects of calcium (Ca) and magnesium (Mg) ions or magnesium ions alone on the embryonic development have been poorly studied in the past.

The purpose of this work was to investigate the effects of elevated Ca and Mg concentrations in the water on the ionic balance of rainbow trout (*Oncorhynchus mykiss*) eggs and fry during acid stress at different developmental stages.

23.2   Materials and methods

Fertilised rainbow trout eggs were obtained from a commercial hatchery (Taimen OY, Lankamaa) on 7 March, and the first acid exposure started about 6 hours after fertilisation. The eggs were reared in one-litre boxes with 100 to 150 eggs in each box. The boxes received water from a proportional diluter at a rate of five cycles per hour (5 l per hour). The test groups comprised a control group which received water directly from an inlet from the River Rutajoki (pH 6.6–6.9, Table 23.1a), an

Table 23.1 (a) Water chemistry of the River Rutajoki and the different salt additions used for the rearing experiments.

pH	6.6–6.9
total hardness (mmol.l^{-1})	0.12
COD_{Mn} (mg.l^{-1} O_2)	9.0
colour (mg.l^{-1} Pt)	50
conductivity (mS.m^{-1})	3.9
alkalinity (mmol.l^{-1})	0.12
Ca ((mg.l^{-1})	3–3.5
Mg (mg.l^{-1})	1.5–2
Fe (μg.l^{-1})	360
Al (total, μg.l^{-1})	43–47
Al (inorganic, μg.l^{-1})	<10

Table 23.1 (b) Salt additions in the acid (pH 4.7) exposures, and resulting variations in Ca and Mg concentration.

	(mg.l^{-1})	Ca (mg.l^{-1})	Mg (mg.l^{-1})
CaCl$_2$	62	20–25	
MgCl$_2$	49		10–15
CaCl$_2$ + MgCl$_2$	111	20–25	10–15
NaCl	126		

acid group (pH 4.7) and additional acid groups with an increased Ca concentration (20–25 mg.l^{-1} Ca), or Mg concentration (10–15 mg.l^{-1} Mg), or both (Table 23.1b).

As these increases were produced by adding the chloride salts of Ca and Mg, an additional acid group was created in which the salt concentration was increased to correspond to the level obtained in the combined Ca and Mg addition by adding NaCl (126 mg.l^{-1}) to the incoming water. Water temperature in the diluter varied between 2 and 5°C up to 15 May, after which it increased to about 8°C by the end of the experiments.

Separate egg exposure groups were used for mortality and ionic measurements. Because of the limit on the number of rearing chambers that could be placed in the diluter, mortality values were recorded only during the exposure period of embryonic development. Eggs were considered to be dead when their colour changed from yellow to opaque (Ingersoll *et al.*, 1990).

Eggs at the eyed stage and newly hatched fry reared in water from the River Rutajoki were exposed by the same procedure. The experiments ended at the terminal yolk resorption stage.

Four to five pooled samples of three eggs or six fry were taken from each group on each sampling occasion; excess water was removed from the surface and the samples were frozen and stored at −20°C until analysed for dry weight and Ca, Mg and chloride concentrations as described by Soivio and Virtanen (1980).

Student's *t*-test for independent variables was used to assess the significance of the differences between the mean ion concentrations recorded in the different

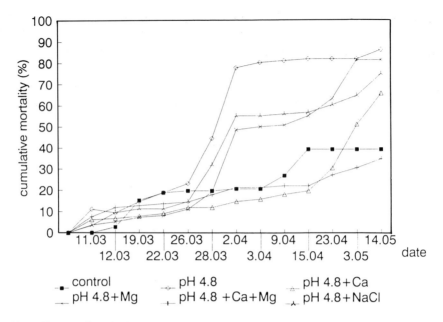

Fig. 23.1 The mortality of rainbow trout eggs during embryonic development in acid exposure with different salt concentrations.
Note: the time between subsequent samples is not constant as is shown in the Figure.

treatments. The chi-squared test was used to determine the significance of the differences in mortality.

23.3   Results

23.3.1   *Exposure throughout embryonic development*

The cumulative mortality in the control group was 40% at the end of the experiment (Fig. 23.1). Acid exposure (pH 4.7) throughout embryonic development (from post-fertilisation until hatching) caused a significant increase in mortality ($P<0.01$) to between 60 and 90% in all the acid treatments except those with elevated Ca and Mg concentrations. In other groups, mortality was more rapid in the presence of acid alone stress and was delayed until the eyed stage with an elevated Ca concentration. Mg and NaCl also reduced the mortality rates to some extent before the eyed stage was reached (Fig. 23.1).

A significant tissue loss of Ca, Mg and Cl occurred in all groups ($P<0.05$) during the first few hours of the water hardening period (Fig. 23.2). No significant differences were found in the egg or body ion concentrations between the treatments or in relation to the control.

Concentrations of calcium, magnesium and chloride up to the hatching stage are shown in Figure 23.3. Calcium concentrations were almost constant. The magnesium concentration decreased in all the groups up to the eyed stage, but increased significantly ($P<0.05$) by the time of hatching. The chloride concentration in the eggs increased significantly ($P<0.05$) between 11 March and 19 March in all treatments and remained at a stable level for the remainder of the exposure period.

Egg dry weight decreased throughout the experiment (from 25.7 ±0.5 to 17.9 ±0.4 mg) and showed no significant differences between the treatments.

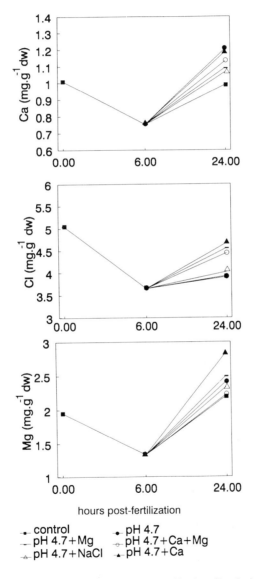

Fig. 23.2 Ionic content of rainbow trout eggs before fertilisation (0-value), after a 6-hour water-hardening period in control water, and after subsequent exposure to acid water at different salt concentrations. Values are means of 4–5 pooled samples of three eggs.

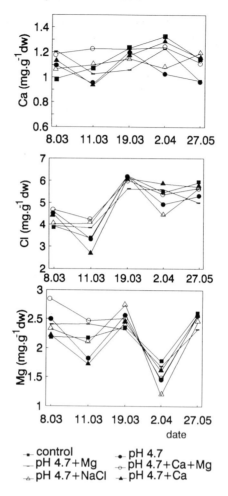

Fig. 23.3 Ionic content of rainbow trout eggs exposed to acid stress throughout the embryonic development. Values are means of 4–5 pooled samples of three eggs. The eggs reached the eyed stage around 15 April.

No differences in development time, or mortality due to partial hatching, occurred in any of the treatments.

23.3.2   *Exposure at the eyed stage*

No significant changes were found during the first 18 days of exposure of the eggs to acid water at the eyed stage (beginning on 15 April). The fry hatched from 3 May onwards and the analyses of samples taken on 24 May and 5 June represent larval whole body determinations including the yolk material (Fig. 23.4).

The loss of the egg capsule and perivitelline fluid on hatching resulted in a loss of magnesium from 2.1–2.4 mg.g^{-1} to 0.9–1.3 mg.g^{-1} (Fig. 23.4), but subsequently the concentration of magnesium increased (until 5 June), although significantly so only in the control group ($P<0.05$). This group had higher concentrations of Ca and Cl in the newly hatched larvae than in the eggs and the amounts increased markedly, by ninefold and threefold, respectively, during the period of yolk absorption (Fig. 23.4). In the acid groups the amount of calcium remained near the base-line level (about 1 mg.g^{-1} Ca), and only a slight increase was found in the chloride concentration (Fig. 23.4).

The final concentrations of all ions at the end of the experiment were significantly

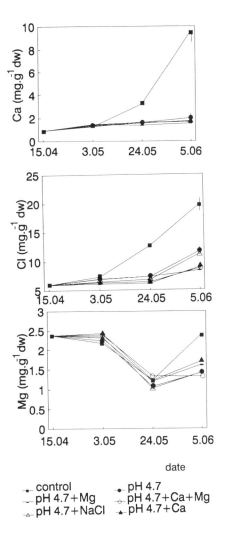

Fig. 23.4 Ionic content of rainbow trout eggs exposed to acid stress at the eyed stage. Values on 15 April and 3 May are from eggs and on 24 May and 5 June from alevins. Values are means of 4–5 pooled samples of three eggs or six alevins. ±SD are indicated by vertical bars at points where significant ($P <0.05$) differences exist.

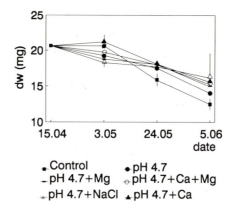

Fig. 23.5 The dry weight of eyed stage eggs (on 15 April and 3 May) and yolk-sac fry (on 24 May and 5 June) in the different treatments.

($P<0.01$) higher in the control group than in the acid groups, but no significant differences were found between the treatments within the acid groups.

The dry weight of the eggs decreased more rapidly in the control group than in the acid groups, being significantly lower ($P<0.05$) than in any acid group on 25 April, and lower than all of them except the NaCl group at the end of the experiment (Fig. 23.5).

23.3.3   *Yolk-sac fry exposure*

The newly hatched yolk-sac fry exposed to acid water showed a net gain in Ca and Cl in the control and acid + NaCl-groups (Fig. 23.6). The concentration of Ca at the end of the exposure was significantly ($P<0.01$) higher in the control group than in the acid groups, where no significant differences existed between the treatments. Chloride concentrations were significantly higher in the control and NaCl groups ($P<0.01$) than in the others (Fig. 23.6).

The Mg concentration in the control group decreased slightly between 22 and 30 May, and then remained at the same level for the remainder of the exposure period. In acid groups, it increased at first ($P<0.05$) and then decreased up to the end of the exposure period (Fig. 23.6). No differences existed between the groups at the end of the exposure period. The final dry weight of the alevins (between 15.9 and 18.9 mg) did not differ significantly between the treatments.

23.4   Discussion

The mortality of eggs exposed to acid water soon after fertilisation increased significantly after three weeks of incubation, before the eyed stage was reached. The high sensitivity of newly fertilised eggs to acid stress reported by Chulakasem *et al.* (1988) and Ingersoll *et al.* (1990) was not seen in these experiments, mainly because of the delay of about 6 hours between fertilisation and the start of exposure; water intake and other possible changes take place during the first few hours after fertilisation (Peterson and Martin-Robichaud, 1982; Rombough and Jensen, 1985). Indeed, no swelling of eggs could be measured microscopically during the first 24 hours in the post-fertilisation exposure stage of any of the present treatments.

The earlier observations of a protective effect of calcium in relation to acid stress (Brown and Lynam, 1981; Rodgers, 1984; Ingersoll *et al.*, 1990; Wood *et al.*, 1990b)

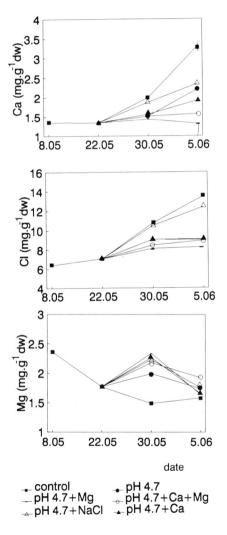

Fig. 23.6 Ionic content of rainbow trout yolk-sac fry exposed to acid stress immediately after hatching. Values are means of 4–5 pooled samples of six alevins. ±SD are indicated by vertical bars at points where significant (*P* <0.05) differences exist.

are not completely supported by the present work, because mortality increased markedly at the eyed stage. Brown and Lynam (1981) carried out their experiment in deionised water comparing Ca concentrations of 0 or 1 mg.l^{-1} with 10 mg.l^{-1}. They found that 1 mg.l^{-1} Ca was sufficient to enable brown trout (*Salmo trutta*) eggs to hatch at pH 4.5 when they were exposed at the eyed stage. However, freshly fertilised eggs at pH 4.5 required 10 mg.l^{-1} Ca to survive to the same extent as the control group. In our natural river waters concentrations of 3.0–3.5 mg.l^{-1} Ca and 1.5–2.0 mg.l^{-1} Mg seem to be sufficient for normal development at pH 6.7 (control). In the acid water, addition of both MgCl$_2$ and CaCl$_2$ was required to reduce the mortality to about the control level.

The mortalities cannot be explained by any differences in ionic composition, and the experiment with added Mg and Ca gave the same ionic results as the other acid treatments, although the mortality here was even lower than that in the control.

At the eyed stage, or as newly hatched fry, the uptake of ions from the surrounding water was mainly dominated by the pH value, with little effect being due to the salt concentration. Similar results were obtained for brook trout (*Salvelinus fontinalis*) alevins by Wood *et al.* (1990a).

Although there were no differences in egg calcium concentration, the greatest effect arising from acid stress at later stages in development was an impairment in the increase in body total calcium, a response similar to the results obtained by a number of authors (e.g. Lacroix *et al.*, 1985; Peterson and Martin-Robichaud, 1986; Gunn and Noakes, 1987; Chulakasem *et al.*, 1988).

The net intake of magnesium found is in contrast with most of the previously reported results where the content during development either decreased (Zeitoun *et al.*, 1976; Peterson and Martin-Robichaud, 1986; Wood *et al.*, 1990b; Cleveland *et al.*, 1991) or remained near to the base-line level (Reader *et al.*, 1989).

The Mg concentration in eggs of rainbow trout (1.33 ±0.22 mg.g^{-1}) on 8 March, after the water hardening period, accounts for only 57% of the 2.33 ±0.22 mg.g^{-1} found on 31 May at the end of the experiment. However, it is clear that the magnesium content increased during the egg phase, which is in agreement with the results of van der Velden (1991), who found a concentration-dependent inhibition of Mg uptake in carp fry exposed to a range of Mg concentrations from 0.1 to 2.5 mg.l^{-1}. As in this study, he concluded that the amount of Mg present in the yolk and perivitelline fluid material was not sufficient for successful development of the egg. He found the critical lower level of magnesium in the water to be around 0.24 mg.l^{-1}, which is much lower than that in our control water. However, at the end of the experiment there was a considerable individual variation in the degree of yolk utilisation, and some individuals may have begun to take in water drinking or even to feed.

A net intake of magnesium was nevertheless clear immediately after water-hardening and during the eyed-egg phase. We are unable to explain whether this increase occurs in the embryo or only in the perivitelline fluid.

The loss of magnesium observed by other authors may be due to the initial concentration gradient between magnesium in the ova and in the rearing water. When comparing results of broadly similar exposures obtained for the same species, variations in the overall chemistry of the ambient water (trace metals, etc.) can lead to different results. Finnish lake and river waters are often low in cations and contain humic substances, which can have a considerable effect on the combined effects of acidity and metals.

The increase in calcium and magnesium concentrations in acidified humic river water to four to six times the natural levels found in most Finnish waterbodies does not seem to have any effect on the inhibition of accumulation of Ca, Cl, or Mg by eggs or fry, but an increase seems to be reasonable in view of the survival of the eggs.

References

Brown, D.J.A., 1982. The effect of pH and calcium on fish and fisheries. *Water, Air and Soil pollution*, **18**: 343–351.

Brown, D.J.A. and S. Lynam, 1981. The effect of sodium and calcium concentrations on the hatching of eggs and the survival of the yolk sac fry of brown trout, *Salmo trutta* L. at low pH. *J.Fish Biol.*, **19**: 205–211.

Chulakasem, W.C., J.A. Nelson and J.J. Magnuson, 1988. Interaction between effects of low pH and low ion concentration on mortality during early development of medaka, *Oryzias latipes*. *Can.J.Zool.*, **67**: 2158–2168.

Cleveland, L. *et al.*, 1991. Sensitivity of brook trout to low pH, low calcium and elevated aluminum concentrations during laboratory pulse exposures. *Aquat.Toxicol.*, **19**: 303–318.

Cutchberson, D.P., 1977. Metabolism of the major mineral elements (Ca, P, Mg, S and also Fe) in relation to requirements. *Comp.Anim.Nutr.*, **2**: 28–86.

Gunn, J.M. and D.L.G. Noakes, 1987. Latent effects of pulse exposure to aluminum and low pH on size, ionic composition, and feeding efficiency of lake trout (*Salvelinus namaycush*) alevins. *Can.J.Fish.Aquat.Sci.*, **44**: 1418–1424.

Ingersoll, C.G., D.R. Mount, D.D. Gulley, T.W. La Point and H.L. Bergman, 1990. Effects of pH, aluminum, and calcium on survival and growth of eggs and fry of brook trout (*Salvelinus fontinalis*). *Can.J.Fish.Aquat.Sci.*, **47**: 1580–1592.

Lacroix, G. L., D.J. Gordon and D.J. Johnston, 1985. Effects of low environmental pH on the survival, growth, and ionic composition of postemergent Atlantic salmon (*Salmo salar*). *Can.J.Fish. Aquat.Sci.*, **42**: 768–775.

Lee, R.M. and S.D. Gerking, 1980. Survival and reproductive performance of the desert pupfish, *Cyprinodon n. nevadensis* (Eigenmann and Eigenmann), in acid waters. *J.Fish Biol.*, **17**: 507–515.

Peterson, R.H. and D.J. Martin-Robichaud, 1982. Water uptake by Atlantic salmon ova as affected by low pH. *Trans.Am.Fish.Soc.*, **111**: 772–774.

Peterson, R.H. and D.J. Martin-Robichaud, 1986. Growth and major inorganic cation budgets of Atlantic salmon alevins at three ambient acidities. *Trans.Am.Fish.Soc.*, **115**: 220–226.

Rask, M., 1984. The effect of low pH on perch, *Perca fluviatilis* L. II. The effect of acidic stress on different developmental stages of perch. *Ann.Zool.Fennici*, **21**: 9–13.

Reader, J.P., N.C. Everall, M.D.J. Sayer and R. Morris, 1989. The effects of eight trace metals in acid soft water on survival, mineral uptake and skeletal calcium deposition in yolk-sac fry of brown trout, *Salmo trutta* L. *J.Fish Biol.*, **35**: 187–198.

Rodgers, D.W., 1984. Ambient pH and calcium concentration as modifiers of growth and calcium dynamics of brook trout, *Salvelinus fontinalis*. *Can.J.Fish.Aquat.Sci.*, **41**: 1774–1780.

Rombough, P.J. and J.O.T. Jensen, 1985. Reduced water uptake and resistance to deformation in acid-exposed eggs of steelhead, *Salmo gairdneri*. *Trans.Am.Fish.Soc.*, **114**: 571–576.

Soivio, A. and E. Virtanen, 1980. Methods for physiological experiments on fish. Ekotoxogologiska metoder för akvatisk miljö. *Nordforsk, Report*, No. 16, 34 pp.

Stolkowski, J., 1977. Magnesium in human and animal breeding. *Rev.Can.Biol.*, **36**: 145–177.

Valtonen, T. and M. Laitinen, 1987. Acid stress in respect to calcium and magnesium concentrations in the plasma of perch during maturation and spawning. *Env.Biol.Fishes*, **22**: 147–154.

van der Velden, J.A., 1991. Magnesium and its transport in tilapia and carp: A study based on nuclear methods. Ph.D. thesis, Technical University of Delft, Delft, Netherlands. 156 pp.

Wacker, W.E.C., 1969. The biochemistry of magnesium. *Ann.N.Y.Acad.Sci.*, **162**: 717–726.

Wood, C.M., D.G. MacDonald, C.G. Ingersoll, D.R. Mount, O.E. Johansson, S. Landsberger and H.L. Bergman, 1990a. Whole body ions of brook trout (*Salvelinus fontinalis*) alevins: responses of yolk-sac and swim-up stages to water acidity, calcium, and aluminum, and recovery effects. *Can.J.Fish.Aquat.Sci.*, **47**: 1604–1615.

Wood, C.M., D.G. MacDonald, C.G. Ingersoll, D.R. Mount, O.E. Johansson, S. Landsberger and H.L. Bergman, 1990b. Effects of water acidity, calcium, and aluminum on whole body ions of brook trout (*Salvelinus fontinalis*) continuously exposed from fertilization to swim-up: a study by instrumental neutron activation analysis. *Can.J.Fish.Aquat.Sci.*, **47**: 1593–1603.

Zeitoun, I.H., D.E. Ullrey, W.G. Bergen and W.T. Magee, 1976. Mineral metabolism during the ontogenesis of rainbow trout (*Salmo gairdneri*). *J.Fish.Res.Board Can.*, **33**: 2587–2591.

Chapter 24
The sensitivity to acidity and aluminium of newly-hatched perch (*Perca fluviatilis*) originating from strains from four lakes with different degrees of acidity

M. VUORINEN,[1] P. J. VUORINEN,[1] M. RASK[2] and J. SUOMELA[1#]

[1] *Finnish Game and Fisheries Research Institute, Fisheries Division, PO Box 202,*
SF-00151 Helsinki, Finland
[2] *Finnish Game and Fisheries Research Institute, Evo State Fisheries and Aquaculture Research Station,*
SF-16970 Evo, Finland
Present address: University of Turku, Department of Biology, SF-20500 Turku, Finland

24.1   Introduction

Rask and Virtanen (1986) have shown that adult perch (*Perca fluviatilis*) taken from an acidic lake had adapted to their acidic environment. In that experiment, perch from the acidic and the circumneutral lakes were acclimated to circumneutral water for three weeks and then exposed for 24 or 72 h to waters at low pH. Measurements of plasma ion concentrations, muscle water content and the blood haematocrit value, showed detectable differences in responses at pH 4.1 and 4.5. Similarly, adult yellow perch (*P. flavescens*) from naturally acid humic lakes survived longer at a lethal pH than did yellow perch from alkaline lakes (Rahel, 1983). Nelson (1990) found differences in the post-exercise metabolic responses of yellow perch from naturally acidic and neutral waters after acclimation to similar conditions for several months before the experiments were carried out.

Adaptational differences in the responses to acidic water between adult fish caught from different watersheds may be a consequence of either natural selection within the population or the acclimatisation of individual fish to acidic water. Heritable differences in the acid tolerance between strains of fish have been documented for brook trout (*Salvelinus fontinalis*; Robinson *et al.*, 1976; Swarts *et al.*, 1978), Atlantic salmon (*Salmo salar*; Schom, 1986) and brown trout (*Salmo trutta*; Rosseland and Skogheim, 1987); these differences were measured in individuals that had not themselves been under the influence of acidic water. Gjerdem (1980) tested 250 brown trout strains in acidic waters from fertilisation to the yolk absorption stage and found large differences in the mortality between strains. Hurley *et al.* (1989) also found that the offspring of brook trout which had

273

originated from an acidic watershed, were more tolerant of acidic water than the offspring of fish from a watershed with neutral water; they exposed brook trout embryos and fry from fertilisation onward, to lethal and sublethal levels of acidity and measured their mortality.

Perch is the most widely distributed species in acidic waters in Finland (Rask and Tuunainen, 1990). In terms of mortality, the most sensitive life phase of perch to acidic water appeared to be the newly-hatched fry (Rask, 1984; Vinogradov and Komov, 1985). Similarly, newly-hatched fry of some other species seemed to be more sensitive to aluminium than embryos still protected by the egg capsule (Tuunainen *et al.*, 1991). In general, aluminium exacerbated the deleterious effects of acidic water, and the effects of acidic water and aluminium on yolk-sac fry of different fish species were increased if the tests were begun just after hatching and if they were then continued, preferably, up to the stage when the fry began to swim (Tuunainen *et al.*, 1991).

The aim of the present study was to clarify whether there were any differences, in terms of tolerance to acidic water and aluminium, between perch strains obtained from small lakes with different degrees of acidity and aluminium concentration. Tests were performed with newly-hatched fry that were the offspring of perch caught from three acidic lakes (pH range 4.29– 5.07 and aluminium concentration 16–254 $\mu g.l^{-1}$) and one circumneutral lake. Two of the study lakes are known to have become acidified recently (Kämäri, 1985; Rask, 1991), and the perch population of the most acidified lake has become affected because of the acidification (Lappalainen *et al.*, 1988).

24.2   Material and methods

The lakes from which the test perch originated are located in southern Finland. Lake Iso Valkjärvi (area 4 ha) has been acidified since the end of the 1800s (Rask, 1991), and L. Pieni Lehmälampi (3 ha) has been recently acidified (Kämäri 1985), but the acidification history of L. Kaitajärvi (9 ha) is not known. L. Valkea Mustajärvi (14 ha) served as a control lake. The water quality of the lakes is shown in Table 24.1. Acidification has affected the reproduction of perch in L. Pieni Lehmälampi; the average mortality of perch embryos in this lake was 35% in spring 1986. This resulted in a low population density and, due to the decreased food competition, an increased growth rate of the perch (Lappalainen *et al.*, 1988). An increased mortality of embryos has also been recorded in Lakes Iso Valkjärvi (15%) and Kaitajärvi (40%) (Tuunainen *et al.*, 1991); but the structure and density of the perch populations in these lakes are normal, as are those in the circumneutral L. Valkea Mustajärvi.

Mature perch were caught by wire traps from the four lakes. Soon after capture, eggs from three female perch from each lake were stripped into a bowl and fertilised with the milt from five male perch from the same lake. Water from the

Table 24.1 Water quality of the four lakes from which the newly-hatched perch used in the tests were obtained. Test solutions were made with water from L. Pahkajärvi. Water analyses were performed using the Finnish Standard Methods (SFS-standards), except for aluminium analysis where the method of LaZerte (1984) was used (number of samples in brackets).

	L. Valkea Mustajärvi	L. Iso Valkjärvi	L. Kaitajärvi	L. Pieni Lehmälampi	L. Pahkajärvi
pH	6.01–6.44	4.84–5.07	4.56–4.77	4.29–4.77	6.45–6.68
	(7)	(5)	(3)	(15)	(2)
Alkalinity, mmol.l^{-1}	0.029–0.081	−0.006–0.002	−0.013–0.011	−0.038–0.017	0.115–0.120
	(7)	(5)	(3)	(15)	(2)
Colour	25–35	10–50	10–10	5–35	35–35
	(7)	(5)	(3)	(15)	(2)
Conductivity, mS.m^{-1}	2.1–2.8	1.5–2.0	1.8–1.9	2.6–3.9	4.7–5.0
	(7)	(5)	(3)	(15)	(2)
Ca^{2+}, mmol.l^{-1}	0.06–0.11	0.03–0.04	0.02–0.03	0.01–0.04	0.11–0.12
	(7)	(5)	(3)	(15)	(2)
COD, mg.l^{-1}	3.60–5.48	6.56–7.92	0.96–1.92	1.36–3.12	4.56–6.24
	(7)	(5)	(3)	(14)	(2)
Fe, µg.l^{-1}	35–544	144–266	15–234	111–431	47–144
	(7)	(5)	(3)	(14)	(2)
Al$_{tot}$, µg.l^{-1}	13–31	35–51	16	129–254	34–37
	(6)	(5)	(1)	(8)	(8)
Al$_{lab}$, µg.l^{-1}	4–12	10–24	8	74–106	15–17
	(4)	(3)	(1)	(4)	(8)

circumneutral lake, L. Valkea Mustajärvi, was used in the fertilisation of the eggs and in their subsequent incubation in the laboratory.

Test solutions with pH values of 4.00, 4.25, 4.50, 4.75, 5.00, 5.25, 5.50 and 5.75 and nominal aluminium concentrations of 0, 100, 200, 300, 400, 600, 800 and 1000 µg.l^{-1} were prepared in polyethylene buckets with the water from the circumneutral L. Pahkajärvi (Table 24.1) which also served as the control water. Aluminium was added as $Al_2(SO_4)_3.18\ H_2O$ (Merck No. 1100) and the pH was adjusted with H_2SO_4 (*p.a.*) using a pH meter (Schott CG 819T; combination electrode Schott Geräte N 62). The pH was checked and adjusted at least three times, and after each acid addition the test solutions were aerated for about one hour. It was necessary to adjust those test solutions with both the highest pH values and the highest aluminium concentrations with NaOH (*p.a.*). The concentrations of total and fast-reactive (labile) aluminium in the test waters were measured by the method of LaZerte (1984), using atomic absorption spectrometry, at the Helsinki University of Technology and are given in Table 24.2.

The laboratory exposure of fry started within a day of hatching. The tests were performed under static conditions in glass jars, with 10 fry in each, in which the water volume of 200 ml exceeded the minimum amount of 2 l.(g of fish)$^{-1}$.day^{-1} recommended by Sprague (1969) for such toxicity tests. The fry of perch taken from the four lakes were exposed for seven days starting at different times

Table 24.2 The measured total and fast-reactive (labile) aluminium concentrations ($\mu g.l^{-1}$) in each of the nominal aluminium concentration and pH of the test waters. Samples were taken at the beginning of the tests and analysed by the method of LaZerte (1984) using atomic absorption spectrometry.

pH	Nominal Al, $\mu g.l^{-1}$															
	0		100		200		300		400		600		800		1000	
	tot	lab	tot	lab	tot	lab	tot	lab	tot	lab	tot	lab	tot	lab	tot	lab
4.00	37	17	120	87	204	136	303	182	388	228	666	357	831	395	1043	414
4.25	34	15	114	80	210	141	292	171	440	236	575	318	779	393	968	422
4.50	36	16	125	70	194	141	292	181	415	232	627	328	761	427	908	394
4.75	35	15	131	76	217	109	301	177	394	210	605	314	815	359	968	439
5.00	35	15	139	77	220	135	289	172	378	209	563	272	760	305	969	334
5.25	34	15	117	75	206	121	275	186	393	212	555	273	558	234	764	292
5.50	35	15	106	70	198	108	274	157	396	201	671	250	444	164	502	232
5.75	34	15	108	74	201	112	292	171	366	222	550	281	329	131	438	202

Table 24.3 Dates of the tests with newly-hatched perch originating from the four lakes, and the temperature (mean $\pm$SE) during the tests.

	L. Valkea Mustajärvi	L. Iso Valkjärvi	L. Kaitajärvi	L. Pieni Lehmälampi
Date	25 May–1 June	25 May–1 June	31 May–7 June	4 June–11 June
T°C	14.1 ±1.0	14.1 ±1.0	16.7 ±0.8	17.1 ±0.8

Table 24.3) because the perch in the more acidic lakes spawned later. The temperature was higher in the later tests (Table 24.3), because it followed the ambient temperature. The fry were not fed, but they used their yolk during the tests. The mortality was observed daily and dead fry were removed.

The LL$_{50}$ (lethal level) values for pH in different aluminium concentrations and the LC$_{50}$ values of aluminium in different pHs for perch were calculated using a computer program supplied by C.E. Stephan (USA, Environmental Protection Agency). The program calculates the results either by probit analysis (Finney, 1971), which were the values principally used, or by nonlinear interpolation.

24.3   Results

During the 7-day test, no appreciable mortality occurred in any of the aluminium test solutions where the pH was greater than 5.0 (Fig. 24.1). At the lowest pH values there were clear differences in the mortality of fry originating from different lakes. Fry originating from the circumneutral L. Valkea Mustajärvi were the most sensitive to acidic water; pH 4.0 was acutely lethal to them and only a few of the fry survived at pH 4.25, even at the lowest aluminium concentrations (Fig. 24.1).

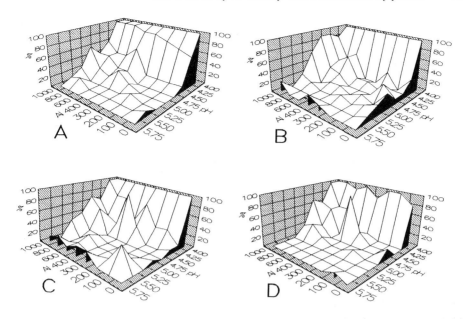

Fig. 24.1 Percentage mortality of newly-hatched perch, originating from four small lakes, during exposure for 7 days to acidic water (pH) and aluminium (μg.l⁻¹). Ten fry were exposed to each test solution. Water quality data for the lakes are shown in Table 24.1. A: L. Valkea Mustajärvi, B: L. Iso Valkjärvi, C: L. Kaitajärvi, D: L. Pieni Lehmälampi.

For the fry originating from the two moderately acidic lakes, L. Iso Valkjärvi and L. Kaitajärvi, a pH of 4.0 was similarly acutely lethal, but at pH 4.25 the mortality was considerably lower. The fry originating from the most acidic lake with the highest aluminium concentration, L. Pieni Lehmälampi, were the most tolerant to low pH; some fry survived even at a pH of 4.0 and no mortality was observed at the lowest aluminium concentrations at pH 4.25 (Fig. 24.1).

The LL_{50} values for pH are presented in Figure 24.2 and their 95% confidence limits are given in Table 24.4. The ranking of the sensitivity of fry to acidity (at the nominal aluminium concentration of 0 μg.l⁻¹) coincides with the acidity of the lakes from which they were caught. The presence of aluminium in the test solutions did not appreciably change the ranking of the sensitivity of fry to low pH. The offspring of the perch from the circumneutral lake (L. Valkea Mustajärvi) were the most sensitive to acidity in nearly all the aluminium concentrations, and in all the aluminium concentrations they were clearly more sensitive than fry from the most acidified lake (L. Pieni Lehmälampi).

Because of insignificant mortalities at pH ≥5 and a high mortality at pH 4.0, valid LC_{50} values of aluminium could not be calculated for all the pH values. However, calculations for a pH 4.25 were possible and 120h–168hLC_{50} values showed that the offspring from the circumneutral lake appeared to be appreciably more sensitive to aluminium than were fry originating from the other lakes (Fig. 24.3 and Table 24.5).

24.4   Discussion

In general, the newly-hatched perch were very tolerant of acidity and aluminium. By comparison with other species which were obtained from circumneutral lakes, newly-hatched perch fry were considerably more tolerant of acid water and aluminium than, for example, newly-hatched pike-perch (*Stizostedion lucioperca*) or roach (*Rutilus rutilus*) fry (Tuunainen *et al.*, 1991; Vuorinen *et al.*, 1993). On the other hand, whitefish (*Coregonus lavaretus pallasi*) yolk-sac fry mortality was comparable to that of perch; pH 4.0 was acutely lethal for whitefish and, depending on the aluminium concentration, mortality was also pronounced at pH 4.25. Pike (*Esox lucius*) yolk-sac fry were even more tolerant of low pH than were perch fry originating from the most acidic lake.

Freda and McDonald (1988) found that the extent of ion loss during exposure to acidic water is the major factor in determining the survival of both acid-tolerant species, such as perch, and acid-sensitive species. In sublethal acidic conditions there is also an increased metabolic demand, because energy is needed to compensate for ionoregulatory and osmotic disorders (McCormick *et al.*, 1989; Leino *et al.*, 1990). On the other hand, the metabolic rate, development and overall activity of the yolk-sac fry of different fish species are reduced by aluminium in acidic water (e.g. Cleveland *et al.*, 1986, Leino *et al.*, 1990; Tuunainen *et al.*, 1991) as well as by many other pollutants (von Westernhagen, 1988). Usually, increased mortality follows such decreases in activity. It is possible that the physiological basis for the difference in acid water tolerance between strains of fish lies in their differing ability to prevent ion loss. In post-spawning brown trout, the earlier mortality during acute exposure to acidic water and aluminium was associated with a higher loss of plasma chloride (Rosseland and Skogheim, 1987). However, the ionic

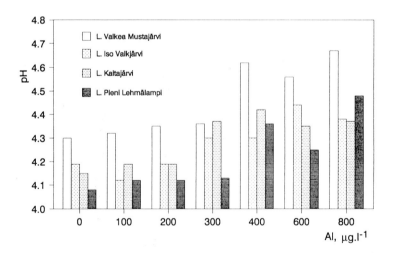

Fig. 24.2 168hLL$_{50}$ values for pH at different aluminium concentrations for newly-hatched perch originating from four small lakes. Water quality data for the lakes are shown in Table 24.1.

Table 24.4 The 168hLL$_{50}$ pH values and 95% confidence limits for each nominal total aluminium concentration in tests with newly-hatched perch originating from four lakes.

Al	L. Valkea Mustajärvi		L. Iso Valkjärvi		L. Kaitajärvi		L. Pieni Lehmälampi	
µg.l^{-1}	LL$_{50}$	95% CL	LL$_{50}$	95% CL	LL$_{50}$	95% CL	LL$_{50}$	95% CL
0	4.30	4.00–4.50	4.19	4.00–5.50	4.15	4.00–4.25	4.08	0–5.00
100	4.32	4.22–4.42	4.12	4.00–5.00	4.19	4.00–4.50	4.12	4.00–4.25
200	4.35	4.00–4.50	4.19	4.00–4.50	4.19	4.00–4.50	4.12	4.00–4.25
300	4.36	4.00–4.50	4.30	4.00–4.50	4.37	4.00–∞	4.13	3.92–4.26
400	4.62	4.47–4.76	4.30	4.00–4.50	4.42	0–∞	4.36	4.00–4.75
600	4.56	4.43–4.68	4.44	4.27–4.58	4.35	4.00–4.75	4.25	4.00–4.50
800	4.67	4.50–4.83	4.37	4.16–4.53	4.37	4.00–∞	4.48	4.29–4.64

regulation mechanisms in yolk-sac fry are somewhat different from those in adults (Alderdice, 1988). Nevertheless, the total body sodium concentration of roach and brown trout yolk-sac fry decreased when exposed to aluminium in acidic water or to very low pH in respect of the species' acid-sensitivity (Reader *et al.*, 1989; Tuunainen *et al.*, 1991).

The tests using newly-hatched perch fry originating from the two most acidic lakes, L. Kaitajärvi and L. Pieni Lehmälampi, were carried out somewhat later

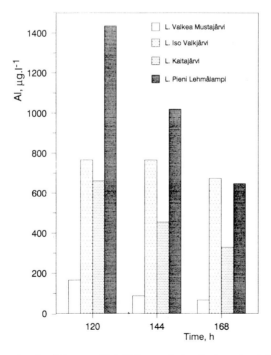

Fig. 24.3 LC$_{50}$ values for aluminium at pH 4.25 for newly-hatched perch originating from four small lakes, for different exposure times. Water quality data for the lakes are shown in Table 24.1.

Table 24.5 The 120–168hLC$_{50}$ values and 95% confidence limits for total aluminium concentration in µg.l^{-1} at pH 4.25 in tests with newly-hatched perch originating from four lakes.

Time	L. Valkea Mustajärvi		L. Iso Valkjärvi		L. Kaitajärvi		L. Pieni Lehmälampi	
(hours)	LC$_{50}$	95% CL	LC$_{50}$	95% CL	LC$_{50}$	95% CL	LC$_{50}$	95% CL
120	166	79–239	766	0–∞	661	414–2189	1436	994–∞
144	88	14–147	766	0–∞	454	273–789	1020	848–2731
168	68	2–132	674	0–∞	329	172–522	648	540–788

than those with newly-hatched fry originating from the other two lakes. This was because the perch spawned later in the more acidic lakes, especially in L. Pieni Lehmälampi (Rask *et al.*, 1990; Vuorinen *et al.*, 1992). Thus, the water temperature was higher during these later tests. An increase in temperature increased the sensitivity of juvenile brook trout (Robinson *et al.*, 1976) and also of newly-hatched whitefish (Tuunainen *et al.*, 1990) to acidic water, possibly because of an increase in metabolic activity associated with the rise in temperature (Rombough, 1988). Aluminium toxicity to salmon fingerlings was found to increase with temperature, and this was attributed to associated changes in the chemistry of aluminium (Poléo *et al.*, 1991). Newly-hatched perch fry, however, were most tolerant of acidic water and aluminium in the test with the highest temperature. Thus, the difference in sensitivity between the perch fry originating from different lakes might have been even more apparent had the test temperatures been the same. The temperature differences between the tests were not large (3°C at most), and all the temperatures were within the optimum range for perch fry (Thorpe, 1977). Therefore, it is probable that temperature differences did not affect the results, or if they did, then the effect was insignificant.

The differences between the strains of newly-hatched perch fry in their tolerance of an acidic environment seem to be genetically determined. The number of perch fry originating from each lake was not high, but the individuals were randomly derived from several parents. The possibility remains, however, that the parental environmental conditions had an effect on eggs during oocyte maturation. The whole oocyte development, as well as oocyte ionoregulation, is under the control of maternal regulatory mechanisms (Alderdice, 1988; Mommsen and Walsh, 1988). The ion concentration in the ovary fluid corresponds to that of the blood plasma of female fish (Mommsen and Walsh, 1988). When the adult perch from lakes with different water acidity and aluminium concentration were studied (Vuorinen *et al.*, 1992), no notable differences in plasma Cl$^-$, Mg^{2+} or haemoglobin concentrations were detected between fish from a circumneutral and from the most acidic lakes; however, the plasma Ca^{2+} concentration was lower and the haematocrit value higher in perch from the acidic lakes. It is unlikely that the exposure of parental perch to acidic/aluminium water had such ionic effects on developing oocytes that could then be reflected in a higher tolerance of fry to acidic/aluminium water; moreover, the eggs were fertilised and incubated in nearly neutral water.

Perch populations seem to be able to adapt to some extent even to relatively rapid anthropogenic acidification. The results of this study indicate that such adaptation could be genetically determined. The physiological basis for the differences in tolerance to acidic/aluminium water between strains of fish needs further investigation.

Acknowledgements

Thanks are due to all who kindly helped in the course of the study. Mr Seppo Peuranen kindly criticised the manuscript and Ms. Kathleen Tipton checked the English language. This study was part of the fisheries subproject of the Finnish Acidification Programme (HAPRO) and was financially supported by the Ministry of Agriculture and Forestry.

References

Alderdice, D.F., 1988. Osmotic and ionic regulation in teleost eggs and larvae. In: Hoar, W.S. and D.J. Randall (Eds.) *Fish Physiology*. Vol. 11. *The Physiology of Developing Fish. Part A: Eggs and Larvae*, pp. 163–251. London, New York, Academic Press.

Cleveland, L., E.E. Little, S.J. Hamilton, D.R. Buckler and J.B. Hunn, 1986. Interactive toxicity of aluminum and acidity to early life stages of brook trout. *Trans.Am.Fish.Soc.*, **115**: 610–620.

Finney, D.J., 1971. *Probit Analysis*. London, New York, Melbourne, Cambridge University Press. 333 pp.

Freda, J. and D.G. McDonald, 1988. Physiological correlates of interspecific variation in acid tolerance in fish. *J.Exp.Biol.*, **136**: 243–258.

Gjerdem, T., 1980. Genetic variation in acid tolerance in brown trout. *Proceedings of the International Conference on the Ecological Impacts of Acid Precipitation*, Norway 1980, SNSF project, p. 308.

Hurley, G.V., T.P. Foyle and W.J. White, 1989. Differences in acid tolerance during the early life stages of three strains of brook trout, *Salvelinus fontinalis*. *Water Air Soil Pollut.*, **46**: 387–398.

Kämäri, J., 1985. A quantitative assessment of lake acidification in Finland. *Aqua Fennica*, **15**: 11–20.

Lappalainen, A., M. Rask and P.J. Vuorinen, 1988. Acidification affects the perch, *Perca fluviatilis*, populations in lakes of southern Finland. *Environ.Biol.Fish.*, **21**: 231–239.

LaZerte, B.D., 1984. Forms of aqueous aluminum in acidified catchments of Central Ontario – a methodological analysis. *Can.J.Fish.Aquat.Sci.*, **41**: 766–776.

Leino, R.L., J.H. McCormick and K.M. Jensen, 1990. Multiple effects of acid and aluminum on brood stock and progeny of fathead minnows, with emphasis on histopathology. *Can.J.Zool.*, **68**: 234–244.

McCormick, J.H., K.M. Jensen and L.E. Anderson, 1989. Chronic effects of low pH and elevated aluminum on survival, maturation, spawning and embryo-larval development of the fathead minnow in soft water. *Water Air Soil Pollut.*, **43**: 293–307.

Mommsen, T.P. and P.J. Walsh, 1988. Vitellogenesis and oocyte assembly. In: Hoar, W.S. and D.J. Randall (Eds.) *Fish Physiology*. Vol.11. *The Physiology of Developing Fish. Part A: Eggs and Larvae*, pp. 347–406. London, New York, Academic Press.

Nelson, J.A., 1990. Muscle metabolite response to exercise and recovery in yellow perch (*Perca flavescens*): Comparisons of populations from naturally acidic and neutral waters. *Physiol.Zool.*, **63**: 886–908.

Poléo, A.B.S., E. Lydersen and I.P. Muniz, 1991. The influence of temperature on aqueous aluminium chemistry and survival of Atlantic salmon (*Salmo salar* L.) fingerlings. *Aquat.Toxicol.*, **21**: 267–278.

Rahel, F.J., 1983. Population differences in acid tolerance between yellow perch, *Perca flavescens*, from naturally acidic and alkaline lakes. *Can.J.Zool.*, **61**: 147–152.

Rask, M., 1984. The effect of low pH on perch, *Perca fluviatilis* L. II. The effect of acidic stress on different development stages of perch. *Ann.Zool.Fennici*, **21**: 9–13.

Rask, M. 1991. Iso Valkjärvi research – an introduction to a multidisciplinary lake liming study. *Finnish Fish.Res.*, **12**: 25–34.

Rask, M. and P. Tuunainen, 1990. Acid-induced changes in fish populations of small Finnish lakes. In: Kauppi, P., *et al.* (Eds.) *Acidification in Finland*, pp. 911–927. Berlin, Heidelberg, New York, Springer-Verlag.

Rask, M. and E. Virtanen, 1986. Responses of perch, *Perca fluviatilis* L., from an acidic and a neutral lake to acidic water. *Water Air Soil Pollut.*, **30**: 537–543.

Rask, M., P.J. Vuorinen and M. Vuorinen, 1990. Delayed spawning of perch, *Perca fluviatilis* L., in acidified lakes. *J.Fish Biol.*, **36**: 317–325.

Reader, J.P., N.C. Everall, M.D.J. Sayer and R. Morris, 1989. The effects of eight trace metals in acid soft water on survival, mineral uptake and skeletal calcium deposition in yolk-sac fry of brown trout, *Salmo trutta* L. *J.Fish Biol.*, **35**: 187–198.

Robinson, G.D., W.A. Dunson, J.E. Wright and G.E. Malmolito, 1976. Differences in low pH tolerance among strains of brook trout (*Salvelinus fontinalis*). *J.Fish Biol.*, **8**: 5–17.

Rombough, P.J., 1988. Respiratory gas exchange, aerobic metabolism, and effects of hypoxia during early life. In: Hoar, W.S. and D.J. Randall (Eds.) *Fish Physiology*. Vol. 11. *The Physiology of Developing Fish. Part A: Eggs and Larvae*, pp. 59–161. London, New York, Academic Press.

Rosseland, B.O. and O.K. Skogheim, 1987. Differences in sensitivity to acidic soft water among strains of brown trout (*Salmo trutta* L.). In: Witters, H. and O. Vanderborght (Eds.) *Ecophysiology of acid stress in aquatic organisms. Ann.Soc.R.Zool.Belg.*, **117**: 255–264.

Schom, C.B., 1986. Genetic, environmental, and maturational effects on Atlantic salmon (*Salmo salar*) survival in acute low pH trials. *Can.J.Fish.Aquatic.Sci.*, **43**: 1547–1555.

Sprague, J.B., 1969. Measurement of pollutant toxicity to fish. I. Bioassay methods for acute toxicity. *Water Res.*, **3**: 793–821.

Swarts, F.A., W.A. Dunson and J.E. Wright, 1978. Genetic and environmental factors involved in increased resistance of brook trout to sulfuric acid solutions and mine acid polluted waters. *Trans.Am.Fish.Soc.*, **107**: 651–677.

Thorpe, J., 1977. Synopsis of biological data on the perch *Perca fluviatilis* Linnaeus, 1758 and *Perca flavescens* Mitchill, 1814. *FAO Fisheries Synopsis*, **113**: 1–138.

Tuunainen, P. *et al.*, 1990. Happaman laskeuman vaikutukset kaloihin ja rapuihin. Raportti vuodelta 1989. English summary: Effects of acidic deposition on fish and crayfish. Report 1989. *Riista- ja kalatalouden tutkimuslaitos. Kalatutkimuksia - Fiskundersökningar*, Vol. 8, 97 p.

Tuunainen, P. *et al.*, 1991. Happaman laskeuman vaikutukset kaloihin ja rapuihin. Loppuraportti. (Abstract: Effects of acidic deposition on fish and crayfish. Final report.). *Suomen Kalatalous*, **57**: 1–44.

Vinogradov, G.A. and V.T. Komov, 1985. Ion regulation in the perch, *Perca fluviatilis*, in connection with the problem of acidification of water bodies. *J.Ichthyol.*, **35**: 53–61.

Vuorinen, P.J. *et al.*, 1992. Reproductive status, blood chemistry, gill histology and growth of perch (*Perca fluviatilis*) in three acidified lakes. *Environ.Pollut.*, **78**: 19–27.

Vuorinen, M., P.J. Vuorinen and S. Peuranen, 1993. Lethal and sublethal threshold values of aluminium and acidity to pike (*Esox lucius*), whitefish (*Coregonus pallasi*), pike-perch (*Stizostedion lucioperca*) and roach (*Rutilus rutilus*) newly-hatched fry. *Sci.Total Envir.* (in press).

von Westernhagen, H., 1988. Sublethal effects of pollutants on fish eggs and larvae. In: Hoar, W.S. and D.J. Randall (Eds.) *Fish Physiology*. Vol. 11. *The Physiology of Developing Fish. Part A: Eggs and Larvae*, pp. 253–346. London, New York, Academic Press.

Chapter 25
The sensitivity to acidification of pike (*Esox lucius*), whitefish (*Coregonus lavaretus*) and roach (*Rutilus rutilus*): comparison of field and laboratory studies

P.J. VUORINEN,[1] M. RASK,[2] M. VUORINEN,[1] S. PEURANEN[1] and J. RAITANIEMI[1]

[1] *Finnish Game and Fisheries Research Institute, Fisheries Division, PO Box 202, SF-00151 Helsinki, Finland*
[2] *Finnish Game and Fisheries Research Institute, Evo State Fisheries and Aquaculture Research Station, SF-16970 Evo, Finland*

25.1   Introduction

Although acidification increases the leaching of a number of metals (Berqkvist, 1987), the concentration of aluminium in acidic lake waters is raised to the greatest extent (Verta *et al.*, 1990). Along with acidification there are also other water quality changes; for example, calcium concentration is lower in acidified lakes than in more neutral ones (Vuorinen *et al.*, 1993b). This is detrimental to fish because calcium ameliorates acid and aluminium toxicity (Brown and Lynam, 1981; Reader *et al.*, 1988). In evaluating the effects of acidification on fish and fisheries, and as well in evaluating the respective laboratory results, it is important to consider other water quality aspects in addition to acidity and aluminium (Magnuson *et al.*, 1984, Tuunainen *et al.*, 1991). In its report of pH values, EIFAC (1969) emphasised the importance of other water quality factors. Wright and Snekvik (1978) found pH and calcium to be the most important water parameters related to fish status. Howells *et al.* (1983) were amongst the first in reviewing the effects of pH and calcium and aluminium concentrations on fish survival and productivity. Since then, some modelling work relating field and laboratory data on the effects of acidification-related parameters on fish has been done (Sadler, 1983; Van Winkle *et al.*, 1986; Breck *et al.*, 1988; Christensen *et al.*, 1988).

The Finnish Acidification Programme (HAPRO) provided information on the effects of anthropogenic acidification on the fish populations of small forest lakes in Finland (Rask and Tuunainen, 1990) and knowledge of the extent of lake acidification and the effects of spring snowmelt on the water quality of small lakes (Forsius *et al.*, 1990; Verta *et al.*, 1990; Vuorinen *et al.*, 1993b). Laboratory tests showed the effects of acidity and aluminium, modified by other water quality factors, on the embryos, newly-hatched fry and adult fish of species inhabiting small Finnish lakes (Vuorinen, 1987; Vuorinen *et al.*, 1990; Tuunainen *et al.*, 1991;

Vuorinen *et al.*, 1992, 1993a, 1994). The commonest fish species in the small forest lakes in Finland are perch (*Perca fluviatilis*), ruffe (*Gymnocephalus cernua*), pike (*Esox lucius*), roach (*Rutilus rutilus*) and, mainly as a stocked species, whitefish (*Coregonus lavaretus*) (Rask and Tuunainen, 1990). Using the data obtained for fish populations and water quality, comparisons have been made of fish presence/absence and various population parameters with water quality factors (Rask, 1989; Rask and Tuunainen, 1990; Tuunainen *et al.*, 1991).

The aim of the present study is to compare the response to acidification of three fish species, based on the results of laboratory tests, to those recorded in the field in population surveys. Pike was selected as one of these three species because it is an acid-tolerant species and roach was selected as an acid-sensitive one (Tuunainen *et al.*, 1991; Vuorinen *et al.*, 1993a). Whitefish was included because of its importance in fisheries management in Finland. The water quality and population survey results given in the present work are derived from data obtained during the HAPRO project by the Finnish Game and Fisheries Research Institute. Laboratory tests were also performed during that study. Sac fry were selected for these comparisons because they have been shown to be the most sensitive life phase to acidity (Mount, 1973; Menendez, 1976), especially in the presence of aluminium (Tuunainen *et al.*, 1991).

25.2   Materials and methods

25.2.1   *Field data*

The fish population data of the present study are based on the surveys of 80 small forest lakes during the HAPRO project in 1985–87. The fish were caught by the standard gill-net series (12–60 mm mesh); for further details of the technique, see Rask and Tuunainen (1990). Roach was detected in 32 lakes, pike in 35 lakes and whitefish in 20 lakes. At least one of the three species was detected in 59 of the 80 test-fished lakes. Roach and pike populations were natural, whereas whitefish were mostly stocked with only two lakes having a natural population.

Samples for water analysis were taken from each lake at the same time as the fish surveys, and in spring during the snowmelt period. Samples were analysed at the laboratory of the Finnish Game and Fisheries Research Institute according to Finnish standard methods for water analysis (SFS-standards). Analyses of total aluminium (Al_{tot}) and fast-reactive aluminium (labile aluminium, Al_{lab}) were made at the Helsinki University of Technology by the method of LaZerte (1984). A summary of water analysis results is given in Table 25.1.

25.2.2   *Toxicity tests*

The nominal pH values in the test waters ranged from 4.00 to 6.00 at intervals of 0.25 pH-units (acidified with *p.a.* sulphuric acid) and nominal aluminium concen-

Table 25.1 Surface area and water quality in lakes in the fish survey. All the data gathered in the years 1985–1988 have been included, whether the samples were collected during the spring snowmelt or in summer.

	Mean ±SE	Min	Max	N
Pike lakes				
Area, km^2	0.22 ±0.03	0.02	0.95	35
pH	5.66 ±0.14	4.56	7.59	35
Alkalinity, $mmol.l^{-1}$	0.059 ±0.017	−0.024	0.371	35
Colour, $mg.l^{-1}$ Pt	40 ±6	9	175	34
Conductivity, $mS.m^{-1}$	3.3 ±0.2	0.8	5.3	35
Total hardness, $mmol.l^{-1}$	0.118 ±0.007	0.030	0.210	35
Ca^{2+}, $mmol.l^{-1}$	0.067 ±0.008	0.010	0.275	35
COD, $mg.l^{-1}$	5.94 ±0.70	1.08	21.3	35
Fe, $\mu g.l^{-1}$	257 ±46	8	1306	35
Al_{tot}, $\mu g.l^{-1}$	143 ±20	7	396	27
Al_{lab}, $\mu g.l^{-1}$	59 ±9	5	148	26
Whitefish lakes				
Area, km^2	0.22 ±0.06	0.01	0.95	20
pH	5.69 ±0.18	4.55	7.59	20
Alkalinity, $mmol.l^{-1}$	0.061 ±0.020	−0.017	0.371	20
Colour, $mg.l^{-1}$ Pt	28 ±5	5	102	20
Conductivity, $mS.m^{-1}$	3.5 ±0.3	1.5	5.7	20
Total hardness, $mmol.l^{-1}$	0.118 ±0.011	0.048	0.210	20
Ca^{2+}, $mmol.l^{-1}$	0.065 ±0.009	0.021	0.150	20
COD, $mg.l^{-1}$	4.23 ±0.62	1.00	12.3	19
Fe, $\mu g.l^{-1}$	192 ±44	16	836	20
Al_{tot}, $\mu g.l^{-1}$	99 ±15	20	201	15
Al_{lab}, $\mu g.l^{-1}$	42 ±7	7	103	15
Roach lakes				
Area, km^2	0.32 ±0.07	0.01	1.94	32
pH	6.10 ±0.12	5.04	7.59	32
Alkalinity, $mmol.l^{-1}$	0.091 ±0.017	0.002	0.371	32
Colour, $mg.l^{-1}$ Pt	38 ±5	10	102	32
Conductivity, $mS.m^{-1}$	3.8 ±0.2	1.9	5.7	32
Total hardness, $mmol.l^{-1}$	0.140 ±0.006	0.080	0.210	32
Ca^{2+}, $mmol.l^{-1}$	0.085 ±0.008	0.020	0.275	32
COD, $mg.l^{-1}$	5.60 ±0.58	1.80	13.0	32
Fe, $\mu g.l^{-1}$	244 ±42	16	846	32
Al_{tot}, $\mu g.l^{-1}$	105 ±19	23	396	24
Al_{lab}, $\mu g.l^{-1}$	42 ±8	5	144	24

trations (with aluminium as $Al_2(SO_4)_3 \times (16-18)H_2O$; Merck No. 1100) were from 0 to 1000 $\mu g.l^{-1}$ usually with an interval of 100 $\mu g.l^{-1}$. In the experiments to compare species sensitivity, the test solutions were made in water from a circum-neutral lake (pH 6.45–6.68, Ca^{2+} 0.11–0.12 $mmol.l^{-1}$, and Al_{tot} 34–37 $\mu g.l^{-1}$); data for the dilution water quality of some other tests discussed in this chapter are given in Table 25.2. The dilution water as such also served as the control water.

The semistatic tests began with each species directly after hatching, and no external feeding was provided for the yolk-sac fry. Fry were exposed for 10 days in

Table 25.2 The 240hEL$_{50}$ pH values for whitefish in four tests with different dilution water qualities in different nominal Al$_{tot}$ concentrations (μg.l^{-1}).

Al	Test A[1]	Test B[2]	Test C[3]	Test D[4]
0	4.40	4.42	5.34	5.18
50	4.55	–	5.76	–
100	4.83	4.39	6.21	5.50
200	4.78	4.42	x	5.44
300	5.01	5.10	x	–
400	4.71	5.50	x	5.48
500	5.08	–	x	–
600	5.31	–	x	5.25
700	5.31	5.57	x	–
800	5.26	–	x	5.82

(1) Ca^{2+}: 0.11 mmol.l^{-1}; Na$^+$: 0.07 mmol.l^{-1}, lake water
(2) Ca^{2+}: 0.12 mmol.l^{-1}; Na$^+$: 0.07 mmol.l^{-1}, diluted lake water
(3) Ca^{2+}: 0.04 mmol.l^{-1}; Na$^+$: 0.06 mmol.l^{-1}, synthetic water, no organic matter
(4) Ca^{2+}: 0.07 mmol.l^{-1}; Na$^+$: 0.09 mmol.l^{-1}, diluted lake water

Note: – = test not made, and x = all fish died by the end of the test.

glass jars with renewal of the test solutions to achieve a replacement rate as proposed by Sprague (1969). The test temperatures corresponded to those of the prevailing natural water. Dead fry were counted and removed daily. Also, fry activity, i.e. the number of swimming or non-swimming, was recorded during the tests. Test results based on these sublethal effects were used for the comparisons of laboratory and field data, because these values are a better measure of the decrease in viability in natural conditions than are the lethal effects (Tuunainen *et al.*, 1991). The test procedures are described in greater detail in Tuunainen *et al.* (1990) and Vuorinen *et al.* (1993a).

25.2.3   *Statistical methods*

Differences in water quality parameters between the lakes inhabited by the three fish species were compared using the one-way analysis of variance coupled with Scheffe's test for the significance of differences between the means at the level of $P<0.05$. Relationships between water characteristics were examined by correlation analysis (Pearson's correlation coefficients). For these calculations, the means of each water quality parameter were first calculated from all the measurements, whether sampled during summer stratification (1–12 samples per lake) or in spring during the snowmelt period (3–9 samples per lake). All the statistical calculations were performed by the Statistical Analysis System (SAS Institute Inc., 1988).

The 10d EC$_{50}$ (effective concentration) values of aluminium at different pH values and the 10d EL$_{50}$ (effective level) values of pH at different aluminium concentrations were calculated by probit analysis (Finney, 1971), or by nonlinear interpolation.

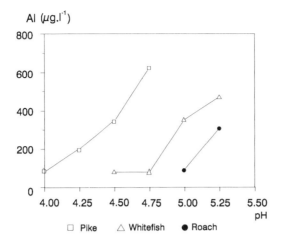

Fig. 25.1 The 10dEC$_{50}$ values for aluminium at different pH levels for the newly-hatched fry of pike, whitefish and roach.

25.3   Results and discussion

25.3.1   *Roach*

Roach is much more sensitive to acidity and aluminium than either pike or whitefish (Figs 25.1 and 25.2). Plotting the mean weight of roach from the catches with the mean pH and mean Al$_{tot}$ reveals a distorted population structure in acidic lakes and especially in acidic lakes with a high aluminium concentration (Fig. 25.3). The mean weight is high in these lakes because the reproduction of roach was apparently not successful in recent years.

The mean weight, mean age and mean length correlated significantly negatively

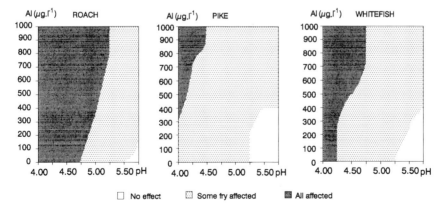

Fig. 25.2 The toxic limit values for acidity and aluminium based on a sublethal effect (swimming activity) for roach, pike and whitefish. The fry were exposed to test solutions for 10 days.

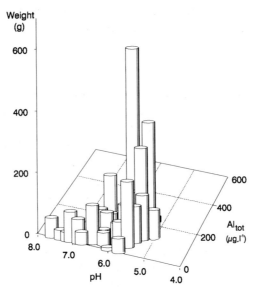

Fig. 25.3 The mean weight of roach in 32 lakes which had different pH levels and aluminium concentrations.

with pH and significantly positively with Al_{tot} and Al_{lab} (Rask, 1989; Rask and Tuunainen, 1990). Roach were not present in lakes with a mean pH of 5 and less (Fig. 25.3, and Rask, 1989) or rarely present in lakes with a mean Al_{tot} >200 $\mu g.l^{-1}$. This is in accordance with the toxicity test results, where few newly-hatched fry survived pHs around 5 with Al_{tot} at about 200 $\mu g.l^{-1}$ (Tuunainen *et al.*, 1991). However, survival was affected at pH 5.5 and even at higher pHs when aluminium was present (Fig. 25.2), and the ionic regulation of newly-hatched roach, seen as the loss of total body sodium, was disturbed in synthetic soft water even at pH 5.75 in Al_{tot} 50 $\mu g.l^{-1}$ (Tuunainen *et al.*, 1991). In fishing surveys, abnormal population structures were found in lakes where the pH was about 5.5 and Al_{tot} 50–80 $\mu g.l^{-1}$ and even at higher pHs when aluminium concentrations were higher (Fig. 25.3).

These data support the proposal of pH 5.5 as the lower tolerance limit for roach by Milbrink and Johansson (1975) and by Almer and Hanson (1980). Hultberg (1988) suggested an even higher tolerance limit, pH 5.8, for roach.

The occurrence of roach in the acidic lakes of the present study also seemed to be dependent on other water qualities. There were roach in only one lake where the water calcium concentration was lower than 0.04 mmol.l^{-1} or conductivity lower than *c.* 2.5 mS.m^{-1} (Fig. 25.4). The difference in this respect is clear in comparison with pike or whitefish whose presence was not related to these water parameters. This indication of the importance of a sufficient water calcium concentration and water conductivity for roach on the basis of these field observations is somewhat puzzling, because calcium and conductivity correlate with pH (Table 25.3). However, in laboratory tests, the embryonic and sac-fry development of cyprinids was more successful in acidic waters containing aluminium when the calcium concentration was higher (M. Vuorinen, unpublished).

25.3.2   *Pike*

Of the three species tested, pike was the most tolerant of acidity and aluminium (Fig. 25.1), and was caught even in highly acidified lakes, the lowest mean pH of which was 4.56 (range 4.36–4.88 and Al_{tot} range 201–319 $\mu g.l^{-1}$ and the highest mean Al_{tot} 339 (range 178–436 $\mu g.l^{-1}$ and pH range 4.48–5.59) (Table 25.1). In addition to water quality, the presence of pike, despite its acid-tolerance, may depend on the morphological and physical characteristics of lakes. Wales and Beggs (1986) found that poor pike catches from waters with a low pH (pH <6.4) in Ontario were solely related to the physical characteristics of the lakes. In the present study, pike were caught only occasionally in the sampling nets. Due to its behaviour and the low density of its populations, it is possible that pike were also present in some of the lakes where none were caught.

Laboratory results indicated that some yolk-sac fry are able to survive even at pH 4 if the Al_{tot} is low (Fig. 25.2). However, at this pH, half of the fry were affected in an aluminium concentration of 80 $\mu g.l^{-1}$ (Fig. 25.1). In a synthetic test medium without an aluminium addition, some pike sac fry survived the 8-day test at pH 4.2 (Johansson and Kihlström, 1975). Some individuals may survive in highly acidified

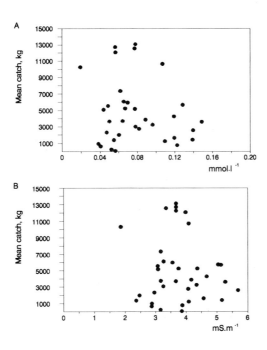

Fig. 25.4 The relationship between mean roach catch per gill-net series in 32 lakes and water calcium concentration (A) and conductivity (B).

Table 25.3 Pearson's correlation coefficients of water quality parameters. The upper right half of the correlation table gives the number of observations.

	pH	Alkal.	Colour	Hardn.	Cond.	Ca	COD	Fe	Al$_{tot}$	Al$_{lab}$
pH		59	58	59	59	59	58	59	47	46
Alkalinity	0.881‡		58	58	58	58	58	58	47	46
Colour	−0.067	0.014		58	58	58	58	58	47	46
Hardness	0.784‡	0.816‡	0.206		59	59	58	59	47	46
Conductivity	0.617‡	0.636‡	0.177	0.864‡		59	58	59	47	46
Ca	0.791‡	0.883‡	0.061	0.859‡	0.799‡		58	59	47	46
COD	−0.071	−0.020	0.932‡	0.134	0.039	−0.017		58	47	46
Fe	−0.137	−0.025	0.868‡	0.148	0.151	0.019	0.850‡		47	46
Al$_{tot}$	−0.484†	−0.360*	0.328*	−0.004	0.169	−0.142	0.359*	0.376†		46
Al$_{lab}$	−0.539‡	−0.410†	0.237	−0.081	0.054	−0.248	0.278	0.312*	0.934‡	

* $P<0.05$,   † $P<0.01$,   ‡ $P<0.001$

conditions because there are wide variations in the tolerances of individual fish (Tuunainen *et al.*, 1991). However, the reproduction of pike, on the basis of sac fry viability in laboratory tests (Fig. 25.2), is somewhat affected at pHs around 5, even where aluminium concentrations are low. This is in agreement with the lower tolerance limit of pH 5 proposed by Milbrink and Johansson (1975) and pH 5.3 suggested by Hultberg (1988). Beamish *et al.* (1975) observed that pike had not released their eggs in lakes that had a pH around 5, as noted after their normal spawning time. This indicates an acidification-induced effect on their reproduction physiology.

25.3.3   Whitefish

Whitefish is less tolerant of acidity and aluminium than pike (Fig. 25.1). In the lakes where whitefish were caught, the mean pH was about the same but the means of Al$_{tot}$ and Al$_{lab}$ were lower (although not significantly) than those of the pike lakes (Table 25.1). Whitefish were caught in 20 of the lakes, but only two of these had natural populations, the remainder having been stocked. The most acidic lake in which whitefish were caught had a mean pH of 4.55 (Al$_{tot}$ 158 μg.l^{-1}) and the lake with the highest aluminium concentration (Al$_{tot}$ 201 μg.l^{-1}) had a mean pH of 5.80. There are no observations of the reproduction of stocked whitefish in the study lakes; most of the lakes do not even have appropriate spawning grounds for whitefish. In these small acidification sensitive lakes, in addition to water quality, the whitefish catch is apparently affected by the stocking density, stocking intervals, fishing and the competition with other fish species for food. In the Ontario lake survey, lake whitefish (*C. clupeaformis*) were captured in lakes with a pH as low as 5, but its occurrence was attributed to the geographical characteristics of the lake rather than to the lake water chemistry (Wales and Beggs, 1986).

The stocking of one-summer-old whitefish in six lakes acidified to different degrees showed that whitefish may survive in lakes where the pH is down to *c.* 4.6

and Al_{tot} about 150 $\mu g.l^{-1}$, although the physiological state of the survivors after three years clearly indicated that they were stressed (Tuunainen *et al.*, 1990; Rask *et al.*, 1992). However, in two highly acidified lakes, stocked one-summer-old whitefish did not survive; one of the lakes had a low pH (4.14–4.91) and very high Al_{tot} (219–581 $\mu g.l^{-1}$) and the other was very oligotrophic with a low pH (4.30–4.91) and low Al_{tot} (0–101 $\mu g.l^{-1}$) (Rask *et al.*, 1992). On the basis of toxicity tests, few whitefish sac fry survived in water with Al_{tot} <300 $\mu g.l^{-1}$ at pH *c.* 4.2, but some were already affected at pH *c.* 5.2 and even at a higher pH if the Al_{tot} concentration was >100 $\mu g.l^{-1}$ (Fig. 25.2).

The presence of whitefish in lakes was not usually related to water qualities other than pH and aluminium. In the laboratory tests, the dilution water quality affected the tolerance of whitefish to acidic water and to aluminium (Table 25.2). For example, in test solutions made up in soft synthetic water with no organic matter (Test C, Table 25.2) all the whitefish sac fry died within 10 days in solutions containing a Al_{tot} ≥200 $\mu g.l^{-1}$ and even at lower aluminium concentrations they did not tolerate pHs below 5.

25.4   General discussion and future research needs

The absence of a species from a small lake does not necessarily indicate the species' sensitivity to acidification because it may never have inhabited the lake, but the presence of a species does give an indication of its tolerance. To evaluate the effects of acidification, fisheries research must inevitably include the examination of population parameters. However, these may not reveal critical water quality factors, and laboratory experimentation is needed for their identification. In addition to water quality, the physiological basis for the effects on the population derived from environmental stress can be investigated by laboratory experiments. Laboratory tests, in turn, omit effects such as competition between species and food availability. Only by combining field and laboratory data can the effects of acidification on fish populations in lakes be efficiently evaluated.

Further investigations of the various physiological bases for the different sensitivities between fish species and between the different life phases to acid and aluminium are required. Also the effects of other water quality factors on acid and aluminium toxicity deserve further study.

Acknowledgements

We thank the many people who have contributed to this work. The English language was checked by Ms Kathleen Tipton. This work is part of the fisheries sub-project of the Finnish Acidification Research Programme (HAPRO) and was financially supported by the Ministry of Agriculture and Forestry.

References

Almer, B. and M. Hanson, 1980. Försurningseffecter i väst kustsjöar (Abstract: Effects of acidification in west coast lakes of Sweden). *Inf.Sötvattenslab.Drottningholm*, **12**. 44 p.

Beamish, R.J. *et al.*, 1975. Long-term acidification of a lake and resulting effects on fishes. *Ambio*, **4**: 98–102.

Berqkvist, B., 1987. Soil solution chemistry and metal budgets of spruce forest ecosystems in S. Sweden. *Water Air Soil Pollut.*, **33**: 131–154.

Breck, J.E. *et al.*, 1988. Potential importance of spatial and temporal heterogeneity in pH, Al, and Ca in allowing survival of a fish population: a model demonstration. *Ecological Modelling*, **41**: 1–16.

Brown, D.J.A. and S. Lynam, 1981. The effect of sodium and calcium concentrations on the hatching of eggs and the survival of the yolk sac fry of brown trout, *Salmo trutta* L. at low pH. *J.Fish Biol.*, **19**: 205–211.

Christensen, S.W., J.E. Breck and W. Van Winkle, 1988. Predicting acidification effects on fish populations, using laboratory data and field information. *Environ.Toxicol.Chem.*, **7**: 735–747.

EIFAC (European Inland Fisheries Advisory Commission), 1969. Water quality criteria for European freshwater fish. Extreme pH values and inland fisheries. *Water Research*, **3**: 593–611.

Finney, D.J., 1971. *Probit Analysis*. Cambridge, Cambridge University Press. 333 pp.

Forsius, M. *et al.*, 1990. Statistical lake survey in Finland: regional estimates of lake acidification. In: Kauppi, P., P. Anttila and K. Kenttämies (Eds.) *Acidification in Finland*, pp. 759–780. Berlin, Heidelberg, New York, Springer-Verlag.

Howells, G.D., D.J.A. Brown and K. Sadler, 1983. Effects of acidity, calcium, and aluminum on fish survival and productivity – a review. *J.Sci.Food.Agric.*, **34**: 559–570.

Hultberg, H., 1988. Critical loads for sulphur to lakes and streams. *Nord*, **15**: 185–200.

Johansson, N. and J.E. Kihlström, 1975. Pikes (*Esox lucius* L.) shown to be affected by low pH values during first weeks after hatching. *Environ.Res.*, **9**: 12–17.

LaZerte, B.D., 1984. Forms of aqueous aluminum in acidified catchments of Central Ontario – a methodological analysis. *Can.J.Fish.Aquat.Sci.*, **41**: 766–776.

Magnuson, J.J., J.P. Baker and E.J. Rahel 1984. A critical assessment of effects of acidification on fisheries in North America. *Phil.Trans.R.Soc.Lond.*, **305**: 501–516.

Menendez, R., 1976. Chronic effects of reduced pH on brook trout (*Salvelinus fontinalis*). *J.Fish.Res.Board Can.*, **33**: 118–123.

Milbrink, G. and N. Johansson, 1975. Some effects of acidification on roe of roach, *Rutilus rutilus* L., and perch, *Perca fluviatilis* L. – with special reference to the Åvaå lake system in Eastern Sweden. *Rept.Inst.Freshw.Res.Drottningholm*, **54**: 52–62.

Mount, D.I., 1973. Chronic effect of low pH on fathead minnow survival, growth and reproduction. *Wat.Res.*, **7**: 987–993.

Rask, M., 1989. Roach, *Rutilus rutilus* L., populations as an indicator of lake acidification. In: Bohac, J. and V. Rozicka (Eds.) *Proc. V Int. Conf. Bioindicatores Deteriorisationis Regionis*, Proc. V. Int. Conf., 23–27 May 1988, Institute of Landscape Ecology CAS, Ceské Budéjovice, pp. 411–417.

Rask, M. and P. Tuunainen, 1990. Acid-induced changes in fish populations of small Finnish lakes. In: Kauppi, P. *et al.* (Eds.) *Acidification in Finland*, pp. 911–927. Berlin, Heidelberg, New York, Springer-Verlag.

Rask, M. *et al.*, 1992. Whitefish stocking in acidified lakes: ecological and physiological responses. *Hydrobiologia*, **243/244**: 277–282.

Reader, J.P., T.R.K. Dalziel and R. Morris, 1988. Growth, mineral uptake and skeletal calcium deposition in brown trout, *Salmo trutta* L., yolk-sac fry exposed to aluminium and manganese in soft acid water. *J.Fish Biol.*, **32**: 607–624.

Sadler, K., 1983. A model relating the results of low pH bioassay experiments to the fishery status of Norwegian lakes. *Freshwater Biology*, **13**: 453–463.

SAS Institute Inc., 1988. *SAS/STAT User's Guide*, Release 6.03 Edition. Cary, NC, SAS Institute Inc. 1028 pp.

Sprague, J.B., 1969. Measurement of pollutant toxicity to fish. I. Bioassay methods for acute toxicity. *Water Res.*, **3**: 793–821.

Tuunainen, P. *et al.*, 1990. Happaman laskeuman vaikutukset kaloihin ja rapuihin. Raportti vuodelta 1989. (English summary: Effects of acidic deposition on fish and crayfish. Report 1989). *Riista- ja kalatalouden tutkimuslaitos. Kalatutkimuksia – Fiskundersökningat*, vol. 8, Helsinki, 97 pp.

Tuunainen, P. *et al.*, 1991. Happaman laskeuman vaikutukset kaloihin ja rapuihin. Loppuraportti. (Abstract: Effects of acidic deposition on fish and crayfish. Final report.). *Suomen Kalatalous*, **57**: 1–44.

Van Winkle, W., S.W. Christensen and J.E. Breck, 1986. Linking laboratory and field responses of fish populations to acidification. *Water Air Soil Pollut.*, **30**: 639–648.

Verta, M. *et al.*, 1990. Trace metals in Finnish headwater lakes – effects of acidification and airborne load. In: Kauppi, P., P. Anttila and K. Kenttämies (Eds.) *Acidification in Finland*, pp. 883–907. Berlin, Heidelberg, New York, Springer-Verlag.

Vuorinen, M., 1987. Effects of exposure to aluminium and acidity on fish fry. In: Anttila, P. and P. Kauppi (Eds.) *Symposium of the Finnish Research Project on Acidification (HAPRO), April 21–24, 1987*. Abstracts. Ministry of the Environment, Ministry of Agriculture and Forestry, Series A, **64**: 88.

Vuorinen, P.J., M. Vuorinen and S. Peuranen, 1990. Long-term exposure of adult whitefish (*Coregonus wartmanni*) to low pH/aluminum: Effects on reproduction, growth, blood composition and gills. In: Kauppi, P., P. Anttila and K. Kenttämies (Eds.) *Acidification in Finland*, pp. 941–961. Berlin, Heidelberg, New York, Springer-Verlag.

Vuorinen, P.J., M. Vuorinen and S. Peuranen, 1992. Reproductive status, blood chemistry, gill histology and growth of perch (*Perca fluviatilis*) in three acidic lakes. *Environ.Pollut.*, **78**: 19–27.

Vuorinen, M., P.J. Vuorinen and S. Peuranen, 1993a. Lethal and sublethal threshold values of aluminium and acidity to pike (*Esox lucius*), whitefish (*Coregonus pallasi*), pike-perch (*Stizostedion lucioperca*) and roach (*Rutilus rutilus*) newly-hatched fry. *Sci.Total Envir.* Suppl. 1993, Part 2: 953–967.

Vuorinen, P.J. *et al.*, 1993b. Water quality during snowmelt and in summer in small Finnish forest lakes sensitive to acidification. *Aqua Fennica* (in press).

Vuorinen, M., P.J. Vuorinen, M. Rask and J. Suomela, 1994. The sensitivity to acidity and aluminium of newly-hatched perch (*Perca fluviatilis*) originating from strains from four lakes with different degrees of acidity (chapter 24, this volume).

Wales, D.L. and G.L. Beggs, 1986. Fish species distribution in relation to lake acidity in Ontario. *Water Air Soil Pollut.*, **30**: 601–609.

Wright, R.F. and E. Snekvik, 1978. Acid precipitation: chemistry and fish populations in 700 lakes in southernmost Norway. *Verh.Internat.Verein.Limnol.*, **20**: 763–775.

Chapter 26
Metal accumulation by Arctic char (*Salvelinus a. alpinus*) in a remote acid alpine lake

R. HOFER, H. PITTRACHER, G. KÖCK and S. WEYRER

Institut für Zoologie, Universität Innsbruck, Technikerstr. 25, A-6020 Innsbruck, Austria

26.1   Introduction

During the last decade the acidification of surface waters has been a major focus for political and scientific activity. This is true for Austria, where a selected number of high mountain lakes were included in a monitoring programme (Psenner *et al.*, 1988). Lake Schwarzsee ob Sölden (SOS), situated at 2799 m a.s.l. in the Ötztaler Alps, is one of the most acidic of the alpine lakes. Its chemistry has been studied during the last decade by Psenner *et al.* (1988); some of the data obtained are given in Table 26.1. During the approximately nine-month period of ice cover, the hypolimnion becomes anoxic. Despite the low pH of the water, aluminum does not reach toxic concentrations.

So far as is known, SOS is the highest lake in the Alps that contains a fishery. Arctic char have been introduced by man, probably as early as the late Middle Ages. The first scientific data obtained for this population were published in 1949 (Steinböck, 1949; Steiner, 1987).

26.2   Material and methods

Vertical water samples were taken from the surface to near to the bottom between June (when the lake was still ice covered) and September. For metal analyses water

Table 26.1 The water chemistry of Schwarzsee ob Sölden (Psenner *et al.*, 1988, and our own measurements).

Conductivity	10.1	$\mu S.cm^{-1}$
pH	5.0–5.35	(the lowest value in June)
Alkalinity	1	$\mu eq.l^{-1}$
Cl	12	$\mu eq.l^{-1}$
Ca	46	$\mu eq.l^{-1}$
Mg	14	$\mu eq.l^{-1}$
Na	4	$\mu eq.l^{-1}$
K	2	$\mu eq.l^{-1}$
Al	10–30	$\mu g.l^{-1}$
Pb	<0.5	$\mu g.l^{-1}$
Cd	0.3–0.06	$\mu g.l^{-1}$ (the highest concentration in June)

was filtered (40 μm), acidified with ultra pure HNO_3 and analysed by atomic absorption spectrophotometry.

The fish were caught with gill nets of different mesh size (set for 1–2 hours in early August 1990 and late August 1991), and samples of gills, kidney and liver were taken for histological and metal analyses. For histology the samples were immediately fixed in buffered formaldehyde, dehydrated in ethanol and embedded in polyethylene glycol methacrylate. Haematoxilin/eosin and May-Grünwald/ Giemsa staining were carried out on 3 μm sections. For metal analyses the samples were dried (60°C), and hydrolysed with HNO_3 (ultra pure) and diluted with distilled water. Cadmium and lead were analysed by atomic absorption spectrophotometry. The opercular bones were used for age determinations.

26.3   Results and discussion

In the deep high mountain lakes of the Alps, a stunted form of Arctic char can be found with a low condition factor and a mean body length of 15–18 cm. A similar body length has also been reported for the char of Lake Schwarzsee ob Sölden (Steinböck, 1949; Steiner, 1987; Fig. 26.1). Fish catches in 1990 and 1991, however, showed a significant increase in size, with specimens measuring up to 28 cm (Fig. 26.1). Since there has been no fishing activity there during the past few years, and no fish younger than 4+ were caught in gill nets of different mesh sizes, it can be assumed that there has been a dramatic decrease in reproductive success during this period. Due to the lower population density, the remaining fish may have

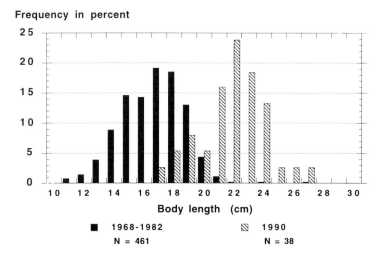

Fig. 26.1 Length–frequency distribution of Arctic char of the Schwarzsee ob Sölden during the period 1968–82 and in summer 1990 (catches from gill nets of different mesh sizes).

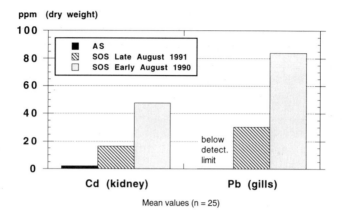

Fig. 26.2   Trace metals in two organs of Arctic char from two Austrian lakes (AS = Achensee, SOS = Schwarzsee ob Sölden).

better feeding conditions now than they did before. In fact, the measured condition factor of the char from Schwarzsee ob Sölden reached 0.76 ±0.09 in 1990 ($n = 10$) and 0.79 ±0.10 in 1991 ($n = 17$), which is not significantly different from that of a normally growing and commercially exploited population in the valley (Lake Achensee: 0.81 ±0.09, $n = 29$).

Due to the low alkalinity (1 μequ.l^{-1}) of the SOS water, the lake and its organisms are vulnerable to the atmospheric input of toxicants such as acids or metals.

At pH values below 7, cadmium exists mainly as the free divalent ion so that this fraction is little affected by further acidification (Campbell and Stokes, 1985). On the other hand, the competition between cadmium and hydrogen ions for binding sites on gill membranes leads to a decrease in accumulation of cadmium with increasing acidification of the water (Campbell and Stokes, 1985; McDonald *et al.*, 1989). However, the fraction of ionic lead, the form most readily assimilated through the gills (Merlini and Pozzi, 1977), increases with decreasing pH. The clear water of the high mountain lakes also reduces the fraction that could be bound onto suspended particles and DOC.

Despite the low concentrations of lead and cadmium in the water (Table 26.1) these metals reached extremely high concentrations in gills (84 ppm Pb) and kidney (47 ppm Cd; Fig. 26.2). Compared to a population in the valley (Achensee, alkaline hard-water lake), those from SOS accumulated on average 25 times more cadmium in the kidney, and about 100 times more lead in the gills. The highest individual concentrations recorded were 178 ppm for cadmium and 160 ppm for lead. In the char of SOS the cadmium concentration of the liver was positively correlated with the age of the fish, whereas the population of Lake Achensee showed a negative correlation (Fig. 26.3). Neither Murphy *et al.* (1978), Wiener and Giesy (1979) nor Hodson *et al.* (1982) could find any correlation between cadmium accumulation and body size or age of the fish.

At the present stage of the investigation there is no obvious explanation for the extremely high tissue concentrations of cadmium and lead in the char of SOS. These concentrations are higher than in fish of other low alkaline lakes (Spry and Wiener, 1991), but more or less similar to the concentrations reported for fish from heavily contaminated waters (Nichols and Scholz, 1989; Köck *et al.*, 1991; Benoit *et al.*, 1976; Holcombe *et al.*, 1976). Although during summer the metal concentration in the water is low, the occurrence of a short but high episodic input during the first event of snow melt in spring (Psenner *et al.*, 1988), when the acid run off also mobilises metals, cannot be excluded. Another source of metals is the diet of the fish, consisting in SOS mainly of chironomids and trichopterans. Indeed, Steinberg *et al.* (1986) found an increased concentration of lead, cadmium and cyanide near to the surface of the sediment of SOS, which reflects an increased atmospheric input during the past decades. However, insect larvae from this lake have not yet been analysed.

Lead is absorbed mainly across the gills, but little seems to be taken up from the diet (Hodson *et al.*, 1978), whereas for cadmium both of these are possible routes of uptake.

A high accumulation of metal in fish tissues might be also explained by a low growth rate due to limited food resources and low temperatures. Bendell-Young *et al.* (1986) attributed variations in cadmium accumulation more to different growth rates of the fish than to differences in the water chemistry. However, most of the char of SOS are in relatively good condition and the liver contains good glycogen levels, even at the end of the nine winter months.

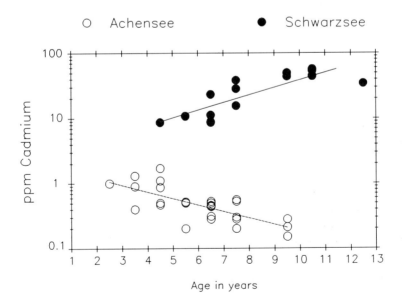

Fig. 26.3 Age-dependent accumulation of cadmium (ppm dry weight) in the liver of Arctic char from Achensee and Schwarzsee ob Sölden.

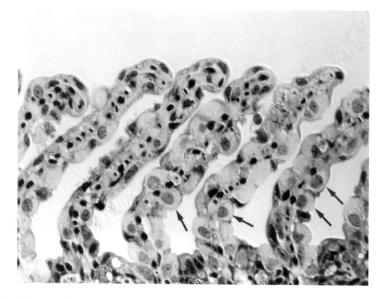

Fig. 26.4 Hypertrophy of chloride cells (arrows) in the gill lamellae of Arctic char from a high mountain lake.

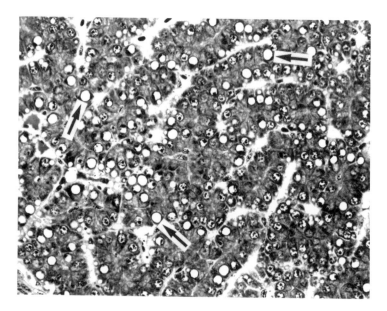

Fig. 26.5   Glycogen vacuoles (arrows) in hepatocyte nuclei of Arctic char from Schwarzsee ob Sölden.

In contrast to a population of Arctic char in a hard-water lake in the valley (Achensee), the char of SOS contained hypertrophic chloride cells (Fig. 26.4) which may compensate for the low ionic strength of the water. It is well known that

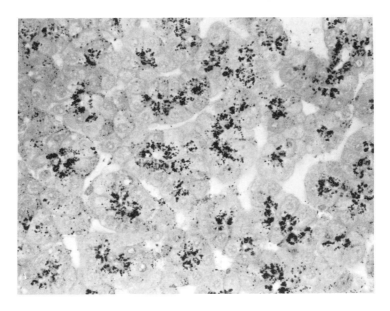

Fig. 26.6 Siderosis in hepatocytes (black dots) of an Arctic char from Schwarzsee ob Sölden (Prussian blue staining).

chloride cells are also capable of resorbing cadmium via the same ionic channels as that for calcium (Verbost *et al.*, 1987). In this way, the chloride cells may contribute to the accumulation of metals in fish tissues.

The adequate stores of glycogen in the liver has been already mentioned. However, $7 \pm 6\%$ (1991) and $15 \pm 7\%$ (1990) of hepatocyte nuclei contained large glycogen vacuoles (Fig. 26.5) and in about 50% of the fish the lysosomes of the hepatocytes contained large quantities of iron (Fig. 26.6), giving rise to a distinct siderosis. The hepatic concentration of iron was positively correlated with the age of the fish. Neither of these pathological changes were seen in the lowland population.

Hyaline droplet degeneration of the first proximal tubules of the kidney was prevalent only after the ice break-up but disappeared during the summer. Hyaline droplets are frequently found in salmonid kidneys and indicate an increased passage of low molecular weight proteins through the glomerular filter.

26.4   Conclusions

Clearly, more research is required in order to understand the input and circulation of metals in high mountain lakes, the route of their uptake by the fish, and the toxic effects of the accumulated metal on fish tissues.

Acknowledgements

Supported by the Austrian Bundesministerium für Land- und Forstwirtschaft. We thank Gun Sonntag for the technical assistance and Joy Wieser for correcting the manuscript.

References

Bendell-Young, L.I., H.H. Harvey and J.F. Young, 1987. Accumulation of cadmium by white suckers (*Catostomus commersoni*) in relation to fish growth and lake acidification. *Can.J.Fish.Aquat.Sci.*, **43**: 806–811.

Benoit, D.A., E.N. Leonard, G.M. Christensen and J.T. Fiandt, 1976. Toxic effect of cadmium on three generations of brook trout (*Salvelinus fontinalis*). *Trans.Am.Fish.Soc.*, **4**: 550–560.

Campbell, P.G.C. and P.M. Stokes, 1985. Acidification and toxicity of metals to aquatic biota. *Can.J.Fish.Aquat.Sci.*, **42**: 2034–2049.

Hodson, P.V., B.R. Blunt and D.J. Spry, 1978. Chronic toxicity of water-borne and dietary lead to rainbow trout (*Salmo gairdneri*) in Lake Ontario water. *Water Res.*, **12**: 869–878.

Hodson, P.V., D.G. Dixon, D.J. Spry, D.M. Whittle and J.B. Sprague, 1982. Effect of growth rate and size of fish on rate of intoxication by waterborne lead. *Can.J.Fish.Aquat.Sci.*, **39**: 1243–1251.

Holcombe, G.W., D.A. Benoit, E.N. Leonard and J.M. McKim, 1976. Long-term effects of lead exposure on three generations of brook trout (*Salvelinus fontinalis*). *J.Fish.Res.Board Can.*, **33**: 1731–1741.

Köck, G., F. Bucher and R. Hofer, 1991. Schwermetalle und Fische: Anforderungen an die Wassergüte. Vienna, Bundesministerium für Land- und Forstwirtschaft. 324 pp.

McDonald, D.G., J.P. Reader and T.R.K. Dalziel, 1989. The combined effects of pH and trace metals on fish ionoregulation. In : Morris, R., *et al.* (Eds.) *Acid Toxicity and Aquatic Animals*, pp. 221–242. Cambridge, Cambridge University Press.

Merlini, M. and G. Pozzi, 1977. Lead and freshwater fishes: part 1 – lead accumulation and water pH. *Environm.Pollut.*, **12**: 167–172.

Murphy, B.R., G.J. Atchison, A.W. McIntosh and D.J. Kolar, 1978. Cadmium and zinc content of fish from an industrial contaminated lake. *J.Fish Biol.*, **13**: 327–335.

Nichols, D.G. and A.T. Scholz, 1989. Concentrations of Cd, Sr, and U in fish and water samples collected from a small stream receiving uranium mine drainage. *J.Freshwater Ecol.*, **5**: 13–25.

Psenner, R., U. Nickus and F. Zapf, 1988. Versauerung von Hochgebirgsseen in kristallinen Einzugsgebieten Tirols und Kärntens. Vienna, Bundesministerium für Land- und Forstwirtschaft. 335 pp.

Spry, D.J. and J.G. Wiener, 1991. Metal bioavailability and toxicity to fish in low-alkalinity lakes: a critical review. *Environm.Pollut.*, **71**: 243–304.

Steinberg, C., W. Beckstette, R. Psenner and N. Schulz, 1986. Chemical sediment stratigraphy of four high alpine lakes in Austria. *Hydrobiologia*, **143**: 343–348.

Steinböck, O., 1949. Der Schwarzsee, 2792 m ü.M, ob Sölden, Ötztal, der höchste Fischsee der Alpen. *Verh.Intern.Ver.theor.angew.Limnol.*, **10**: 442–450.

Steiner, V., 1987. Die Hochgebirgsseen Tirols aus fischereilicher Sicht. Reinhaltung der Tiroler Gewässer. Innsbruck, Amt der Tiroler Landesregierung. 213 pp.

Verbost, P.M., G. Flik, R.A.C. Lock and S.E. Wendelaar Bonga, 1987. Cadmium inhibition of Ca^{2+} uptake in rainbow trout gills. *Am.J.Physiol.*, **253**: 216–221.

Wiener, J.G. and J.P.Giesy, Jr. 1979. Concentrations of Cd, Cu, Mn, Pb and Zn in fish in a highly organic softwater pond. *J.Fish.Res.Board Can.*, **36**: 270–279.

Chapter 27

Effects of episodic acid runoff on the abundance of fish fry of spring spawning fish species and the perch (*Perca fluviatilis*) stock in the estuary of River Kyrönjoki

R. HUDD,[1] A. LESKELÄ,[1] J. KJELLMAN,[1] M. RAHIKAINEN[2] and P. KARÅS[3]

[1] *Finnish Game and Fisheries Research Institute, Merenkurkku Fisheries Research Station, Korsholmanpuistikko 16, SF-65100 Vaasa, Finland*

[2] *Finnish Game and Fisheries Research Institute, PO Box 202, SF-00151 Helsinki, Finland*

[3] *National Board of Fisheries Sweden, Institute of Coastal Research, PO Box 584, S-74071 Öregrund, Sweden*

27.1   Introduction

Due to rapid land upheaval, all of the coasts in the Gulf of Bothnia have until recently been part of the sea bed. Because of the high concentration of sulphur in seawater, all newly formed sediments also have high concentrations of this element (Ericsson, 1982). In particular, there are rich sulphuric layers in the sediments formed during the Litorina Sea phase of the Baltic (Purokoski, 1959; Sevola, 1979; Erviö, 1975) and in the sediments formed in estuaries (Rosberg, 1895). The high organic production, due to favourable climatic factors during the Litorina phase (*c* 5000 BC) and to the high organic production in estuaries in general, is the cause of these sulphur rich deposits.

When the sulphuric deposits are exposed to air as a result of water engineering work, such as ditching, excavation and drainage pumping, the sulphur becomes water soluble and enters the water as sulphuric acid. There are high concentrations of several metals in the former sediment and these can then become dissolved (Tiitinen, 1981; Alasaarela, 1983). Because of large-scale engineering work in the watercourses along the coast of Finland, there have been consequent large changes in the fish stocks and fisheries there (Hildén *et al.*, 1982).

Müller (1982) and Lehtonen and Hudd (1990) have drawn attention to the importance of the rivers and estuaries for the reproduction of fish stocks along the coast of the Gulf of Bothnia. The beneficial factors are early and stable warming, a nutrient-rich environment and the shelter provided by the rich vegetation and turbidity. The acidity of the coastal soils and sediments has been known since the nineteenth century (e.g. Rosberg, 1895). Although there have been mass mortalities of fish (Anonymous, 1896; Hudd *et al.*, 1984), no long-term monitoring of the fish stocks and their reproductive success has been undertaken until the 1980s.

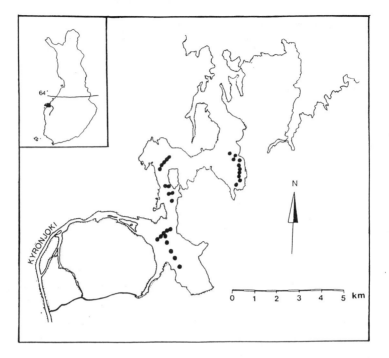

Fig. 27.1 The River Kyrönjoki estuary and the fry sample seining stations 1980–90.

Since engineering works and especially excavation of the watercourses are likely to continue, it is important to monitor and make impact assessments of the reproductive success of the fish stocks. This chapter deals with the abundance of fry from spring-spawning fish stocks of the River Kyrönjoki estuary (shown in Fig. 27.1, Table 27.1) and the effect on the year-class success of the variation in fry abundance caused by periodic acidification.

27.2   Material and methods

27.2.1   *Acidification and summer temperature during the study period*

Usually the lowest pH values are found during the latter part of the spring flood and at the beginning of the autumn flood. There are considerable differences from year to year in the extent and duration of the acidification. Occasionally a rapid fall in pH can be caused by rainfall and temporary pumping of drainage water. The drainage pumping also causes large variations in the pH level within the area. In the pumped water, pH values 3–4 have been measured and the associated concentrations of metals have been very high, e.g. aluminium concentrations of several tens of milligrams per litre have been recorded (Water District of Vaasa, unpubl.). During the study period the lowest pH values were measured in the spring of 1983,

Table 27.1 Hydrological data for the River Kyrönjoki.

Drainage area	4920 km^2			
Lakes, % of drainage area	1.1			
Alum soils, % of drainage area	10			

	min	mean	max		
Acidity (mmol.l^{-1})	0.04	0.30	1.42		
Alkalinity (mmol.l^{-1}	0.0	0.15	0.60		

	HQ (1/20)	MHQ	MQ	MNQ	NQ
Discharge (m^3.s^{-1})	480	295	43	4.0	1.9

HQ (1/20) = highest water discharge in a 20 year period. MHQ = mean highest water discharge. MQ = mean water discharge. MNQ = mean lowest water discharge. NQ = lowest water discharge recorded.

1985, 1986, and 1987. The duration of the acidic episode was longest in the years 1980, 1985, and 1987 (Fig. 27.2). The study period included years in which the air temperatures varied considerably during the spring and summer. The coldest summers of the study period were 1981, 1985 and 1987 and the warmest 1980, 1983 and 1984. Early high temperatures were recorded in the summers of 1989 and 1990; latest warming was in the summers of 1981 and 1985 (Fig. 27.2).

27.2.2   *Collection of fry*

The project was started with a spatial survey of the distribution and abundance of fish fry in 1980–1982. Using the information from this survey 30 sampling stations were chosen (Fig. 27.1). These stations were chosen so that the habitats of the phytophilic spring-spawning species would be included. The time of fry sampling was fixed at the middle of the summer period when the fish were still catchable with the gear used, and the migration out of the estuary had not yet started. The fishing gear used were small beach seines (Table 27.2) that were drawn by a small boat. The length of the haul was standardised at 20 m. The width of the haul was determined by the length of the boat, i.e. 4 m. The number of hauls at the sampling stations varied from 46 to 286 per year (Table 27.3). The fry were preserved in alcohol (*c.* 80%) and their length measured in the laboratory. The catch per unit effort is given as individuals per haul (Hudd *et al.*, 1984; Urho *et al.*, 1990; Hudd and Leskelä; 1992).

27.2.3   *Comparison between fry abundance, potential abundance and year-class strength of the perch stock*

It is known that the recruitment of the European perch (*Perca fluviatilis*) depends on the temperature conditions during the first summer and this determines the strength of the year class in the northern Baltic (Neuman, 1974; Böhling *et al.*,

1991). The observed fry abundance of perch in this study was plotted against an index derived from a bioenergetic model (Karås, 1987) based on temperature and day length. As background values for hatching time and potential growth, the temperature data (Fig. 27.2) from the River Kyrönjoki were used. It was assumed that the food supply and predation were not limiting factors.

The spawning stock of the perch in the river was monitored by wire-trap catch samples and by catch statistics provided by the Finnish Game and Fisheries Research Institute (Table 27.3). To determine the dependence of year-class strength on the abiotic factors of pH and temperature, the water quality was expressed as annual indices. The pH index calculation was based on the number of days with a pH value under 5.0 and 5.5 (Formula 1) between May and August. The correlation as well as the regression analyses were adapted for calculating the number of 3-year-old specimens of a year-class. The number of 3-year-olds were calculated by Pope's Virtual Population Analyses (VPA) (Gulland, 1975;

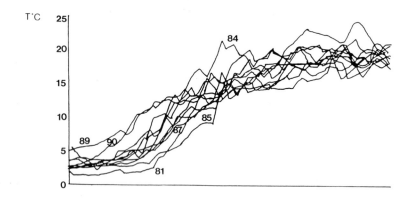

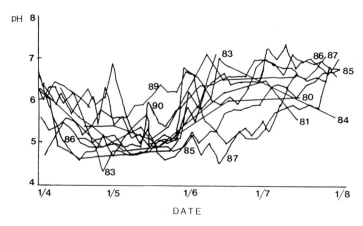

Fig. 27.2 Temperature and pH data for the River Kyrönjoki, April–July, during the study period (1980–90).

Table 27.2   Dimensions of the beach seines used in the River Kyrönjoki estuary 1980–90.

Year	Wing length (m)	Bag Length (m)	Bag Depth (m)	Wing mesh (mm)	Bag mesh (mm)
1980	9	2.5	1.2	5	1
1981–90	9	3.5	2.5	5	1

Table 27.3   The number of hauls at the fry sampling stations, the weight of perch in wire trap catch samples, and the annual total yield of perch in the River Kyrönjoki estuary 1980–90, annual pH index and bioenergetic index.

Year	Number of hauls	Perch in catch samples (kg)	Perch annual river total (kg)	pH index	Bioenergetic index
1980	49		93 900	45.0	129
1981	97	166	80 800	72.5	55
1982	46	132	47 344	80.0	73
1983	180	142	43 418	52.5	116
1984	76	149	47 180	58.0	139
1985	120	150	35 121	40.0	55
1986	150	154	25 928	67.0	99
1987	66	265	10 617	14.5	69
1988	89	332	28 027	70.5	151
1989	120	377	39 447	93.0	94
1990	89	504	54 439	77.0	133

Ricker, 1983). To determine the regression of stock dependence on pH and temperature the pH and bioenergetic indices were used and the stock size converted to a logarithmic scale (Hennemuth *et al.*, 1980).

Formula 1. Calculation of the pH index

$$\text{pH index} = A - (b \times \text{pH}<5.0) - (c \times 5.0<\text{pH}<5.5)$$

where   A = Days from 1 May to 1 August (= 93)
        b = 2
        c = 0.5

27.3   Results and discussion

27.3.1   *Annual abundance of fry*

The springs of 1985 and 1987 were the coldest during the study period, which partly explains the associated low abundance of fry in most species. In 1987, the acidic period in the river lasted for longer than in the other years, and the lowest measured pH was 4.5. In 1985, the river acidity was close to average so the exceptionally low abundance of fry was probably due to the cold weather conditions. The springs of 1980, 1981, 1983, 1984 and 1986 were relatively warm. However, the abundance of fry was low in 1983 and 1984. This was particularly so in the year 1983 which was more acidic than in most of the other years of the study period, and this could have led to a low abundance. On the other hand, in the warm spring of 1980 abundance of perch and roach fry was moderate in spite of the high acidity of the river water. The highest abundances of fry were observed in 1982, 1986, 1989 and 1990 (Fig. 27.3). In the years 1982, 1989 and 1990 the acidity in the river was less severe with average or slightly above average temperatures (Fig. 27.2).

Generally, perch was the most dominant species in the seine catches, with roach and bream the second most numerous. In 1983, when abundance of all the fish species was very low, roach dominated the catch of fry, and the relative abundance of pike-perch fry was exceptionally high. The most acidic period in 1983 occurred relatively early in the year. Therefore, roach which spawn later than perch in the River Kyrönjoki were not so severely affected by the acidic water. Pike-perch spawn even later than roach and were also not as seriously affected. The spring of 1983 was warm and the temperature in the estuary rose evenly, which was beneficial for the fry which had survived the acidic period. In 1984 and 1985 the relative numbers of smelt were exceptionally high in the seine catches. In 1985, in which there was a cold and late spring and an average acidity (as based on this 11-year survey), there were very few fry of species other than smelt and perch. In 1987, when the spring was late and cold and the water very acidic, there was a clear dominance of perch. The abundance of all fry was very low in 1987, but the relative numbers of pike-perch were higher than in most of the other years. In the year 1990, with low acidity and moderate temperatures, the abundance of bream fry was much higher than in previous years (Figs 27.2 and 27.3).

27.3.2   *Correlation between the abundance of fry and year-class strength of perch*

The number of 3-year-old fish could be calculated for year-classes 1980–87. The strength of later year-classes than 1987 could not be estimated because no age groups have yet been recruited to the catch samples. The VPA showed a high fluctuation of year-class strength, with two dominant year-classes, 1982 and 1986, and one fairly strong year-class in 1980. This gave a correlation between seine catch per unit effort (cpue) and the number of 3-year-olds of 0.82 ($P = 0.01$) with Pearson's correlation analyses, whereas the correlation between cpue of perch fry and the bioenergetic index was −0.29 with a low probability ($P = 0.42$). The multi-regressional model explained 75% of the year-class fluctuations, with a high probability ($P = 0.03$). The pH index alone explained 66% of these fluctuations (Fig. 27.4).

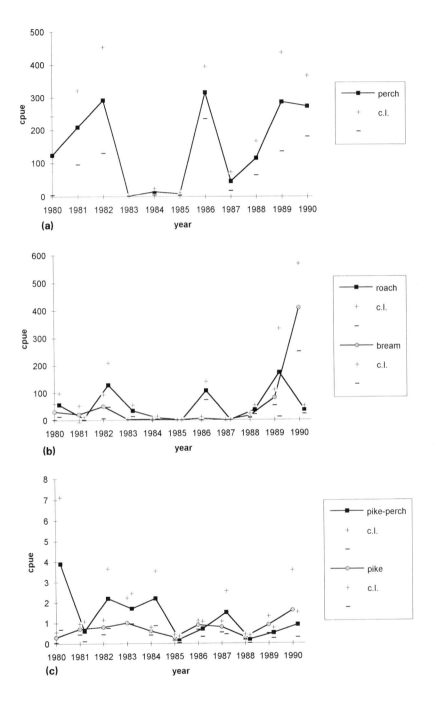

Fig. 27.3   Annual abundance of fry of (a) perch, (b) roach and bream, and (c) pike and pike-perch with 95% confidence limits.

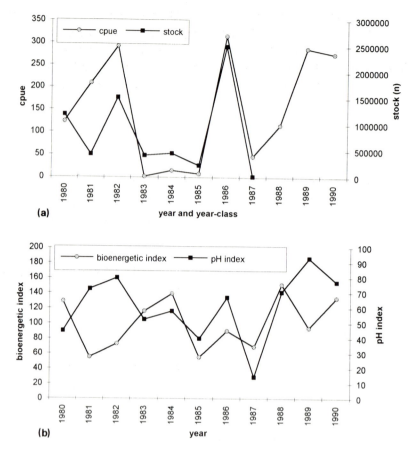

Fig. 27.4   (a) Year-class strength (stock) and seine cpue of perch, and (b) pH index and bioenergetic index for the River Kyrönjoki.

Temperature has been shown to affect survival within the first year and thereby the year-class strength of perch in the Baltic (Neuman, 1974; Karås, 1987). Rahikainen and Karås (in prep.) have verified the estimates of normalised year-class strengths of perch calculated by the bioenergetic index. The bioenergetic index explained 89% of the year-class strength calculated by a VPA in the clean waters of Taivassalo, in the northern Archipelago Sea of the Baltic Sea. Therefore, it can be concluded that water temperature strongly affects the year-class strength of perch in areas without other environmental disturbances. Disturbances, such as acidity in the River Kyrönjoki, may reduce the recruitment to such an extent that the influence of temperature is of a minor importance. This shows that watercourse engineering works can have a considerable influence on the perch population of the River Kyrönjoki.

It is clear that water acidity is the limiting factor for reproduction, and also that temperature affects the recruitment. Both in 1980 and 1986 the conditions gave rise to stronger year-classes than might be assumed by the pH index, whereas 1981 and 1982 gave weaker year-classes, which may depend on the bioenergetic indices. The year of 1984 on the other hand gave rise to one of the weakest year-classes even though it had the highest bioenergetic index and a good pH index. Although the model is not complete, it does provide a functional instrument to estimate the year-class strength of perch.

27.4   Conclusions

The good correlation between the abundance of perch fry in the seine catch and the year-class strength shows that such seinings have a high predictive value. Therefore, they can also serve as a good monitoring tool for environmental impact analysis. Since the derived pH index explained 66% of the year-class fluctuations, it is also clear that the major reason for year-class fluctuations of the perch stock of the River Kyrönjoki is the periodic acidification and that natural abiotic regulation mechanisms such as temperature are of a lesser importance.

Acknowledgements

In the years 1980–82 and 1987–90 the project was performed in collaboration with the Water District of Vaasa as a fishery investigation for water court (management) purposes. The temperature and pH measurements are made by the Water District of Vaasa and the City of Vaasa's agricultural laboratory. We also wish to thank the Eteläpohjanmaan Kulttuurirahasto foundation for providing grants.

References

Alasaarela, E., 1983. Acidity problems caused by flood control works of the river Kyrönjoki. *Publ.Water Res.Inst.*, **49**: 3–16.

Anonymous, 1896. *Fiskeritidskrift för Finland*, **5**: 12–13.

Böhling, P., R. Hudd, H. Lehtonen, P. Karås, E. Neuman and G. Thoresson, 1991. Variations in year-class strength of different perch (*Perca fluviatilis*) populations in the Baltic Sea with special reference to temperature and pollution. *Can.J.Fish.Aquat.Sci.*, **48**: 1181–1187.

Ericsson, E., 1982. Inverkan av landhöjningen på kustnära vattensystems hydrologiska funktioner. In: Landhöjning och kustbygdsförändring. Luleå, Symposiepublikation, Vol. 2: 8–15.

Erviö, R., 1975. Agricultural land with a high sulphur content in the drainage basin of the Kyrönjoki. *Maataloustieteellinen aikakauskirja*, **47**: 550–561.

Gulland, J.A., 1975. *Fish Stock Assessment*. FAO/Wiley Series on food and agriculture, Vol. 1. 223 pp.

Hennemuth, R.C., J.E. Palmer and B.E. Brown, 1980. A statistical description of recruitment in eighteen selected fish stocks. *J.Northw.Atlant.Fish.Sci.*, **1**: 101–111.

Hildén, M., R. Hudd and H. Lehtonen, 1982. The effects of environmental changes on the fisheries and fish stocks in the Archipelago Sea and the Finnish part of the Gulf of Bothnia. *Aqua Fennica*, **12**: 47–58.

Hudd, R. and A. Leskelä, 1992. Kevätkutuisten kalojen poikastuotanto Kyrönjoen suistossa vuosina 1980–1990. Finnish National Board of Waters and Environment. 51 pp. (English summary).

Hudd, R., M. Hildén, L. Urho, M. Axell and L. Jåfs, 1984. Kyrönjoen suisto- ja vaikutusalueen kalatalousselvitys 1980–1982. National Board of Waters, Vol. 242 A. 277 pp. (English summary).

Karås, P., 1987. Food consumption, growth and recruitment in perch (*Perca fluviatilis* L.). Ph.D. thesis, University of Uppsala, Sweden. 142 pp.

Lehtonen, H. and R. Hudd, 1990. The importance of estuaries for the reproduction of freshwater fish in the Gulf of Bothnia. In: van Densen, W., B. Steinmetz and R. Hughes (Eds.) *Management of Fresh Water Fisheries*, pp. 82–89. Proceedings of FAO/EIFAC Symposium, Göteborg, 31 May– 3 June 1988. Wageningen, Pudoc. 649 pp.

Müller, K., 1982. Jungfischwanderungen zur Bottensee. *Arch.Hydrobiol.*, **95**: 271–282.

Neuman, E., 1974. The effects of temperature on the growth and year-class strength of perch (*Perca fluviatilis* L.) in some Baltic archipelagoes. *Inf.Sötvattenslab.Drottningholm*, Vol. 6. 104 pp.

Purokoski, P., 1959. Rannikkoseudun rikkipitoisista maista. *Agrogeologisia julkaisuja*, **74**: 1–27.

Ricker, W.E., 1983. Computation and interpretation of biological statistics of fish populations. *Bull.Fish.Res.Board Can.*, Vol. 191. 382 pp.

Rosberg, J., 1895. Bottenvikens finska delta. Academic dissertation, Helsinki University, 255 p. + tables.

Sevola, P., 1979. Pohjanmaan ongelmasavet – muinaismeren pohjaliejut. *Suomen luonto*, **38**(3): 102–106.

Tiitinen, R., 1981. Vesien happamuuteen vaikuttavista tekijöistä alunamaa-alueilla. Vesihallituksen monistesarja. *Vaasan vesipiirin vesitoimisto*, Vol. 79. 56 pp.

Urho, L., M. Hildén and R. Hudd, 1990. Fish reproduction and the impact of acidification in the Kyrönjoki River estuary in the Baltic Sea. *Environm.Biol.Fishes*, **27**: 273–283.

Chapter 28
Aluminium toxicity and restoration of a brown trout fishery in a limed acid upland lake (Loch Fleet, Galloway, Scotland)

G. HOWELLS,[1] T.R.K. DALZIEL[2] and A.W.H. TURNPENNY[3]

[1] *Department of Zoology, University of Cambridge, Downing Street, Cambridge CB3 3EJ, UK*
[2] *PowerGen plc, Power Technology, Ratcliffe-on-Soar, Nottingham NG11 0EE, UK*
[3] *Fawley Aquatic Research Laboratories Ltd., Marine Laboratory, Fawley, Southampton SO4 1TW, UK*

28.1   Introduction

28.1.1   *Water quality and fishery status*

The acidity of waters of low ionic strength is linked with poor or lost fisheries in areas of sufficient acid deposition (Wright and Snekvik, 1979). While acidity *per se* is toxic to freshwater fish at levels below pH 5 (Alabaster and Lloyd, 1982), poor fishery status is reported in many less acid water bodies where water quality is characterised by the presence of a variety of trace metals. Aluminium, leached from poor soils by acid anions, is often elevated in such waters.

Acute toxicity of acid waters with high aluminium concentrations has been demonstrated in laboratory tests and as a result of acid episodes recorded in the field (Andersson and Nyberg, 1984; Skogheim and Rosseland, 1984). Less rigorous, but persistent, conditions lead to sub-lethal effects on growth and skeletal development (Reader *et al.*, 1988), gill osmoregulatory function (Potts and MacWilliams, 1989) and tissue and blood homeostasis (Cameron, 1989; Wood, 1989; MacDonald *et al.*, 1989). The role of potentially toxic trace metals, also present in such waters in the UK (Turnpenny *et al.*, 1987) is uncertain.

28.1.2   *Aluminium toxicity*

The mode of toxic action of aluminium on aquatic life depends on its physical and chemical state in the prevailing ambient conditions. Aluminium in solution is amphoteric and can form both inorganic and organic complexes, tending to polymerise (Driscoll and Schecher, 1988). These properties encourage the formation of various molecular species, dependent largely on pH, but some other water components are also critical (Howells *et al.*, 1990) and mitigate aluminium toxicity by protecting physiological processes or by interacting with the aluminium to produce less toxic complexes. For example, calcium concentration has been shown to be important in reducing aluminium toxicity in the field and the laboratory.

311

Aluminium forms inorganic complexes with fluoride, sulphate and silicate, and organic complexes (such as with citrate) also occur naturally. Silicic acid confers protection to fish from aluminium; acute toxicity of soluble inorganic aluminium to Atlantic salmon (*Salmo salar*) fry was entirely eliminated by an equivalent 13:1 ratio of Si:Al (Birchall *et al.*, 1989). The presence of silicic acid in natural waters may also explain the presence of fish in some where total aluminium concentrations are high.

In humic waters, dissolved aluminium tends to form polymeric species (Backes and Tipping, 1987); such organically complexed aluminium is often the predominant soluble form of aluminium and is relatively non-toxic to most aquatic life. Field and laboratory observations of Nova Scotian stream waters with high humic content (DOC >10 mg.l^{-1}) indicates that acidity rather than aluminium is the toxic agent controlling Atlantic salmon presence in these waters (Lacroix and Kan, 1986; Lacroix and Townsend, 1987).

28.1.3   *Acid mitigation projects*

Acid mitigation projects can provide information on the quantified response of the ecosystem to acidification and reversal following the acid mitigation, including fish recovery (Howells and Dalziel, 1992; Thornelof and Degerman, 1991; Gubala and Driscoll, 1991; Hindar and Rosseland, 1991; Stoner and Donald, 1991; Bergquist, 1991). Such a project currently being undertaken is the Loch Fleet Project (SW Scotland, UK) which started in 1984.

28.2   The Loch Fleet Project

The principal objective of the Loch Fleet Project was to improve the prevailing acid waters of the lake and its tributary streams by application of fine-ground limestone to areas of the catchment (Fig. 28.1). Liming was carried out in 1986 and 1987, resulting in a sustained improvement in water quality, sufficient for trout restoration (Howells and Dalziel, 1992). Water quality data – including acidity, alkalinity, calcium, DOC, aluminium fractions and trace metals – were collected from 1984 through to the time of writing (May 1992). Following the improvement in water quality, brown trout (*Salmo trutta fario*) from three stocks were reintroduced in 1987 and 1988. Since stocking, annual surveys of the trout population have been carried out, allowing assessment of growth, condition, stock and spawning performance.

28.2.1   *Target water quality*

Earlier field and laboratory studies on brown trout response to acid waters provide a target water quality for successful re-establishment of a brown trout fishery. This was set at pH >6, a calcium concentration >2 mg.l^{-1}, and a total aluminium

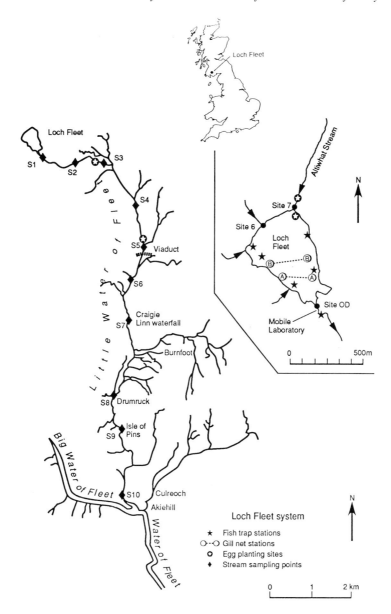

Fig. 28.1 Loch Fleet catchment.

concentration <0.1 mg.l^{-1}. This was intended as a 'mean' or sustained target, but brief and occasional episodes of poorer water quality might be expected in tributary streams which provide spawning and nursery areas. The long-term survival of the stocked population will depend on how long the target conditions can be maintained. A forecast is provided by estimating calcium fluxes from treated catchment areas following liming, and relating these to water quality (Dalziel *et al.*, 1992a).

Table 28.1   Loch Fleet water chemistry, pre- and post-liming.

Component	Pre-liming 1985	Post-liming 1989
pH	4.53	>6.0
Hydrogen (μg.l^{-1})	29.0	0.33
Calcium	0.92	3.16
Aluminium	0.20	0.08
Silicate	0.76	0.58
TOC	6.1	5.8
Copper	0.01	ND
Zinc	0.04	0.03
Iron	0.15	0.10
Manganese	0.20	0.08

Units: mg.l^{-1} except hydrogen (methods of sampling and analysis are described in Dalziel *et al.*, 1992a).

28.2.2   *Water quality before and after liming*

Pre- and post-liming water quality characteristics are summarised in Table 28.1. It is clear that conditions before liming would be toxic.

After limestone application to parts of the catchment in April 1986 and April 1987, lake water quality improved, exceeding the target described above. Total aluminium was reduced and the toxic inorganic monomeric fraction fell to a very low level (Fig. 28.2). Silicate and TOC, as expected, showed no significant change; in both cases the levels observed fell below those considered as effective in countering aluminium toxicity. Copper, zinc and iron declined to concentrations below those reported as toxic to brown trout (Dalziel *et al.*, 1992b).

Liming of the catchment was restricted to only some parts (or sectors), each receiving a different dose (tonnes.ha^{-1}) and/or a different mode of application (dry powder, slurry, pellets) and so conditions in the drainage from treated areas varied (Howells and Dalziel, 1992). Only one limed sector provided a stream suitable for trout spawning, and water quality there also met the target conditions for all life stages (Dalziel *et al.*, 1992b).

28.2.3   *Fishery status prior to liming*

An assessment of water quality prior to liming was provided by a field bioassay between 1984 and 1986 (Turnpenny *et al.*, 1988). Trout eggs, taken from spawning fish nearby, were fertilised and planted out in gravel beds around the lake, using recoverable plastic mesh boxes so that survival could be determined. Other life stages, including newly-hatched fry and yearling fish, were held in fish tanks fed by stream waters, and their survival monitored. In all cases, survival rates were poor (Table 28.2), confirming that a wild population would not have been viable.

A brown trout fishery was present in the Fleet system, including its headwater lake, prior to 1950s, yielding an annual catch of 100–150 trout with a mean weight

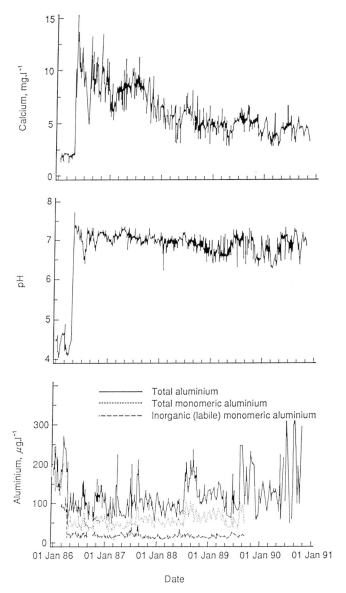

Fig. 28.2 Loch Fleet water quality – Ca, pH, Al – post-liming.
(**A**) Altiwhat.

of 500 g. After 1955, the catch rate declined, with a few larger fish being caught, indicating recruitment failure. By 1975, no catches were reported. Further downstream, records show a parallel decline in sea trout (*Salmo trutta trutta*) catches, from several hundred fish each year for 1930–60 to less than 100 per year (Turnpenny, 1992). There is no systematic record of water quality during these periods, but the record of diatom remnants in the lake sediments indicates that the lake did

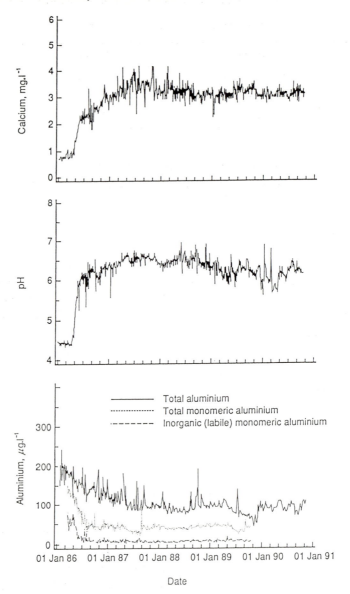

Fig. 28.2   Loch Fleet water quality – Ca, pH, Al – post-liming.
(**B**) Loch outlet.

not acidify until 1975 (Anderson *et al.*, 1986). However, calcium concentrations must always have been low and aluminium and trace metals possibly high.

A survey of the Fleet system in 1984–85 (Turnpenny *et al.*, 1988) revealed a very poor fishery status, with no fish detected in the lake itself, and only eels (*Anguilla anguilla* (L.)) at low densities (3–5 per 100 m^2) over the first 7 km downstream. At this point (Craigie Linn), a 5 m high waterfall marks the boundary between

Table 28.2 Survival of brown trout life stages in 1984–85, prior to liming.

Life stage	Observation	Fleet streams	Controls
Eggs	Survival to hatch	10–20%	86–90%
Yolk-sac fry	Median period of survival	3–10 days	>12 days
Yearlings	Median period of survival	8–98 days	>180 days

underlying granite (upstream) and greywacke (downstream) geologies. Below the fall, juvenile brown trout were present in low densities (1–5 per 100 m^2) down to the confluence with the larger Water of Fleet.

28.2.4   *Trout restocking programme*

Six months after the lime applications in April 1986, when the chemistry of the stream drainage and lake outlet returned to a quality suitable for fish, field survival trials were repeated, this time to include adult fish, placed in a floating cage within the lake. High survival rates with all life stages (Table 28.3) indicated that restocking would be successful.

Table 28.3 Survival of brown trout life stages in 1986–87, following lime application.

Life stage	Observation	Fleet waters	Controls
Eggs	Survival to hatching	69% (±17)	66% (±14)
Yolk-sac fry	Survival over 18 days	100%	100%
Yearling fish	Survival over 180 days	100%	100%
Adult fish	Survival over 180 days	100%	100%

The lake was restocked with brown trout in April 1987, initially at a low density of 3.2 kg.ha^{-1} in order to avoid excessive pressure on the limited invertebrate community. The stocking included fish from three, independent, local sources to ensure an expanded gene pool. A mixture of I, II and III+ age groups was introduced to provide a succession of spawning age classes in due course, and to expedite attainment of an equilibrium age structure. With favourable response to this first stocking, a second was carried out in July 1988, at a rate of 2.3 kg.ha^{-1}. The same sources and age distribution of stock were used. Since then, no further stock fish have been added to the system.

28.2.5   *Spawning and population expansion*

A spawning run was observed in 1987, the first season following stocking. In November, fish traps in the Altiwhat stream (main tributary, Fig. 28.1) and the lake outlet captured a strong run (61 in all), comprising almost all the 'eligible' III+ group fish and a few younger ones introduced earlier that year. Spawning activity was observed and large numbers of trout fry emerged in the following spring. The same spawning success was evident in each subsequent season, with an increasing number of spawners each year (Table 28.4). Since 1989, counts have been made by electronic fish counters installed at the Altiwhat stream and lake outlets.

With successful spawning, the population of younger age classes has expanded rapidly. Annual sampling has been undertaken by netting and rod-and-line fishing in the lake. Fin clip marks in the primary introduced stock distinguished new recruits from the indigenous stock, and by the summer of 1991, of some 70 fish recaptured in a one-day fly fishing exercise, none bore the marks of the original stocking. A quantitative estimate of the trout stock has yet to be made, but evidence indicates that a thriving population now exists.

Table 28.4   Counts of spawners entering the Altiwhat stream and the Loch Fleet outlet during autumn 1987–91.

Location	1987	1988	1989	1990	1991
Altiwhat	50	57	57	320	>1000*
Outlet	10	1	44	71	30

* Total movement

In the downstream Little Water of Fleet, annual summer electro-fishing surveys demonstrate the resurgence of fish populations there, with trout repopulating the stream to Craigie Linn, albeit at low population densities (Table 28.5). The eel population has also increased. Absence of trout of reproductive size has limited population expansion, which, so far, has been driven by immigration downstream.

28.2.6   *Growth, condition and dietary analysis*

Samples of Loch Fleet trout obtained from a variety of methods – netting, rod-and-line fishing, trapping – have provided information on growth performance, condition and diet. The tagging of individual fish has added to growth and condition data. Recaptures of some of the original July 1988 stock in September 1988, indicated an average 20% weight increase over the 77-day interval. Subsequent captures of fish of varied age class, predominantly those grown from indigenous spawned fish, provides a growth curve (Fig. 28.3) which can be compared favourably with that for fish from other Scottish lakes. Predictions of growth of trout fed maximum rations based on the Loch Fleet temperature regime (Elliott, 1975) are also comparable, indicating that food supply is not limiting. Growth of trout recaptured from the upper Little Water of Fleet has been analysed similarly and confirms that diet is not limiting. Comparison with trout from a selection of 41

Table 28.5   Population densities of brown trout, Fleet system, 1985–91.

Location	1985	1989	1990	1991
Outlet 0.05 km	0	0.040	0.044	0.14
Lime tanks 1.0 km	0	0.16	0.17	0.60
First bridge 2.1 km	0	0.021	0.14	0.14
Viaduct 4.6 km	0	0.025	0.011	0.01
C. Linn above 7.1 km	0	0.003	NF	0
C. Linn below 7.2 km	0.01	0.030	NF	0.04
Drumruck 9.1 km	0.05	0.19	0.08	0.04
Culreoch 11.5 km	0.02	0.30	0.08	0.10

Numbers.m^{-2} (excludes 0-group); NF = not fished. Distances are from lake outlet.

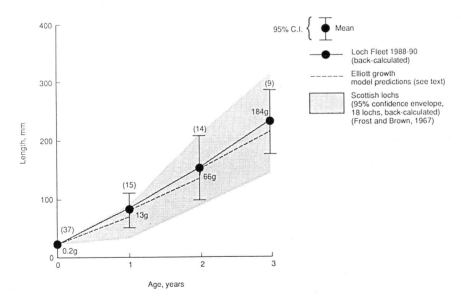

Fig. 28.3   Brown trout growth in limed Loch Fleet, compared with other Scottish lakes (number of fish in brackets).

other upland streams in UK (Turnpenny *et al.*, 1987) shows that rates of growth were good (Fig. 28.4). Condition factors (K) for trout captured from the lake (Table 28.6) remain at about 1.5.

Diets of captured trout have been analysed to determine the taxonomic breakdown of invertebrate groups (Figure 28.5). This indicates a high dependence on chironomids and terrestrial insects, the latter especially in rod-and-line caught fish, perhaps owing to their mode of capture. An important conclusion is that fish are catholic in their tastes and not wholly reliant on autochthonous food supplies, so that population growth is relatively independent of the supply of aquatic invertebrates.

28.3   Future prognosis and conclusions

28.3.1   *Liming effectiveness*

The calcium carbonate supplied by lime applications at Loch Fleet is expected to assure suitable water quality (including pH and aluminium levels) for some time to come. Calcium fluxes from lime treated sectors of the catchment and for the whole lake provide estimates of the time over which conditions suitable for trout will continue. These suggest that the lake itself will be able to maintain satisfactory conditions at least to the end of the century. The conditions in the Altiwhat stream (limed at a lower dose than that of a wetland source area) look likely soon to fall below target water quality (Figure 28.6), particularly during high flows associated

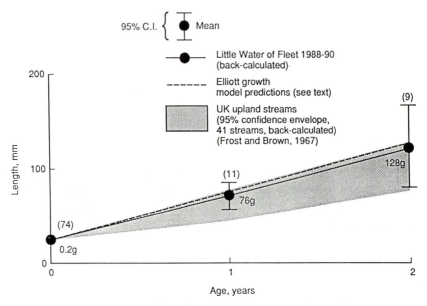

Fig. 28.4 Brown trout growth in Loch Fleet streams, compared with UK upland streams (number of fish in brackets).

Table 28.6 Condition factors of brown trout caught in Loch Fleet, 1988–91.

Year	1988 (Stocked)	1989	1990	1991
K (mean)	1.58	1.63	1.33	1.47
SD	0.22	0.38	0.38	0.10
Number	30	7	7	70

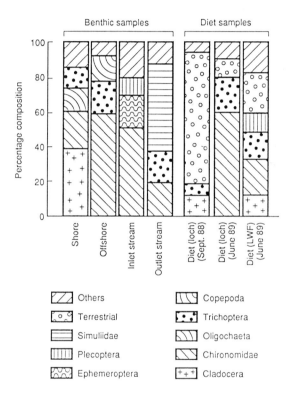

Fig. 28.5 Brown trout gut contents.

with snow melt or heavy rain (Dalziel *et al.*, 1992a). If such episodes occur during the early development of fry, loss of recruitment will follow, even though yearling and older fish may survive in the lake. A contribution of fry from a recently constructed spawning bed at the lake outlet may be able to maintain recruitment to the lake stock.

28.3.2   *Strain selection*

Fishery management together with catchment lime treatment could potentially extend the recovery of the Fleet system. Nothing is known of the stock provided by

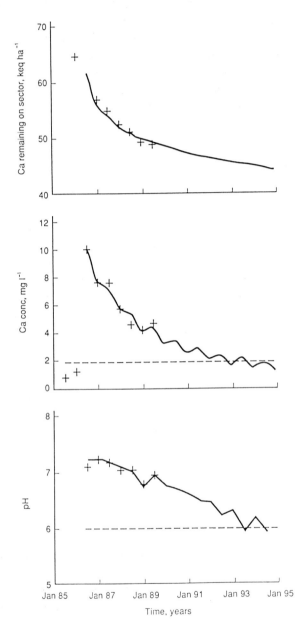

Fig. 28.6   Liming effectiveness predictions – pH, Ca – in the Altiwhat stream.

the fishery managers during the 1950s decline (or earlier). However, it is clear that separate strains of brown trout have different tolerance to acidic conditions. Even within local stocks, survival of acid exposure varied significantly (Turnpenny *et al.*, 1988). Recent observations on survival and development of Norwegian strains and a Scottish strain exposed to acidity and aluminium have shown that the latter compares poorly with Norwegian strains at 10 weeks post-hatch with adverse effects on body mineral content and the degree of skeletal calcification (Dalziel and Lynam, 1992).

28.3.3   *Fish population response to liming*

The recovery of the fish community of limed lakes and streams varies with the natural conditions, and also with the style of lime application. Where a lake turnover or stream flow is rapid, direct liming of waters produces only a transitory effect, possibly sufficient to protect spawning stock and young fry. At some sites repeated lime applications have to be made to maintain suitable water quality for fish. More stable and sustained conditions result from catchment liming, as at Loch Fleet. Recovery of the fish populations is often slow without restocking – in lakes downwind of the Sudbury smelter (Canada), massive emission reductions in 1970 quickly improved lake water quality, but fish populations began to recover only in 1982, and even now only half the lakes are suitable for lake trout (Gunn and Keller, 1990). Recovery of the acid treated Lake 223 (Canada), following reduced acid dosing, led to water quality returning to its previous status after three years. However, fish populations are also slow in recovering, with some species still absent in 1987 and trout recruitment poor (Baker *et al.*, 1990). Water quality improvements in limed Swedish lakes has led to a recolonisation by some fish species over a 13-year period, but minnow, Arctic char and brown trout are slow to do so (Bergquist, 1991).

28.3.4   *Acid waters and fishery management*

A combination of catchment liming and fishery management has led, at Loch Fleet, to sustained target water quality and brown trout recovery at this upland site. Water quality improved rapidly after liming, and included reduction of acidity, raised calcium concentrations, and reduced levels of toxic aluminium and trace metals. Restocking with local trout strains has quickly established an indigenous spawning population and growth and condition is good. The limited spawning potential of the tributary stream has been enhanced by construction of an artificial spawning run at the lake outflow. Satisfactory conditions for trout within the lake are likely to be maintained, at least to the end of the decade.

28.4   Summary

Water quality conditions sufficient for brown trout have been maintained in a limed upland lake for five years after limestone applications to the catchment. A pH >6.0, calcium >2 mg.l^{-1} and total aluminium 0.1 mg.l^{-1} is matched by good growth and condition, as well as annual recruitment to the population. The combination of catchment liming and fishery restocking has led to the sustained recovery of the former brown trout fishery at this site.

Acknowledgements

The Loch Fleet Project was supported by the Central Electricity Generating Board, South of Scotland Electricity Board, North of Scotland Hydro-Electric Board and National Coal Board (now National Power, PowerGen, ScottishPower, Scottish Hydro-Electric, British Coal).

References

Alabaster, J.S. and R. Lloyd, 1982. *Water Quality Criteria for Freshwater Fish*, 2nd edn. London, Butterworth.

Anderson, N.J. *et al.*, 1986. Palaeological evidence for the acidification of Loch Fleet. Department of Geography, University College, London, Working Paper no. 17, 71 pp.

Andersson, P. and P. Nyberg, 1984. Experiments with brown trout (*Salmo trutta*) during spring in mountain streams at low pH and elevated levels of iron, manganese and aluminium. *Rept.Inst.Freshw.Res.Drottningholm*, **61**: 34–47.

Backes, C.A. and E. Tipping, 1987. Aluminum complexation by an aquatic humic fraction under acidic conditions. *Water Res.*, **21**: 211–216.

Baker, J.P. *et al.*, 1990. Biological effects of changes in surface water acid–base chemistry. Washington DC, NAPA–Report No. 13. 331 pp.

Bergquist, N.C., 1991. Extinction and natural recolonization of fish in acidified and limed lakes. *J.Freshw.Res.*, **66**: 50–62.

Birchall, J.D. *et al.*, 1989. Acute toxicity of aluminium to fish eliminates in silicon-rich acid waters. *Nature*, **338**: 146–148.

Cameron, J.N., 1989. Acid–base regulation in fishes: 2 Biological responses and limitations. In: Morris, R. *et al.* (Eds.) *Acid Toxicity and Aquatic Animals*, pp. 99–112. Cambridge, Cambridge University Press.

Dalziel, T.R.K. and S. Lynam, 1992. Survival and development of four strains of Norwegian trout and one strain of Scottish trout (*Salmo trutta*) exposed to different concentrations of aluminium at two pH levels. PowerGen Report PT/92/330007/R.

Dalziel, T.R.K. *et al.*, 1992a. Targets and timescales of liming treatments. In: Howells, G. and T.R.K. Dalziel (Eds.) *Restoring Acid Waters: the Loch Fleet Project*, pp. 365–391 (Chapter 16). London, New York, Elsevier.

Dalziel, T.R.K., M.V. Proctor and K. Paterson, 1992b. Water quality of surface waters: before and after liming. In: Howells, G. and T.R.K. Dalziel (Eds.) *Restoring Acid Waters*, pp. 229–257 (Chapter 12). London, New York, Elsevier.

Driscoll, C.T. and W.D. Schecher, 1988. Aluminum in the environment. In: Siegel, H. and A. Sigel (Eds.) *Metal Ions in Biological Systems*, pp. 59–120. New York, Basel, Dekker.

Elliott, J.M., 1975. The growth rate of brown trout (*Salmo trutta* L.) fed on maximum rations. *J.Anim.Ecol.*, **44**: 805–821.

Frost, W.E. and M.E. Brown, 1967. *The Trout*. London, Collins.

Gubala, C.P. and C.T. Driscoll, 1991. Watershed liming as a strategy to mitigate acidic deposition in the Adirondack region of New York. In: Olem, H. *et al.* (Eds.) *International Lake and Watershed Liming Practices*, pp. 145–160. Washington DC, Terrene Institute.

Gunn, J.M. and W. Keller, 1990. Biological recovery of acid-stressed lakes near Coniston, Canada, following reduction of industrial emissions of sulphur. In: International Conference on Acidic Deposition: Its Nature and Impacts, Glasgow, 16–21 September 1990, Abstract p.151.

Hindar, A. and B.O. Rosseland, 1991. Liming strategies for Norwegian lakes. In: Olem, H. *et al.* (Eds.) *International Lake and Watershed Liming Practices*, pp. 173–192. Washington DC, Terrene Institute.

Howells, G. and T.R.K. Dalziel (Eds.), 1992. *Restoring Acid Waters: the Loch Fleet Project*. London, New York, Elsevier.

Howells, G. *et al.*, 1990. EIFAC water quality criteria for European freshwater fish: report on aluminium. *Chemistry and Ecology*, **4**: 117–173.

Lacroix, G.L. and K.T. Kan, 1986. Speciation of aluminum in acidic rivers of Nova Scotia supporting Atlantic salmon: a methodological examination. *Can.Tech.Rept.Fish.Aq.Sci.*, No. 1501. 12pp.

Lacroix, G.L. and D.R. Townsend, 1987. Responses of juvenile Atlantic salmon (*Salmo salar*) to episodic increases in acidity of Nova Scotian rivers. *Can.J.Fish.Aquat.Sci.*, **44**: 1475–1484.

MacDonald, D.G., J.P. Reader and T.R.K. Dalziel, 1989. The combined effects of pH and trace metals on fish ionoregulation. In: Morris, R. *et al.* (Eds.) *Acid Toxicity and Aquatic Animals*, pp. 221–242. Cambridge, Cambridge University Press.

Potts, W.T.W. and P.G. McWilliams, 1989. The effects of hydrogen and aluminium ions on fish gills. In: Morris, R. *et al.* (Eds.) *Acid Toxicity and Aquatic Animals*, pp. 201–220. Cambridge, Cambridge University Press.

Reader, J.R., T.R.K. Dalziel and R. Morris, 1988. Growth, mineral uptake and skeletal calcium deposition in brown trout, *Salmo trutta* L., yolk-sac fry exposed to aluminium and manganese in soft acid water. *J.Fish Biol.*, **32**: 607–624.

Skogheim, O.K. and B.O. Rosseland, 1984. A comparative study on salmonid fish species in acid aluminium-rich water. *Rept.Inst.Freshw.Res.Drottningholm*, **61**: 177–185.

Stoner, J.H. and A.P. Donald, 1991. Watershed liming – the Welsh experience. In: Olem, H. *et al.* (Eds.) *International Lake and Watershed Liming Practices*, pp. 193–210. Washington DC, Terrene Institute.

Thornelof, E. and E. Degerman, 1991. Lake liming in Sweden – case studies and general experiences. In: Olem, H. *et al.* (Eds.) *International Lake and Watershed Liming Practices*, pp. 41–60. Washington DC, Terrene Institute.

Turnpenny, A.W.H., 1992. Fishery restoration after liming. In: Howells, G. and T.R.K. Dalziel (Eds.) *Restoring Acid Waters*, pp. 259–287 (Chapter 13). London, New York, Elsevier.

Turnpenny, A.W.H. *et al.*, 1987. The fish populations of some streams in Wales and northern England in relation to acidity and associated factors, *J.Fish Biol.*, **31**: 415–434.

Turnpenny, A.W.H. *et al.*, 1988. Factors limiting fish populations in the Loch Fleet system, an acidic drainage system in southwest Scotland. *J.Fish Biol.*, **32**: 101–118.

Wood, C.M., 1989. The physiological problems of fish in acid waters. In: Morris, R. *et al.* (Eds.) *Acid Toxicity and Aquatic Animals*, pp. 125–152. Cambridge, Cambridge University Press.

Wright, R.F. and E. Snekvik, 1979. Acid precipitation: chemistry and fish populations in 700 lakes in southernmost Norway. *Verh.Internat.Verein.Limnol.*, **20**: 765–775.

Chapter 29
Observations on the development of fish populations in small acidified lakes in southern Finland during a four-year period after liming

J. RAITANIEMI[1] and M. RASK[2]

[1] Finnish Game and Fisheries Research Institute, Fisheries Division, PO Box 202, SF-00151 Helsinki, Finland
[2] Finnish Game and Fisheries Research Institute, Evo State Fisheries and Aquaculture Research Station, SF-16970 Evo, Finland

29.1   Introduction

Because of different catchment characteristics a considerable number of Finnish lakes have a naturally low alkalinity and are sensitive to acid deposition. It is estimated that 12% of Finnish lakes are acidic (ANC $\leq$0). Of these 4900 lakes (surface area 274 km^2), 45% are probably naturally acidic due to high concentrations of organic matter (Forsius, 1992). Those that are acidified due to airborne pollutants are mostly small headwater lakes situated in southern and central parts of the country. Fish populations affected by acidification are fairly common in lakes near the southern coast, south-eastern border, and the city of Tampere.

More than 100 Finnish lakes and ponds have been limed to reduce the effects of acidity (e.g. Alasaarela *et al.*, 1990). However, in most cases only chemical studies have been carried out and there are few biological data on the effects of liming. This paper summarises the findings for the structure of fish populations in eight small acidified lakes that were examined before or soon after liming in 1986 and 1987, and again in 1989 and 1991.

29.2   Material and methods

29.2.1   *The lakes studied*

The lakes studied are situated in two areas in southern Finland, lakes Havisevanjärvi, Kalliojärvi, Matalajärvi, and Rukojärvi (10 to 20 km north-east of the centre of Tampere) and lakes Iso Hanhilampi, Salminen, Syväjärvi, and Suurilampi in Miehikkälä, Ylämaa, and Taipalsaari, all of which are located close to the south-eastern border (Table 29.1).

The drainage areas of the lakes are characterised by rocky coniferous forests and/or ditched bogs. Suurilampi is situated on a ridge, close to a residential area. The vegetation in the shallow areas of the lakes consists of species like *Nuphar*

Table 29.1 Physical characteristics of lakes studied. Retention times are from Oravainen (1983), Silvo and Weppling (1989), and Water and Environment District of Tampere.

Lake	Area (ha)	Altitude (m)	Mean retention time (months)
Havisevanjärvi	37	117.7	6
Kalliojärvi	12	c.130	82
Matalajärvi	72	141.5	12
Rukojärvi	11	142.5	10
Iso Hanhilampi	15	48.3	11
Salminen	19	52.0	14
Suurilampi	4	77.7	16
Syväjärvi	26	35.1	42

lutea, Sparganium sp., *Isoetes* sp., and *Lobelia dortmanna. Equisetum fluviatile* was found in Havisevanjärvi and Rukojärvi. Matalajärvi is connected to a larger lake, Paalijärvi, by a narrow channel.

Before neutralisation the pH values were 5.3 to 5.7 in most lakes during the summer (Table 29.2); Salminen, however, was more neutral with a pH range of 5.7 to 6.2 (Oravainen, 1983, 1985; Silvo and Weppling, 1989).

The minimum pH values of the lakes have not been measured, but in the data from about 80 lakes of corresponding size and catchment area the lowest values have usually occurred in April during the snow melt period. At this time the pH is usually lower by 0.3 to 0.9 pH units and alkalinity by 0.03 to 0.05 mmol.l^{-1} than the summer values; however, the variance between years can be considerable.

The history of acidification has been examined by palaeolimnological methods only in Matalajärvi which was shown to be acidified by acid precipitation (Tolonen *et al.*, 1986). For the other lakes, the decreasing trend of the roach populations (Section 29.2.2) suggests a recent acidification, although the respective roles of precipitation and land use (bog ditching, etc.) cannot be separately identified.

The methods used for the liming of each lake are described in Raitaniemi and Rask (1990), and more details are given in Silvo and Weppling (1989) and Alasaarela *et al.* (1990). In July–August 1989, the alkalinity of Suurilampi and Kalliojärvi was still above 0.1 mmol.l^{-1}, while lowest values of 0.04 mmol.l^{-1} were found in Rukojärvi and Iso Hanhilampi. In August 1991 the alkalinity values were 0–0.02 mmol.l^{-1} lower than in 1989 (Table 29.2).

29.2.2   *Fish populations*

According to local informants, the populations of roach (*Rutilus rutilus*) had become sparse before the neutralisation of Havisevanjärvi, Matalajärvi, Rukojärvi, Salminen and Suurilampi. Before neutralisation, roach were believed to have disappeared completely from Kalliojärvi, where the last individuals were observed in the beginning of the 1960s, and from Syväjärvi, where the roach died after the bogs in the drainage area of the lake had been ditched at the beginning of the 1970s.

Table 29.2 The quality of surface water in the lakes before liming, and in 1989 and 1991 (mostly summer values). The sample from the stream flowing into Havisevanjärvi was taken in 1989 above the lime doser. Most of the analyses have been made in the laboratory of the Finnish Game and Fisheries Research Institute, Fisheries Division, according to Finnish standard methods for water analysis (SFS-standards).

Lake and year	pH	Alk. $(mmol.l^{-1})$	Colour $(mg.l^{-1}$ Pt)	Cond. $(mS.m^{-1})$	Hardn. $(mmol.l^{-1})$	Ca $(mmol.l^{-1})$	COD $(mg.l^{-1})$	Al_{tot} $(\mu g.l^{-1})$
Havisevanjärvi								
April 1983[π]	5.1	*0.01	100	3.6		0.05	15.0	220
Hav.stream 1989	5.9	0.06	160	2.9	0.09	0.06		321
1989	6.6	0.08	80	3.6	0.14	0.10	11.2	228
1991	6.4	0.06	85	3.6	0.20	0.04	13.6	218
Kalliojärvi 1984[•]	5.5	<0.01	[π]25	3.3		0.05	2.4	70
1989	7.0	0.10	10	3.6	0.16	0.10	4.6	22
1991	6.5	0.09	5	3.6	0.19	0.09	4.2	10
Matalajärvi 1982[π]	5.0		80	2.5		0.03	9.3	170
1989	6.3	0.05	40	2.3	0.10	0.05	7.4	57
1991	6.5	0.05	25	2.7	0.20	0.05	7.2	31
Rukojärvi 1982*	5.3	0.02	100	2.6		[π]0.05	[π]14.0	[π]430
1989	6.0	0.04	80	2.4	0.11	0.05	10.1	186
1991	5.9	0.03	65	2.5	0.26	0.06	11.8	195
Iso Hanhilampi 1987[#]	5.3		80	3.7			11.0	
1989	6.2	0.04	40	3.6	0.13	0.10	9.5	206
1991	5.7	0.03	50	3.4	0.28	0.08	8.4	262
Salminen 1986	6.4		20	4.3	0.14	0.08	6.4	49
1989	6.5	0.05	15	3.9	0.13	0.08	5.1	44
1991	6.3	0.04	15	4.0	0.30	0.07	5.7	67
Suurilampi 1986	5.3	0.03	5	2.0	0.07	0.03	2.3	50
1989	6.9	0.16	15	3.4	0.14	0.12	4.8	59
1991	6.5	0.16	10	2.9	0.31	0.11	4.1	10
Syväjärvi spring 1987[#]	5.4	0.02	10	3.8			3.0	
1989	6.8	0.08	10	3.5	0.14	0.10	4.2	12
1991	6.1	0.07	10	3.4	0.25	0.09	3.2	11

[#]   values from Silvo and Weppling (1989)
*   values from Oravainen (1983)
[•]   values from Oravainen (1985)
[π]   values from the Water and Environment District of Tampere (Ca, COD and Al of Rukojärvi Oct. 1986)

Another Cyprinid that can no longer be identified also occurred in Kalliojärvi, but it disappeared before roach. Other changes in the fish species composition of the lakes are not known to us.

Surveys of the fish populations were made using a series of gill nets of varying mesh sizes (details of sampling techniques, and age and growth determinations, are in Raitaniemi and Rask, 1990). The growth of roach and perch (*Perca fluviatilis*), hatched after liming, was compared to the pre-neutralisation data for older age classes at corresponding ages (Student's *t*-test). The dependence of the growth of different year classes of perch on liming and temperature was tested by two-way ANOVA.

29.3   Results

29.3.1   *The catches*

Perch has remained the dominant species in the catches from seven out of eight lakes in 1986–91. Roach were found in six lakes, and in one of them, Suurilampi, they occupied the dominant place after neutralisation. An increase in the numbers of roach in relation to perch was also observed in Rukojärvi and Havisevanjärvi. Ruffe (*Gymnocephalus cernua*), which was found in the catch from six lakes, has remained about as numerous after liming as before. Other, less numerous species in the catch are pike (*Esox lucius*, 5 lakes), stocked whitefish (*Coregonus lavaretus*, 6 lakes), rudd (*Scardinius erythrophthalmus*, 1 lake), vendace (*Coregonus albula*, 1 lake), crucian carp (*Carassius carassius*, 2 lakes), and stocked bream (*Abramis brama*, 1 lake). Rudd appeared in the catch from Suurilampi in 1991. No changes in the numbers of the other species could be detected (Figure 29.1). Most of the whitefish that were caught had been stocked before the liming (Kalliojärvi, Matalajärvi, Iso Hanhilampi, and Salminen).

29.3.2   *Effects on reproduction*

A clear increase in the populations of roach was found in Suurilampi and Rukojärvi. The roach populations of both lakes are dominated by the year-class hatched after liming. The rudd of Suurilampi consisted of the two year-classes from 1987 and 1988. A probable increase was also detected in Havisevanjärvi where young fish formed a considerable part of the roach population (Figure 29.2). Local anglers also caught more roach, both small and large, from Havisevanjärvi in 1989 than since the beginning of the 1970s. There were also a few young roach in the catch from Salminen, where older roach hatched before liming have not been subsequently caught.

  A strong year-class of perch was hatched in the warm year of 1988, but in the years just after liming, 1986 (Havisevanjärvi) and 1987 (Kalliojärvi and Syväjärvi), the year-classes were small or about average in the lakes inspected.

29.3.3   *Growth*

The roach hatched after the neutralisation in Suurilampi and Havisevanjärvi grew faster than had the older ones at the same age. The growth of the roach hatched a year or two before liming was faster after liming than that of the older fish at the same age before liming in Matalajärvi; in Salminen, however, statistically significant differences in growth rates were not found (Figure 29.3).

Four out of five old (i.e. >3 years) roach caught from Suurilampi had grown more in the summer after liming than in the year before. Among the other catches where the growth of old roach after liming could be measured (Matalajärvi 1983 and Havisevanjärvi 1987), some fish in Havisevanjärvi had increased their growth in 1987 and 1988, and some not until 1988.

The growth of different year-classes of perch varied between the lakes (Figure 29.4). The dependence of growth on temperature was most noticeable during the first summer, and could, for example, be seen when comparing the year-classes of a cool summer such as 1987 with the warm one of 1988. Both the strength and growth of the year-classes of perch were higher in 1988. Although temperature was a more

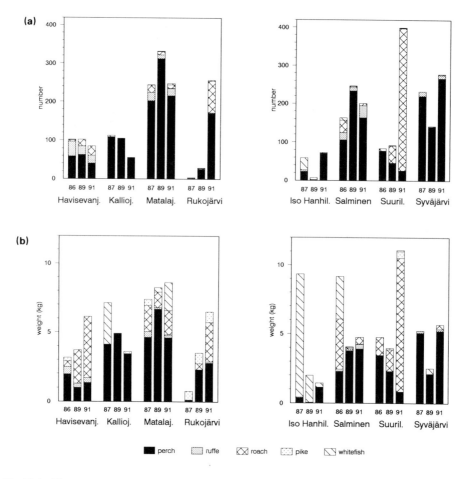

Fig. 29.1 The experimental catch (a) and yield (b) of fish from the lakes studied, before or in the year of liming (1986 or 1987), 2 or 3 years after liming (1989), and 4 or 5 years after liming (1991). In addition, there was one crucian carp in the 1987 catch from Havisevanjärvi (182 g), and one vendace in the 1989 catch (54 g) and two vendace in the 1991 catch (77 g) from Matalajärvi. Nine rudd (258 g) were also in the 1991 catch from Suurilampi, and one bream (232 g) in the 1991 catch from Iso Hanhilampi.

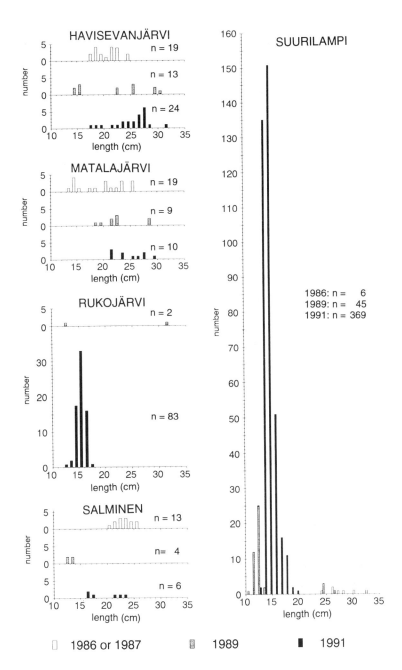

Fig. 29.2 The length distributions of roach in the catch from the lakes. The distribution of 1986 in Havisevanjärvi consists of fish from five nettings.

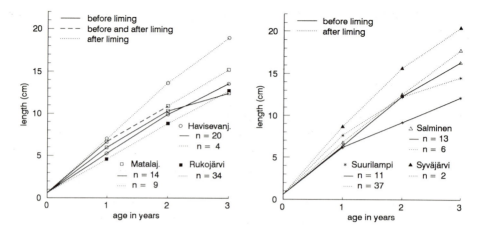

Fig. 29.3 The growth of roach in the lakes before and after liming. The growth of roach in Havisevanjärvi and Suurilampi was significantly faster after liming than before ($P < 0.001$). In Matalajärvi the roach born 1 or 2 years before liming (1986 and 1987, broken line) also grew faster in the summer after liming than older roach at the same age before liming ($P < 0.001$).

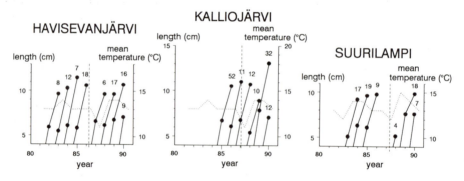

Fig. 29.4 The average growth of different year-classes of perch during their first and second year in three lakes. The liming is marked with a vertical broken line for each lake. The yearly mean air temperature of the growing period in the area (May–September, Tampere Härmälä and Lappeenranta Airport) is marked as a dashed line. The numbers of fish used in the calculations are marked above the dots. The significance of the effect of temperature (t) and liming (l) on the growth during the first summer was tested with two-way ANOVA in Havisevanjärvi (t: $P < 0.05$, l: $P < 0.01$), Kalliojärvi (t: $P < 0.001$, l: could not be tested), and Suurilampi (t: $P < 0.001$, l: $P < 0.05$, t*l: $P < 0.05$).

significant factor, liming also seemed to have a slight effect on the growth of young perch.

29.4   Discussion

On the basis of the studies included in the Finnish Acidification Project (HAPRO), roach is usually the most affected species among the fish communities of acidified lakes. From laboratory experiments, roach also seems to be one of the most acid-sensitive species (Tuunainen *et al.*, 1991, Vuorinen *et al.*, 1994). Roach populations have been observed to be clearly affected by acidity at pH 5.5 to 6.0. In these populations, young individuals are either few in number or absent (Almer *et al.*, 1974; Hultberg, 1985; Rask and Tuunainen, 1990; Tuunainen *et al.*, 1991).

In addition, several other fish species, especially perch, pike, and ruffe, but also such species as vendace, whitefish, burbot (*Lota lota*), and bream, have been affected by acidification (Tuunainen *et al.*, 1991). In some cases, fish species living in waters affected by acidification have been reported to have survived better after lime treatment of the water (Bengtsson *et al.*, 1980; Hasselrot and Hultberg, 1984; Nyberg *et al.*, 1986).

Recovery of a roach population similar to that observed in Suurilampi has also been described in a Swedish lake by Eriksson *et al.* (1983). The recovery in Suurilampi was probably associated with a sufficiently elevated alkalinity (0.16 mmol.l^{-1} still present in August 1991). In the other lakes with lower alkalinity values, the conditions have been probably more unstable and the success of roach more or less due to chance.

It is probable that in limed lakes, especially those with an alkalinity lower than about 0.10–0.15 mmol.l^{-1}, the acidic water flowing into the lakes during periods of high runoff can still affect the survival of the most sensitive species, particularly their eggs and fry, despite a higher pH in the summertime. The time of snow melt in the spring is considered to be the most critical period for the fish in limed lakes (Bengtsson *et al.*, 1980, Booth *et al.*, 1986). The early spring peak of acidity may also affect the gonad development of fish, even though the spawning, and thus the occurrence of most sensitive life stages of embryos and fry, takes place later in the spring. In some of the lakes within this study, low pH values have been measured in the springtime, for example, in Havisevanjärvi as low as 4.9, and in Matalajärvi 5.2–5.5 (J. Havu, pers. comm.). Such values are too low for roach to thrive (Tuunainen *et al.*, 1991; Vuorinen *et al.*, 1994).

The reason for the increase in the total catch of Rukojärvi in 1991 was probably that, exceptionally, the place where the nets were laid was changed, following the advice of a local inhabitant. However, his personal experience of the disappearance of roach before liming and their reappearance after liming indicated that a change in the roach population had indeed occurred. In Suurilampi the decrease in the catch of perch was apparently due to competition by roach.

Among the lakes where some recovery of the roach population was detected after liming, a probable decrease in Al_{tot} was found only in the humic lake Rukojärvi. The measured Al_{tot} value before liming, 430 $\mu g.l^{-1}$, is high despite the protecting effects of complexation between aluminium compounds and dissolved organic carbon (cf. Hutchinson and Sprague, 1987). Thus the decrease of aluminium content could have enabled the reproduction of roach despite the small increase in alkalinity after liming. In Havisevanjärvi the presence of humic substances probably enabled the survival and reproduction of roach after liming despite the high aluminium content, but aluminium may still have affected their reproduction and development as was observed in Suurilampi. In laboratory experiments aluminium (>100 $\mu g.l^{-1}$) affected the survival of newly hatched roach at pH ≤ 6.0 (Tuunainen *et al.*, 1991; Vuorinen *et al.*, 1994).

The increase in the growth of roach after neutralisation, as recorded in Suurilampi, may have been due to changes in the zooplankton and benthic invertebrate communities. In some studies of Swedish lakes, the richness in species composition and the number of planktonic crustaceans and benthic invertebrates increased after the lakes were limed (Hultberg and Andersson, 1982, Eriksson *et al.*, 1983). A decreased acid stress after neutralisation may also have contributed to the increase in growth. Acid stress has been shown to reduce the growth of some salmonids (Edwards and Hjeldnes, 1977; Rodgers, 1984) and whitefish (Vuorinen *et al.*, 1990). The increasing growth of some old roach in 1987, and some in 1988, in Havisevanjärvi was probably due to immigration of roach in succeeding years from the lower lake in the same water system (Raitaniemi and Rask, 1990).

Disturbances in the reproduction of perch are usually found in waters with pH lower than 5.0–5.5 (Runn *et al.*, 1977; Lappalainen *et al.*, 1988; Raitaniemi *et al.*, 1988), which is generally more acid than the lakes in this study were before liming. It is probable, therefore, that the pre-liming acidity of these lakes had little effect on the perch populations, and so neither did neutralisation. Eriksson and Tengelin (1987) found significantly increased catches of perch only in limed lakes which had a pH <4.9 before liming. However, Nyberg *et al.* (1986) obtained after liming double the catch of perch from lakes where roach also coexisted, so these lakes had probably had a pH higher than 5 before liming.

In Swedish perch populations with a normal reproduction and age composition, liming has sometimes led to a slight increase in growth rates, especially for older perch, but often no such effects have been observed (Nyberg, 1984; Nyberg *et al.*, 1986). In our study the mean temperature of the growing season seemed to regulate the growth of at least younger age-classes in such a way as to mask the potential effect of liming.

Therefore, in at least some of our acidification-prone lakes, liming has proved to be a successful way to maintain or restore the populations of even the most sensitive fish species, when an adequate method for liming is used. From the fisheries point of view, liming should be a part of a general programme of action for acidic lakes together with, for example, the introduction of sport fish. We believe that the increase in roach populations is not the response awaited by sports fishermen.

Acknowledgements

We would like to thank the staff of the Finnish Game and Fisheries Research Institute, Fisheries Division for working facilities. A. Lappalainen, L. Nuora and A. Järvinen took part in the test nettings. K. Nyberg made the age and growth determinations in 1991. H. Halme checked the language.

References

Alasaarela, E., J. Havu, K. Heikkinen and K. Weppling, 1990. Neutralization of acidified watercourses. In: Kauppi, P., K. Kenttämies and P. Anttila (Eds.) *Acidification in Finland*, pp. 1117–1126. Berlin, Heidelberg, Springer-Verlag.

Almer, B. *et al.*, 1974. Effects of acidification on Swedish lakes. *Ambio*, **3**: 30–36.

Bengtsson, B., W. Dickson and P. Nyberg, 1980. Liming acid lakes in Sweden. *Ambio*, **9**: 34–36.

Booth, G.M., J.G. Hamilton and L.M. Molot, 1986. Liming in Ontario: Short-term biological and chemical changes. *Water, Air and Soil Pollution*, **31**: 709–720.

Edwards, D. and S. Hjeldnes, 1977. Growth and survival of salmonids in water of different pH. SNSF-project, Norway, FR 10/77, 12 pp.

Eriksson, F. *et al.*, 1983. Ecological effects of lime treatment of acidified lakes and rivers in Sweden. *Hydrobiologia*, **101**: 145–164.

Eriksson, M.O.G. and B. Tengelin, 1987. Short-term effects of liming on perch *Perca fluviatilis* populations in acidified lakes in South-West Sweden. *Hydrobiologia*, **146**: 187–191.

Forsius, M., 1992. Acidification of lakes in Finland: regional estimates of lake chemistry and critical loads. Publications of the Water and Environment Research Institute. National Board of Waters and the Environment, Finland, Vol. 10. 37 pp.

Hasselrot, B. and H. Hultberg, 1984. Liming of acidified Swedish lakes and streams and its consequences for aquatic ecosystems. *Fisheries*, **9**(1): 4–9.

Hultberg, H., 1985. Changes in fish populations and water chemistry in lake Gårdsjön and neighbouring lakes during the last century. *Ecol.Bull.*, **37**: 64–72.

Hultberg, H. and I.B. Andersson, 1982. Liming of acidified lakes: Induced long-term changes. *Water, Air and Soil Pollution*, **18**: 311–331.

Hutchinson, N.J. and J.B. Sprague, 1987. Reduced lethality of Al, Zn, and Cu mixtures to American flagfish by complexation with humic substances in acidified soft waters. *Environ.Toxicol.Chem.*, **6**: 755–765.

Lappalainen, A., M. Rask and P.J. Vuorinen, 1988. Acidification affects the perch, *Perca fluviatilis*, populations in lakes of southern Finland. *Environ.Biol.Fish.*, **21**(3): 231–239.

Nyberg, P., 1984. Effects of liming on fisheries. *Phil.Trans.R.Soc.Lond.B*, **305**(11): 549–568.

Nyberg, P., M. Appelberg and E. Degerman, 1986. Effects of liming on crayfish and fish in Sweden. *Water, Air and Soil Pollution*, **31**: 669–687.

Oravainen, R., 1983. Kangasalan kunnan alueella sijaitsevien järvien perustutkimus 1982–1983 (The basic research of the lakes situating in Kangasala commune area 1982–1983; in Finnish). Tampere, Kokemäenjoen vesistön vesiensuoje-luyhdistys r.y.

Oravainen, R., 1985. Tampereen kaupungin järvien happamoitumis-selvitys 1984–1985 (The acidification study of the lakes in Tampere area 1984–1985; in Finnish). Tampere, Kokemäenjoen vesistön vesiensuojelu-yhdistys r.y. 175, 63 pp.

Raitaniemi, J. and M. Rask, 1990. Preliminary observations on the effects of liming to the fish populations of small acidic lakes in southern Finland. *Aqua Fennica*, **20**(1): 115–123.

Raitaniemi, J., M. Rask and P.J. Vuorinen, 1988. The growth of perch, *Perca fluviatilis* L., in small Finnish lakes at different stages of acidification. *Ann.Zool.Fennici*, **25**: 209–219.

Rask, M. and P. Tuunainen, 1990. Acid-induced changes in fish populations of small Finnish lakes. In: Kauppi, P., *et al.* (Eds.) *Acidification in Finland*, pp. 911–927. Berlin, Heidelberg, Springer-Verlag.

Rodgers, D.W., 1984. Ambient pH and calcium concentration as modifiers of growth and calcium dynamics of brook trout, *Salvelinus fontinalis*. *Can.J.Fish.Aquat.Sci.*, **41**: 1774–1780.

Runn, P., N. Johansson and G. Milbrink, 1977. Some effects of low pH on the hatchability of eggs of perch, *Perca fluviatilis* L. *Zoon*, **5**: 115–125.

Silvo, K. and K. Weppling, 1989. Pienvesistöjen kalkituskokeet Kymen läänissä 1986–1987 (Liming experiments of small lakes in South Eastern Finland 1986–1987; in Finnish, English summary). Helsinki, Vesi- ja ympäristö-hallituksen monistesarja, Vol. 151. 47 pp.

Tolonen, K. *et al.*, 1986. Acidification of small lakes in Finland documented by sedimentary diatom and chrysophycean remains. *Developments in Hydrobiology*, **29**: 169–199.

Tuunainen, P. *et al.*, 1991. Happaman laskeuman vaikutukset kaloihin ja rapuihin. Loppuraportti (Effects of acidic deposition on fish and crayfish. Final Report; in Finnish, English summary and legends). *Suomen Kalatalous*, **57**: 1–44.

Vuorinen, P.J., M. Vuorinen and S. Peuranen, 1990. Long-term exposure of adult whitefish (*Coregonus wartmanni*) to low pH/aluminium: effects on reproduction, growth, blood composition and gills. In: Kauppi, P., K. Kenttämies and P. Anttila (Eds.) *Acidification in Finland*, pp. 941–961. Berlin, Heidelberg, Springer-Verlag.

Vuorinen, P.J. *et al.*, 1994. The sensitivity to acidification of pike (*Esox lucius*), whitefish (*Coregonus lavaretus*) and roach (*Rutilus rutilus*). Comparison of field and laboratory studies. Chapter 25, this volume.

SECTION D
POPULATION AND COMMUNITY
EFFECTS

The relatively few papers included in this section (three out of the five presented to the Symposium) do not reflect the comparative level of activity in this area of research. As stated in the Introduction, the separation of the papers into Sections is to some extent artificial, and a number of contributions to previous Sections (especially Section C) include information on field effects. The following papers have field effects as their main focus, but the topics are clearly linked to those covered in the preceding papers.

Physicochemical analytical methods can never detect and identify all the polluting loads that occur in the environment, so that bioassays and bioindicators with endpoints such as mortality, growth rates, reproduction, induction of enzymatic systems or physiological alterations and changes in behaviour are required for the monitoring of dangerous substances in effluents and waterways. Some cases of the integration of effect-related parameters were given in this session.

For example it was shown that morphological changes in cyprinid fish gills can be useful for monitoring water pollution. The effect-related parameter methaemoglobin concentration in fish blood seems to be a good bioindicator for pollution for surface water by nitrite. However, methaemoglobin concentrations in fish blood expressed in absolute values are of less importance in fish physiology than its relative concentration since methaemoglobin is unable to transport oxygen and so at high relative concentration causes hypoxia.

Monitoring of pollutants, e.g. heavy metals (Cu, Zn, Pb, Cd), and chlorinated hydrocarbons (DDT, DDD, DDE, HCH, PCB) and their residues in fish of Hungarian water bodies showed that chemical contamination there does not reach a level which could acutely damage fish health and remains below the permissible values from the point of view of human consumption.

Finally, there is a real need for biological test systems (*in situ* bioassays) and on-line monitoring systems to identify situations where there may be damage to the waterways and their fish population. Only systems such as these are capable of recording the integrated effects caused by complex mixtures of harmful substances which may be released into the aquatic environment.

P.-D. Hansen, Session Chairman
L. Astic, Session Vice-Chairperson

Chapter 30
Fish gills as a monitor of sublethal and chronic effects of pollution

V. POLEKSIĆ and V. MITROVIĆ-TUTUNDŽIĆ

Faculty of Agriculture, University of Belgrade, Belgrade, former Yugoslavia

30.1   Introduction

In a degraded aquatic environment, particularly where pollutants occur at chronic and sublethal concentrations, changes in the structure and function of aquatic organisms occur more frequently than their mass mortality. Therefore, one of the possible methods for assessing the effects of pollutants on freshwater fish is to examine their organs for morphological changes.

Gills are a well-known target organ in fish, being the first to react to unfavourable environmental conditions (Lemke and Mount, 1963; Mallatt, 1985; Mitrović-Tutundžić and Poleksí, 1986; Bruno and Ellis, 1988; Couillard *et al.*, 1988; Temmink *et al.*, 1989). Vital functions are performed by the gills (e.g. respiration, osmoregulation and excretion); their permanent contact with the aquatic environment and the very large surface area of the secondary epithelium, which is not as protected as that of the skin and mouth, are the main reasons for the particular sensitivity of fish gills.

More than 20 years ago, when attempting to review the scattered and rather meagre literature data on the chronic effects of pollution on fish, we tried to formulate the concept of the term 'sublethal effects of pollution', including direct and indirect long-term effects on fish populations arising from damage to individual fish from unfavourable ecosystem changes (Mitrović, 1972).

Since then we have continued to study the morphological changes and damage in fish gills within natural fish populations from various Serbian rivers which are polluted to differing degrees, within fish from fish farms which receive mildly to moderately polluted water, and within fish from toxicity tests.

In this chapter we will give a brief review of some of the results obtained for fish from different locations, and attempt to describe and evaluate the type and intensity of morphological changes and damage, and correlate these to the intensity of pollution. Since most of the results reviewed here have been published in Yugoslavian journals, or are unpublished, we believe that some of the information will not be widely known.

30.1.1   *Case studies*

(a)   Fish kills in the River Jadro

In a very successful salmonid fish farm in Solin which has an excellent water supply from the River Jadro and an annual rainbow trout production of about 500 tonnes.ha^{-1}, increasing fish mortalities have occurred since the end of the 1970s, especially during summer months. In investigating the possible cause for this mortality, it was found that used oils, organic solvents, detergents and acids were occasionally discharged into the river from a small lorry service station situated upstream of the fish farm water supply. A histological analysis showed severe damage to the fish gills, although all other vital systems, except for some minor skin lesions, were normal. In 1980, from the springtime when fingerlings from the nearby hatchery supplied with clean water were transferred into the fish farm rearing ponds, up to the period of increased mortality at the end of summer, histological examination of the fish gills were carried out every two weeks. It was found that the fingerlings had normal healthy gills but that gill damage was then progressive and became very severe at the period of increased mortality, which was when the water temperature was at its highest (up to 20°C).

These findings were not published because we could not obtain sufficiently accurate data on the actual concentrations of oils in ponds which varied with the work being done at the service station, but the concentrations of mineral oils and detergents in the effluent were quite high (293 mg.l^{-1} fat, 74 mg.l^{-1} mineral oils and 4.4 mg.l^{-1} detergents). In the River Jadro endemic trout (*Salmo krkensis*) were still present, but the gills of the few fish which were examined were severely damaged. In 1981 the pollution of the river was stopped and the mortalities ceased.

(b)   Fish kills in the Sava in 1990

In 1989, a histological study of fish gills was carried out on fish caught at different locations in the lower part of the River Sava; pronounced alterations and damage were found in the gills of fish from almost all the sites.

In spring of 1990, for a period of about a month, there occurred in this part of the Sava an increased mortality of large mature fish, mainly Danubian wels (*Silurus glanis*). At this time chemical analyses showed that the water quality was quite good (corresponding to II class or β-mesosaprobic); at other periods, depending on the water flow the quality varies from mildly to heavily polluted (III–IV class or α-mesosaprobic to polysaprobic). By carrying out additional analyses of the dead fish, the water and the bottom sediments it was found that although the concentrations of heavy metals and some persistent pesticides in the water were much lower than the permissible levels, they were much higher in the sediments and the fish. Using the histological data and the analytical results for the period of the fish kills, it was concluded that the mortality occurred when a very sudden temperature

Table 30.1   Rivers in Serbia investigated 1977–90.

	1977	1978	1979	1980	1981	1982	1983	1984	1985	1986	1987	1988	1989	1990
Velika Morava and its tributaries	+	+	+											
Južna Morava and its tributaries				+	+	+	+							
Zapadna Morava and its tributaries								+	+					
Timok river basin					+	+	+	+						
Lower reaches of the Sava and its tributaries										+	+	+	+	+

rise (unusual for early spring) occurred, and the fish became very active after a winter spent resting on the river bed and, weakened by chronic poisoning, died.

30.2   Fish populations investigated by histological analysis

In order to investigate as many fish gills as possible, we carried out a histological analysis on the gills of fish from three different groups of populations of Cyprinids:

(1)   Natural fish populations (mainly barbel, *Barbus barbus*, and chub, *Leuciscus cephalus*) from the largest rivers in Serbia;

(2)   Cultured mirror carp (*Cyprinus carpio*) populations from four Cyprinid fish farms;

(3)   Mirror carp fry populations from toxicity tests.

30.2.1   *Natural fish populations*

Since 1977 we have investigated gills from natural fish populations from almost all the river systems in Serbia (Table 30.1). This formed part of a study of the chronic effects of pollution on fish populations which was included in the project 'Study of the pollution of surface and ground waters in Serbia, and the protection measures'.

We have investigated different sectors of the rivers, from the upper regions (mostly Salmonid), through to the middle reaches, to the lower stretches (mostly Cyprinid). The degree of pollution in these rivers varies with the fluctuation in water level throughout the year. Except for the headwaters, the rivers investigated were moderately to heavily polluted, mostly retaining the characteristics of a second-class water quality (β-mesosaprobic, changing occasionally to α-mesosaprobic or even polysaprobic level) with some areas where toxic pollution occurred (e.g. locations in Timok, Južna Morava and Zapadna Morava), and a few fishless areas (e.g. in the Veliki Timok, Zapadna Morava and Borska rivers) (Mitrović-Tutundžić *et al.*, 1982; Grubić *et al.*, 1982; Mitrović-Tutundžić *et al.*, 1985; Poleksić *et al.*, 1988).

30.2.2   *Carp populations from fish farms*

As a part of the project 'Investigation in aquaculture development' during the period 1986–89, we have investigated four Cyprinid fish farms. The gills of carp from this specific pond ecosystem (i.e. shallow, warm, eutrophic water) were examined to find whether there was a connection between gill morphology and the water quality which was analysed at the same time. The investigations were carried out in the ponds Mika Alas, Ečka (Belo Jezero), Baranda (Sakule lake) and Živača.

Results of the physical, chemical and biological parameters studied have shown that changes in the chemical characteristics of water and bottom sediments, and in the structure and composition of plankton and bottom fauna have occurred in all ponds. The changes were of different magnitude in each of these ponds. Among the most important physicochemical changes in all of them, however, was the formation of thick bottom sediments, and the associated increase in the organic matter content and degradation products, which caused a deterioration in the oxygen regime. In Mika Alas, Sakule and Živača the quantity of fish food organisms available decreased during the most important period of the growing season, and blooms of some groups of algae (which never build up high densities in ponds with good water quality) occurred (Blagojević and Mitrović-Tutundžić, 1991; Mitrović-Tutundžić and Vidmanić, 1991).

30.2.3   *Fish from toxicity tests*

The structural changes in carp gills that occurred in sublethal bioassays with several pollutants were analysed in order to see whether certain lesions occur after exposure to specific pollutants. In contrast to the situation in rivers and fish ponds, where the environmental degradation is due to a permanent or sporadic uncontrolled pollution of differing intensity and type, in laboratory bioassays it is possible to study the effects of pollutants on test organisms exposed under controlled conditions.

Using established test procedure guidelines (OECD No. 203, 1983/1987, Anonymous, 1983) 14-day semistatic sublethal toxicity tests were carried out, followed (in the test with copper sulphate) by a 'recovery' period of the same duration. The dilution water was dechlorinated and aerated Belgrade tap-water of a medium hardness (about 12.5° dH) and with average values of pH 7.3 and conductivity 470 μS.cm^{-1}. In our laboratory, tests are mostly carried out on pesticides (at acute and subacute concentrations), but in this chapter we are presenting only the results for copper sulphate.

30.3   Histological analysis and classification

Gills of fish from the three above-mentioned population groups were removed immediately after they were caught and sacrificed, and then fixed in 4% neutral formaldehyde. They were prepared for microscopical examination using standard histological techniques and a haematoxylin/eosin stain. Structural alterations in the gill are not type-specific but depend on the chemical concentration (i.e. the intensity of the irritant); therefore, the type and severity of changes are determined by the intensity of the pollutant, especially in the case of low and moderate concentrations (Mitrović, 1972; Temmink *et al.*, 1983; Mallatt, 1985; Mitrović-Tutundžić and Poleksić, 1986).

As fish are poikilothermic aquatic vertebrates, they have a limited variety of tissue and thus their pathological response is relatively restricted (Roberts, 1989). However, the characteristics of the fish respiratory and osmoregulatory apparatus described in the Introduction make the study of structural changes in the gills a method of choice in the investigation of sublethal and chronic effects of pollution on freshwater fish morphology.

30.3.1   *Review of the literature*

Since the appearance of the earliest works on fish gill pathology (Osburn, 1910, cited in Eller, 1975), the majority of subsequent studies dealt with changes caused by known pollutants, usually obtained under laboratory conditions. Of more than 100 studies published up to 1985, only six were on changes found in field studies (Mallatt, 1985).

There have been attempts to classify fish gill structural changes. To our knowledge the first classification of 'gill diseases' was published in 1957 by Wood and Yasutake, dividing them into nutritional and bacterial gill diseases.

The first review on this subject, published by Eller in 1975, presented an overview of freshwater gill lesions and the classification of causative agents.

In *Fish Pathology* (Roberts, 1989), the classification of gill lesions is based on three types of pathological responses: (1) lamellar oedema, (2) lamellar hyperplasia, and (3) lamellar fusion.

Hibiya (1982) also classified changes in gill morphology into three categories: (1) degenerative changes, (2) circulation anomalies, and (3) progressive degeneration.

A most detailed description and a classification of fish gill structural changes was given by Mallatt; he made a statistical review of the literature, compared the data according to several criteria, and proposed 15 classes of irritant-induced gill alterations (Mallatt, 1985).

30.3.2   *Proposal of the classification of freshwater fish structural changes*

Investigation of morphological changes of fish gills made over several years allowed us to construct a classification of alterations that appear in Cyprinid fish gills under the effect of unfavourable environmental conditions.

In respect of the normal morphological structure, we can distinguish 26 different types of gill lesion. We have classified these lesions according to two criteria.

First criterion

The first criterion classifies gill lesions, based on the type and location of the damaged gill tissue, into five main groups:

(a) hypertrophy and hyperplasia of gill epithelia and related changes,
(b) changes in the mucous and/or chloride cells,
(c) gill parasites,
(d) blood vessel changes,
(e) terminal stages.

Second criterion

The second criterion – of severity, is based on the scope for repair of the lesions, i.e. the possibility that a normal morphological structure will be restored after an improvement in the environmental conditions, or the cessation of pollution.

With regard to this second criterion we have classified gill lesions into three progressive stages:

First stage: Changes that do not damage the gill tissues to such an extent that with an improvement in environmental conditions the reconstruction of normal gill structure and function cannot occur. Under unchanged environmental conditions such lesions can persist, but in the case of long-term exposure, the changes will probably progress to the second stage.

Second stage: Changes that are more severe, leading to effects on the associated tissue function. Second-stage lesions are repairable in the event of water quality amelioration, but, if large areas of gill are damaged or in chronic pollution situations, then, if the level of pollution increases, or with a deterioration in other environmental conditions (temperature, pH, DO, etc.), the changes could endanger the functions of the gill and could lead, in chronic pollution situations, to changes of the third stage.

Third stage: Restoration of the structure of the gills is not possible when alterations of the third stage occur. Even with an improvement in water quality or the cessation of toxic exposure, changes occurring at this stage will lead, sooner or later, to damage of vital gill functions, and even mortality.

Table 30.2 contains a list of the 26 types of Cyprinid gill lesions that we propose, together with a classification of the changes according to the criteria used.

30.3.3   *Mathematical equation for the calculation of the degree of gill damage*

Within the second criterion of classification, we have attempted to quantify the degree of change observed in a single fish gill. We assumed empirically that the kinetics of the changes seen have an exponential growth. For this reason we assigned corresponding values (stage indices) to the three different stages of change:

Table 30.2   List of gill lesions.

	Stage
(a) Hypertrophy and hyperplasia of gill epithelia	
Hypertrophy of respiratory epithelium	I
Lifting of respiratory epithelial cells	I
Leukocyte infiltration of gill epithelium	I
Thinning of respiratory epithelium	I
Rupture and peeling of the lamellar epithelium	II
Focal hyperplasia of epithelial cells	I
Hyperplasia from the base to approximately half the length of the secondary lamella	I
Irregular ('chaotic') hyperplasia of epithelial cells	I
Fusion of the tips of secondary lamellae	I
Hyperplasia of sponge-like eosinophilic cells	I
Fusion of the primary lamellae tips	I
Uncontrolled thickening of proliferated tissue	II
Fusion of several secondary lamellae	I
Shortening of secondary lamellae	I
Complete fusion of all the secondary lamellae	II
(b) Changes in mucous and/or chloride cells	
Hypertrophy and hyperplasia of mucous cells	I
Empty mucous cells or their disappearance	I
Hypertrophy and hyperplasia of chloride cells	I
Chloride cells present in secondary lamellae	I
(c) Blood vessel changes	
Lamellar telangiectasis	I
Filament blood vessel enlargement	I
Haemorrhages with rupture of epithelium	II
Stasis	II
(d) Gill parasites	I
(e) Terminal stages	
Scar tissue – fibrosis	III
Necrosis	III

(a) for the first stage: 10^0
(b) for the second stage: 10^1
(c) for the third stage: 10^2

Of the total of 26 types of gill change, 19 belong to the first stage, five to the second and two to the third.

The sum of the number of lesion types within each of the three stages multiplied by the stage index as above represents the numerical value of the degree of damage in a single fish gill, i.e.

$$I = \sum_{i=1}^{19} a_i + 10 \sum_{i=1}^{5} b_i + 10^2 \sum_{i=1}^{2} c_i$$

where I is   the degree of changes in a single fish gill
       a =   first stage alterations
       b =   second stage alterations
       c =   third stage alterations

This method of calculating a value of I makes it possible to compare the degree of tissue change in a large number of fish from different situations of pollution, and to correlate the intensity of pollution with the intensity of the changes found.

30.3.4   *Application of the mathematical equation to derive categories of gill damage*

The gill tissue of each fish was submitted to a histological examination followed by a calculation of the degree of changes observed (I values). In analysing the data obtained, we have tried to develop a scale of numerical values of I, in order to evaluate the degree of damage in each gill examined. From these results it became clear that gills of fish from the same location, or from the same fish pond, or from the same pollutant concentration (as the function of the time of exposure) had similar I values. This made it possible to compare the severity of the changes with the intensity of pollution.

In our experience, the scale of the I values and the associated effects is as follows:

I values	*Effects*
0–10	Functionally normal gills
11–20	Slightly to moderately damaged gills
21–50	Moderately to heavily damaged gills
>100	Irreparably damaged gills

The absence of the category representing an I range of 51–100 needs an explanation. In our investigations, we never obtained such I values; this might support our hypothesis of the exponential nature of the development of gill lesions.

After the gills were examined and the degree of change calculated, we calculated the frequency of the four categories of gill damage within the population groups sampled. Such analyses were carried out on:

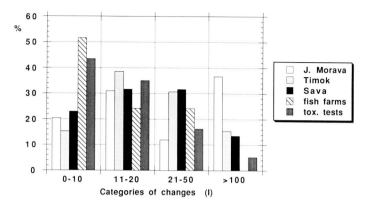

Fig. 30.1 Frequency of the four categories of change in the fish populations examined.

(a) 49 fish from the Južna Morava, 26 fish from the Timok river basin, 44 fish from the lower reaches of the Sava (total of 119 fish from natural populations);
(b) 33 fish from four fish ponds;
(c) 92 fish from toxicity tests with acute and subacute concentrations of copper sulphate. Student's *t*-test was used for the analysis of statistical significance of the data obtained.

Figure 30.1 shows the frequency of the four categories of changes found in the populations sampled. Data given for natural populations are the aggregated results from all the sites which were investigated; in that way sites with different levels of pollution have been included, thus reflecting the average state throughout the river length. Samples were usually collected during the period of low (autumn) water levels.

From Figure 30.1 it can be seen that in the Južna Morava there was about 20% of fish with functionally normal gills ($I = 0–10$). Fish with such gills were from the less polluted locations. About 43% of fish gills were damaged, but with reversible changes. A relatively high percentage (about 37%) of fish had irreversibly damaged gills, and these were caught in the most heavily polluted parts of the Južna Morava and its tributaries.

In the Timok river basin, 15% of the fish examined had a more or less normal gill structure and all were from the Trgoviški Timok. Thirty-nine per cent of fish had *I* values between 11 and 20, and 31% from 21 to 50, making a total of 70% of fish with reversible effects. Fifteen per cent of fish had irreversibly damaged gills, and these were from the most polluted rivers containing mixed inorganic and organic pollution (Crni, Beli and Veliki Timok).

In the lower reaches of the Sava and its tributaries, as many as 23% of fish had normal gill structures. More than 60% of fish had slightly to heavily damaged gills, but with reversible effects, and only 14% had gills that were irreversibly damaged.

All these results are in agreement with the results of the water quality investigations made at the same time.

Half of the fish from fish farms had functionally normal gills, and about 50% of the pond carp gills examined were reversibly affected. No fish was found with terminal effects, which agrees with the results from other methods of water quality assessment.

In the toxicity tests with copper sulphate, fish from all the acute and subacute concentrations as well as those from the control, two 'no effect' concentrations and the recovery tests, were combined in the test fish group to avoid bias. Within this group, more than 40% had normal gills, and about 35% of the gills were slightly affected. Sixteen per cent of the gills from the toxicity tests were moderately to heavily damaged, and 5% were irreversibly affected.

30.4   Discussion

The list of lesions given in Table 30.2 arising from the histological programme contains 26 types of gill alteration. Such a detailed list is given in order to emphasise the large number of symptoms that can occur in fish gills, and which are detectable by light microscopy and standard staining techniques. Some of the lesions are, in fact, only different histological appearances, or differing degrees of the same process. For example:

(a) Hyperplasia is represented by several different 'lesions' depending on the mechanism, or the rapidity of occurrence, or the location and the manner of spreading over the gill structure.

(b) Different histological symptoms can appear simultaneously or separately as part of the inflammatory reaction. Although not recognised by Mallatt (1985), lesions such as the lifting of the respiratory epithelium, leukocyte infiltration, some of the blood vessels changes, and oedema indicate an acute inflammation, as well as the hyperplasia and scar processes which are chronic effects.

(c) Among the blood vessel effects, a distinction has been made between lamellar telangiectasis and stasis because, in our opinion, it is possible from a histological examination to see telangiectasis as a dilation of the terminal blood vessel of the secondary lamella (marginal channel) (Evans, 1987; Roberts, 1989), and stasis in this and other blood vessels as a congestion of blood cells (Mallatt, 1985).

(d) A similar distinction (using their different histological appearance) was made for the two lesions designated as terminal stages. Although necrosis could be preceded by the scarring process (mostly in sublethal situations), this lesion can also occur in most of the highly toxic (lethal) exposures.

In our investigations we also calculated the frequency of lesions in the population studied (data not shown), because this frequency, when compared with different types of pollution could give an indication of the cause of poisoning or the persistence of pollution. However, at times the frequency of some of the lesions sometimes seemed to be independent of the pollutional situation. It is obvious that some of the symptoms listed are not, or are rarely encountered, in some fish populations (parasites in fish used in toxicity tests, terminal stages in commercial fish ponds). By definition, toxicity tests are carried out under specific pathogen-free (SPF) conditions, and the water quality of fish ponds should never be so poor as to lead to significant mortality. However, some lesions are present regardless of the population status and pollutional situation.

In more than 50% of all the gills examined, lifting of the respiratory epithelium was found, as well as other changes. The same applies to complete fusion, which was found in 30–40% of all the gills examined. In both cases there was no statistically significant difference between the populations sampled. The explanation may be that lifting of the epithelium, as well as massive hyperplasia which leads to a complete fusion, are typical defence mechanisms of the gills in that both increase the barrier between water and blood. Epithelial lifting is thought to be an initial response of the branchial apparatus (Smart, 1976; Segers *et al.*, 1984) and can be induced by low doses of toxicants (Roberts, 1989), while the fusion of all the secondary lamellae is induced by higher doses of toxicants (Temmink *et al.*, 1989; Poleksić, unpublished results), or as a 'final' result of hyperplasia in long-term sublethal poisoning.

For the classification of symptoms we used the criterion of reversibility, as found in our toxicity tests and from data in the literature. Four categories of gill damage were established, and the results have shown that our system of classification could be used as an additional means of estimating the average level of pollution in watercourses. In order to see whether this hypothesis was correct we calculated the frequency of occurrence of the categories of gill damage (Fig. 30.1). The results obtained confirmed that, in the rivers studied, chronic toxic and mixed pollution was present because a lower-than-normal percentage of fish had functionally normal gills; also, that among other effects, the irreversible changes were present in a relatively high percentage of fish, especially in those from the Južna Morava and other heavily polluted parts of the rivers studied. Statistical analysis showed that fish from the Sava and its tributaries had gills which were damaged to a lesser extent than those from the Timok and the Južna Morava, but this finding could be misleading because it is possible for fish from the Sava river to migrate into the Danube, or to other unpolluted parts of the biggest Yugoslav river or tributaries and vice versa. The data from the chemical and biological investigations of the Sava river support this conclusion because the water quality varies between the second and the fourth class throughout the year, depending on the water flow.

More than 50% of the gills from pond fish were functionally normal which, together with those which were slightly to moderately damaged, makes a total of more than 70% with normal and slightly damaged gills. This percentage corresponds to another finding from this overall study (data not shown) in that about 70% of the gills from farmed fish had portions with a normal morphological structure. Also, the most frequent lesions found in pond fish gills belonged to the first stage, while among the second stage alterations, only complete lamellar fusion and blood vessel stasis were found at a higher frequency (39% and 24% respectively). A high percentage of normal gills, and the absence of those irreversibly changed, indicate that the water of these ponds was still of an acceptable quality, although some parameters (O_2, NH_3) occasionally exceeded the maximum permissible concentrations, leading to the appearance of the so-called EDG (environmental gill disease; Klontz *et al.*, 1985). This uncontrolled thickening of proliferated tissue was commonly found in the gills of carp from the ponds with the poorest water quality and a high stock density.

It must be emphasised that the frequency of occurrence of categories of gill damage in the toxicity tests with $CuSO_4$ was calculated from a single sample containing all the fish that were used, including the control fish and fish from the recovery tests. Again, these results showed that the intensity of gill damage depends on the pollutant concentration and on the time of exposure as well as on the time of recovery in clean water.

30.5   Conclusions

These results show that structural change in fish gills can be used for monitoring the sublethal and chronic effects of pollutants, particularly in those cases where other methods of assessment are not satisfactory, and to complement the assessment of the average level of pollution.

It should be emphasised, however, that the results show that fish gills can maintain their vital functions even when some lamellae are heavily damaged; this finding was also reported by Brown *et al.* (1968).

Therefore, we propose that morphological changes in fish gills should become one of the methods used for water quality assessment in sublethal and chronic situations, with the following conditions;

(a) A minimum of 10 fish per location should be analysed and the mean value of *I* calculated;
(b) The types of gill structure change must always be uniformly assessed;
(c) The values obtained for *I* should be presented together with the results of other methods of assessment;
(d) The mode of life and type of feeding of the fish must be taken into consideration.

The study of fish gill structural changes could also be used to investigate the effects of specific pollutants on fish and for a prediction of further effects on fish communities in some chronically polluted rivers.

In subacute and chronic toxicity tests, fish gill morphological changes could also be studied together with other parameters (e.g. biochemical, physiological, behavioural). This could be a relatively sensitive method for estimating the harmful effects of different concentrations of a specific pollutant, and the long-term damage to fish exposed to different levels for a limited period.

A more precise measure for gill damage might be obtained by morphometric analysis, and the use of electron microscopy, or at least different staining techniques for light microscopy. An attempt to estimate the proportion of gill area affected, compared to that functionally normal (isolated areas of damage is a relatively common finding) could also increase the precision of the analysis (R. Lloyd, personal communication).

We would expect that similar results will be obtainable with other fish species, but more information must be gained on their normal gill histology.

Fish gill structural changes can also be used in water quality monitoring where the most satisfactory results will be obtained with fish held in cages.

References

Anonymous, 1983. OECD Guideline for testing of chemicals No. 203. Fish acute toxicity test. Organization for Economic Cooperation and Development, Paris, 1983, and Eco.87.1.(Update of Guideline 203), OECD, 1987.

Blagojević, S. and V. Mitrović-Tutundžić, 1991. Study of the environmental conditions in four Cyprinid fish farms. I. Principal physical and chemical conditions of water and bottom sediments of fish ponds. *Ichthyologia*, **23**(1): 1–15.

Brown, V.M., V.V. Mitrović and G.T.C. Stark, 1968. Effects of chronic exposure to zinc on toxicity of a mixture of detergent and zinc. *Water Res.*, **2**: 255–263.

Bruno, D.W. and A.R. Ellis, 1988. Histopathological effects in Atlantic salmon, *Salmo salar* L., attributed to the use of tributyltin antifoulant. *Aquaculture*, **72**: 15–20.

Couillard, C.M., R.A. Berman and J.C. Panisset, 1988. Histopathology of rainbow trout exposed to a bleached kraft pulp mill effluent. *Arch.Environ.Contam.Toxicol.*, **17**: 319–323.

Eller, L.L., 1975. Gill lesions in freshwater teleosts. In: *The Pathology of Fishes*, pp. 305–331. Wisconsin, Ribelin and Migaki.

Evans, D.H., 1987. The fish gill: site of action and model for toxic effects of environmental pollutants. *Environ.Health.Perspect.*, **71**: 47–58.

Grubić, G., D. Janković and V. Mitrović-Tutundžić, 1982. Uticaj zagadivanja suspendovanim materijama rudnika uglja Rembas na ihtiofaunu Resave, pritoke Velike Morave. *Ekologija*, **17**(1): 39–53.

Hibiya, T., 1982. *An Atlas of Fish Histology. Normal and Pathological Features*. Tokyo, Stuttgart, New York, Kodansha, Gustav Fischer Verlag.

Klontz, G.W., B.C. Stewart and D.W. Eib, 1985. On the etiology and pathophysiology of environmental gill disease in juvenile salmonids. In: *Fish and Shellfish Pathology*. London, Academic Press.

Lemke, A.E. and D.I. Mount, 1963. Some effects of alkyl benzene sulfonate on the bluegill, *Lepomis macrochirus*. *Trans.Am.Fish.Soc.*, **92**(4): 372–378.

Mallatt, J., 1985. Fish gill structural changes induced by toxicants and other irritants: a statistical review. *Can.J.Fish.Aquat.Sci.*, **42**: 630–648.

Mitrović, V.V., 1972. Sublethal effects of pollutants on fish. In: *Marine Pollution and Sea Life*, pp. 252–257. Oxford, Fishing News Books.

Mitrović-Tutundžić, V. and V. Poleksić, 1986. Uticaj zagadjenja na histološku gradju škrga riba. *Pesticidi*, **3/1986**: 125–130.

Mitrovič-Tutundžić, V. and L. Vidmanić, 1991. Study of the environmental conditions in four Cyprinid fish farms. II. Biological characteristics of ponds. *Ichthyologia*, **23**(1): 37–45.

Mitrović-Tutundžić, V., D. Janković and I. Elezović, 1982. Chronic effects of pollution on the ichthyofauna of the Velika Morava river. *Ichthyologia*, **14**(2): 135–146.

Mitrović-Tutundžić, V., V. Poleksić and D. Janković, 1985. Uticaj zagadjenja na škrge riba u vodama sliva Timoka. *Ichthyologia*, **17**(1): 13–27.

Poleksić, V. *et al.*, 1988. Kontaminacija donjeg dela toka Save pesticidima i morfološke promene na škrgama prirodnih populacija riba. *Pesticidi*, **3**(1): 11–17.

Roberts, R.J., 1989. *Fish Pathology*. London, Bailliere Tindall. 467pp.

Segers, J.H.L. *et al.*, 1984. Morphological changes in the gill of carp (*Cyprinus carpio* L.) exposed to acutely toxic concentrations of methyl bromide. *Water Res.*, **18**(11): 1437–1441.

Smart, G., 1976. The effect of ammonia exposure on gill structure of the rainbow trout *(Salmo gairdneri)*. *J.Fish Biol.*, **8**: 471–475.

Temmink, J.H.M. *et al.*, 1983. An ultrastructural study of chromate-induced hyperplasia in the gill of rainbow trout (*Salmo gairdneri*). *Aquat.Toxicol.*, **4**: 165–179.

Temmink, J.H.M. *et al.*, 1989. Acute and subacute toxicity of bark tannins in carp (*Cyprinus carpio*). *Water Res.*, **23**(3): 341–344.

Wood, E. M. and T. Yasutake, 1957. Histopathology of fish. V. Gill disease. *Progr.Fish-Cult.*, **19**: 7–13.

Chapter 31
The use of methaemoglobin concentration to measure sublethal effects in fish

J. PALÁČKOVÁ [1] and Z. ADÁMEK[2]

[1] *Department of Fisheries and Hydrobiology, University of Agriculture, Zemědělská 1,*
613 00 Brno, Czech Republic
[2] *Research Institute of Fish Culture and Hydrobiology, 389 25 Vodňany, Czech Republic*

31.1   Introduction

A deterioration in water quality can be caused by the presence of a very wide range of substances and result in adverse effects on the physiological and biochemical processes in aquatic organisms. Among these substances, nitrite is of considerable importance due to its toxic effects and its formation in organically polluted water.

The mechanism of the toxic action of nitrite in fish has not yet been clearly established. Nitrite, an intermediate in the oxidation of ammonium to nitrate or, more frequently, a product of nitrate reduction under anaerobic conditions, oxidises haemoglobin to methaemoglobin which then lacks the capacity to bind oxygen reversibly. Nitrite may thus cause an internal hypoxia in fish.

The toxicity of nitrite to fish depends on many endogenous and exogenous factors, the importance and interactions of which have been the topics of many studies (Wedemeyer and Yasutake, 1978; Tomasso *et al.*, 1979; Browser *et al.*, 1983). Of special importance is the fact that the uptake of nitrite by fish is dependant on the competition between nitrite and chloride within the active chloride uptake mechanism in the gills (Williams and Eddy, 1986; Paláčková and Mareš, 1989).

Methaemoglobin can be formed in fish blood in the absence of nitrite and its natural physiological concentration is maintained by a methaemoglobin–reductase system capable of changing methaemoglobin to haemoglobin (Cameron, 1971). 'Normal' physiological levels of methaemoglobin in fish blood are considered to be specific for individual fish species (Brown and McLeay, 1975; Smith and Russo, 1975; Tomasso *et al.*, 1979).

Methaemoglobin concentration in red blood cells of fish can also be considered as a relatively stable parameter, depending on environmental conditions. The levels are little affected by other haematological parameters such as, for example, haemoglobin concentration, haematocrit value and number of reticulocytes (Cameron, 1971).

The objective of this study was to assess the level of methaemoglobinaemia in populations of some fish species under natural conditions of different water quality. Special consideration was given to its relationship to nitrite (NO_2^-) concentration.

In some cases, fish (carp fingerlings) kept in submerged cages in field study localities were examined.

31.2   Localities

The fish sampled were obtained from different surface water bodies:

- fish farms (localities A, B, C)
- brooks (localities D, E, I, J)
- eutrophic artificial lakes (localities F, G, H)
- a river (locality K).

31.3   Material and methods

Fish sampled for the investigation were caught by different methods: gill nets (localities F, G, H), electrofishing (localities D, E), seine nets (localities A, B, C) and from experimental submerged cages (localities I, J, K). However, the methods did not differ within the species sampled.

The blood was sampled by cardiopuncture using heparinised syringes and needles (Jirásek *et al.*, 1980). The concentration of haemoglobin was measured by the cyanhaemoglobin method, and the methaemoglobin concentration was determined by measuring changes in absorption after addition of cyanide and/or ferricyanide to a diluted haemolysed blood sample, following the 'Unified methods of haematological investigations of fish' (Svobodová *et al.*, 1986). Nitrite ion concentration was measured by the azo dye method of the 'Unified methods of chemical analyses of water' (1965). Statistical evaluation of results was performed using Student's *t*-test.

31.4   Results and discussion

The average values of methaemoglobin concentration in blood of six fish species under investigation are presented in Table 31.1. The water bodies in which the sampled fish had developed were not strongly polluted, neither during previous years nor at the time of the investigation. Also, the hydrochemical parameters except for the nitrite concentrations were comparatively well balanced. At no time did the levels of nitrite in the waters reach the lethal limits. The water quality of the individual localities is therefore characterised only by the nitrite concentration for the purposes of the study, since it was the primary factor in the investigation.

Both species specificity and a direct dependence on nitrite concentration in water are clearly shown from the methaemoglobin concentrations found in the blood of the sampled fish (Table 31.1). When comparing these values for different fish

Table 31.1 Changes in methaemoglobin concentration in some fish species according to nitrite concentration in water.

Fish species	Locality	$N-NO_2$ $(mg.l^{-1})$	Fish weight $(g.ind^{-1})$	Haemoglobin $(g.l^{-1})$	Methaemoglobin $(g.l^{-1})$	Methaemoglobin (% total Hb)
Rainbow trout (*O. mykiss*)	A	0.011	228.7 ±10.9	77.72 ±8.62	9.15 ±3.12B[†]C[‡]	12.07 ±5.19B[†]C[‡]
	B	0.030	216.8 ±41.0	51.65 ±6.91	12.47 ±2.13C[‡]	24.11 ±2.08C[‡]
	C	0.060	247.4 ±23.6	97.50 ±20.95	30.42 ±5.86	32.13 ±8.12
Brown trout (*S. trutta fario*)	D	0.080	208.0 ±21.4	72.96 ±24.34	13.17 ±4.91	24.26 ±3.62
	E	0.086	148.1 ±28.3	62.45 ± 6.97	15.91 ±4.60	25.06 ±5.74
Roach (*R. rutilus*)	F	0.037	54.5 ±5.3	60.66 ±4.18	3.31 ±1.55G*H[‡]	5.37 ±1.32H[‡]
	G	0.048	28.4 ±3.4	53.07 ±13.68	4.62 ±1.49	8.63 ±3.22
	G	0.079	47.2 ±6.5	84.92 ±6.63	5.66 ±1.99	6.77 ±2.62
	H	0.291	49.6 ±4.8	69.11 ±13.95	13.57 ±3.91G[‡]	20.28 ±6.92G[‡]
Bleak (*A. alburnus*)	F	0.037	50.2 ±7.4	80.76 ±16.27	6.69 ±3.70	8.17 ±3.83
	G	0.048	49.7 ±9.6	80.37 ±11.02	7.34 ±4.55	8.75 ±4.61
	F	0.068	66.6 ±9.8	69.56 ±4.46	8.79 ±3.56	12.57 ±4.84
Carp fingerlings (*C. carpio*)	I	0.030	57.2 ±6.8	59.36 ±8.11	4.96 ±1.81J[†]	8.29 ±2.55J[‡]
	J	0.060	27.0 ±6.7	54.71 ±14.15	6.17 ±2.73K[†]	11.36 ±4.54K[†]
	K	0.114	18.1 ±1.4	69.97 ±6.95	15.22 ±7.04I*	21.27 ±7.80I*
Pike (*E. lucius*)	H	0.182	1358 ±306	66.81 ±9.50	23.16 ±6.26	32.10 ±7.98
	H	0.291	1418 ±382	68.48 ±19.19	26.35 ±7.94	38.29 ±4.60

Note: Statistically significant difference within the same fish species on different localities: * $P < 0.05$, [†] $P < 0.01$, [‡] $P < 0.001$

species inhabiting the same water, or in other localities with a comparable nitrite concentration (0.030–0.037 mg.l^{-1} N–NO$_2$), the lowest level of methaemoglobin was recorded in the blood of roach (*Rutilus rutilus*) (3.31 ±1.55 g.l^{-1}) and carp (*Cyprinus carpio*) fingerlings (4.96 ±1.81 g.l^{-1}), followed by bleak (*Alburnus alburnus*) with 6.69 ±3.70 g.l^{-1}.

The highest susceptibility to methaemoglobinemia was found in rainbow trout (*Oncorhynchus mykiss*) where the level of methaemoglobin in the blood was 12.47 ±2.13 g.l^{-1} under comparable conditions. The same species dependence is found where the nitrite concentrations in water are higher. The methaemoglobin level in the blood of brown trout (*Salmo trutta fario*) and pike (*Esox lucius*) was not assessed under the same environmental concentrations of nitrite given above but, on the basis of the results obtained, a lower susceptibility to methaemoglobinaemia can be expected for brown trout in comparison with rainbow trout.

When evaluating the significance of these differences in the methaemoglobin concentration in the blood of the fish sampled from the localities under study, the relative sensitivity of individual fish species to environmental water quality can be estimated. The following relationships were found when comparing the methaemoglobin concentrations found in fish blood from the different localities where the nitrite concentrations ranged from 0.03 to 0.08 mg.l^{-1} N–NO$_2$:

The methaemoglobin concentration in the blood of rainbow trout from locality C which had double the nitrite concentration compared to locality B, was 2.4 times higher than the methaemoglobin concentration in the blood of fish from the latter location; this difference was statistically highly significant ($P < 0.001$). A similar significant difference ($P < 0.01$) was found between carp fingerlings from localities I and J, although this was an increase of only 1.2 times. A significantly higher methaemoglobin concentration (1.7 times) was found ($P < 0.05$) in the blood of roach from locality G than in those from locality F which had a 2.1 times higher nitrite concentration.

The differences between the methaemoglobin concentrations in blood of other fish species originating from different localities were not statistically significant. For example, bleak from locality F which had a 1.8 times higher nitrite concentration in water compared to other sites in this locality were found to have their methaemoglobin concentration increased by only 1.3 times. These apparent anomalies might be due to the presence of higher concentrations of some anions which are known to reduce the effect of nitrite on fish. The current knowledge about the controversial action of chloride, bromide, bicarbonate and others has been summarised by Lewis and Morris (1986). On the other hand, we did not find an effect of increased chloride concentrations on methaemoglobinaemia in young carp and tilapia under experimental conditions (Paláčková and Mareš, 1989).

When trying to rank the susceptibility of various fish species to sublethal nitrite concentrations, rainbow trout seem to be the most sensitive. However, methaemoglobin concentrations in fish blood expressed in absolute values are of lesser importance in fish physiology than is the comparative proportion of the total haemoglobin content because it is this fraction of the haemoglobin which is unable to act as an oxygen carrier and at sufficiently high levels will cause hypoxia.

Our results can be compared with published data only in the case of rainbow trout because the other fish species included in our study have not been investigated in the same way by other workers. However, the data published previously give a wide spectrum of physiologically 'normal' values for the proportion of methaemoglobin in the total haemoglobin content; Cameron (1971) reported a proportion of 2.9% in a wild stock of rainbow trout and 17% in a hatchery stock without mentioning whether these caused any adverse effects.

In summarising the results we have obtained from localities with average nitrite concentration lower than 0.03 mg.l^{-1} N–NO$_2$, the following values of methaemoglobin concentration (and percentage of total haemoglobin) can be adopted as physiologically acceptable for these fish species: rainbow trout 11 g.l^{-1} (20%), carp fingerlings 4 g.l^{-1} (8%), two-year-old carp 8 g.l^{-1} (10%), and grass carp 6 g.l^{-1} (9%).

31.5   Conclusions

The measurement of the methaemoglobin concentration in fish blood can be recommended as a sensitive biological indicator of the water pollution by nitrite. Because of their high susceptibility to induced methaemoglobinaemia, salmonid species seem to be the most suitable for such a purpose under natural field conditions.

References

Bowser, P.R. *et al.*, 1983. Methemoglobinemia in channel catfish: Methods of prevention. *Prog.Fish Cult.*, **3**: 154–158.

Brown, D.A. and D.A. McLeay, 1975. Effect of nitrite on methemoglobin and total hemoglobin of juvenile rainbow trout. *Prog.Fish Cult.*, **37**: 36–38.

Cameron, J.N., 1971. Methemoglobin in erythrocytes of rainbow trout. *Comp.Biochem.Physiol.*, **40A**: 743–749.

Jirásek, J., D. Pravda and A.Hampl, 1980. An effective method of blood sampling for mass hematological examination of young fish. *Acta Univ.Agr.(Brno)*, **1**: 175–182.

Lewis, W.L. and D.P. Morris, 1986. Toxicity of nitrite to fish: a review. *Trans.Am.Fish.Soc.*, **115**: 183–195.

Paláčková, J. and J. Mareš, 1989. The effect of chloride concentration on methemoglobinemia in carp (*Cyprinus carpio*) and tilapia (*Oreochromis niloticus*) fingerlings. Second Ichthyohematological Conference, Litomysl: 37–45.

Smith, C.E. and R.C. Russo, 1975. Nitrite induced methemoglobinemia in rainbow trout. *Prog.Fish Cult.*, **37**: 150–152.

Svobodová, Z., D. Pravda and J. Paláčková, 1986. Jednotné metody hematologického vyšetřování ryb. (Unified methods of haematological examination of fish.) VÚRH Vodňany, Edice Metodik.

Tomasso, J.R., B.A. Simco and K.B. Davis, 1979. Chloride inhibition of nitrite induced methemoglobinemia in channel catfish. *J.Fish.Res.Board Can.*, **36**: 1141–1144.

Unified methods of chemical analyses of water, 1965. Prague, SNTL. 449 pp.

Wedemeyer, G.A. and W.T. Yasutake, 1978. Prevention and treatment of nitrite toxicity in juvenile steelhead trout. *J.Fish.Res.Board Can.*, **36**: 822–827.

Williams, E.M. and F.B. Eddy, 1986. Chloride uptake in freshwater teleosts and its relationship to nitrite uptake and toxicity. *J.Comp.Physiol.*, **B156**: 867–872.

Chapter 32

Monitoring system for investigation of heavy metal and chlorinated hydrocarbon pollution of fish in natural waters and fish ponds

J. SZAKOLCZAI,[1] J. RAMOTSA,[2] M. MIKLOVICS[2] and G. CSABA[2]

[1] *University of Veterinary Science, PO Box 2, H-1400 Budapest, Hungary*
[2] *Central Veterinary Institute, PO Box 2, H-1581 Budapest, Hungary*

32.1   Introduction

Good quality food for consumption can only be produced in an environment free from contamination. A considerable amount of information on the extent of environmental contamination within a given area can be obtained by examining the water bodies there, since these are likely to contain all the contaminants of local importance. However, the levels of these contaminants in the water are continuously changing; therefore, these investigations do not always provide a reliable indicator of the general situation. Plants and animals (including fish) that live in water provide a much more reliable source of information on the levels of environmental contamination.

Of the total Hungarian surface water volume, 96% is derived from neighbouring countries. This water supply can be found in the valleys and watershed area of the Rivers Danube, Tisza and Dráva. About 13% of the total supply of water is used in agriculture for fish culture and irrigation. About 30,000 of the approximately 150,000 hectares of water area are used for fish ponds and storage lakes. The annual yield of fish production is 36–38 thousand tonnes, of which 25 thousand tonnes are produced in fish ponds and the remainder come from natural waters.

The general quality of the water is affected by organic contamination (which can be characterised by the chemical oxygen demand), oil contamination and nitrogenous compounds. Apart from some exceptional cases, the concentration of harmful substances (e.g. toxic metals, pesticides, etc.) and the level of radioactive contamination remain generally below the limits permitted. Nevertheless, about 190–200 cases of severe water contamination occur each year; of these, 'only' 50–70 result in a mortality of fish.

Attempts to control environmental pollution began in 1965 when about 500 tonnes of fish, primarily pike-perch, died in Lake Balaton. Because of a lack of appropriate experience and of toxicological as well as analytical facilities, it took about six months before the conclusion could be drawn, primarily from histopathological studies, that the deaths were due to pollution by chlorinated hydrocarbons (e.g. aldrin, dieldrin and DDT).

Lake Balaton is one of the most important natural resources of Hungary. It is a centre of interest from the point of view of environmental protection, fishing and angling. Its commercial fish production is 1200–1400 tonnes per year; thus the Balaton fisheries are also important in producing food for human consumption. A mortality of Balaton fish is of considerable public concern; therefore it is essential that the various toxic components associated with the Balaton aquatic environment should be investigated. A mortality of Balaton fish occurred again in 1975, and this provided a stimulus for the allocation of some financial resources to begin a monitoring programme.

32.2   Material and methods

The basis of the monitoring system is as follows. Investigations were carried out between 1976 and 1990. At the beginning of the programme, samples were taken monthly between March and October, and subsequently on four occasions (in March, June, September, December) per year. On every occasion three fish (3-years-old or older) of each species were examined. The fish were captured by nets, and randomly selected from the catch. The species examined were mainly common carp (*Cyprinus carpio*), common bream (*Abramis brama*), pike-perch (*Stizostedion lucioperca*), silver carp (*Hypophthalmichthys molitrix*), bighead (*Aristichthys nobilis*) and eel (*Anguilla anguilla*) collected from Lakes Balaton and Velence, the Rivers Danube and Tisza, and from the five largest fish farm ponds located in different regions of Hungary. A total of nearly 3000 fish specimens were examined. The examination consisted of an external inspection, weighing and dissection, and a detailed parasitological, microbiological, histological examination and toxicological analysis.

Histological sections were prepared from liver, kidney, and intestinal tissue, and sometimes from skin. The sections were stained with haematoxylin-eosin, Sudan III and PAS stains. Samples for toxicological analysis were taken from the liver and muscle and sometimes from the gills and kidney and from the intestinal contents. The atomic absorption AOAC methods were used to determine the heavy metal concentrations in the fish. Initially only copper and zinc were measured, because these were used as active ingredients of pesticides (fungicides) used in vineyards. Since 1982, however, cadmium and lead have also been measured as a result of Müller's (1981) data on Lake Balaton and River Zala. Chlorinated hydrocarbon pollution was investigated by using gas-liquid chromatography on samples collected from that part of the dorsal musculature which is rich in fat, from both sides of the dorsal fin. Results of the external and histopathological examination and toxicological analysis were compared.

We attempted to induce a seasonal fluctuation in the copper (Cu) and zinc (Zn) levels of groups of common carp. Each group contained 10 fish of about 300–400 g body weight, collected from a fish farm. For three months the fish were fed either a

Table 32.1 Copper and zinc residues in fish from Hungarian waters (in mg.kg^{-1} wet weight).

		Min–max	
		Copper	Zinc
Natural waters			
Pike-perch	liver	1.76 – 9.85	14.20 – 35.75
	muscle	0.53 – 2.79	3.18 – 5.72
Common	liver	8.17 – 35.72	29.13 – 87.20
bream	muscle	0.43 – 2.07	3.17 – 6.72
Common	liver	2.89 – 35.79	34.17 – 742.40
carp	muscle	0.18 – 1.93	5.85 – 23.10
Silver	liver	2.18 – 28.13	34.75 – 55.30
carp	muscle	1.37 – 3.17	5.79 – 28.87
Bighead	liver	8.13 – 32.10	32.10 – 40.08
	muscle	0.53 – 2.18	4.26 – 6.44
Eel	liver	2.11 – 7.95	13.12 – 33.99
	muscle	0.48 – 2.63	2.69 – 4.17
Fish ponds			
Common	liver	7.62 – 33.18	35.13 – 212.40
carp	muscle	0.32 – 2.02	5.18 – 23.79
Allowed values for fish quality			
	liver	60.00	80.00
	muscle	10.00	60.00

complete carp or trout food: the carp food contained 18.8 ppm Cu and 57.5 ppm Zn, and the trout food 56.9 ppm Cu and 230.0 ppm Zn. At the start of the feeding programme, some of the carp were killed and examined as controls. Halfway through this study, five fish were killed, and the remaining five fish, which had until then received trout food, were then fed with carp food. At the end of the experiment all fish were killed and examined by the methods mentioned above.

Heavy metal and chlorinated hydrocarbon residues were evaluated on the basis of values set for human consumption by order of the Ministry of Health (see Tables 32.1 and 32.2).

32.3   Results

The following are the main results obtained from the monitoring programme.

(1)   When a sudden mortality occurs in a fish population, the monitoring system allows us to reliably distinguish between losses due to toxic effects and those caused by diseases. When the circumstances give rise to a suspicion of a toxic cause, a comparison of the results with those of samples taken at the same place earlier, can be used to establish whether or not environmental contamination has occurred.

Table 32.2 Maximum levels of toxic heavy metal and chlorinated hydrocarbon residues in fish from Hungarian waters (in mg.kg^{-1} wet weight).

	Lead	Cadmium	*p,p'-DDT	**HCH	HCB	PCB
Natural waters						
Pike-perch	0.41	0.19	0.162	0.168	0.311	0.045
Common bream	0.50	0.16	0.183	0.097	0.036	0.043
Common carp	0.51	0.18	0.127	0.093	0.019	0.047
Silver carp	0.57	0.21	0.937	0.478	0.042	0.073
Bighead	0.43	0.17	1.116	0.273	0.072	0.093
Eel	0.68	0.22	0.787	0.018	0.076	0.058
Fish ponds						
Common carp	0.72	0.19	0.237	0.171	0.052	0.047
Silver carp	0.55	0.17	2.250	0.789	0.092	0.077
Bighead	0.43	0.20	2.953	0.128	0.057	0.071
Allowed values						
for fish quality	2.00	0.30	3.000	2.500	0.500	2.000

* sum of p,p'-DDT, p,p'-DDD, p,p'-DDE
** sum of alpha-, beta-, gamma-HCH

(2) On the basis of the data which we have collected, we can be certain that at present the chemical contamination of the Hungarian environment does not reach a level which could cause acute damage to fish health. Heavy metal and chlorinated hydrocarbon contamination of the fish remains below the values considered to be unacceptable from the point of view of their suitability for human consumption as set by the Ministry of Health in Orders No. 4/1979, 15/1982, 8/1985, and 32/1989.

(3) Copper and zinc levels (Table 32.1), particularly in the liver, vary between fish species in a characteristic manner. This is accompanied by a slight seasonal fluctuation from year to year. Copper and zinc residues (mainly in the liver) measured in winter, spring and early summer were consistently higher (less so in the common bream and more so in the common carp) than those found in the late summer and in the autumn. In the intestinal contents of the carp a maximum of 13 ppm of Cu and 178 ppm of Zn was found in the winter, while only 4 ppm of Cu and 18 ppm of Zn were present in summer. However, in the pike-perch no such seasonal fluctuation was observed.

  Zinc concentrations were many times higher than the corresponding copper concentrations. In the common bream, and especially in the common carp, the levels of Zn residues were higher than those found in pike-perch and in the other fish listed earlier. Zinc residues exceeded the limit set for human consumption in more than 20% of the cases, primarily in the liver of common carp.

  The data from the experiment which was conducted to model the seasonal fluctuation of copper and zinc concentration, did not consistently indicate an accumulation of these metals. Perhaps food with a higher metal content should be fed to the fish for a longer period in order to elucidate the problem of seasonal fluctuations.

(4) Lead and cadmium residues were very low in all cases (Table 32.2). There were no differences between omnivorous carp and herbivorous silver carp taken from the same location. There were no significant differences between samples of the same fish species taken from different locations.

(5) As a function of age, chlorinated hydrocarbon contamination in fish from farm ponds is more severe than in fish living in natural waters. This underlines the primary role of agriculture in causing environmental contamination (Table 32.2). DDT was found in a very low percentage of fish while the occurrence of its metabolite DDE was significantly higher. A seasonal fluctuation was not found in case of these residues. The level of chlorinated hydrocarbons found has decreased significantly in fish, when compared to the levels found in the 1960s.

(6) Older fish, principally those living in natural waters, often show hepatic degeneration to a varying degree: 23–26% of the common bream, common carp and pike perch specimens and 50% of the eel showed such effects. Histologically, there is a diffuse pathological and necrobiotic fatty infiltration in the liver, usually accompanied by a glycogen deficiency. In many instances this process is irreversible, as seen by a disruption of the reticular fibres. However, we have not been able to establish any relationship between the quantity of residues measured in the various organs of the fish and the external and histopathological changes (hepatic degeneration, diffuse pathological and necrobiotic fatty infiltration in the liver).

32.4   Discussion

On the basis of the monitoring experience and the test results the following conclusions can be drawn.

Fish can be considered as suitable for assessing the level of environmental contamination, not only from the research point of view but also from a practical aspect. If a sudden mortality occurs in a fish population, and disease can be ruled out as a cause, a drastic change in some environmental factor (local water pollution, faulty fisheries technology) is probably the underlying reason for the losses. If the deaths are seen immediately they occur and the competent authorities are notified, the causes can be elucidated by a careful consideration of all the circumstances.

From the investigations of heavy metals, it can be seen that Cu, Zn, Pb and Cd pollution of the Hungarian aquatic environment is not yet high enough to cause acute toxicity to fishes. The wide variation found between the omnivorous carp and the bream showed that high levels of Zn may accumulate in invertebrates and plants in some habitats in the water, resulting in a significant increase of Zn levels in carp. This conclusion was drawn from an analysis of the intestinal contents, which calls attention to the possibility that seasonal fluctuations are the consequence of feeding. The presence of Zn levels which exceed the limits set for human consumption causes a significantly greater problem which would repay further investigation.

At present, the possible losses caused by microtoxicoses (sublethal effects) are not easy to assess. For example, a high proportion of older fish is affected by hepatic degeneration, but as yet no obvious explanation exists as to the cause underlying this process; it may be supposed that it is a consequence of chemical contamination, or a natural result of the ageing process. The irreversible processes in the liver focused our attention on the possible role played by various microtoxicoses (e.g. chlorinated hydrocarbons, heavy metals, etc.). In experiments to simulate different microtoxicoses by exposing fish to sublethal amounts of heavy metals, malathion, phenoxy-acetic acid, and deltametrin, we found that as well as some other characteristic changes (hyperaemia and incipient neuronal degeneration in the brain, and destruction of the respiratory epithelium of the gills) there was a correlation between the time taken to die and the severity of hepatic degeneration. Therefore, hepatic degeneration can be considered as a factor which seriously impairs the organism's viability. While this may not represent a hazard to the life of the individual, it may well be of decisive importance so far as the survival of the population is concerned. Further research is required on the events that lead to the development of this condition.

References

Miklovics, M., E. Kovács-Gayer and J. Szakolczai, 1985. Accumulation and effect of heavy metals in the fishes of Lake Balaton. Symp.Biol.Hungarica (Heavy metals in water organisms) Vol. 29: 111–117.

Müller, G., 1981. Heavy metals and nutrients in sediments of Lake Balaton, Hungary. *Envir.Technol.Lett.*, **2**: 39–48.

Ramotsa, J., J. Szakolczai and E. Kovács-Gayer, 1990. Study of the chlorinated hydrocarbon pollution of fishes in Lake Balaton. *Magy.Áo.Lapja.*, **45**: 359–361.

Szakolczai, J., 1981. 'Internal' structural changes of the fish population of Lake Balaton caused by internal and external factors. Newer results of the investigation of Lake Balaton II., VEAB Monographs, Vol. 16: 227–283.

Conclusions

The papers presented at this Symposium represented only a partial coverage of the work being carried out in this field. However, some general conclusions can be made in the context of the objectives of the Symposium.

The numerous studies at the cellular and organ level tend to be driven in part by scientific curiosity, rather than by the need to provide information of value to the protection of fisheries. The possibility to extrapolate from the effects measured to predict effects at higher levels of biological organisation seems to be uncertain. The determination of the stage at which the measured effects at this level become 'harmful' has not been a part of these investigations in the past, and this should be given some priority in future. Also, research at this level of biological organisation should be encouraged if it is directed towards providing a better knowledge of the primary toxic effects of chemicals, e.g. for predictions of mixture toxicity.

Studies carried out at the individual level of organisation are more capable of being used to predict pollution effects at the community level, although much of the work is directed primarily towards the measurement of the hazardous properties of existing and new chemicals. However, there is a need to incorporate information on sensitive life stages of fish (e.g. from FELS tests) into models to predict effects on fish populations. Work at the cell and organ level of organisation may provide information which can be used to identify and classify those chemicals with specific toxic actions to which a wide range of species sensitivity exists and which may be correlated with wide acute-to-chronic toxicity ratios.

Responses at the cellular, organ and individual level can be used as bioassays of water quality. They can provide information on the presence of harmful substances in the water which may not be included in chemical monitoring programmes. Also, they may be used to identify the presence of specific chemicals or groups of chemicals in the water. The use of such bioassays should be encouraged. The linkage between the observed effect and harm to fish is not strictly necessary for such bioassay purposes; therefore, unless there is evidence to the contrary, the occurrence of effects only indicates the presence of biologically active concentrations of chemicals (or significant deviations of environmental parameters) in the water and should not be taken as evidence of damage to the fish community.

Therefore, measurements of effects on natural communities should be encouraged if they lead to the acquisition of good data which (a) enable these effects to be quantified and correlated with concentrations of chemicals in the aquatic environment or in fish tissue and (b) enable the effects to be quantitatively correlated with the extent of damage to the fish population. Emphasis should be given to the need for a comprehensive chemical analytical programme to be integrated into such studies.

The example of the research on the effect of acidification of waters (including elevated levels of aluminium) on fisheries, which incorporated and integrated information obtained from effects at all levels of biological organisation, and from chemical monitoring should be used as a model of what can be, and should be, achieved in such studies. This experience should be used to develop guidelines for investigations into other types of pollutional situations, and should provide confidence in the possibility of constructing predictive models which incorporate data on sublethal and chronic effects of pollutants on fish for environmental protection.

R. Müller, Symposium Chairman
R. Lloyd, Symposium Convenor

Glossary of abbreviations

AAS	atomic absorption spectrophotometry
ACR	acute-chronic toxicity ration
ACTH	adrenocorticotropic hormone
ANC	acid neutralising capacity
COD	chemical oxygen demand
DBTC	di-n-butyltindichloride
DMSO	dimethyl sulphoxide
DNP	2,4-dinitrophenol
DO	dissolved oxygen
DOC	dissolved organic carbon
DTDMAC	ditallow dimethyl ammonium chloride
EC$_{50}$	effective concentration for 50% of test organisms
EE$_2$	17α-ethynylestradiol
EL$_{50}$	effective level for 50% of test organisms
ELS	early life stage
ELT	embyro-larval test
ER	endoplasmatic reticulum
FELS	fish early life stage
GSI	gonadosomatic index
H&E	haematoxilin and eosin stain
HCH	hexachlorocyclohexane
HSI	hepatosomatic index
LC$_{50}$	lethal concentration for 50% of test organisms
LD$_{50}$	lethal dose for 50% of test organisms
LL$_{50}$	lethal level for 50% of test organisms
LOEC	lowest observable effect concentration
MATC	maximum acceptable toxicant concentration
MCH	mean corpuscular haemoglobin
MCHC	mean corpuscular haemoglobin concentration
MCV	mean corpuscular volume (of red blood cells)
MPO	myeloperoxidase
MT	metallothionein
NBT	nitro blue tetrazolium
NOEC	no observable effect concentration
PCB	polychlorinated biphenyl

PCP	pentachlorophenol
RER	rough endoplasmatic reticulum
SD	standard deviation
SE	standard error
SEM	standard error of the mean
SER	smooth endoplasmatic reticulum
TBTQ	bis(tri-n-butyltin)oxide
TOC	total organic carbon
VLDL	very low density lipoprotein
VTG	vitellogenin

Index

Books published by
Fishing News Books

Free catalogue available on request from Fishing News Books, Blackwell Scientific Publications Ltd, Osney Mead, Oxford OX2 0EL, England

Abalone farming
Abalone of the world
Advances in fish science and technology
Aquaculture and the environment
Aquaculture & water resources management
Aquaculture development – progress and prospects
Aquaculture: principles and practices
Aquaculture in Taiwan
Aquaculture systems
Aquaculture training manual
Aquatic ecology
Aquatic microbiology
Aquatic weed control
Atlantic salmon: its future
The Atlantic salmon: natural history etc.
Bacterial diseases of fish
Better angling with simple science
Bioeconomic analysis of fisheries
British freshwater fishes
Broodstock management and egg and larval quality
Business management in fisheries and aquaculture
Cage aquaculture
Calculations for fishing gear designs
Carp farming
Carp and pond fish culture
Catch effort sampling strategies
Commercial fishing methods
Common fisheries policy
Control of fish quality
Crab and lobster fishing
The crayfish
Crustacean farming
Culture of bivalve molluscs
Design of small fishing vessels
Developments in electric fishing
Developments in fisheries research in Scotland
Dynamics of marine ecosystems
Ecology of fresh waters
The economics of salmon aquaculture
The edible crab and its fishery in British waters
Eel culture
Engineering, economics and fisheries management
The European fishing handbook 1993–94
FAO catalogue of fishing gear designs
FAO catalogue of small scale fishing gear
Fibre ropes for fishing gear
Fish catching methods of the world
Fisheries biology, assessment and management
Fisheries oceanography and ecology
Fisheries of Australia
Fisheries sonar
Fishermen's handbook
Fisherman's workbook
Fishery development experiences
Fishery products and processing
Fishing and stock fluctuations
Fishing boats and their equipment
Fishing boats of the world 1
Fishing boats of the world 2
Fishing boats of the world 3
Fishing ports and markets
Fishing with electricity
Fishing with light
Freshwater fisheries management
Fundamentals of aquatic ecology
Glossary of UK fishing gear terms

Handbook of trout and salmon diseases
A history of marine fish culture in Europe and North America
How to make and set nets
The Icelandic fisheries
Inland aquaculture development handbook
Intensive fish farming
Introduction to fishery by-products
The law of aquaculture: the law relating to the farming of fish and shellfish in Great Britain
A living from lobsters
Longline fishing
Making and managing a trout lake
Managerial effectiveness in fisheries and aquaculture
Marine climate, weather and fisheries
Marine fish behaviour in capture and abundance estimation
Marine fisheries ecosystem
Marketing: a practical guide for fish farmers
Marketing in fisheries and aquaculture
Mending of fishing nets
Modern deep sea trawling gear
More Scottish fishing craft and their work
Multilingual dictionary of fish and fish products
Multilingual dictionary of fishing vessels/safety on board
Multilingual dictionary of fishing gear
Multilingual illustrated dictionary of aquatic animals & plants
Navigation primer for fishermen
Netting materials for fishing gear
Net work exercises
Ocean forum
Pair trawling and pair seining
Pelagic and semi-pelagic trawling gear
Pelagic fish: the resource and its exploitation
Penaeid shrimps — their biology and management
Planning of aquaculture development
Pollution and freshwater fish
Purse seining manual
Recent advances in aquaculture IV
Recent advances in aquaculture V
Refrigeration on fishing vessels
Rehabilitation of freshwater fisheries
The rivers handbook, volume 1
The rivers handbook, volume 2
Salmon and trout farming in Norway
Salmon aquaculture
Salmon farming handbook
Salmon in the sea/new enhancement strategies
Scallop and queen fisheries in the British Isles
Scallop farming
Seafood science and technology
Seine fishing
Shrimp capture and culture fisheries of the US
Spiny lobster management
Squid jigging from small boats
Stability and trim of fishing vessels and other small ships
The state of the marine environment
Stock assessment in inland fisheries
Study of the sea
Sublethal and chronic toxic effects of pollution on freshwater fish
Textbook of fish culture
Trends in fish utilization
Trends in ichthyology
Trout farming handbook
Tuna fishing with pole and line